JUST ANOTHER SQUARE DANCE CALLER

AUTHORIZED BIOGRAPHY OF MARSHALL FLIPPO

Source: Neeca Flippo

by Larada Horner-Miller

To buy books in quantity for corporate use or incentives, call **(505) 323-7098** or e-mail
larada@icloud.com

ISBN-13: 978-0-9966144-3-6 (Horner Publishing Company)

ISBN-10:

✿ Created with Vellum

DEDICATIONS

Larada's Dedication

- To Lin for his support throughout this project
- To Harold and Elva Horner for passing on their love for square dancing to me
- To the Marshall Flippo family for encouraging him to live his dream
- And to all the square dance callers, cuers, and dancers who loved Flippo

Marshall's Dedication

- To Neeca, the love of my life
- To John, my best friend and son
- To all the callers, cuers and dancers in the world who enriched my world

EPIGRAPH

"The old-time dances are not coming back," Shaw said. "They've never gone."[1]

Flippo Calling to a Crowd. Source: Neeca Flippo

---

1. Bob Osgood, *As I Saw It.* [Kindle iPad version] (2017) 1360.

CONTENTS

FOREWORD

I remember my first-grade teacher going around the room and asking each of us what our fathers did for a living. There were lawyers, doctors, truck drivers, and the like, but when she got to me, I proclaimed my dad was a square dance *caller*![1] The whole room busted out laughing.

Restraining her own giggles, the teacher informed me that square dancing was a hobby, not something someone did for a living, but I insisted, with only a hint of doubt in my young voice. She asked where he went in the mornings and what kind of uniform he wore. He wore a bolo tie and cowboy boots, but I was certain that if I mentioned that, I would have been laughed at again.

Being a square dance *caller* was the only job I knew my dad to have. He was one of the best in the world, but of course he would never say that. People who danced to his calls always made a point to tell me how much he meant to them and how much they loved him.

I never cared for school and didn't plan on taking any more, so when I graduated high school, I was thrilled. Unfortunately, shortly after, my mom told me that instead of just working at our resort, Kirkwood Lodge, I was going to need to go out and get a real job. This was a responsibility I had never considered, nor thought to consider.

Noticing I was reeling from the revelation, my mom suggested that I go on tour with my dad. She has always been there to rescue me when needed. Going on tour seemed to me a great deal better than getting a real job or going to more school. The plan was to do three months out east, come home for Christmas, and finish with three months out west. Dad made room in the car for my boom box and a few dozen t-shirts, and we were off.

Dad loved everything about touring, and we loved being on the road. We reveled in making good time on a trip (we took this very seriously), getting "smokie" and "statie" reports from the CB radio, finding the cheapest motels in the best locations, and finding the best coffee and breakfast in town. The only thing he didn't like was doing laundry. He taught me how to do it, and it was clear this was my main purpose in being on the trip. I am still using those skills today at FlipBack, our boutique resale store.

Dad made a point to introduce me right away at the dances. I was shy and tended to mumble, but no one cared about that. I was Marshall Flippo's son, and that made me royalty and an instant friend of anyone that knew my dad. We both had great memories of that tour. I got to see another side of my dad, and I learned more on that trip than I could have ever learned in school.

When my dad told me Larada was planning on writing a book about him, I was ecstatic. I had always thought his life would make a great book, and I was immediately on board. He was a little harder to sell. He didn't want the cover to mention square dancing, or have a picture of him on it, and he figured the book would be better if he didn't talk about himself. Fortunately, Larada won him over. I could tell, the more they worked together, he began to look forward to their weekly interviews. He would even take notes during the week of things he wanted to go over or something he thought might be interesting. I hope you enjoy this book as much as he and Larada did in putting it together.

John Flippo
June 5, 2019

John, Shelly and Flippo ready to go on the lake! Source: John Flippo

---

1. **Caller** — A person who prompts dance figures in such dances as line dance, square dance, and contra dance.

ACKNOWLEDGMENTS

The square and round dance world came out in full force to support this book. An individual thank you goes out to the following people:

- John Flippo helped me throughout this project by answering questions, being a beta reader, and cheering me on.
- Neeca Flippo shared about her life with Flippo any time I asked.
- Stan Jeffus scanned Neeca's three photo albums/scrapbooks and sent me a CD with them on it, which made this task much easier.
- Paul Cote gave me permission to use "Another Square Dance Caller" in the title and to include the lyrics in this book.
- Gary Shoemake was Flippo's go-to guy and supplied endless Flippo information.
- Mike Seastrom helped with important information specifically about Bob Osgood, Flippo, and California dancing. He agreed to read an advance copy.
- Jerry Junck was one of my cheerleaders and helped with technical square dance information. He agreed to read an advance copy.
- Tony Oxendine agreed to read an advance copy.
- WASCA Historians Jeff and Bobbi Fuhr researched the years that Flippo called at WASCA and sent me all the flyers for those festivals.
- The Marshall Flippo Fan Club supplied answers to questions I had, especially Tom Miller and Ken Ritucci.
- Beta Readers: Chuck Weiss, Sally Nolen, John Flippo, and Mary Sheehan Johnson corrected grammar and spelling errors and also any square and round dance misinformation.
- East Mountain Writing Group: Cody, Chelsea, and Marty encouraged

me through the whole project with critiques, revisions, and hours of help!

- Masaharu "Doc" Hiraga connected me to Japan and Flippo's Japanese experience.
- Vic and Debbie Ceder allowed me to use their original list of Flippo's recordings as a starting point.
- Jeff Kaminski enthusiastically allowed me to use a picture of Chula Vista Resorts, Wisconsin Dells, Wisconsin on the cover.
- Mark Newton shared an original call sheet of "The Auctioneer."
- Bryan and Kenta Swift helped with the cover.
- Kris Jensen helped with information about Challenge levels of square dancing.
- Callers, cuers, and dancers shared their favorite Flippo story.

I couldn't have done this book without you!

DEAR READER

Welcome to Marshall Flippo and the World of Square Dancing

Marshall Flippo early in his calling career. Source: Neeca Flippo

Star, legend—all words used to describe Marshall Flippo in the square dance world, yet when we started this project, he made me promise that I didn't portray him as a hero. His humble spirit spoke volumes about his view.

Marshall Flippo died on Sunday, November 4, 2018. He called actively until he was ninety years old, having a sixty-four-year career in the field he loved. During his heyday, he worked at Kirkwood Lodge in Osage Beach, Missouri, for half of the year, calling seven nights a week and the other half he toured the United States, calling usually six nights a week for forty-two years. He endured this grueling schedule because he did what he loved! He returned to his Texas roots as often as he could and called the anniversary dance for the Grand Squares Square Dance Club in San Antonio, Texas for forty-four years. He had long-term relationships with many dancers, clubs, and festivals all over the world.

He truly was a Renaissance man. The rough times of the depression and the subsequent recession formed Marshall Flippo, forcing the Flippo family to move several times around the Abilene area, searching for lower rental costs and better housing. As a *caller*[1], he spent six months of a year for forty-two years traveling the country and the world, a gypsy. Did the frequent moves during his early years set him up for this lifestyle?

It was 1944, and Flippo focused on World War II. He volunteered at seventeen, influenced by the war's impact on his country and his surroundings. Flippo's oldest sister and best friend enlisted, leading the way for him, so his patriotism shifted the direction of this young Texan's life away from finishing high school and out to the world.

After his service to his country, Flippo returned to Abilene, Texas and met the love of his life, Neeca. A happenstance career that fell into place because of a serendipitous square dance vacation to Kirkwood Lodge in the Lake of the Ozarks of Missouri ultimately changed his life forever.

His career spanned six decades, and he loved every minute. He came to the activity a bashful young Texan and felt the formula for his success was "he was the luckiest man in the world—at the right place at the right time." This powerful theme weaves its way through his life story, from getting rides home to Abilene, Texas with his friend, Thurman Curry, to his naval training in San Diego, California and his baseball career, to all the ins and outs of his successful square dance calling career.

❧

During a large part of our interviews, we looked at three albums/scrapbooks Neeca, Flippo's first wife, made for him. She documented a major part of his successful career, so I often reference him looking at a picture from one of these albums/scrapbooks.

More than anything, Marshall Flippo wanted you to laugh in reading his biography. His life was joy-filled, and he wanted you to experience that through his stories.

I knew him as "Flippo" or "Flip." Often when he spoke to himself in our conversations, that's how he referred to himself, as well. I will use Marshall sparingly in this book, not out of dishonor, but because "Flippo" is what we called this man we loved.

Flippo was a Texan through and through, with a unique story to tell. I would do him a disservice if I didn't include some of his linguistic differences. I've tried to capture his syntax, his Texas twang, and his words in a way that you can hear him telling his story to you. Flippo often sang the end of a sentence—truly a *caller* and master storyteller. I include these so the reader can hear his Texas twang, again not to disrespect him.

This biography is the remembrances of a ninety-year-old man. I've tried to verify all the Navy stories with historical fact. I did seek out truth when in doubt from those who might know. I couldn't verify the rest of the book because many of the key players are dead. So in saying that, these are Flippo's stories and memories; he was accurate in many places but admitted in others he just didn't know for sure. So let's go with that!

Since Flippo was the source for this book's stories, when he said things like "Bill Hagadorn said," I didn't do a quote within a quote, but wrote it as a direct quote of Bill or whoever Flip was quoting.

There's a glossary of square dance and round dance terminology, Appendix I, in the back of the book, and I italicized all dance terms in the text to signal the reader. For easy reading and reference, any terms will be in the Footnotes once at the end of each chapter. For more expanded definitions for some calls, see the glossary.

Now look over our shoulders as we look at his life through the albums and scrapbooks. Enjoy his pictures and meet Marshall Flippo!

Larada Horner-Miller and Marshall Flippo. Source: Larada Horner-Miller

---

1. Caller — A person who prompts dance figures in such dances as line dance, square dance, and contra dance

ANOTHER SQUARE DANCE CALLER
LYRICS

Another Square Dance Caller[1] **– Lyrics**[2]

OPENER - MIDDLE BREAK - CLOSER
Sides face, grand square
*Please don't say I look like Willie Nelson
If you do I'll sit right down and cry
But if you say I sing like Gary Shoemake
Then I know that all you folks are on my side
circle left

I'm just another square dance caller
Trying to make my living with a song
promenade
Maybe one day I'll get to Nashville
But you know that doggone road is so long

FIGURE
Heads promenade and get about halfway
Down the middle and do the right & left thru
Flutter wheel cross the floor, sweep 1/4 more
Pass thru and do the right & left thru
Swing thru and now let the boys run right
Half tag, swing and promenade
Maybe one day I'll get to Nashville
But you know that doggone road is so long

ALTERNATE LYRICS

Some folks say I call like Kenny Bower
I say Kenny Bower calls like me
But Kenny sells a million of every single song
I must be doing something wrong

Dolly Parton sings just like an angel
She sings as pretty as can be
I'll never be as famous as sweet Dolly
She has two big advantages on me

SEQUENCE: (Opener, figure heads twice, break, figure sides twice, closer)[3]

---

1. Flippo sang this song as his last song in Abilene, Texas on his "Farewell to the Road' on September 5, 2016 and again during the evening in Sierra Vista, Arizona on New Year's Eve, 2017. The playfulness of the lyrics, peppered with references to two special square dance callers and lifelong friends (Gary Shoemake and Kenny Bower), exhibited Flippo's nature.
2. May 29, 2019 – Permission from Paul Cote, Owner of Chaparral Records to reprint these lyrics.
3. Listen to a 30 Second Sample: https://www.ceder.net/recorddb/viewsingle.php?RecordId=280

A TRIBUTE TO THOSE WHO'VE GONE

M arshall Flippo wanted to honor the deceased *callers*[1] who helped him.
He said, "All those guys were deceased and, unbeknownst to them, helped me a lot because I stole stuff from them."

In his geographical style of reminiscing, Flippo stated, "I want to go down the whole list [*caller* & *cuer*[2] list we created], and I'm going to go plum across the country to different *callers* that have now gone but have helped me along the way. I'm going to go all the way from the west coast, all the way to the east coast, talking about these *callers*."

His humor continued with a chuckle, even as he talked about dear friends that are gone. "Some of them are still dead. They're still dead!"

Flippo dedicated another chapter to funny stories about his *caller* and *cuer* friends, but he specifically wanted this list before "Marshall Flippo was born . . ."

Abilene *Callers*

"I was lucky to be amongst J. C. Wilson, Betty Casey, and Bob Sumrall," Flippo shared about the cadre of *callers* in Abilene who helped him get started.

Betty Casey

Early on in our discussions, I realized the impor-tance of Betty Casey to Flippo's calling career—she was his mentor and teacher. He referenced her books, *Dance Across Texas* and the *Complete Book of Square and Round Dancing,* so often, so I bought them.

He shared, "I wrote the foreword to it [*Complete Book of Square and Round Dancing*]."

Betty Casey's signautre.
Source: Neeca Flippo

7

When I asked him about who he'd like to write the foreword to this book, he immediately said, "Betty Casey," then sighed and said, "She's gone."

Flip talked about her often—no funny stories but his major support. He shared, "I was lucky to have Betty Casey as my teacher. She had gone to, the same time that Bob Osgood, [see below] went, Pappy Shaw's in Colorado Springs."

"Lloyd 'Pappy' Shaw was an educator, and is generally credited with bringing about the broad revival of square dancing in America."[3]

"Betty Casey, she meant the world to me."

Betty told him once, "Flippo, come over to the house if you want to, and I've got a wire recorder." Because of her Texas hospitality, she opened her home and heart to this young *caller*.

Flippo explained, "Now, wire recorder was before the tape recorder. The quality was God-awful, but you could tell what I was saying. When I first heard myself, I told Betty, 'I'm quitting.'" If she heard him do something wrong, she straightened him out.

She assured him that the recorder didn't do him justice, but he could learn from it. He added, "And so I drove over to her house every once in a while and hear myself on that recorder, that wire recorder. She was a nice, nice person! Of course, you've seen the books, I guess, that she wrote."

In one of the three albums/scrapbooks Neeca, Flippo's wife, created, Betty is quoted in an article about Flippo: "Betty tells of the endless hours Flip used to spend in going over and over his calls in the early days. She referred to him as a perfectionist, and it is this quality of dedication which has had much to do with his success over the years."

Another keepsake in one album/scrapbook was a note from Betty: "I'm so proud of your calling and business successes. Heard many, many compliments on the dance you called here. I feel privileged to have been the one to launch you and the career which you've developed on your own in national proportions of acclaim and accomplishment. Love, Betty."

J. C. Wilson

If Flippo identified one man who helped him the most, it was J. C. (Joel) Wilson. J. C. is the first *caller* he danced to besides Betty Casey. Flip also identified J. C. as the other person he'd like to write the foreword to this book.

He shared, "J. C. usually called on Thursday nights, and so sometimes we'd go and sometimes we wouldn't. That was downtown at the YMCA. He had excellent, excellent rhythm, and he helped me with my rhythm. He had such a beautiful voice and lots of volume. He helped me a lot with my calling, and he never did get out of town. He was well-known in town, and people just booked him all the time like the utility companies and stuff like that. They'd hire him because he was good on *one-nighters*.[4] I've never seen anybody that could beat him on *one-nighters*, and he just made you have a good time."

8

Flip added, "J. C. stole a lot of *patter*[5]—the words you put in between your calls. He had all these thangs like, 'Chase that rabbit. Chase that squirrel.' He'd say, 'Up the river, go down the bend.' He had these jingles he got off of the Burma-Shave signs alongside the highway. Those signs metered out. I started picking some of those up [like] 'Ningo, bingo, six penny high, little pig, a big pig, root hog or die.'" These jingles became Flippo's trademark.

In a conversation, Flippo asked J. C. where he went to college?

J. C. said, "I went to college at McMurray."

Flippo exclaimed with a chuckle, "Oh, God. McMurray." This took him back to when he was a kid. McMurray College was about five blocks from where he lived, and all the kids from Wylie would hang around the campus. The football players would get them into the football games as their brothers. "So anywhere from six to ten kids played around on the campus."

In this background story, Flippo's connection with McMurray centered around some guy asking the kids if they had animals.

The young Flippo replied, "I got a dog."

The guy said, "Oh, good, good."

Flippo added, "Then the other kids had a dog. One ole boy had a goat, and so they were different kinds of animals. Thar was about eight or nine of us that had animals. I 'member two dogs got into a fight, but anyway they got them separated."

Joe (J. C.) Wilson. Source: https://hamilfamilyfuneralhome.com/tribute/details/2052/Joel-Wilson/obituary.html

Flippo returned to J. C.'s conversation, "Oh, J. C., I used to hang around that campus a lot."

He said, "Well, it was good to me."

Flippo described him, "J. C. was crippled. He had one leg a lot shorter than the other, but he had a voice that was booming. I saw him call to fifteen squares [without a microphone] one time out thar dancing. He had that kind of voice that booms out."

Flip remembered, "I was in the opera at McMurray. I guess this was a part of the opera. Anyway, all we had to do was lead our dogs around the front of the stage and then back the other way." Flippo added this description, "It was an amphitheater outside on the grounds of the university or college at that time. It's a university now."

This information got J. C.'s attention. He questioned, "What do you mean you were in the opera at McMurray?"

"Well, we led dogs around. Ten or twelve of us had different animals."

J. C. exclaimed, "Flippo, I was the star of that opera."

"You're kidding me!"

"No."

"Well, I 'member a guy up thar yelling."

9

J. C. exclaimed, "Damn it, I was singing."

He realized they had never mentioned McMurray before, then he lavished compliments on J. C. and his calling. "I wish he was still alive—bless his heart. I tell you—ah, boy. People dying off that I don't have hardly any kinfolk left or anythang."

Bob Sumrall

When Flippo started talking about Bob, he wanted to make sure I spelled his name right, "Bob Sumrall. S-U-M-R-A-L-L, I thank."

He remembered, "So, Bob and J. C. called a dance down at the Y, and it was really crowded. I thank, only time I danced to Bob was when he was calling with J. C. But I was lucky to have him in the background that knew somethang."

Flippo called Bob "the granddaddy of square dancing in Abilene, Texas." He remembered, Bob "wrote a couple of books. He had a lot of foresight in his writing. He was a good 'un."

Because of Flippo's reference, I bought Bob's books on eBay, and they came in plastic sleeves to protect them—vintage treasures.

Bob Sumrall. Source: Necia Harp

In thinking about Bob, Flip repeated his name a couple times and continued, "I only danced to Bob a couple times because when I started, he was kinda fading out. Bob was a very smooth *caller*, very smooth. Bob knew a lot of *patter*."

When asked if Bob influenced him, Flip said, "From hearing him call, I picked up stuff that, you know, just one *caller* picking up somethang from another *caller*. His delivery or the way he treated people or stuff like that. I probably picked up somethang from him."

Owen Renfro

Flippo shared, "I had a good friend thar, was a good *caller*, started about the same time I did. We were good friends. His name was Owen Renfro, and so unbeknownst to him, I stole some from him."

He continued with a cough, "Owen was a good, great *caller* thar in Abilene. He started calling before I did, and he had a couple flourishing clubs thar. We traveled quite a bit. They'd go with us to a dance somewhere that I was calling, or I'd go with them somewhere to a dance he was calling. God, that's way back through. Owen and Opal Renfro. Opal and Owen are both gone now. They were older than Neeca and I but good, really good people."

When I asked if he stole or borrowed material from Owen, Flip replied with a laugh, "I'm sure I did. I stole everythang I could from different callers. We got to call this 'Research' instead of stealing."

Other *Callers*
Bob Osgood[6]

Bob Osgood. Source: http://www.sdfne.org/bob-becky-osgood/

Early on in our interviews, I asked Flippo what was his favorite festival. Without hesitation, he answered, "Asilomar because of Bob Osgood. Him and Becky run Asilomar with an iron fist. I thank it's why I liked it so well. You learned so much from Osgood 'cause him and Becky went to Colorado Springs where ole Pappy Shaw was. I was lucky to meet Bob Osgood, I swear to God."

He added, "Bob Osgood taught Chuck Jones, creator of Bugs Bunny, how to square dance. Bob Osgood taught quite a few Hollywood stars how to dance."

In one of Flippo's photo albums/scrapbooks was a cartoon of Bob Osgood—with his eye patch and sitting at a typewriter. This cartoon of Bob was a part of the headline for his article, "As I See It," in his monthly square dance magazine, *Sets in Order*.

Flippo shared many more memories and information about Asilomar and the Osgoods. See in Chapter 15, Asilomar.

Bob Osgood's banner for "As I See It" column. Source: *Sets in Order,* December 1985

Bob Page[7]

Flippo did the Asilomar weekend with Bob Page when Osgood first hired him, and they did it for quite a few years. He lived over in Hayward, California and had a good club over there called Gingham Squares, one of the top in the Bay Area. Bob and Nita Page also owned a travel agency and a bar. Flip added, "Anyway, a good, good caller—a good friend."

He added, "Frank Lane and Barbara Lane and Neeca and I always stayed with them in Hayward when we were calling in the Bay Area. I was thar in their home when he come home and said, 'Nita, I have high blood pressure,' and that's what he finally died of. But wasn't real soon—two or three years later he died and that's what caused it."

Flippo sang Bob's name, "Bob had a bar, a whiskey bar, just a bar. And I forget who run his bar, but he was very seldom thar. When the topless thang hit San Francisco on Broadway Street. Now Broadway wasn't like the major street of San Francisco —Market was, but Broadway was where all the nightclubs were and all the topless dancers."

Bob had to call, and Flip was leaving in a couple nights, so he wanted Flippo to go over to Broadway and the topless nightclubs.

Flip explained, "They took Carol Doda to court for dancing that way, and she won. And when she won, that's when all the topless thangs started. They had topless shoe shine girls and everythang—shine your boot."

Bob & Nita Page. Source: http://www.sdfne.org

So, Bob said, "You and Nita go on over thar. I'll show up later on." With a chuckle, Flippo explained, "So, we went over thar and we did go to Carol Doda's—Nita and I did, and then we went on down to another one that had three chairs at one little table. The table wasn't about two feet wide and probably a yard and a half long and three people sit around it, you know, and drink whiskey and whatever, and so, ole Bob showed up, and his eyes were bugged out, you know."

And Flippo told him, "Bob, you know, after you're in here a while, they don't bop to you."

He said, "Flippo, you know you can always get up and go outside and come back in."

With a laugh, he added, "So, we enjoyed the topless girls, and Carol, C-A-R-O-L Doda, D-O-D-A, I thank. Carol Doda. She was the one that got it all started because they took her to court for doing it, and she won, and so, after she won, it just broke loose."[8]

Arnie Kronenberger[9]

Arnie always had Flip into LA every year for the Rinkidinks, his club. He'd have anywhere from one hundred to one hundred twenty-five squares there.

One time Arnie called Flip and said, "We've got over a hundred sold already." Flippo explained that the proceeds of that dance always went to a Korean boy that they were raising. Arnie told Flippo that this year they would have a good MC, Chuck Jones who created Bugs Bunny.

Flippo continued, "He introduced me, and his introduction was so damn funny.

People were almost on the floor, and he could see when I was going downhill. He'd get up thar and tell another funny story, so I had a real easy dance that night."

As Flip thought about his dear friend, he laughed, "Kronenberger's story. I can't tell that one!"

Flippo worried about the language in this story, but I assured him we could tell it carefully: "When Kronenberger called at Kirkwood, after the dance, we'd go down in the game room and shoot the bull with a bunch of his followers, and we'd have that ole room almost full, and we wouldn't let Arnie tell that real dirty joke until Friday, the last night.

"Arnie's joke went: This ole boy belonged to a Limerick Club in Illinois, and the Limerick Club had a contest, and this ole boy come in first in the contest, his limerick did. So they took up money for him and sent him out to LA, and he went out thar and won the national. So they's having the International in Oslo, Norway, so the Limerick Club in Illinois worked and worked—took in enough money to fly him over thar for the International Limerick contest."

Arnie Kronenberger. Source: http://www.sdfne.org/arnie-kronenberger/

Flip continued the joke laughing, "So, he went over, and he came back."

The limerick club members said, "How'd you come in? Did you win first?"

"No, I didn't win first."

"Well, how about second?"

"No, the words were too bad. I could not. You wouldn't believe how bad the words were over thar in those limericks."

And they said, "Well, you didn't win first or second with your dirty limerick?"

"No, I didn't even show."

"You didn't even show! What came in third?"

"Oh," he said, "I can't tell you—too many dirty words."

They said, "Now, wait a minute. We took up money for you to go over thar and try to win the International First prize limerick. You won't tell us the first one. It's got too many dirty words. You won't tell us the second place."

He replied, "Well, second one and the first come in are almost the same, so I can't tell you either one of them, really, as far as dirty words go."

And they said, "Listen, we sent you over thar now. Tell us what came in third."

He said, "If you'll let me substitute 'ta dum' for some of the dirty words, I'll tell you."

"Well," they said, "okay."

He said, "Okay. It starts out:
Ta dum, ta dum
Ta dum, ta dum, ta dum

Dum, ta dum, F**k Tom! Ta dum, Ta dum!

At this point, Flippo's laughing like crazy. "Did you get it?" Then he said, "The F word was the clean one."

Flippo ended, "That's the only clean one—the rest of 'em were all dirty."

He continued about Arnie's joke-telling at Kirkwood, "Well, on Sunday night we had ole timers. We were all down thar, saying 'hello' to each other and hadn't seen each other in a year."

Arnie made an announcement, "We're having a lot of fun in the game room. Come on down here."

"Well, a bunch of 'em from the Bible area came in, and they stayed the whole time. So, we were really watching our stories."

So Kronenberger said, "Let me tell my story."

Flippo said, "No, no, you can't tell your story when they come in here. Maybe they won't come back tomorrow night. Sure enough, here they come. Arnie starts in on this limerick story."

Flip knew it had the F word in it, so he said, "No, Arnie, wait 'til Friday."

"Nay, I'm telling now."

Flip continued, "So he told it. As soon as he got through, they all got up and left."

He said, "Damn it. I should have told that last night."

Flippo continued, "Arnie was a really good friend. I roomed with him later on at WASCA on the east coast."

Bob Van Antwerp[10]

When Bob retired from the Long Beach Recreational, they moved up to Lake Tahoe. He called Flippo, and he went up and called one dance for him there a long time ago. Flip added, "He's dead now and so is Roberta, his wife."

"He was such a neat person. I mean, well put together and always dressed spic and span. Dressed like he just stepped out of a band box. He usually had a tie on—very seldom you saw him without a tie, a square dance tie, and Roberta was one of a kind. Bob was always a friendly guy and a very, very good caller and a very good organizer, and stuff like that. I don't know of anythang real funny with Bob."

Bob Van Antwerp. Source: https://www.ceder.net/recorddb/artist_viewsingle.php?RecordId=28

Joe Lewis. Source: https://www.ceder.net/recorddb/artist_viewsingle.
php?RecordId=366

Joe Lewis[11]

Joe Lewis played the accordion and called at the same time, and he had built in a guitar, a piano, and vibes, so he sounded like a whole band. Flippo added, "I don't know how he could call and know where his fingers are going at the same time. I don't know how he did that, but he'd play that damn thang, *hash numbers*[12] and also *singing calls.*[13] I had trouble just a-standing up."

Look for more stories about Joe in Chapter 31.

Bill Castner. Source: *American Squares,* January 1964

Bill Castner

Flippo shared, "I knew Bill Castner real well. Bill had some extra exhibition group over thar around Hayward, California. What's that other name? Anyway, little towns over thar, across the Bay from San Fran."

He continued, "I don't know whether he moved up. I don't thank he lives in

Tucson anymore. He won that thang at the National—they won it for a long time. He was the caller and leader of that group. They were really flashy. They had a square dance club, so I called for that club, oh God, ten or twelve years, I guess. I got to know some of them, but Bill Castner was a great caller, a great caller. He weighed about maybe 450—somewhere in thar. Big guy. Him and Dick Houlton, they were both real big like that. They had a weekend they called 'Two Ton Weekend.'"

---

1. **Caller** — A person who prompts dance figures in such dances as line dance, square dance, and contra dance
2. **Cuer** — Leader at the front of the ballroom [hall] who tells the dancers, as they dance, what steps to do.
3. Wikipedia, "Lloyd Shaw (educator)," June 17, 2019, https://en.wikipedia.org/wiki/Lloyd_Shaw_(educator)
4. **One-nighters** — A one evening square dance that has a party atmosphere and a few *Basics* are taught. The objective is to get people up dancing and having a good time.
5. **Patter** - A single tune, used by a caller as background for a series of calls, with no lyrics accompanying the music. Couples are moved into a variety of formations, but brought back to their home positions before the next set of calls.
6. CALLERLAB, an international caller's association, was Bob Osgood's brain child.
7. Bob Page was one of the original 11 who formed CALLERLAB.
8. Wikipedia, "Carol Doda," March 17, 2020, https://en.wikipedia.org/wiki/Carol_Doda)
9. Arnie was one of the original 11 who formed CALLERLAB.
10. Bob Van Antwerp was one of the original 11 who formed CALLERLAB.
11. Joe was one of the original 11 who formed CALLERLAB.
12. **Hash Numbers** — Same as Patter — A single tune, used by a caller as background for a series of calls, with no lyrics accompanying the music. Couples are moved into a variety of formations, but brought back to their home positions before the next set of calls.
13. **Singing Calls** — The caller sings parts of the songs. See glossary for more.

ONE OF FLIPPO'S FAVORITE DIRTY JOKES!

Flippo had definite ideas on how he wanted his biography to begin. He instructed the exact placement of this joke: "Somewhere or the other before you start in on Marshall was born, whatever."

I assured Flippo that we could word it so we could include it, so here's the other way he wanted to start off his biography—with a laugh!

"I thank that I'm going to tell some dirty joke or somethang on the front. I have a real good story that a caller's wife told me the first time I met her and her husband. It was in Lincoln, Nebraska. I was calling in Lincoln that night, and I was staying with Bill and Phyllis Speidel, and probably Phyllis was one of the better cooks in America. So, every time I was calling in Lincoln, I always stayed with them. I was dreaming of one of Phyllis's good meals.

"But when I got thar, they said, 'Hey, we're going to go meet a young couple, a young caller that's starting to get out now amongst other cities. His calling is very good. And we're to meet them at a restaurant.'

"So, I thought, 'Well, thar went a good meal.'

"Anyway, we met them before the dance at the restaurant, and the caller's wife was sitting next to me, and I guess we'd ordered. It seemed like it was right at the first, right after I met them. We had just met them, said hello and said a few thangs.

"She says to me, 'Flip, did you hear about the six guys that went about three quarters the way up this mountain going hunting for deer?'"

Flippo thought to himself, "What is it?" and then he said, "No, I hadn't heard that."

She said, "They were hunting for deer, and they were up thar three days. They had this little cabin up thar, and it had six cots in it. That's where they slept. They was up thar for about three days and hadn't seen a deer yet."

Flippo's laughter sprinkled throughout the retelling of this favorite story.

17

"So, they were kind of discouraged, so one of them said, 'Let's go down to the foot of the mountain to that bar down thar and have us a couple of beers.' So, they went down thar and got drunk that night. They headed back up the mountain and were drunk as skunks. They finally got back to the cabin. They threw their clothes off. They had on—we called them long handles. I don't know what you call them. They had that flap in the back. I've heard them called different thangs. We called them long handles anyway. They took all their clothes off, and they just fell onto the cots and went to sleep.

"At 3:30 a.m. this ole boy woke and he had to go to the crapper—not number one, but number two. He had to relieve himself."

With a chuckle, he added, "And I don't know whether to say that word or not, but he had to . . . He went to the door, opened the door, and thar was a blizzard blowing, and it was snowing going sideways. And he thought, 'I ain't going out thar in a dad-gum snow like that, take my pants down in that dang gum cold weather.'

"He saw his buddy over thar sleeping on his stomach, and he thought, 'Oh, yeah.' So, he went over thar and very quietly undone this ole boy's flap and pulled it down. Put one foot on one side of the cot, one foot on the other, squatted down thar, and took a big crap.'"

Flippo's laughter exploded at this point. "I don't know how we can say that, but anyway, he got off, buttoned that flap back up, you know, and went on about his sleep.

"The next morning, he heard this guy talking to another guy saying, 'I'm ruined. Looky here, I'm ruined.'"

"His buddy says, 'Well, you're not ruined. We all have accidents. Good Lord a mercy.'

"He said, 'Yeah, I'm ruined.'

"His friend recounted, 'No, we all make mistakes, have errors. That's just life. You're not ruined. Don't even thank about it.'

"He repeated, 'I'm ruined. I'm ruined.'

"And the guy said, 'I'm telling you—you're not ruined! Why do you thank you're ruined?'

"He said, 'Oh, yes, I am! Looky here. Look at it. I haven't eaten corn in twenty years.'"

Flippo said, "I thought, 'Well, this is my kind of woman!' And of course, the caller's wife jumps on me every time I tell that. I always give her credit for it. She said, 'Quit telling it and giving me credit for it.'"

As our laughter subsided in the telling of this story, he repeated the punch line like any good storyteller does, "I haven't eaten corn in twenty years!" and we chuckled once more.

PROLOGUE

F lippo had planned to write his own prologue but never did. He did say when we talked about it, "I could thank you for writing the book."

He also added in our last conversation, "I'd rather say summin' about Blue Star Records because I thank I told how it kinda started at Merrbach's and everythang, but I want to give 'em, Blue Star, a big credit because it's like Kirkwood, you know, I just lucked out thar, so I wish I'd wrote . . ."

Was it luck? Being in the right place at the right time? How did Marshall Flippo become a world-renowned square dance caller? He repeatedly credited his success to luck, but I would offer more: his humility, talent, hard work, and personality.

Marshal Flippo certainly wasn't "Just Another Square Dance Caller," but in his mind, he was. Early in our conversations about this book, he said, "Don't make me a hero," so with that in mind, we adopted the title of this book. This book is his biography, but also it is the history of square dancing and its evolution from the late '50s through 2018.

Flip became a close friend to me. That's what he did. He met dancers, remembered names, and gave women a kiss every time he saw them. Because of his calling prowess, Flip became a favorite of many. His friendships grew and grew over the years for those reasons. Over the past twenty-five years, our own friendship grew.

For over a year, I interviewed Flip for this book. As I recall that memorable raspy voice, I want you to hear what I heard: his soft Texas drawl, how he sang many of his responses, his chuckles and laughter at reminiscing, and his intense interest in the production of this book. The book was my idea, not his, but we often talked about the ins and outs of publication, and he had set ideas. I learned in my research after he died that he had written a chapter in a textbook for Bob Osgood—no wonder he had knowledge of book formatting!

He wanted hard back copies, and it couldn't be as thick as Bob Osgood's book, *As I Saw It*. After looking at the first four transcribed interviews on paper, he demanded all those "I's" taken out. Another demand was, "Get rid of all those 'giggles,'" which made me laugh. When I sent him a copy of the first four transcribed interviews, I had put the word "giggles" in parentheses anytime he laughed. I told him I would take them out but somehow let the reader know when he laughed or giggled—he was okay with that! And finally, he didn't want his picture on the cover, but John, Neeca, and I love the picture we selected, and Flip was warming to the idea before he died.

In taking out the "I's," I will tell you his story, often quoting him with his Texas pronunciation of words sprinkled throughout, but at times in my words as I interpreted his life—I guess that's what a biographer does. This is not voodoo. I'm not searching for any deep psychological meanings. I want to honor a humble man who didn't want to be made "a superstar."

I had been warned early on by a caller friend that Flippo would hijack the interviews if I let him, and he did. But what happened was when he revisited his favorite topics and retold stories, he went deeper, sharing more vivid details, so we wandered through his life going from the Navy to Kirkwood to his favorite story about Frank Lane. My job then became to group together the similar stories and fuse them together.

I asked Flip to describe himself in one of our phone interviews, and that stopped him for a moment.

Then he chuckled, "A little short squirt with lots of luck! That's about it!" He added to this description: "A little short squirt— after all, a lot of people didn't know me when I had hair." He laughed again and

Young Marshall Flippo. Source: Neeca Flippo

repeated the phrase a couple more times—to hear the sound of it. I could tell as he repeated it, he was pleased with his answer! Flippo wanted you to laugh with him —not a contrived snicker but deep belly laughs like he did so often when a story bounced back into his memory.

Also, early on in our interviews, Flip described himself as being bashful, which was hard for me to imagine. Here was a man who shook hands with all the men in the dance hall and kissed every lady.

Even though he didn't want to be a square dance hero, Flippo has become an icon, a legend in the square dance world. His calling career spanned six decades. He's seen square dance come into its heyday and experienced its decline over the last twenty or so years.

He stands center stage in the history of square dancing. Today you may know him as the elder statesman of square dancing with a raspy voice, great choreography, and funny, colorful stories, but Flippo was a pioneer and a star with over two hundred records and twenty-five albums. He crisscrossed the United States yearly for forty-two years, traveled abroad numerous times, and met and loved dancers and callers all over the world.

Marshall also stood at the crossroad of square dance history. His mentors, Betty Casey and Bob Osgood, learned at the feet of Lloyd "Pappy" Shaw, and Flippo carried that message onto the next several generations of callers, bridging the old and the new. Pappy Shaw emphasized to callers he trained "clarity, rhythm, and command."[1]

He also stressed smooth dancing and said, "Dance tall. Raise your shoulders, pull your dining room back, tuck in your sitting room. Now you're beginning to look like square dancers.[2]

Pappy Shaw founded a new attitude about Western square dancing.

"This is the true dance of America. It comes from so many directions; it is the spirit of the West. It borrows much from its overseas ancestors who brought their dance with them when they came to this country. Like other things American, it mixes and borrows from the world and makes it purely an American dance." [3]

Flippo absorbed Shaw's philosophy from Betty and Bob and passed it on as often as he could.

About a third of the way through our interviews, Flippo asked me, "Somethang else I wanted to ask you. Are you sorry that you started this? It seems like it's a lot of work for you."

I was shocked and assured him, "NO! No, this has been so much fun. No, are you kidding me? No, no, no! I'm really enjoying it." He didn't realize the precious gift he had given—sharing his life's stories with me.

This book celebrates Marshall Flippo's life, his family, and his devotion to and love for square dancing and its people. Flippo is a noted storyteller, so enjoy the stories he tells about other caller friends and also the stories his close friends shared about him. Also, be sure there are two sides to each story told by Flippo and his friends, and I do have both sides of some of these hilarious stories. If you know Flippo, some of the stories will be on the racy side, but that's Flip!

Many of you dancers reading this book knew him in his later years—the elder statesman of square dancing. His scratchy voice surprised many new dancers when they were told he was someone they didn't want to miss as a caller, but when the music started and he called, his choreography and thought process soon enlightened them to his expertise in the field. Yes, you may have known the older Marshall with a raspy voice—let's look at his life and how he became the most famous world-known caller ever and what formed him.

Flippo identified himself as being "lucky—being at the right place at the right time," and that was his explanation for his successes, but there's more to it than that. One lucky event led to the next and to the next and the next!

This book is a conversation between Flip and me about his life. Grab a cup of coffee and join us at the table. It's funny mostly; sad in places, but mostly fun. That's the way Flip lived his life!

---

1. Osgood, Bob. *As I Saw It*. [Kindle iPad version] (Humbug Enterprises, 2017).
2. Osgood, Bob. *As I Saw It*. [Kindle iPad version] (Humbug Enterprises, 2017).
3. Osgood, Bob. *As I Saw It*. [Kindle iPad version] (Humbug Enterprises, 2017).

GROWING UP A TEXAN

Source: John Flippo

1

CHILDHOOD

Marshall Doyle Flippo was born on September 2, 1927 in Tuscola, Texas. Flippo's early life centered around his immediate family: Dad, Mama, Helen, and Onita. "My parents' names were Roy and Gus. Her name was Gertrude, but everybody—her nieces, nephews—called her Gus. I don't know if Gus is short for Gertrude or not."

Even if you knew Marshall well, you probably didn't know his middle name.

Flip shared, "I never did like it much, you know, and my sisters, when they'd get mad at me, 'Marshall Doyle!' My dad give me that name, I understand. His name was Roy Marshall Flippo, and he give me the Marshall. I don't know where the Doyle came from." He questioned whether we should use it at all but his final decision was, "Well, you can use it at the very beginning. You can do that, but you'd only use it once, right?"

Baby Flippo with his dad, Roy Flippo. Source: John Flippo

When asked about childhood pictures, he thought for a moment and identified one in *Sets in Order,* a square dance magazine, and the reader had to guess the caller. They had them on the front page or cover.

25

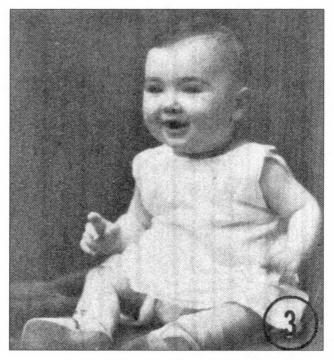

Flippo's baby picture. Source: *Sets in Order*, July 1963

He added, "I have a picture of me and my son and my dad—three generations. I have one of my mother, but we're not all together."

Flippo's Sisters

Flippo was the middle child with an older sister, Helen June, who was seven years older, and a younger sister, Onita, who was four years younger.

Flip said, "We got along really well, yeah. We'd get mad at each other, you know, and start throwing shoes or stuff at each other, but basically, we loved each other, and we knew it. Both of them have passed."

Flippo loved his two sisters, Helen June and Onita.

He remembered his younger sister, "Onita was four years younger than me, and she was the one that was priceless. She never met a stranger in her life. You seen people when they laugh, it makes you laugh? She had one of those laughs. She started laughing at somethang, and you wouldn't even know what the hell you were laughing at when you starting laughing. She was a very good, dear person."

Helen June Flippo front row, fourth from the left. Army Nurse Corp in France World War 2. Source: John Flippo

In describing his older sister, Flippo shared, "Helen was a nurse. She signed up right when the war started. She ended up over thar with ole Patton. I went home one time on leave, and she got home on leave. I had two little ole ribbons and two little ole stars in them. She had medals down to her waist on both sides of her dress coat. I took mine off and never did wear them again, but she wouldn't talk too much about it. Helen did say she dove under a lot of trucks. She personally met Patton one time and got to talk to him."

Helen survived the war, but when she went to Austin for her granddaughter's high school graduation, she tripped and fell down the stairs and broke her neck. She lived about six months after that. Flip created a CD for her sharing many childhood memories to bolster her spirit—a thoughtful brother.

Sadly, Flip shared, "She was such a good gal, too. She was seven years older than me and always treated me like the same age."

"I wish Helen hadn't had to die because she had some good stories. She was kind of like me—she was kind of shy. Onita was the only one that really had a personality. Now my younger sister died with cancer."

Homes

"Well, I lived on our farm in Tuscola, Texas. I's born thar, and I lived thar two years.

Then Flippo added with his great sense of humor, "Then I took Daddy and Mother to Abilene." He described his childhood home as "just an old farmhouse that my grandmother owned, and it was an eighty-acre farm out in Tuscola. It was just a typical old farmhouse."

The grandmother who owned the farm was his dad's mother. "Her last name was Marshall." So that's from where his first name came.

She was very old and died before they moved to Abilene. Flip didn't remember her at all but did see pictures of her. He said, "She looked like in the pictures kinda a tall woman, but straight as a board. I never heard too much about her husband, and all my grand folks. After she died, my grand-folks were all gone, and I was only two, so I didn't know any of my grandparents."

Family Farmhouse in Tuscola, Texas.
Source: John Flippo

They tried to keep the farm. On one Sunday, his family found out the house on the farm burned down, so they drove out to the eighty-acre farm to see the wreckage. Flippo didn't have much to say about this devastating loss.

Not wanting to lose connection with it, the Flippos went back and visited the farm often.

The Flippo family moved often—twice in Tuscola then to Abilene, seventeen miles north and six miles from Buffalo Gap, by horse-drawn wagon. Then they moved six times, and he recalled every house, almost every address, and even his neighbors. His ability to recall memories from so long ago amazed me.

During the Depression, every time Flippo's dad found a better house or price, they would move. The first house he remembered was where his younger sister, Onita was born, 1425 Cedar Street, Abilene, Texas. At this time, Abilene was a small town of 27,000 people. The rent was $27 a month.

They stayed there awhile, until Marshall's dad found another place to live on the south side of Abilene for $26 a month. They didn't stay long here, but Flippo still remembered, "Jones and Stubbs lived across the street. This house was by a trailer," but he didn't identify their significance. Amazing that he could remember their names.

Then they moved to 11th Street and Alta Vista in the College Heights area. In this neighborhood, the houses were made of stucco with wide driveways, but the neighbor's house was close. Flippo remembered he was in the third grade at this time. One night his mama and older sister couldn't sleep because of a neighbor up at 3:00 a.m., chopping ice.

The Flippo family moved again, this time to 19th street. This housing was cheaper, and this put the children in the Wylie Consolidated school system.

Not long after, another move occurred to one block behind their previous home.

As Flippo reminisced about his family, their homes, and his childhood, precious memories of the family's first car came to him. His dad bought a Model T car when Flippo was in the sixth grade, so they'd go to Buffalo Gap to see his mother's side of the family, the Stocktons. He had two uncles, Uncle Charlie and Uncle Bill, who lived there.

On the way back home, they had to go up Mud Hill, a steep incline for a Model T. Once, his dad got it going fast and hit the wooden bridge, and it stopped, so his dad ended up backing it up the hill then. Neeca remembered Flippo retelling this story "every time we traveled that road. It really is just a small hill, but it must have looked big when Flip was a child."

Flippo's dad had a big impact on him. So much so that when he rode his tricycle as a child, he used hand signals to turn left or right after watching his dad drive.

On Sunday, October 30, 1938, while they lived on Fulton Street, Flippo and his family heard the famous H. G. Wells' Mars invasion program on the radio. It was performed and broadcast live as a Halloween episode. Many listeners missed the introduction that stated this was only a dramatization of H. G. Wells's novel, *The War of the Worlds*. Spread throughout the broadcast, they had news updates that placed the invasion in New Jersey and then New York City. This left the listeners believing that the Martians had landed. The bewildered Flippos peered out of the house looking for Martians or the end of the world. His younger sister, Onita, peeked out with him. Flippo's cousin, Lanelle, took part in this memorable evening.

Looking out the window, at first they saw no cars. Then car lights turned down Fulton Street and turned around and came another way. A black cat crossed in front. Lanelle's dad turned around and came back to the house. Did they think the lights were aliens?

According to Marshall, "That's where we saw the world come to an end. We's all out thar lookin." The eleven-year-old Flippo shared his innocence in this frightening experience that caught many Americans off-guard.

Family and Faith

The church played a major role in the Flippo family.

"Mama is in heaven for sure," Flippo sang the end of the sentence in true caller fashion. "She was a good one—Dad was, too. I went to church three times a week until I come in the Navy, so we'd go to church every Sunday morning, Sunday night, and Wednesday night prayer meeting. We attended the Oak Street Methodist Church at one time, and then all the congregation moved over to a brand-new church that the guys had built, and the new church was called Fairmont Methodist—a big rock church. They made a beautiful church—had a basement and everythang, and it eventually burned, but that's just a few years ago."

He continued talking about the present-day church. Neeca, his ex-wife, goes there now. "She said some of the old congregation was still thar." He commented that he wouldn't know anyone that belongs to that church now.

When asked if church was a big part of his childhood, he responded, "Ah, yes, yes, yes. I got a whippin' for saying 'Goll-lee' one time in front of a school bus with a bunch of kids yelling, 'Hit him. Hit him, Mrs. Flippo! Hit him, hit him. Hit him harder. Hit him harder. Hey, Flippo's gettin' a whippin'. Flippo's gettin' a whippin'.'"

We both laughed as he recounted the story: "I'll tell you how it happened.

Anyway, the bus stopped in front of our house, and we had about ten guys and girls, you know, young kids get on the bus thar, and it was stopped thar, and so a lot of the kids in the neighborhood would get on the bus when it stopped. So, then one morning when the bus pulled up thar, and I headed toward the bus. I had hay fever a lot when I was a kid, and I realized I didn't have a handkerchief, so I said, 'Mama, I don't have my handkerchief.'

"'Oh, I shall git ya one.' So, she got one. She said, 'I couldn't find a man's, but here's your sister's.'"

Flippo exclaimed, "Goll-lee, a woman's handkerchief!"

She asked, "What did you say?"

He answered, "A woman's handkerchief!"

"No," she declared, "you said a bad word. Go get a limb off that peach tree over thar."

"So, I got a whippin' out thar in front of that damn bus with those kids yelling, 'Hit him harder, Mrs. Flippo. He's going around in a circle. So are you!'"

Our laughter ended the story. I asked how old he was then, and he thought for a moment and asked questions about grade levels and ages. Finally, he decided, "It's somewhere around ten or eleven."

As he thought about his childhood discipline, he added, "Dad very seldom whipped me, but the one time he whipped me, I'll never forget. It's always bad when Mama says, 'I'm not gonna do anythang to you. Just wait 'til your Daddy gets home.' So, you got all afternoon thanking, 'Ah, no! What's gonna happen?' But Dad didn't whip me much, but Mama, Mama, you said a bad word, you're gonna get it."

He continued his reminiscing about his parents, "Mama was at one time a Nazarene, which, you know, they believe in tongues, shouting, and stuff like that, saying 'Amen.' When I knew her, she's a Methodist. She was Nazarene 'fore I came along. She never did shout in the Methodist church. But a really Christian woman. She'd go to the Missionary Society on Tuesday afternoon and stuff like that, and she couldn't drive, so somebody come by and pick her up or she'd walk. But I thank if anybody ever got to heaven, she's one of 'em. And Dad, too. Dad couldn't say anythang bad around her. Why, she'd divorce him in a minute."

His laughter exploded. "But she didn't believe in divorces, so I don't know what she'd a done."

Flippo couldn't say enough about his parents. "But I thank Dad knew better to say bad words around Mama. I never did hear Dad say a bad word really, so they were pretty good, pretty close."

"Her folks were Nazarene—Uncle Charlie and Uncle Bill. They lived in Buffalo Gap. Uncle Bill had ten kids and 'A'nt Anner.' We called her Anner. 'A'nt Anner.' Uncle Charlie had seven or eight children. They lived about four miles from each other."

When asked about the name "A'nt Anner," Flip shared, "I guess it was Anna, probably. Well, I'm quite sure it was, and I don't know why we called her Anner. It was like my Mama's name was Gertrude Eugenia, and they always called her Gus, Aunt Gus. That was my mother."

Flippo recalled a story about Uncle Bill. "I 'member over at Uncle Bill's crowding around the radio when the World Series was on. Babe Ruth was playing

—Lou Gehrig. We're all gathered around the radio like we were seeing it, and those kids were all my cousins, and they're mostly all gone now except Herbert's still alive and Lola. Most of 'em are all gone." Often Flippo reflected through his reminiscing that so many relatives and friends had passed away—being ninety-one years old when we talked, he had lost so many.

Flippo Family Work Ethics

Flippo's mom got up at three-thirty or four every morning and fixed his dad's breakfast. He had to go to work at five-thirty. "Every morning for all the time I knew her, she'd git up, make his breakfast. Good woman—Four foot ten—and looooong hair. It'd go down past her butt, yeah, but she never did wear it out. She always wore it in a knot. And then sometimes, she'd have me braid her hair. I was pretty good braider, too. What's that other one? Not braiding, but thar's some other one."

We brainstormed what he meant, and he came up with it, "I'm talking about plaiting. Plaiting was easier than braiding, but I could plait her hair, but it was very seldom we did."

As he recalled seeing her long hair for the first time down, he chuckled. "She wore it mostly in a knot, and you'd never see her wear it out anywhere with it long like it was, but I thank the first time I saw it was she's getting ready for church, and she hadn't done it up in a knot yet. I said, 'My, you got lots of hair.'"

Flippo's dad worked for Ben E. Keith. He was hired during the Depression, and four-year-old Flippo happened to be with him. "He was going every morning at 4:00 a.m. looking for work because this is the Depression. Thar was no work.

"Jobs were scarce. He'd get up at 4:00 a.m. and get in about 5:00 p.m. Dad was a super man. He was just a dear person. Anyway, he'd go, and he'd try to find a job until 5:00 p.m. and then he'd come home. Now all the time that I knew them, Mama would get up at 4:00 a.m. and fix his breakfast. When he went to work for Ben E. Keith, it was Abilene Fruit and Vegetable at the time that he got hired. And then they changed it to Ben E. Keith. It was a fruit and vegetable company out of Fort Worth. And now they're all over the country.

"But anyway, we'd go to some places twice. I say we, I only went with him once, but I happened to be lucky enough to be thar when they hired him. So, we went early to Ben E. Keith's because they were delivering food in the city. They'd get up early of a morning and get a good start on it.

"He'd asked me the night before, 'Do you want to go with me in the morning?'"

Eagerly Flippo replied, "Yeah. Yeah."

Flippo laughed as he thought about it, "So anyway, he said, 'Okay, you got to be up at 4:30.'"

So he got up at 4:30 a.m. His mama made breakfast. He and his dad got in the car and stopped at a couple places, and then they went to Abilene Fruit and Vegetable, which is now Ben E. Keith. They didn't have a job, so they continued all day. Before they went home that night, Flippo's dad went back by Ben E. Keith, and they asked, "Can you drive a truck?" Flippo laughed outright at this question.

Flippo's dad answered, "Yes, I can drive a truck."

"They instructed, 'Well, come in at 4:30 in the morning. You've got a job. We had a truck driver die just about four hours ago.'"

"So, Dad said, 'I'll be here.' And of course, he was.'"

"He worked for them for thirty-seven years. I believe he had a thirty-six year 'Safe Driver's Award.' And he had so many chances to better himself, but he said, 'No. Staying right here. They hired me during the Depression when I really needed it. I ain't changing jobs.' So, he stayed with them, and he was a good man."

Flippo's musing about his parents warmed my heart. "She's a really a good woman, and Dad was a good guy, too. I just love 'em both, but we were not a huggin' family. I remember Dad hugging me when I was baptized. You know, you gotta stand up thar, and people come by, you know. I thought, 'Ah, here come Mother and Dad. Oh, my.' Mama hugged me, and Dad hugged me, too. I was so surprised. I don't know where my kissin' came in or where it started, but we were not what ya call a huggin' or kissin' family. I don't really recall kissing my mama. Surely, I did, but anyway, we were not that lovey-dovey."

We talked about how families are all different and he continued, "We loved each other. I had two good sisters, and I's just lucky, lucky. I got a joke about Lucky."

Flippo's humor always prevailed, so I asked him, "You do?"

"Yeah. I can't remember how it goes," which caused a belly laugh from both of us.

School Life at Wylie

Besides his family's strong influence, Flippo's school experience at Wylie, a consolidated school, grades 1 – 11, also shaped this young man.

Flippo remembered his mother and older sister taking him to school. With a September birthday, his parents wondered when to enroll him into school, so they waited a year. Flippo started first grade at the age of seven.

The Flippos continued to move. "Dad found another cheaper one on Forest Drive. It's South 20th now, but it was Forest Drive at that time—1941, I believe. Forest Drive, and that's when I started going to school at Wylie—more about Wylie later on."

Flippo and his sister had to ride the bus to Wylie. "We only had eleven grades. I know they have twelve now." Flippo also remembered, "The superintendent of the school was Frank Careson. He was [also] the superintendent of Wylie Consolidated School District. Our Ag/FFA teacher was his brother."

School Age Flippo. Source: John Flippo

Wylie was where Flippo was when he joined the Navy when he was senior. That's what they called eleventh graders then.

Flippo's favorite class in school was "probably spelling."

"I know that Mrs. Shepard was, I believe, the sixth-grade teacher. A lot of thangs happened to me in sixth grade. I know Mrs. Shepard was the spelling teacher, and she marked some of my words with an X, and I looked and I looked, and they were spelled right. So, I questioned her on it, and she said, 'Oh, I made a mistake, Marshall.' Do you know, she never did put an X on one of my words again after that." He chuckled in thinking about this incident. "But anyway, yeah, I like spelling."

His interest in spelling continued throughout our interviews—he would spell out any names he thought I might not know and repeated the correct spelling for "Wylie" several times for me up to our last interview. What an amazing ability!

Flip enjoyed his school years reflecting that he had a good teacher, then added, "All my teachers were good, really. I can't thank of a bad one."

Flippo chuckled a couple times. "You thank of funny thangs that happened when you hadn't thought of them in a long time."

With encouragement, he continued, "An ole boy named Raymond Sherman had a juice harp. A cop stopped the bus driver. Raymond was in the back, and this highway patrol was talking to the bus driver. I don't thank the bus driver done anythang. Anyway, he didn't get a ticket. Raymond was back thar twanging and making noise, 'me, my, me, me' the whole time. That's just one of those funny thangs."

Flippo had fun in school.

Rayburn Landers was the coach and sixth grade teacher, and at that time they had ink wells in their desks. Somebody had a bottle of ink they couldn't open. Flippo recounted what happened: "So it goes all way around the room and all these kids trying to open it. I'm sitting on the front because Rayburn says, 'This is where you sit. You don't sit in the back.' So I was sitting up front, and this ink bottle was going around the room. Everybody tried it, and it got back over to Rayburn. We called him 'Coach.' Coach had it. He said, 'Flip, here it is. I can't open it.' I thought, 'Boy, I'm going to be the strongest one.' I took this damn bottle, gave it a big yank, and ink went everywhere. He'd opened it. He got down on the floor laughing. I had ink all over me and that ole ink won't come out."

As Flippo often did in his storytelling, he repeated key phrases from the story, "'Here, Flip, I can't get this thang open.'" And "Man, I give it a big yank!" He also added, "Rayburn was a good guy."

When he got home, his mother asked, "What in the world happened?"

"I spilled some ink."

"I can see that."

When Flippo finished seventh grade, which was Grammar School, he recalled with a laugh a class trip they took. This week-long bus trip was a celebration of the end of Grammar School, and they went to Austin, Houston, "San Antone," and Galveston.

Mrs. Burgess and Mrs. Shepard were the chaperones of thirty-two students. This trip had a strong effect on Flippo in a couple ways.

"First time I'd seen the ocean, yes ma'am. And that wasn't really the ocean. That was the Gulf of Mexico. Looked kinda like the ocean to me. That was really a trip. I started smoking on that trip—been smoking ever since."

Flippo laughed at my chuckles at this revelation, then he named a couple of the possible culprits that started him smoking. Finally, he came up with the person, "Oh, I know who it was. It was Dan Snow. He smoked at home, and he'd been smoking I don't know how long. Sometimes he'd come and spend the night with me, and we'd sleep outside on the front yard or in the back porch or whatever. I liked to go and stay with him because his folks knew he smoked, and so we could smoke in the house, and we'd light our cigarettes by those ole oil lamps, you know. They didn't have electricity. So, we'd light, and I could almost buy me an ole oil lamp to get one more taste of that." Flippo's soft sigh and chuckle at this memory warmed my heart.

He continued the description, "You tasted when you lit that cigarette with an oil lamp. Just put it up to the top of the oil lamp, you know, and lit your cigarette. But, so I thank he's the one give me a cigarette on that trip. I guess he showed me how to inhale and everythang. Anyway. I got hooked on 'em."

Something tragic happened on that same trip. "My buddy liked to drown in Galveston, Glen Sheldon. We're out thar in the surf, and I's out thar I thought pretty far, and I'd just learned to swim. Here comes ole Glen right by me. I said, 'How you doing, Glen?' His eyes were this big. And I thought, 'What's wrong with that guy?' And boy, here comes the bus driver swimming like a fish and went out thar and grabbed ole Glen. He's in an undercurrent and couldn't get out of it. He'd a drowned if that bus driver hadn't saved him."

They had a good trip though. Flippo mused, "That's a long way down thar."

Being the president of his class from seventh grade all the way up through high school, Flippo was a leader at his school. He minimized this by saying, "I thank I's the only one who would take it, but I didn't do anythang." With a chuckle, he added, "They had to have somebody, I guess."

The school system was different then: eighth, ninth, tenth, and eleventh grades were high school—no twelfth. "We only had seven grades in grammar school, and then we had four grades in high school. The eleventh was called the senior year, and the eighth was freshmen. That was at Wylie."

"A funny thang I might have told you about my Aunt Pearl. I was very bashful, and my younger sister, Onita, was outgoing. My Aunt Pearl said, 'Marshall, you'd better be careful. She'll catch you in school,' and so I said, 'I don't thank she'll ever catch me.'" But Flippo quit school before his senior year to go into the navy. He took an equivalency test when they were in Puget Sound to finish high school then returned to Wylie four years later, and it turned out his Aunt Pearl had been right. By the time he got out of the Navy, Onita had finished school. "We got our diplomas on the same day . . . . I graduated right along with her."

SCHOOL DAYS 1943-'44
Wylie

Source: John Flippo

With a chuckle, he recalled, "And Pearl said, 'I told you.'"

His love for sports started at Wylie where he played baseball and football. Flippo played shortstop in baseball. In football, Flippo played tailback and quarterback. A lot of schools were small at that time, so they played six-man football. They played Butterfield, Tuscalo, and Lawn. Flippo spelled out Lawn to make sure I spelled it correctly.

Flippo's childhood was focused on his family and school, with the church playing a major role, as well. His west Texas upbringing was filled with laughter, love, and good times. And was unfortunately cut short by the raging World War II.

Roy and Gertrude Flippo with June. Source: John Flippo

16 year-old Flippo with his dog, Rusty. Source: John Flippo

June, Flippo with Roy Flippo in the 70s. Source: John Flippo

THE TEXAN BECOMES A SAILOR

Source: John Flippo

2

YOU'RE IN THE NAVY NOW!

World War II began on September 1, 1939 and ended on September 2, 1945. In 1944, the war was intensifying. Flippo's sister, Helen, had already joined and was serving. Patriotism flourished across the country with Flippo experiencing his own version in his small west Texas town.

"I joined the Navy when I turned seventeen in 1944." After Flippo shared this, he sat quiet—his thoughtful silence spoke volumes.

In reviewing the part in the first interview about him joining the Navy, I mistakenly thought he had falsified his records to join.

Quickly he answered, "Whoa, whoa, whoa!! What did you say about the records?"

From his tone, I realized I had made a mistake. "I thought you told me that you falsified your records when you were seventeen. That's how you got into . . ."

He interrupted me with a resounding, "No!"

So he explained what happened. "Well, Dad had to sign for me, but we didn't falsify it. I got in. Daddy signed for me, and I went in on my seventeenth birthday. I didn't falsify anythang."

Flippo remembered back to when he was still at home, and R. H. 'Hub' Evans came home from the war after joining the Marines. He was a year ahead of Flip in school. When he came home on leave, he wore his dress Marine uniform. Flip said, "My God, looked good, ya know. He came out to school at Wylie, but anyway, he had quit his senior year. He came out thar, and he had his Marine uniform on, really 'snappy.'"

The thought of this tickled Flippo. Hub reassured him it would be a lot of fun, he hadn't been in the war yet, but he was headed that way. Hub faced Iwo Jima, which was a hard time.

Flippo went home from school and told his Mom and Dad, he was going to quit school and join the Marines.

His dad objected, "You don't want to join the Marines."

Flippo's parents continued: "Are you sure? You're a young guy, and you're probably not thanking straight."

"No, I want to join the service."

He remembered, "Well, Hub said it's tough but said it's really good for ya and everythang, and I was kinda patriotic, too."

With a chuckle, Flippo shared about his deep patriotism. "This is silly here, but I slept on the back porch, and I'd play the radio all night long. Well, some of those stations go off with the 'Star-Spangled Banner.' I would git out of bed and stand up in the dark.

"Anyway, I had to have Dad and Mother's consent to join when I was seventeen, and so they consented. It was some kinda defensive spirit. You really learn discipline and stuff like that.

He wanted to go to the Marines because he liked that uniform, but somehow he got sidetracked to the Navy. So, he joined the Navy on his seventeenth birthday, and he got out his twenty-first birthday, September 2, 1948 four years later.

Flippo's described his parents' farewell: "We said goodbye at the railroad station. My sister had been in the service for a while, so they were used to this."

Inducted in Dallas

So, the young Flippo left Abilene with a bunch from the area and went to Dallas on the T & P Railway, where they were inducted. "Then we came back through Abilene, and Momma and Dad were at the train station. They hugged me and everythang, and we just kept goin' all the way to San Diego on the old T & P and then the S & P Railroad, and one ole car that I's on had a square wheel right under me."

I laughed at his comment, and he joined my laughter. "And anyway, funny thangs happen when we were being inducted. Thar's a whole bunch of us in thar, and an ole boy from—oh, where was he from? Anyway, close to Abilene, he kept goin' to sleep. They'd hotfootin' him—hotfootin' him." Flippo let out a chuckle.

"Well, we were all sitting around in a kinda big circle, and they'd take one in every once in a while. It'd been a long while, and they'd take another person in. Anyway, he's over thar falling asleep, and every time he'd fall asleep, somebody'd hotfoot him."

When Flippo laughed again, I finally had to ask for an explanation of "hotfootin." Another laugh escaped before he explained, "They'd put a match in his shoe and light that match, and they would burn down. Yeah, pretty hot for him, and he'd stomp his foot, you know. Sometimes the match would fall out. But he wouldn't wake completely up, so one ole boy went over thar, and he put about ten matches around his feet, and tied his shoestrings together, and, so, he lit all those damn matches. Oh, I wish I could remember his name right off. Anyway, well, when it got that hot, he jumped up and started to walk. Well, hell, he fell straight down, you know. He's the best sport in the world, and he just laughed about it, but of course, we all got a big laugh out of it."

The story continued with more chuckles from Flippo. "And then, they put us on that ole T & P Railroad, goes right down through the middle of Abilene. It's the Texas & Pacific, just like Southern Pacific. This is Texas & Pacific. We had so much damn fun on that train. I can't thank of any particular thang, but I 'member laughing all the way to San Diego, the guys doing different thangs."

Boot Camp

With a cough, Flippo said, "I thought, 'Well, I'm going to like this.' I got to boot camp, and God dang, I tell you, it was tougher than hell, and I guess I did pretty good. The last inspection that we had we lined up, and our 'Boats 'n Bait' was ahead, but got most of the marching and all that kind of stuff, you know."

I asked, "Who?

Flippo replied, "Boats 'n Bait."

I asked for an explanation.

His response was sharp. "Honey, don't tell me how to spell it—boats and bait. You could find it in some Navy literature, I'm sure. Boatswain—I thank it's B-O-A-T-S-W-A-I-N. I'm not sure. Well, he got the ole first lieutenant, but he was the head of our company, and so the last inspection we had. You know, they taught us how to roll up or down our clothes and all that kinda stuff. Give us a sea bag and all that. But he got to me, and he looked at me, and he said, 'Who are you?'"

Flippo told him.

He asked, "You been in this company all along?"

And Flippo answered, "Yes, Sir."

He replied, "Well, I guess you's alright. I never did have to chew you out 'cause I don't remember seeing you." Flippo enjoyed this comment about his good behavior.

Leave After Boot Camp

After boot camp, Flippo had leave for nine days, and then they went back to the Naval Training Center in San Diego. That's when they started shipping sailors out to different ships. "But I guess I had as about as good as I could have. It was really fun being with different guys, learning 'em and then becoming friends. And so, I was enjoying it alright, and even on the first ship, the USS *Lander*. We caught it out of San Francisco, and I wasn't too worried about seasickness, but I got seasick between San Francisco and Hawaii one time, and then the rest of time I's in the Navy, I didn't get seasick again.

Flippo shared his tactic when you get seasick, "You're fighting somebody else for a garbage can."

As he thought about this, Flippo's belly laugh was infectious. Flip added that when he was seasick, you'd hear him shouting on the ship, "Git out of my way! I got to go! Wait 'til I git through."

Even though he had that bout with seasickness, Flippo added, "I'm gonna like this, I thank. I like the sea, like the ocean, like the water, and I liked Hawaii when I got thar."

ॐ

People have always been important to Flippo, so two adventuresome sailors, Thurman Curry and Harold Snodgrass, livened up his traveling home and back to San Diego.

ॐ

Thurman Curry

Thurman Curry became one of Flippo's best friends and their experiences of hitchhiking from San Diego to Abilene definitely highlights a different time and concern about safety.

Flip was on the ship with Thurman Curry, and they both lived in Abilene.

As he thought of Thurman, he remembered, "My best buddy when I was at 1425 Cedar, Abilene, Texas was a black kid. My best buddy in the Navy, and you know I can't thank of his first name because we didn't know their first names. Freeman—last name was Freeman. Freeman was black, and so was Thurman."

Because they didn't have a car, Thurman and Flippo hitchhiked to Abilene from San Diego between boot camp and Amphibious Training. It took them three rides. Flippo added, "Nowadays, I wouldn't hitchhike to save my neck. And nobody would pick you up nowadays, anyway."

As Flip related this story, it reminded me of my childhood when we picked up hitchhikers on the lonely fifty-mile road to Trinidad, Colorado and never thought a thing about it. Times have changed so much.

Flippo knew Thurman before the service but had "no earthly recollection" how. "The only thang I know is we ended up on the same ship. Thurman Curry. C-U-R-R-Y."

Flippo and Thurman palled around and went on leave together. They left out of San Diego and were out on El Cajon Boulevard, "way out thar where thar's no houses or nothing on the outskirts of San Diego, and I've tried to find that place where we were on the highway. We were in our Navy whites. We decided if we'd wear them, we'd have more luck."

Flippo often identified the times in his life where luck played out, but in this situation, you have to wonder how lucky these two decked-out sailors really were.

When he became a caller, Flippo returned to San Diego and went back, "to El Cajon Boulevard to about the place I thought we's hitchhiking, and nothing but tall buildings out thar now. Ah, it had grown, grown, grown, way past where we were, and we were out of town. Ole trees planted out thar about as big as your finger, and so we sat thar about—man, I don't remember how we got out thar. Someway we got out thar."

So, they waited, until at some point Flippo had to go to the bathroom. He said, "Thurman, I've gotta go."

Thurman asked, "Where you going to go? Thar's nothing but those little ole trees out thar.'"

Flippo replied, "Man, I'm starting to hurt."

42

Thurman noted, "Well, let's wait for ten more cars," and Flippo added, "so the ninth one picked us up."

First Ride

By the time the ninth car picked them up, Flippo thought he was going to burst. "We were two bashful kids, and so we were sitting in the back. [The driver] and her husband were up front. We get to El Centro, she stopped the car, and the ole man got out—wasn't old. He was twenty-five or thirty. He got out."

Flippo thought, "Oh, man, he's going to the bushes. I'm going to follow him." But Flippo was out of luck. "He walked around the car. She scooted over, and he started driving."

"So, I was hurting plum up to my chest, and ole Thurman's laughing like hell. We got to Yuma."

They stated, "Now, we're going to spend the night here." They let them out there by the highway. Flippo spied a service station on the east corner, so he went to the first service station, "I guess I needed it so bad, I don't know, not too much at all come out, and I was still hurting. We walked across the street to another station, and I guess I peed for five minutes. What a relief! It must have stretched my bladder because I got all the way to Abilene 'fore I ever had to pee again."

They didn't have very much money, but they did buy a sandwich, got back out on the highway, and at about the fourth or fifth car, a guy picked them up.

Second Ride

The driver asked them where they were headed.

In unison Flippo and Thurman answered, "Abilene, Texas."

"Well, I'll take you to El Paso."

Flippo shared, "You know from Yuma to El Paso is a good long trip."

"Either one of you drive?"

Again, they responded together, "Yeah, both of us drive."

The driver seemed relieved. "Okay."

Flippo added to the story, "We drove the car for that ole boy. He got in the back seat and went to sleep. You know, you wouldn't do that nowadays to save your day. And anyway, he got thar, back in the hole." Thurman drove awhile. They pulled in and got us some gasoline, and there weren't many convenience stores at that time, so they had to watch out. They got the gasoline, the car owner snored almost all the way to El Paso, and he woke up at Las Cruces.

He questioned them about how long he slept.

Thurman answered, "Yeah, we stopped twice. You never did wake up, but you were snoring."

"Oh," he commented, "boy, I'm really ready to go on to San Antone. You'll have more luck here than out thar where it splits. Thar's nothing out thar at all."

So, he took them on up the highway to Van Horn, let them out, and they spent nine hours looking for another ride. Flippo realized they probably missed a ride or two in Van Horn because they looked for a place that had a coke. After they got back out, they were hitchhiking a little.

Thurman stated, "I'm hungry."

From where they got the coke, way on down the street, Flip saw a sign that said "Cafe." And so, they walked there and had something to eat and probably missed some rides. They got three excellent rides, even though they had to wait nine hours, it was worth it for this couple.

Third Ride

They did finally get a good ride with a man and his wife.

The man asked, "Where you boys going?"

These two answered together again, "We're headed to Abilene.'"

The driver assured them he was going right through there, and they would have a ride all the way. The driver and his wife planned to spend the night in Big Spring. They had reservations downtown at a hotel. They were going to leave early in the morning.

He added, "I'll let you out here on the highway. If you guys want to spend the night, we'll be glad to take you home. We'll have breakfast and everythang in the morning. We'll take you on."

Flippo described their situation, "Thar weren't many motels at that time. Very nice couple. So, we pooled the money we had left. I thank I had eleven dollars or somethang. Thurman had somethang. We pooled our money to pay for the hotel room, which was nine dollars, and so, the next morning they let us have breakfast, and the man paid for the breakfast. I know I had two eggs, bacon, and no hash browns, but I did have some French fries, and it was eighty-five cents. That's counting the coffee, too."

The hospitality of this couple warmed Flippo's heart. "He grabbed the check, paid for it, so anyway, we took off to Abilene."

As we entered Abilene, the driver asked, "Now, where do you all live?"

Flippo explained, "Well, Thurman lived over on the north side. I lived on the south side."

Thurman refused, "No, no, no. You don't need to take us home. If you'll let us out in downtown Abilene, we'll have our folks come and get us."

Flippo recounted, "So that's what they did. They let us out downtown—I forget exactly around Woolworth's, I thank, or Grant's Department Store. I believe it was Woolworth, and so we called our folks and they came got us. What a nice couple!"

In remembering, Flippo wished he'd gotten their name and their address so he could have at least sent them a card. He added, "It was a good ride, so we got thar in three rides, and every one of the rides were really good."

As I listened to Flippo's hilarious hitchhiking stories with Thurman, I saw the adventuresome young man shining through his words and attitude and marveled at his acceptance of long waits and strangers taking care of him and Thurman. They handled the situation of not having a car, and more importantly they arrived home to Abilene safe and sound.

. . .

Harold Snodgrass

Thurman and Flippo's return trip to San Diego was totally different. Harold Snodgrass got leave the same time they did. The three of them had buddied around for a long while.

Harold told Flippo and Thurman, "Now, you guys, don't you get a bus ticket or anythang back. I'm going to come through Abilene, and I'll have me a brand-new car, and we'll just all go out thar together."

Flippo sang this whole phrase: "Ole Harold said, 'I'm coming by in a new car.'"

Harold promised to be back through there in a car, and they had a ride to San Diego.

&

Flippo's voice took on a relaxed tone as he described the setup, "We had to report back to San Diego. So, Ole Harold came by about a week before we had to leave. He had an ole '35 Ford, so we would go out to little ole towns around lookin' for girls and that damn thang would break down."

Thurman predicted, "Hell, we'll never get back to San Diego in this thang." Flippo laughed out loud at this memory.

Young Flippo, the Sailor. Source: John Flippo

So, the three sailors put on their uniforms went looking for girls in these little

45

towns around Abilene like Sweetwater, Anson, Tuscola, and Buffalo Gap. Flip added, "We'd always have our uniforms on, thanking maybe we catch a look—we'd catch anythang."

Flippo described this trio, "But we were bashful as hell. The girls would almost have to ask us. Every time we get in one of those little ole towns, that damn car would break down, so we'd work on it and work on it. I was no mechanic, and Thurman wasn't either, but ole Harold kinda knew what was going on, so he'd get that ole car started again."

"So, the time came for us to leave." Flippo sang the word leave.

Flippo thought, "Oh, no! We's going to San Diego in this thang."

So they packed all of their bags in the back of that undependable car and took off. They had Harold up front and Thurman up front, and they switched drivers about every 150 miles, rotated around. Surprisingly, the ole car kept running. They left Abilene, and twenty-seven hours later they were in San Diego. That car made it all the whole way, and Harold kept it. It was a good one on the road, but not in Abilene.

"We had one little incident. Harold went to sleep when he was driving, and he hit one of those sawhorses that was blocking the highway, and he didn't stop in time, and we hit a ditch." Flippo chuckled as he remembered.

Thurman was lying down in the back, and it knocked him off to the floor. Flippo was sitting in the passenger seat, and his head hit the roof of the car and startled him awake.

Flippo questioned Harold about what happened.

"Oh," Harold answered. "I kinda went to sleep, went through the blockade, and hit the ditch."

At that point, Flippo exclaimed, "Well, good Lord! I cannot see."

He couldn't see anything because the hood went up with the impact.

Flippo explained, "It knocked the hood up. So, he got out, and I's still sitting thar, sleepy, you know, and the last thang I 'member is him. He slammed that hood down, and it wouldn't stay down. He got up on it, and he was jumping up and down on it, and I went back to sleep."

The next thing Flip knew, they were on US Highway 80, headed to San Diego. The car made it all the way without any trouble except when he went through that barricade. "That's the only little bobble we had, and I went to sleep while he got that car back on the ole highway. I don't know how he did it, and Thurman was asleep in the back seat, so it didn't bother us too much. He had that ole car and sold it. Boy, that was really good: a sailor with a car. Really good, and especially in those days."

Flippo remembered another fun activity they had with Harold's car. He'd let the air out of all the tires, they'd get on that "dad-gum trolley track—streetcar track—and the wheels just fit that damn trolley track. He'd just turn loose of the steering wheel, and we'd head down that trolley track and that ole car—you couldn't get it to stop. We'd go over everythang the track took us through." As Flippo remembered the fun they had with that ole '35, he laughed and laughed.

Another time they drove to Tijuana, Mexico. "I 'member we went up in some mountains. We went up in thar and thar's a big ole fire over thar. It was like a campground, and we went over thar and some people over thar, way up in the mountains."

The campers asked, "How you sailor boys doing? Could we buy you one here? We're just camping out. We're fixing to have some hot dogs." As Flippo remembered this little venture across the border, he laughed.

The trio joined them. He described their experience. "So anyway, we had a good time with those people up thar, and then we went back, put the ole car on the track again, took off towards the ship. I don't know how long."

Flippo described Harold's car after their shenanigans with a chuckle. "It looked like it might have been through two or three wars. Ole car just run like a top." He was surprised when Harold told him about the sale. Harold said, "Well, I almost got what I paid for it."

Flippo couldn't believe the difference in the money. Harold lived in Tennessee, so the difference in the price from Tennessee out to San Diego was quite high, so he got almost whatever he paid for the car.

Back to San Diego & Amphib Training

After returning to San Diego, Flippo had to do KP duty for a week serving breakfast and lunch and "stuff like that."

"They asked if anybody wanted to be in the 'Amphibs,' and I held up my hand. I had never even heard the word 'Amphibs.' Coronado Island was our Amphibious training base; it was before the bridge was built."

Flippo in front of the Coronado Hotel. Source: John Flippo

He noted, "That base is still here. And so is that hotel." Flippo shared that he always wanted to buy a home on Coronado Island, but he commented, "No, no, no, no! It's too much money."

This training dictated where Flippo would end up during the war. They took their amphibious training there because it had a really good surf. He remembered one time, they did their training in that surf getting in and out off of beaches. He was on one of the little landing boats with a crew of four, and Flippo was one of the four on the little boats that had a ramp in front. In other words, they'd go in and land, drop that ramp, and the troops would all come out of it.

Now, they had bigger ships that would do the same, but these were little ones.

Flippo related, "I forget how many we had on the USS *Lander*, but we had a bunch, and they'd be dropped down to the ocean, filled up with troops, and then we'd go in. We couldn't turn around and go forward out of that surf. You had to back all the way out because if you turned around, those big ole waves would hit that ramp and knock it down inside the boat after you'd left your troops on the beach. You couldn't turn around. You had to back all the way out. So, we had a good coxswain on our little ole boat. We backed out. We had no problems."

During their night time duty in training, they picked up downed pilots who were on maneuvers night flying and landing on a carrier at night, and so when they missed, they'd picked them up if they could find them. The Secretary of Navy came out once, and he wanted to see some maneuvers. "The day he wanted to see maneuvers, it was raining like hell, and the weather was God awful, but he says, 'Go ahead and do it. You might have to do it the same way.'"

The story continued, "Oh, man! I'll never forget that day. Anyway, we went in, and our coxswain on our boat was very good, so we took our troops in and landed, and then he backed out. Well, thar was a lot of them weren't good enough, and they broached their boat and, of course, thar's boats all over the beach that were broached and washed back up on the beach and stuff like that. I thank he could have wanted it every week, but it was a pretty bad day. We lost some sailors on that thang."

As Flippo headed toward war duty and all the unpredictable events he would face, this amphibious training prepared him for his wartime assignment aboard the USS *Lander*.

3

USS LANDER

USS Lander — Copyright. Source: https://www.navsource.org/archives/10/03/
03178.htm

Flippo had referenced a war book of his, *USS LANDER 1945*, and he lent it to
me, hoping I'd read it so we could discuss it. He referred to it often when the
war came up. "And this war book is going to tell you what all I did in the war. After
the war, I can fill you in what I did. I was in two more years after the war, so I
played baseball, but I can fill that in later on." And he did.

When I had looked through Flippo's Navy book, *USS LANDER 1945,* I saw several pictures of the crew by divisions so, I asked him which division he was in so I could feature it in this book.

His response was priceless. "I was in the Bakers and Cooks. I don't remember what our division was named, but I was a baker in the Navy. I don't know whether they didn't thank we was important or just skipped us or didn't know we were thar."

So, he was not in any of the division pictures, but Flippo is in one picture in his Navy book, *USS LANDER 1945*, which was, "When I'm cleaning the colander thar. I thank I'm up on a stool. I'm very, very young. I'm seventeen years old."

He commented about seeing seventeen-- old boys now. "Surely, I didn't do that," he would think.

Flippo Cleaning a Colander. Source: *USS LANDER 1945*

After reading Flippo's Navy book, I regret not reading it fully before he died so he could elaborate on what it said. Because he referenced it so often, I've used it to fill in Flippo's Navy stories as needed.

The United States' military focus between 1944 and 1945 was the Asiatic-Pacific Theater. The USS *Lander*, a destroyer tender (APA 178) [Attack Transport – Troop][1] participated in two major campaigns in the Asiatic-Pacific Theater: Iwo Jima operation: assault and occupation of Iwo Jima, 6 to 16 March 1945; and Okinawa operation: assault and occupation of Okinawa, 7 to 11 June 1945.[2]

Flippo knew specifics about the USS *Lander*, "See the ship was just built in Seattle, and it was a new ship and a lot of those were built by old what's-his-face. Damn. It is a shipbuilder." I confirmed on the Internet, and the builder was Oregon Shipbuilding Corporation.

Flippo's Navy book described the USS *Lander*:

> These highly powered, Kaiser-built, Victory ship hulls, stacked high with landing craft and anti-aircraft weapons were admirably suited to carry our fighting men to hostile beachheads. Thoroughly trained in California and again in Hawaiian waters, the *Lander* was prepared and expected to land invasion forces first on the island stepping stones to Japan and finally on the shores of the empire.[3]

The young, inexperienced seventeen-year-old Flippo was in the majority on the USS *Lander*. "We were, for the most part, a green crew."[4] Seventy-five percent of the sailors on the ship had never been to sea!

After amphibious training, Flippo was assigned to the USS *Lander*, and they picked his new ship up in San Pedro near San Diego on December 29, 1944.[5]

They picked up the rest of the ship's personnel and took off. Flip remembered one guy.

He stated, "I ain't going to war."

And Flippo asked, "Why?"

He repeated, "I ain't going to war."

"Well, you're in the war right now."

"Yep. When the ship goes, I ain't going."

Flippo asked, "What are you going to do, jump off?"

"No, I have seasickness."

When they pulled along the dock in San Francisco, Flippo didn't feel sick, but the sailor was sick as a dog.

And he continued, "I'm going to have to have shore duty because I've got seasickness."

The sick sailor got a medical leave, and he didn't go with the ship, but Flip thought it was legitimate. "He was puking every other minute."

With a chuckle, Flippo recalled getting seasick once between San Francisco and Hawaii. "I got to Hawaii, and I became very sick. I 'member waking up of a morning, and I had like indigestion. It was like a big piece of meat lodged in my stomach." He laughed about it now, but the seriousness of the situation for a seventeen-year-old away from home came through.

Young Flippo as a sailor. Source: John Flippo

"And it felt like a brick. And so, I went and ate the chow, breakfast, and I went back up and I felt like, 'Man, I'm going to throw up.' So, I got pretty close to a GI can, and I did throw up.

"Boy, after I threw up," Flippo laughed, "I felt so good."

And Flippo thought, "Oh, man, whatever it was came up, but the hurt started back." Then he thought, "Uh oh."

So, Flippo went to sick bay because he had appendicitis. They sent him over to Base Eight hospital in Honolulu and took his appendix out the same day. "That little old nurse sitting thar. She was a-waiting. She came in thar."

Flippo said to the nurse, "I got to go to the bathroom."

She asserted, "Well, get up and go to the bathroom."

Flippo remarked with disbelief, "Well, they just cut on me and took my appendix out."

She retorted, "That's alright. Go on."

Again, Flippo laughed. "So, I got up. It was hard to walk. And so, I walked back thar to the crapper, and I walked back to my bed. And I was thar overnight, and my ship was sailing the next day."

Flippo thought, "Well, I'm not going to be on that ship." He added, "Now I believe it was about eleven or twelve o'clock in the morning the doctor came."

Flippo told the doctor, "My ship leaves, I believe, tonight."

The doctor assured him he would be on it.

Flippo questioned him, "How am I going to be on it?"

The doctor instructed him to get up, put his clothes in his sea bag, and a bus would be out front. He told him to take his sea bag out there.

Flippo described this event. "Well, your sea bag had all the clothes you ever had owned when you was in the service. It was heavy."

Even though we were on the phone, I could almost see Flippo shaking his head in disbelief. I certainly was!

Flippo asked the doctor, "Shall I carry it?"

"Yeah, carry it on out there." I cringed—he just had surgery!

With a laugh, Flippo added, "Anyway, I's afraid I's gonna miss that ship, but I didn't."

It was hard to believe, but Flippo kept laughing as he told this story relating how different his appendectomy was from his dad's! His dad stayed in the hospital two weeks. "But anyway, I got out of thar carrying my sea bag to the bus. The damn bus took me down to the dock. I caught a little ole boat out to the ship, and I had to drag that damn sea bag up the gangplank. And thar was an ole boy behind me. I never will forget him. An ole boy named Smitty Smith—damn, his first name started with an N. Anyway, he was behind me."

Smitty saw Flip's dilemma and offered to carry his heavy bag for him.

Flippo exclaimed, "Damn right." With a chuckle, he added, "We became real close friends." He continued, "But anyway, he carried that up to the top of the gangplank for me, and then we became quite good friends. When I was transferred after the war, I run into him again at DesPac[6], and he'd been one of them off of another destroyer who had been picked to play on the baseball team."

Flippo ended the story with, "Anyway, I made it."

Route Traveled on USS *Lander*

When Flippo recounted the route the USS *Lander* took so many years ago, he left out names of several ports and islands. The itinerary from his Navy book showed the specific places they stopped. (See Appendix B.) He remembered they went to Eniwetok, took off to Guam, and went to the Marshall Islands. "And you know, every time we sailed, nobody knew where we's going, so, we'd always guess, 'Where we going next?'"

He didn't go straight from Iwo Jima to Okinawa. They returned to Hawaii before going to Okinawa, and he only spent four days in Okinawa on the USS *Lander*. Later, he returned on the USS *Piedmont* and stayed about eleven months.

Iwo Jima

Flippo remembered the name "Iwo Jima" came up and thought, "Nah, we ain't going thar." And then the next day, "Hey, I thank we're going to Iwo Jima."

"No, we're not going to thar."

Next day, again, "Boy, I believe we're headed to Iwo Jima." And with a chuckle, he added, "I asked, 'How do you know that?'"

The sailor answered, "I just feel it in my bones." He ended this thought with a laugh.

Flippo was just talking to a friend, and so sure enough, they went there, but "they didn't do too much at Iwo Jima." He recalled being anchored out there, and they carried something in other than troops. "But don't seem like we carried many Marines. We carried mainly Army, so, I don't thank the Army was up in thar as much as the Marines were."

Flippo sailed to Iwo Jima knowing that his buddy, Hub Evans, was there, and he had it pretty tough at Iwo Jima. Flip didn't have it so bad because he was down on the beach. "That beach was funny because it was like quicksand almost. They had trouble getting up and down the beach because they'd sunk in. They bombarded it for a long while. They didn't thank thar would be anybody left on it, but they were all in caves. They had a hell of a time with it. It was Marines mainly."

Flippo and I never talked about it, but I wonder how he felt when they picked up wounded Marines, and he scanned the crowd for his friend. It must have been torture, but he never said anything.

Flippo's Navy book portrayed the Navy's involvement differently there than Flippo's experience.

> Preparations were underway for participation in training operations off Maui when we received a change of orders. We were assigned to a task unit, which was to pick up casualties from the Iwo Jima operation which was then in progress. These casualties plus a thousand or so battle-weary Marines were evacuated to Maui in the Hawaiian Islands.[7]

The Navy book revealed,

> It was not long before we learned that we were to proceed to Iwo Jima as part of a larger group. We had not expected to be sent to a theatre of combat operations without having participated in training operations in the Hawaiian area. The need, however, was urgent. The fanatic Jap defense at Iwo had caused far more than anticipated casualties, and it was imperative that these Marines be evacuated quickly.[8]

"We continued steaming throughout the day awaiting orders. During the ensuing eight days we steamed back and forth while our wake traced a rectangular furrow in the sea. Everyone became restless: for there is nothing more tedious than sailing nowhere." [9]

"After a long period of tracing rectangles in the sea, we received welcome orders which sent us toward Iwo Jima . . . . As we approached Iwo, we could see star shells bursting in the black sky. We passed barren, uninhabited Minami Iwo, and with the breaking of dawn, Mount Suribachi came into view.[10]

They watched as the battle roared.

"White crosses, marking the cemetery of the 4th Marine Division, made an even more significant impression."[11]

"From some foxhole, a Marine pressed the button of his Walkie-Talkie. He broadcast the terse message, 'Germany has surrendered.' This started a flow of rumor, which culminated in a big celebration. Thousands of rounds of ammunition, large and small, were fired into the air before it was learned that the rumor was false."[12]

"On March 16th, we received the formal notice that organized resistance on Iwo Jima had ceased. Some of the Marines slated for passage on the *Lander* never came aboard because some Japs in the northeastern tip of the island ignored this notice."[13]

After this, the *Lander* had an uneventful return to Hawaii.

Flippo got in at the tail end of the war. Iwo had calmed down some, but they were still fighting when the *Lander* arrived. The fighting was way off from them, and they stayed there a couple days and then took off for Okinawa.

The Battle of Iwo Jima lasted from February 19 – March 26, 1945. The USS *Lander* arrived there on March 14 and left six days later.

Okinawa

When they "took off for Okinawa," Flippo said, the journey took a couple months, and they had several stops along the way: Guam, back to Eniwetok, Pearl Harbor, Maui, back to Pearl Harbor, Maalaea Bay (Maui), back to Pearl Harbor, Honolulu, back to Eniwetok, Ulithi, and then Okinawa.[14]

The USS *Lander* arrived in Okinawa June 7, 1945 and stayed three days.[15]

Again, the speculative conversation started.

Somebody threw out the question, "Where we going?"

"Oh, I don't know. I thank we're going to Okinawa."

"No, no, no, no, no." Flippo remembered chuckling, "Anyway, this goes on for a few days, you know."

Somebody shared he had been looking at the map.

Flippo asked, "Yep. What'd you see?"

The sailor replied, "I saw Okinawa."

Another sailor realized Okinawa was the last little island they would hit because the next island was Japan—no more little islands like Okinawa or Iwo Jima.

So, they did end up going to Okinawa.

Flippo's Navy book described what they faced in Okinawa:

"Summary reports were coming in daily from Okinawa bringing news of an increasing number of ships damaged or sunk by Kamikaze planes. Here, if any place, we felt that enemy planes or submarines would be contacted."[16]

Flippo saw a Kamikaze hit a ship nearby. It went down the after stack[17] of the USS *Louisville* in Okinawa's Naha harbor.

Here's what the USS *Lander* encountered when they arrived at Okinawa:

Fighting was still in progress on the southern tip of Okinawa. An old battleship and a cruiser were stationed below Naha leisurely shelling inland objectives. Small spotting aircraft hovered in the area. Alongside our ship, the *Louisville* rode at anchor with one stack split open like a spent firecracker where she had been hit by Kamikaze plane a few days before.[18]

Flippo's Navy book identified what they experienced in Okinawa: "We had been warned to expect enemy air raids at sunset."[19]

Flippo added, "We also had to 'make smoke.' When I say, 'Make smoke,' is all the ships were able to make smoke for disguise, you know. They couldn't see where we were at. Their planes couldn't find out where our ship was. Japanese Betty was one of their big airplanes and they flew over the harbor, and it was a way high, and the ole LSD's [Landing Ship Dock][20] and ships like mine that had five 'H guns.' They'd shoot and you'd see the tracers go about halfway up to that plane, and then they'd fall off. They wouldn't even get close to that airplane, but that airplane was a Japanese plane called the Betty. I thank it was thar for reconnaissance or somethang like that. It just flew over the harbor one time, and it was gone. It was a way, way up thar. Japanese Betty was a large Japan bomber."

Interesting tactics were used here to hide these monstrous destroyer tenders from the enemy.

"The order was given 'Smoke boats, make smoke.' It became impossible to move because it was impossible to see. The zinc compound in the smoke pots filled lungs with acrid, choking air. Many felt the smoke to be more of a nuisance than the enemy planes in the vicinity."[21]

Okinawa is where they picked up a hundred Japanese prisoners. "Another troopship was—I forget the name of it—but they had a hundred, too. No, a hundred, too—a hundred, also!" We both laughed at his play on the word, "too!"

The prisoners had been living in caves and Flippo guessed that they hadn't bathed in probably a year. They had a hundred on their ship that they planned to take to Hawaii and a hundred on another APA [Attack Transport – Troop].[22]

They were pulling out of Naha harbor, out of Okinawa, and Tokyo Rose, a Japanese radio personality who aimed propaganda at U. S. Troops,[23] came on the radio. They could pick her up on their shortwave and always listened to her. She knew they listened to her. "She always knew stuff before we ever knew it in the bottom of the ship. I's going by the communication guy or whatever he was, and he hollered at me and said, 'Come in and listen to this,' and it was her talking in good English. She said, 'Thar's two troopships with a hundred prisoners apiece leaving out of Naha harbor headed to Hawaii. We know where they are. We got our sights on them. I hate to mention it to them, but they will never make it. They'll never make Hawaii. They will be torpedoed.' I don't know how she knew that so quickly, before we even pulled up anchor. It was unbelievable. Now this is still during the wartime."

The mention of Hawaii caused Flippo to sidetrack with this story, "So, as we were sailing out of Okinawa, we were taking these prisoners to Hawaii, so we's all hepped up about going back to Hawaii where I stood in line over a block for a whore house one time. I thought, 'Boy, I'm doing a hell of a job on her.' I heard a crunch and I looked up, and she was eating an apple. A hell of a job! Those were busy girls."

He repeated the line, "Hell of a job!" in this side story.

The prisoner story continued: "The two ships get out thar about a day's time or two days, and all of a sudden our ship comes to a halt, still in the water, and we look over, and the other ship had, too. Now we thought, 'What the hell's up?'"

The answer came, "Well, lucky for us, the captain comes on and says, 'Boys, we are transferring all of our prisoners over to the other ship. We're headed to Tsing-tao, China.' For whatever reason, I have no earthly idee, but our captain outranked the other captain on the other ship, so, we got to go to Tsingtao, China, which is across the Equator."

As they prepared to go to China, they took all of their prisoners off and put them on the other ship. "Boy, that was loaded down. We spent about four hours of our sailing time looking for one more prisoner 'cause all we could count was 99, and everybody got mad, and they figured one of 'em had jumped overboard. So, either one of them jumped—said to hell with it—overboard, or we lost one or miscounted—one or the other." This exchange happened at Ulithi on June 18, 1945.

The other ship loaded with the prisoners was torpedoed, but it didn't sink. They made it all the way to Hawaii, even though it was crippled and listing really bad. So, it did get torpedoed, and Tokyo Rose was correct.

China

His adventure continued, "We took off for Tsingtao, China. That's where, you know, it shows crossing the Equator and all that stuff."

Flip tried to spell Tsingtao for me and did an admirable job, but after stumbling a little, he reneged and said, "You might look on a map or somethang for the right spelling of it." But then he came through with the correct spelling, "T-S-I-N-G—Sing. Tao—T-A-O. Tsingtao, China."

"So, we went over to Tsingtao." Flippo, ever the caller, sang, "Tsingtao."

They got off on liberty[24] and were on shore duty. Of course, they hit the first cafe they could find to have some Chinese food. "And, Larada, when we walked through the door of this restaurant, above the bar in the back, like straight ahead of you, a monstrous, monstrous mural of a swan screwing a woman, and she's all spread out thar, and it had its wings all out thar and everythang. It was right up above the bar."

It must have really shocked the impressionable young sailor for Flippo to remember this so many years later.

So, this group of six got a booth and ordered food, having no idea what they ordered. After ordering, BANG—a bullet went right above their heads. Here come the waitresses and waiter, running toward them and turning over tables to get them to safety. They finally figured they should follow them, and the wait staff took them back into the kitchen. They told these frightened sailors the National-ists and the Communists were having a street fight outside and that's where the bullet came from.

Flippo thought, "God, dog!"

His breathing got heavy here as he told his story, as it did any time he talked for an extended length of time.

The wait staff clarified, "We'll let you know when it clears."

Flippo forgot how long they stayed. "Not a good while, but a little while." Flippo continued, "So, anyway we got back out thar, and I don't remember much about it. I was just a little ole kid. Why we went thar I have no earthly idee."

The Equator

The map in Flippo's Navy book showed them crossing the Equator near the Manus Admiralty Islands. On June 19, 1945, Flippo participated in a rowdy tradition of the sea: the first time crossing of the Equator, which changed sailors from "rancorous and scurvy landlubbers, beachcombers and pollywogs" into "Shellbacks" through an initiation.[25]

In the initiation, they ran a gauntlet. They were given "De Woiks."[26] The Navy book didn't explain what this meant but left it to your imagination!

They went across the Equator, which was fun to Flip. He got beat up because he was a "Pollywog," a guy that's never been across the Equator. "They initiate you pretty good."

I loved that Flippo said, "I looked for when I crossed the Equator." Even though the elderly Flip recounted this, did the young Flippo think there was going to be a marker of some kind?

"You had to go down that damn line. They hit ya with a shillelagh, and so, none of 'em really were vicious, thank the Lord!"

The initiation was they were "Pollywogs" until they went through that "damn line," then they became "Shellbacks."

The ones that had went cross before, they're the ones that manned the shillelaghs. They had a water hose on us and spraying the hell out of us. The executive officer had to go through, too. He had never been across, but the ole captain had quite a few times, I thank, Captain Sweeney. It's in that book (*USS LANDER 1945*).[27]

In a conversation, the absence of any Navy pictures of Flippo came up. "It seemed like I saw a picture of me somewhere else. I thank it was on our gun position." John sent me several pictures of Flippo in the Navy that were not in his Navy book.

Flippo's Navy book makes no mention of their side trip to China—maybe for security reasons. Its absence makes you wonder.

Back to the War

After the China trip, they went on those maneuvers to invade Japan, and they picked up some troops somewhere, but Flip wasn't sure where.

The USS *Lander* docked at many little islands, and they went to Hawaii and picked up some American soldiers and headed back to the South Pacific.

Again, they sailed, and nobody knew where they were headed. They passed several little islands, but Flippo remembered one specifically, "Mog Mog—little ole really small island, and all the ships anchored out in thar and took their small boats and went over to Mog Mog because it was loaded with beer. And it was just a beer island what it was, so, anyway, we'd go over and have a lotta fun over thar. Now, we went to different islands out thar."

The USS *Lander* stopped at several ports in the Philippines. Flippo's Navy book showed they sailed by Manila and the sight was horrible.

"The Harbor was filled with sunken ships. Fire had gutted many buildings. Manila, once a proud and beautiful city, now was a burned out shell."[28]

Flippo continued, "So, that's when we went on the big ole maneuvers. I'm sure —of course, everybody was sure, too, we were fixing to hit Japan, and thar's every kind of ship in the world thar—as far as you could see. You couldn't see nothing but ships from battleships, carriers, destroyers, cruisers, and troopships. Any kind of ship you want to know—landing ships. We were out thar with a bunch of ships. Then I 'member the Atomic Bomb was dropped. And another one was dropped. I was out in the Pacific when they were dropped. Ole Harry Truman dropped a bomb on them." Flippo added, "We didn't get that much news 'til an hour or so later. They literally knocked off two cities—Hiroshima and Nagasaki. And then they give up. The war ended on maneuvers to invade Japan."

The war officially ended September 2, 1945.

Japan

The USS *Lander* didn't arrive in Japan until September 25, 1945 for one day, then they did excursions out and came back to Japan in October for five days.

After the war, they took troops into Japan at Yokosuka Harbor. "It's spelled Y-O-K-O-S-U-C-K-A. We pronounced it Yo-kosucka. The Japanese pronounced it Yo-kos-ka—[Yokosuka, from the Internet]—a ways thar from Tokyo. We were on maneuvers to invade Tokyo or Japan when the war ended, and we took our troops in that we were going to take in to fight. Our troops became occupational forces, and we didn't stay thar too long."

Flippo remembered the Japanese people with much affection. "The Japanese people were so good to us thar. When we first got in thar and went ashore, we had to wear our sidearms for a couple days. I thank that lasted for two days, and they saw that the Japanese people were going to be nice to us, so we didn't have to wear the sidearms anymore. Now I was on shore duty—SP duty, shore patrol duty—over thar in Kamakura."

Flip was on shore patrol duty in Kamakura and met a Japanese girl. "We later on became pretty good friends. In fact, when I'd go ashore on liberty, well, I'd go see her and take her cigarettes and soap and stuff like that. I 'member when I wasn't going back anymore. We was fixin' to go decommission our ship. Well, I 'member she walked out of the gate with me. Her family had a big home thar, and so she walked out the gate, and I guess both of us were around the same age— seventeen or eighteen years old. And I remember us both crying."

Always concerned about the accuracy of his memories, Flippo ended our conversation with, "I'm probably really off on some of it, but when I edit the book, I'll straighten some of it out." His laughter rang in my ear then and does now as I wish he had the chance to edit this book and see it published.

They went around and through the Panama and went to Norfolk, Virginia, where they saw signs on the grass at the courthouse. "Dogs and sailors, stay off the grass." When Flippo told this story, he sang "Norfolk, Virginia" a second time—he loved to repeat phrases, names, punch lines, and sing keywords.

Flippo was on the USS *Lander* about a year—from the end of December 1944 to the end of December 1945.

On March 26, 1946,[29] they decommissioned the ship there right after the war, "And I went home," he sang the word home, "for a thirteen- to fourteen-day leave."

He took a Greyhound bus, spending the night in Memphis, then he went on into Abilene and spent twelve days there.

1st Row L to R: A Young Flippo Onboard, Flippo with ship in background. 2nd Row L to R: Young Flippo onboard with gun, Young Flippo with two other sailors. Source: John Flippo

1. Wikipedia, "Attack transport," February 14, 2020, https://en.wikipedia.org/wiki/Attack_transport
2. Revolvy, "USS Lander (APA-178)," September 10, 2018, https://www.revolvy.com/page/USS-Lander-(APA%252D178)
3. Ensign B. K. Issacs, Jr., USNR., *USS LANDER 1945* (1945): 1.
4. Ensign B. K. Issacs, Jr., USNR., *USS LANDER 1945* (1945): 2.
5. Ensign B. K. Issacs, Jr., USNR., *USS LANDER 1945* (1945).
6. **DesPac** — Destroyers of the Pacific baseball team took two guys off of all of the destroyers who had baseball teams and formed a team.
7. Ensign B. K. Issacs, Jr., USNR., *USS LANDER 1945* (1945): 3.
8. Ensign B. K. Issacs, Jr., USNR., *USS LANDER 1945*, Iwo Jima (1945): 1.
9. Ensign B. K. Issacs, Jr., USNR., *USS LANDER 1945*, Iwo Jima (1945): 1.
10. Ensign B. K. Issacs, Jr., USNR., *USS LANDER 1945*, Iwo Jima (1945): 1.
11. Ensign B. K. Issacs, Jr., USNR., *USS LANDER, 1945*, Iwo Jima (1945): 2.
12. Ensign B. K. Issacs, Jr., USNR., *USS LANDER 1945*, Iwo Jima (1945): 3.
13. Ensign B. K. Issacs, Jr., USNR., *USS LANDER 1945*, Iwo Jima (1945): 3.
14. Ensign B. K. Issacs, Jr., USNR., *USS LANDER 1945*, (1945).
15. Ensign B. K. Issacs, Jr., USNR., *USS LANDER 1945*, (1945).
16. Ensign B. K. Issacs, Jr., USNR., *USS LANDER 1945*, Okinawa (1945): 1.
17. **After Stack** — used to expel boiler steam and smoke or engine exhaust. Wikipedia, "Funnel (ship)," February 24, 2020, https://en.wikipedia.org/wiki/Funnel_(ship)
18. Ensign B. K. Issacs, Jr., USNR., *USS LANDER 1945*, Okinawa (1945): 1.
19. Ensign B. K. Issacs, Jr., USNR., *USS LANDER 1945*, Okinawa (1945): 1.
20. Wikipedia, "Dock landing ship," December 18, 2019, https://en.wikipedia.org/wiki/Dock_landing_ship
21. Ensign B. K. Issacs, Jr., USNR., *USS LANDER 1945*, Okinawa (1945): 2.
22. Wikipedia, "Attack transport," February 14, 2020, https://en.wikipedia.org/wiki/Attack_transport
23. Biography, "Tokyo Rose," April 19, 2019, https://www.biography.com/military-figure/tokyo-rose
24. **Liberty** — Shore leave is the leave that professional sailors get to spend on dry land. It is also known as "liberty" within the United States Navy, United States Coast Guard, and Marine Corps. Wikipedia, "Shore leave," February 2, 2020, https://en.wikipedia.org/wiki/Shore_leave
25. Ensign B. K. Issacs, Jr., USNR., *USS LANDER 1945*, Davey Jones (1945): 2.
26. Ensign B. K. Issacs, Jr., USNR., *USS LANDER 1945*, Equator (1945).
27. Ensign B. K. Issacs, Jr., USNR., *USS LANDER 1945*, Equator (1945).
28. Ensign B. K. Issacs, Jr., USNR., *USS LANDER 1945* (1945).
29. "NavSource Online: Amphibious Photo Archive," May 5, 2017, https://www.navsource.org/archives/10/03/03178.htm

4

THREE MORE SHIPS AND BASEBALL

When Lin and I met Flippo for our original face-to-face meeting in Tucson, Arizona in 2017, Flip's interest in the World Series dominated the night. When we did meet at a Texas Steakhouse, it just happened to have multiple TV screens in a 360-degree viewing range.

Flippo's behavior when we moved from the restaurant to his home should have been another clue. His side comments about the game came from a deeper knowledge than the average baseball fan, and that surprised me. I had no idea of his involvement in baseball until after that first interview that night. When a question would come up about one of the plays, he would say, "That old shoe was still sliding." [1] "He didn't put his apron down." [2]

I found out that night that baseball had played a major role in Flippo's life. He played baseball in high school and went on to play the last two years of his Navy service.

USS *Piedmont*

USS *Piedmont* — Copyright. Source: http://www.navsource.org/archives/09/03/0317.htm

Flippo in Japan. Source: John Flippo

After his leave, the Navy sent Flip back overseas, and he ended up at Yokosuka Harbor again, right back to Japan, right in the same harbor where he had left a month before. He was aboard a destroyer tender, USS *Piedmont*.

"Went right back to the same harbor," Flippo sang harbor and added "where we had left out of. I was on the *Piedmont* for about eleven months."

He met a Japanese girl named Tamiko (Tah-mee-co). "T-A-M-I-K-O." They later became pretty good friends. In fact, he was there eleven months.

While Flippo thought about Tamiko from so many years ago, he shared an aside about a current square dance caller. "And ole Harue over in—you know the Japanese girl from Sierra Vista?"

Harue told Flippo her grandmother was named Tamiko.

He reflected, "You might be my granddaughter—no, you'd have to be my great-granddaughter."

Flippo added, "But we were just joking around. But her grandmother was named Tamiko."

As we thought about the possibility of this coincidence, we pondered the possibility.

With a chuckle, Flippo agreed, "Yeah. Small world, yeah!"

❧

Flippo played baseball in Japan after World War II. Source: John Flippo

Flippo's sports career started on the USS *Piedmont*. He played more than baseball, playing football for the *Piedmont* team. They played some Army team over in Yokohama at Lou Gehrig stadium, named after Gehrig because he'd toured over there before the war. This stadium was also a football stadium. "Anyway, our football team played the Army team in that stadium in Yokohama and got beat 38-7. I remember that. That was football." During a second telling of this story, he chuckled. "Got beat 38-nothing. We didn't do too good." Seventy years later, the score is irrelevant—they lost!

1946 Baseball Team played in Japan. Source: John Flippo

Japan, August 31, 1946
        Piedmont Baseball
            Team
1st Row, Left to Right:
Raymond, McGhee, Cracola, Lewis,
& Scribner,
2nd Row:
Paquette, (maneger), Cambell,
Flippo, Pruitt, Carmack, Means,
Montini, Smith, ‡‡

Source: John Flippo

They also formed a baseball team, then he was transferred to a destroyer, USS *Wiltsie*.

USS Wiltsie — Copyright. Source: http://www.navsource.org/
archives/05/716.htm

USS *Wiltsie*

Flippo was transferred from the USS *Piedmont* to the USS *Wiltsie*, another destroyer tender. They had a baseball team on that ship, and they were pretty good, beating other destroyers. So, the Navy decided they'd make a team: DesPac, standing for "Destroyers of Pacific." They took two guys off of all of the destroyers who had baseball teams. "They had a big high falutin' coach, and I forgot his name. He was pretty well known at that time. Anyway, they picked me and Joe Paquette off of our destroyer."

Flippo spelled out how he thought Paquette would be spelled for me, "P-A-Q-U-E-T-T-E—I don't have any idee."

Paquette was a left-handed pitcher, a good pitcher. "I thank he was from Boston or that area. So, they took the two of us off of thar and put us on the USS *Dixie*."

USS *Dixie*

USS Dixie — Copyright. Source: http://www.navsource.org/archives/
09/03/0314.htm

65

Flippo ended his Naval career on the USS *Dixie*. His new assignment was another destroyer tender, a big ship.

"We had some really good players on that dad-gum team, and some of them had been in the major leagues, you know, before they were in the Service, and either way we had a pretty damn good team. I wasn't much. I was just the 'utility infielder,' and I played shortstop most of the time. So, the first two years was the war time, and then after that, it was beach time. That's when I played baseball. So, we played Navy teams or Army teams who had baseball teams. So, it wasn't too long after the war."

There was a pause as Flippo struggled a little remembering. "I'm trying to thank where in the world. I know we ended up in San Diego, and we played baseball at Navy Field thar. The *Dixie* was anchored out in the San Diego harbor. We were playing all teams up and down the coast thar, and we got to play some pretty big teams. Even one time, we played the Padres, which is a major league team thar in San Diego. We played the San Francisco—it's the Giants now, but it was the Seals."

They could choose to either stay on the USS *Dixie* or at Navy Field in the barracks, so they usually stayed at Navy Field, "because we usually worked out early of a morning. I say early—around ten o'clock, but we had liberty at night."

Flippo added the reason they stayed on the ship was because they could go and do anything they wanted to, but when they ran out of money, they'd usually go back to the ship. They practiced in the daytime and sometimes they played a ball game there. When they ran out of money, they'd go back to the ship, "and they fed us [baseball players] back in a room by their selves with gooooood food, I mean good food."

The last two years Flippo was in the Navy, he played a lot of baseball; basically, all he did was play baseball.

Flippo's time in the Navy was drawing to a close, but "The guys [Navy] wanted me to ship over—you know—reenlist and stuff like that."

They told him if he shipped over, all he would do is play baseball.

Flippo sang, "Yeah, I thank I'm going home. I'm kinda homesick."

The Navy recruiter whined, "Oh, stay in."

Flippo matched his whine with, "Nooo, I ain't gonna stay in." Flippo shared that he'd heard the small towns around Abilene had grown in his four-year absence and that added to his desire to go home.

Flippo won this discussion and realized if he had shipped over, "I'd had been right in the middle of that Korean thang, and I wouldn't be playing baseball. So, I ended up for two years in a really good service—just playing baseball—that was it."

He sat quietly for a moment and added, "This was a good duty, I mean good duty if you want to believe that—Wow.

Honorable Discharge

Navy Department · United States of America

from the Armed Forces of the United States of America

This is to certify that

MARSHALL DOYLE FLIPPO COMMISSARYMAN THIRD CLASS, USN

was Honorably Discharged from the

United States Navy

on the 2nd day of SEPTEMBER 1948. This certificate is awarded as a testimonial of Honest and Faithful Service

Filed for record September 17, 1948
Mrs. Chester Hutcheson, County Clerk,
Taylor County, Texas
By ________ Deputy.

R. S. LAMB,
Captain, U. S. Navy,
Commanding Officer.

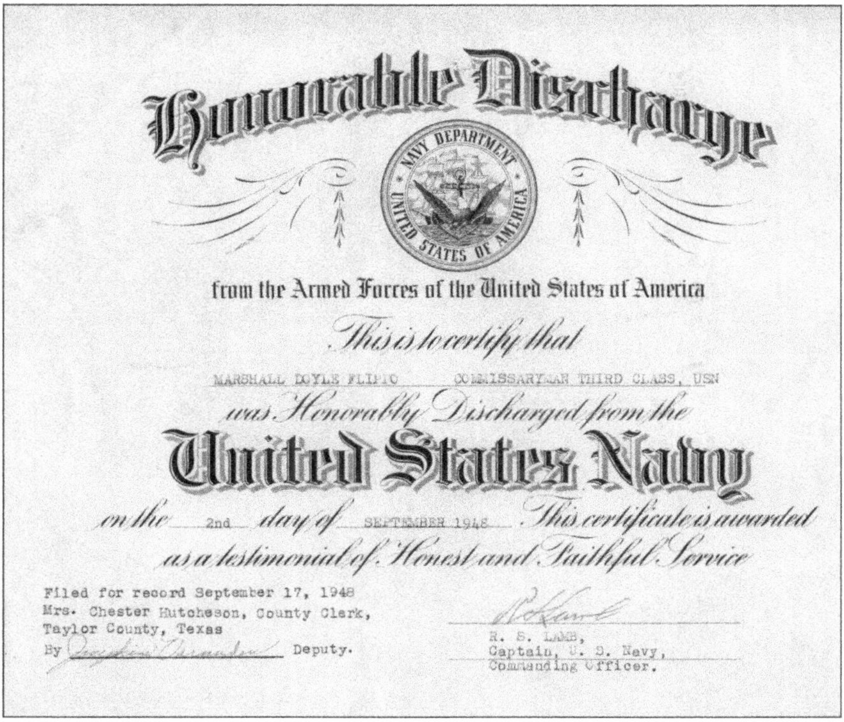

Source: John Flippo

When his time was up, he was still on the *Dixie* and was discharged at Camp Pendleton, north of San Diego. "That's where I was let out of the Navy. But anyway, I was discharged, and I went back to Abilene."

Flippo's naval career ended after four remarkable years. I admire his patriotism that sent him off to war at as such a young age, yet in true Flippo style, he enjoyed the experience.

---

1. "That old shoe was still sliding" mean "The baseball player's foot was sliding for some time!"
2. "He didn't put his apron down" means "He didn't put his glove down to stop the ball."

AFTER THE NAVY

Source: John Flippo

5

FALLING IN LOVE WITH NEECA AND MORE BASEBALL

F lippo repeated this often: "When I met Neeca and married her was probably one of the luckiest thangs." Again, he felt luck had played a big part in his life.

As we neared the end of our first interview, he said, "See I met Neeca after the service. That was '49. I got out of the Navy in '48."

Flippo enjoyed the telling and retelling of how he met Neeca. First time he told the story was in our first interview, face-to-face, and Flip became animated relishing the memories. The air felt electric with his words. When he returned to this story over the phone, I could hear the emotion in his voice.

Flip was discharged and went back to Abilene. He went skating one night, and a group was playing broom ball, "which is hockey with a broom and a big ole rag wadded up. So, we had two teams playing broom ball in a skating rink. And man, I went after that damn puck, which was a big ole bunch of cloth, and I slid into the side, and thar was a bunch of people thar. They were looking down at me like, 'you're a fool,' and thar's this one girl in particular, and she really looked like, 'man, you're crazy,' and that was Neeca. Now, I looked up and saw her looking down, and I continued the ball game.

"When I got through with the broom ball, I saw girls—thar was four or five of them. They weren't skating. They were leaving. They were just watchers really. One of them's name was Edna McMann or somethang like that. I don't know the girls Neeca was with."

A Young Marshall Flippo in 1949. Source: John Flippo

After that, he returned to the skating rink, but Neeca wasn't there the next time either, but the time after that she was. "I saw her, and of course, our eyes met again. I was skating at this time, and I skated over to the rail."

Flippo asked, "Hey, what's your name?"

She answered, "Neeca."

"Holy mackerel! How do you spell it?" With a chuckle, he added, "And then she spelled it wrong. [Then she spelled it right.]"

"It's N, double E, C, A. That C is a soft C, so it's pronounced like an S, so it's pronounced Neeca."

Flippo asked her if she wanted to get a coke afterward but she told him she was with friends.

"Well, are you in a car?"

"Yeah, we're in a car."

"How old are you?"

"Seventeen."

"I look at seventeen-year-old girls now and I's like, 'Surely not.'" As he thought about her age today, I could just see Flip shook his head and made a face.

Flippo asked a second time about getting a coke afterward, and she agreed.

So they started dating. Then he took her and introduced her to his parents, and they liked her. She took him and introduced him to her folks. Flippo thought her folks were just dear people. Their names were Fred and Floy Redus. Her dad worked for Texas Electric Company, a big electric company in Texas. Her mom was a housekeeper.

Flip didn't have a car, but his dad had a '35 Dodge, so he let him use it. "Do you know how much I'd take with me on a date? Two bucks! Two dollars, and that would buy us a movie and also a snack and a coke. Isn't that unbelievable!"

Their courtship continued, "So anyway, we got to dancing and we got pretty heavy with it [dating], so I asked her to marry me."

Flippo asked Neeca to marry him in the Majestic movie house, in Abilene. He had an engagement ring and tried to put it on her finger, the wrong finger.

Neeca exclaimed him, "Flippo, what are you doing?"

"Well, I'm trying to put this engagement ring on. You said okay."

"Well, you got the wrong finger."

They went together "a good while." They married February 25, 1949 [verified by Neeca] and divorced forty-two years later. Flippo was twenty-one, and Neeca was seventeen when they got married.

Flippo got out of the Navy September 1948, so as he pointed out, "I wasn't out too long 'til I got married."

"She's one of the best women I've ever known."

The Flippos' Wedding

With a chuckle, Flippo described their wedding. "I didn't have no car, so my best man, Thurman Lee Curry from the Navy, lent me his car. We went on a one-day honeymoon to San Angelo, Texas, which was eighty-nine miles away."

Flippo was also best man for Thurman's wedding.

Thurman asked Flippo where they were going on their honeymoon.

Flippo clarified, "Thurman, we don't have but one day."

He stated, "Well, you don't have no car."

Flippo responded, "Yeah."

Thurman offered, "You can borrow mine."

After Neeca and Flip got married, the newlyweds borrowed his car and went to San Angelo for their honeymoon. "I remember we's getting close to San Angelo, and the lights went out in the car. This is night time. We got married around seven or eight at night. We took off, and our folks were thar at the wedding, you know, and everythang. Thurman and his wife, Betty, were thar. I don't know anythang about mechanical or electricity or anythang, but I pulled off the road, and I stopped about twenty yards from a culvert. We couldn't see anythang when I pulled off. I just pulled off, stopped as quick as I could."

Neeca asked, "What's going to happen now?"

Flippo replied, "I don't know. I'm going to get out and lift that hood up and see."

He got out of the car and lifted the hood up. "I had no earthly idee, so thar's some wires thar, so I grabbed hold of the wires, and when I started to kinda pull on the wires, the lights came on."

Neeca yelled, "Don't touch nothing. Don't touch nothing else. Let's go."

So they went on in, and the lights stayed on until they got into San Angelo. After settling into the motel, they went to a movie. "All I had for my honeymoon was a twenty-dollar bill. We had breakfast—I don't know what we did the rest of the morning, probably sex, and then we got out of the motel Sunday about noon. We had to go back to Abilene, 'cause we both went to work Monday morning. She was an operator at Bell telephone, Southwest Bell. I worked at a bakery. We took off back to Abilene, and it became dark again, and I flipped the lights on, they came on, so I don't know. I guess I moved the right wire."

Bringing up Thurman made Flippo wonder about him. He lost track of Thurman and Betty, but his deep connection to his friends motivated him to find them. They lived in the Dallas area. He called them, and Thurman had died in his 80s, but Betty was still alive.

Flippo ended this sidetrack with, "And what a great friend he was! And he wasn't a baseball player or anythang, you know."

Mead's Bakery

For their first home, the newlyweds lived in a pretty big apartment downtown where Neeca's folks lived. Flippo didn't have a car, so she'd walk one way to the telephone company where she worked, about five blocks, and he walked the other way about six blocks to Mead's bakery where he worked.

Flippo's connection to Mead's Bakery went back to his childhood. When he was in school, he worked there. He had worked in some service stations before, putting air in tires and washing windshields before he was twelve. Flip went to work there when he was twelve at 17 1/2 cents an hour. Mead's Bakery was one of the two biggest bakeries in Abilene with Mrs. Beard being the other.

When he first worked for Mead's Bakery, Flip built boxes for them to put bread in. The first night he worked there, Flippo worked all night long building those boxes. It was on a Friday or Saturday night. He went to work there in the night time, and early in the morning, when he got off work, he walked two blocks to the bus stop. Flippo created an alarm clock for himself: he held a nickel in his hand, and when he sat down on the curb waiting for the bus, he would fall asleep. When that nickel fell down, it would wake him up. Then he took the bus out to within about four blocks of his home.

Flippo wrapped bread for a long time. He thought wrapping the bread was "everythang." The bread is put on a conveyor, and it goes through a slasher, and then when it gets through the slicer, you take it and wrap it. He wrapped bread for a good while and made cinnamon rolls. "I 'member icing the cinnamon rolls. Then when I went in the service, I told them that I'd worked in a bakery, so they made a baker out of me."

Reminiscing about his pay when he married, he said, "It wasn't very much, but it was probably enough for our family, and she did pretty good at the telephone company."

The Flippos' Early Marriage

In their early marriage, Flippo and Neeca were saving money "hand-over-hand 'cause I was walking to work. She was walking to work. We were downtown, so we could walk to the movie theater."

One time Neeca asked him what he did in the Navy.

Flippo answered, "I was a baker."

Then she asked what he baked.

He replied, "I baked the cakes and cookies and everythang. Bread."

She continued her query, "Well, why were you a baker?"

Flippo answered, "I don't know. Because I guess I told them I worked for a baker, and that's what I was on the ship, a baker, but I did have a gun position."

So, she stated, "Well, I'm going to bake a cake."

He added, "But she didn't know how to make icing."

Flippo chuckled. "I can make icing." He added, "So I cut this icing formula down from 582 men to two people. Put it on thar. The cake looked pretty good."

So, they went to the movie, and she had put it in the windowsill. When they returned, she went ahead of Flip into the apartment and walked into the kitchen.

Neeca shouted, "Oh, good, good, good!"

Flippo thought, "Oh boy. That cake turned out good." He added, "I walk around the corner and thar's probably a thousand pissants on that damn cake, and it looked terrible. It fell and the icing was just thin as hell. Ants all over it."

She added, "Oh, good, good! We won't have to eat it."

Flippo laughed. "She says she's not a good cook, but she's a pretty good cook. Her momma was a great cook. My mama was super-duper. I tried to get her recipes from June, my sister. My two sisters are dead, and I didn't get the recipes, but I've talked to one of my sister's daughters."

And Flippo asked his niece if she had any recipes from her grandmother.

She replied, "No, I don't think she had very many. She just reached down and put some salt in and pepper and stuff like that."

And Flippo added, "They all did back then. If I could just get ahold of it, I'd love to make my mom's potato salad and candied yams. And oh, God, I tell you. Just melt in your mouth, but she was an excellent cook, my momma, and so was her mother."

Playing Baseball for the Abilene A's

Baseball played a significant role in Flippo's Navy life. His interest in baseball began during school at Wylie and continued after the Navy in Abilene.

Abilene A's—Flippo is front row, second from the right. Source: John Flippo

After they were married, Flippo played for the Abilene A's, a semi-pro baseball team. There were so many guys wanting to play that they had major leagues and the minor league. Abilene was in a C league. They played softball during the week, and then they played regular baseball on Sundays.

They played all those little towns around Abilene, and then they would go to Brownwood every year for a state softball tournament. "We never did win that sucker, but we came in second one time. Now I talked it over with Neeca: I thank most of those guys are gone now. John Ray Harrison was our first baseman—left-handed, tall, lanky guy—who later on became the mayor of Pasadena, Texas. I 'member we visited him at his office in Pasadena—Mayor Harrison!"

Mayor Harrison gave them a little tiny baseball bat. "John [Flippo's son] was with me, just a little ole kid. This was late—holy mackerel! His wife was named Barbara. They had a little kid named Johnny, and we'd go over to Brownwood each year to play in the state tournament. And John Ray was really a good first baseman, a good ballplayer and good hitter and everythang. John Ray and Barbara come by and got Neeca and I, and we were going over to Brownwood a day early, so we get to Cross Plains. This was before [our] John came along."

Flippo remembered going to Brownwood for one of the annual tournaments. All those softball teams from Texas would congregate there, and it was a double elimination tournament. "I thank the time that we came in second was the time that we lost the very first game we played, so we only had one more left, you know, and if we lost another one, we were out of it, but we went all the way to the finals, and the team from down south of Houston. They beat us, so we came in second."

Abilene A's—Flippo is front row, second from the right. Source: John Flippo

Flippo got sidetracked again with another story. "Anyway, got another story. On the way thar, we get to Cross Plains, and we're on this highway, and we're supposed to turn right, right out of town on another highway takes us up to Brownwood. Brownwood was about seventy-eighty miles from Abilene. So we get to Cross Plains, and we get to this highway and Barbara says, 'You're missing the highway,' and he turned real fast and lost control of the car, and we were just going zigzag down the highway. Thank the Lord thar wasn't no other car around. And he got control of it again, and I 'member Johnny saying, 'Hey Daddy, do that again!'"

Flip's laughter exploded at young Johnny's comment and this memory. As I laughed, I could see a young boy seeing this as a fun experience.

With another small laugh, Flippo returned to the team information and listed his team players. "We did have a pretty good ball team, the Abilene A's. Now the ole boys that were on that team was—if I can 'member all their names. I know Wally Jordan was the catcher. I know he's deceased. Eddy Dun was the main pitcher. We had two or three pitchers. First baseman was John Ray Harrison. It was George Williams played second base, good ballplayer. And his brother played, too. I played shortstop, and J. D. Moore played third base. And then we had Donald Williams played left field. Ah, left fielder was Derek Eyes."

With a laugh, he clarified the two left fielders. "I know Don Williams played out in the outfield. I thank he played left field when he wasn't pitching, and then him and Eddy Dun would swap off. If one of them pitched, the other one played the outfield."

Flip had trouble remembering Charlie, the manager', last name. At one point he said, "I kept getting it mixed up with Charlie Procter [the *round dance cuer*]."[1] Neeca helped out on that name: "Charlie Chapman was the manager and then played center field."

Charlie was more than the manager of the team. In the right field, they had two or three players that they would use. One was John Ray Harrison's brother, Robert Harrison, who played right field and who Flippo thought was killed in an accident in Houston. Center fielder was Charlie, who was also their manager. Flippo said he was a good guy and a good player. He was also one of their pitchers in hard ball.

They played two or three games every week at night time, and then on Sunday they played baseball in the day time.

When Flip had trouble remembering names, his sense of humor always prevailed, "Anyway, the right fielder was, I have no idee. Who played right field? Somebody! I'll try to thank of it."

The Flippo's First House

Flippo returned to his life with Neeca. They were saving money because all they ever spent it on was a movie and some groceries, and even though they weren't making much, they saved a lot.

Young Flippo on motorcycle. Source: John Flippo

Neeca shared, "This photo was taken in front of our friend's house. They went for a ride on it and were gone for what seemed like a long time. They told us it turned over when they tried to turn around—they were bruised but nothing serious. We had a model A first and then the motorcycle. He rode it to work when he worked at Mead's Baker. It was 1949 or 1950."

So, they saved enough to buy a car. "We bought a car, and from then on, we were broke. I kept working at the bakery, and my wife was probably as frugal as anybody. She's just that good with money."

Now when they got married, the Flippos lived in an apartment and went different ways. They heard about the GI bill,[2] so they bought a house out on 1918 Marshall Street. "It just had been built, and I always liked that house. We were paying $50 per month on it 'til we paid it out. They were building the houses small and everythang. She fixed that sucker up. Boy, really nice, and I worked in the front yard—not too good. We had a pretty good lawn with that St. Augustine grass. And then she fixed the backyard up. It was unbelievable."

Neeca shared, "We bought the house new in 1949 on the GI Bill and paid $7200 with payments of $50 per month for twenty-five years. We sold it in 2006. We did a lot of improvements over the fifty-five years." Flip loved the house and would drive by every time he was in Abilene.

Flippo reflected about Neeca. "You know, I couldn't have found a better woman—just the best woman in the world. She is really, really a good person, and I screwed our marriage up after forty-two years. But anyway, that's another story."

Thinking about their personalities, Flippo chuckled. "We were about as shy as a person can get. I come out of my shell—she came out quite a bit, too! If she knows somethang, she's good. But we were so bashful and backwards."

He reminisced about one specific example of their shyness, "I 'member one time we were downtown, and we run around a corner, and she was kinda looking in the window."

Flippo remarked, "Hey, thar's a couple of square dancers coming down the street." He explained, "They was about a block away [on the same side of the street]."

Neeca stated, "Let's get across the street."

"So, we went across the street, but that's how bashful we were."

Flippo and Neeca were a shy couple when they married, but square dancing changed all that. That's one reason it meant so much to them!

---

1. **Round dance cue**r — Leader at the front of the ballroom [hall] who tells the dancers, as they dance, what steps to do.
2. **GI Bill** — any of various Congressional bills enacted to provide funds for college educations, home-buying loans, and other benefits for armed-services veterans. "Dictionary.com," 2020, https://www.dictionary.com/browse/gi-bill

ABILENE: WHERE IT ALMOST DIDN'T START

Wagon Wheel, Abilene, Texas. Source: Larada Horner-Miller

6

ABILENE: WHERE IT ALMOST DIDN'T START

M arshall Flippo's calling career could easily have not happened. In fact,
Flippo missed his first night of square dance lessons. Initially he couldn't
connect with the music and find the beat. Being a shy man by nature, his tempera-
ment could have stopped him from becoming the well-known caller who's so well-
loved. Just one of these could have been fatal, but Flippo faced all three and over-
came the challenge placed before him.

Square Dance Lessons Almost Missed

It all began with a statement in 1951 from Neeca, "Hey, we're going square
dancing."

Flippo questioned her sudden interest.

"Thar's a lady downtown that's a caller. She's starting a new square dance class,
and we're going. And I've talked to Hazel."

Neeca had joined forces with Hub's wife, Hazel, and knew she would talk Hub
into joining in on this new adventure. He was Flippo's best friend.

Flippo described his experience, "That night, I can 'member it just like I was
sitting here. That night we went to the square dance. We was pulling up to the
square dance."

Hub shared, "Flippo, I'm more scared right now than I was on Iwo Jima." Hub
was in the Marines, and he had it tough at Iwo Jima, like all the Marines did. But
Flippo was in the Navy, and his time in Iwo Jima wasn't as tough as Hub's.

With a laugh, Flippo answered him, "Yeah me, too."

So they pulled alongside the curb and looked in, and they were already dancing.

Hub stated, "They've already started. I ain't going in."

Flippo agreed with him.

Neeca exclaimed, "No, no, no, they just started."

Flippo asserted, "No, we're not going. It done started," and they drove off.

They returned the next week on time with Hub and Hazel and Flippo's little sister, Onita, and her husband, Roy Dale Williams.

"And the first *right and left grand*[1] I'll guarantee you is what sold me. For some reason, I like to touch people, so that was pretty good. You know you go on that *right and left grand*, shaking hands with everybody. So Neeca and I were very, very shy, if you can believe it."

Sent out to Dance

Betty Casey, a well-known caller, taught square dancing in her living room, which held about three squares. That's what she had when she taught Flippo and Neeca. Her husband was named John. The Flippos only had ten lessons before Betty sent them out to square dance. You only needed ten lessons at that time.

After their square dance lessons, Betty told them, "Now, go down to the YMCA. Thar's a guy named J. C. Wilson calling, and he won't hurt you. Other words, he'll call stuff that you know, and you'll get through it and everythang. And he'll be good to you."

So they went, and there "was just a mob of people, I mean to tell you. I guess twenty-five squares outside on the patio. It was summertime. J. C. was calling, and we got up. We took four couples with us: my sister, Onita, and husband, me and Neeca, Hub and Hazel, and another couple that was in class, and we just graduated. We got up that first *tip*.[2] I never will forget it in my life. We was a way in the back, away from everybody."

Joe (J. C.) Wilson. Source: https://hamilfamilyfuneralhome.com/tribute/details/2052/Joel-Wilson/obituary.html

J. C. called, "*Join hands, circle to the left.*[3] *Now wash those clothes and wring them out*[4] *and hang them on the line, sunny side out.*"[5]

Betty hadn't taught them this one, so they looked at each other. Flip thought Neeca said, "Let's sit down." So, they sat down, "and that damn J. C. turned the music off."

He announced, "Folks, I just seen a square sat down over thar. Would you go get them?"

Flippo added with a laugh, "And God, strangers coming up thar and getting us. I never did see my wife again until the end of the dance, so they split us all up, and we had one hell of a good time, you know."

Flip recalled that first evening with precision, "And then he let an ole boy call the last *tip* with him named Walt Faulkner. Walt was deaf, but he'd put his hand on the bass fiddle. Back in the '50s, all we had was bands—no records. Walt Faulkner was a damn good *caller*."[6]

J. C. included these new dancers, showing them true square dance hospitality, and that ended Flippo's first night out as a square dancer.

A Chicken Coop in 1952

When asked about why Flippo started calling, he answered, "I thought, 'Maybe I can do this in time.' I loved to sing. I was out of lessons about a year before I ever started. Thar was two square dance clubs, and they were both full. They both had waiting lists for people to get in. The list wasn't that long, probably ten to twelve couples. So, we put our names in for that one downtown. They could only dance twenty-five squares."

Ed Hall, who was in their class and lived out at Wylie, announced, "I have an ole chicken coop that would probably dance three squares. I'll clean that thang out if ya'll wanna come out thar, but I can't take more than twelve couples."

So, twelve couples signed up to go out there, and they danced out there every Friday night to records, and "thar weren't many out at that time that were good to dance to."

Flippo identified the recorded *callers* they danced to: "Joe Lewis had the best ones. And Les Gotcher had some that were really hard. He was a *hash*[7] *caller* from California and toured the whole country—probably the tops in his time."

Fenton "Jonesy" Jones, a nationally known *caller*, had some, but there was no way they could dance them. Come to find out, Jonesy played in a band in LA. He picked up the lingo and said, "I believe I can do this," so he just got up and called a whole bunch of stuff. He didn't even know what worked into what. He just knew the words he'd heard *callers* use, and he recorded with Capitol Records. There was no way they could dance to those. And later on, he learned to square dance and then to call and then became a very good *caller*.

They danced to records for quite a while, and then they would have a band come in. Most of the Fridays they danced to a two-piece band. At that time, if you said, we're going to have a record dance, nobody'd come. People liked live music. So, they'd have a two-piece band and the fiddle player. There were very few people recording at that time.

One night someone had a suggestion. "Thar's twelve of us here. Why don't we all learn to call? And we won't have to have a record or a band, so we'll just be our own *caller*."

So that's the way it started. Flippo remembered the first one he called. *Singing calls*[8] didn't appeal to him too much at that time, so he learned *patter*.[9] First one he learned was '*Dip and Dive.*'[10] So, they all learned some kind of calls. "Some guys were good. I wasn't one of the good ones."

Trouble with the Beat

Flippo faced his first problem with calling.

At one point, Neeca told him, "You can't stay on beat. What's wrong with you? Can you pat your foot to the music?"

"Yeah," Flippo explained. He had a "Turkey in the Straw" record, and he would go in the front bedroom of their house because they had no furniture in there and he had a little record player. "I believe it was a Califone. So, I'd get in thar, and she'd come in."

And she'd say, "Flip, you're not on the beat. I know good and well you can pat your foot to the music."

"Yeah."

She'd say, "Well, start patting that foot to the music. Don't do anythang—just keep patting it. When it hits the floor, you say '*Bow to your partner, corners all*,'[11] and just stay on the beat."

"Well, I had a hell of a time with that."

Flippo Ventures Out with His Calling

So, they danced out at the Chicken Coop a long while. Then they got taken in by one of those clubs in Abilene, the Crosstrail. Somebody set it up. At dances then, there wasn't one *caller* calling a dance. If you attended the dance and wanted to call, you could call, so it was multiple *callers* all the time.

J. C. Wilson and Bob Sumrall had a dance together. Flippo never doubted why they went. It was the first time they danced to just one or two *callers*. Usually it was everybody. And so, the format for that dance was three *calls a tip*. They enjoyed that dance with Bob Sumrall. Bob was an excellent *caller*, and so was J. C.

Flippo went back to the Crosstrail and had his calling debut outside of the Chicken Coop.

"They asked me to call one night. So, now the *figers* [figures][12] we used back thar— we had no lists or anythang."

Today we have five levels of square dancing with a list of calls at each level, so this was a simpler time in square dancing.

Bob Sumrall. Source: Necia Harp

So, Flippo called, "*Bow to your partner and corners all. Circle to the left, go around the hall*,"[13] and he was on beat. "*Wash your clothes and wring them out. Hang them on the line, sunny side out.*"

"Well, at that point thar, what you did was kinda keep four in the middle and then turn around and turn your partner under where you'd both be facing out. '*Hang them on the line, sunny side out*,' so we'd be circling out."

"The call goes '*break with the left, pull the right hand lady under*.'[14] That's your partner. '*Circle to the left and ya go like thunder*.'"[15] Well, Flip had them circling out, and he remembered Neeca was in the way back of the hall.

Remembering, he chuckled and sang this part, "So I said, '*Wash those clothes, wring them out. Hang them on the line, sunny side out. Turn the corner by the left, and do a dosado,*' we called it. It was partner left, corner right, and so they were facing out. I'd left somethang out: '*pull the right hand lady under, and then do a dosado.*"

When Flip made the mistake, he saw Neeca turn around and head for the restroom. So, he had to go back and start over.

Always the historian, Flip clarified how the call, *dosado,* changed and morphed into the *do paso* we know today. The *dosado* at that time was popular with callers and "[they] would put in a lot of *hash* like, '*A chicken in the bread pan picking out dough,*' and stuff like that. And he'd just keep calling and he'd keep calling."

That *dosado was similar to do paso* but shorter. The caller ended the *dosado* with "turn your partner by the left with a courtesy turn and promenade home. Then that turned into a *do paso*—partner left, corner right, partner left and courtesy turn."

A Trip Out of Town

Flippo heard about this *caller* over at Cisco, Texas—Melton Luttrell. Dancers said, "Boy, he's really good. He's got a real good band." So three couples got in the car and drove over there. "Sure enough, boy, it was one hell of a good dance. The music was good. The hall was just beautiful. They had ole boarded windows. You lifted those boarded windows up and get the fresh air through thar. And a great smooth floor. And a great band and a great caller. We went over thar every second and fourth Tuesday. We'd get some other people to go with us. Sometimes we'd take two or three cars."

So, Allen and Ruth Cox, friends of Flippo's, and Doug and Jackie Copeland went up there a couple times. Usually the group traveled in the same car, but sometimes they

Melton Luttrell. Source: https://www.ceder.net/callerdb/viewsingle.php?RecordId=2528

had different people with them. They went up to Melton one time when he was calling, and they told him that Flippo started calling.

Melton stated, "Oh, hell, I'll get him up here. Come up here."

So Flippo had his first out-of-town debut! The hall was full of people, and that was when Flip was really having trouble with staying on the beat. Flip was scared to death when he got up there. The band helped him a lot because every time he got offbeat, they'd pick him up.

Before they left the dance to go home, Flip saw the Coxes and Copelands talking to Melton. He asked, 'What did Melton say?'"

And they shared, "Melton told me to tell you, 'Don't give up your day job.'"

The next time they went, Melton asked Flippo to call again. "I guess he just thought he'd be goodhearted and get him up thar and he'll stay offbeat again, but I accidentally stayed on beat all the way through it."

Melton came to Flip and complimented him. "Man, that was a lot better than you were. Have you been practicing?"

"I don't like to practice."

He instructed, "Well, get in a square."

Melton had been to Herb Greggerson's school, and Greg told him, "Get in a square and call a call that you know. Call it in a square, not out loud but silently, under your breath." Flippo found this hard to do, but when he did try it, he succeeded in not calling out loud and disrupting the caller's calls. And so finally, Flip started working on it that way.

Flippo summed it up, "Now, let's see Betty Casey, J. C. Wilson, Bob Sumrall, Dick Van Hook, and Bill Golligher called in Abilene. They were the main callers in Abilene at that time."

In 1953, Flippo taught square dancing for the Abilene Recreation Department and the YMCA. He also had the Marshall Flippo's Square Dance Exhibition Group made up of young dancers. He remembered, "They were a lot younger than me and were from all around Abilene, Texas."

Square dancing had become central to their lives.

From the Hayloft to The Wagon Wheel Square Dance Hall

In 1954, Flippo rented "The Hayloft" to teach square dance lessons in Abilene. Between 1956 and 1961, he taught beginner square dance classes at the YMCA.

They danced at "The Hayloft," but they foresaw problems there. "It wasn't nothing but a room over an ole garage, and it was a good floor. We were afraid the floor would give out and fall down onto the garage. It'd hold about thirteen squares. Sure enough, it never did fall down."

When they danced down at the Y, people would say, "Oh, wish we had a building."

Wagon Wheel, Abilene, Texas. Source: Larada Horner-Miller

This wish came true in 1958. Four couples—Larken and Mabel Drake, Ed and Delona Fishel, Bill and Helen Smothers, and Neeca and Flippo—bought the quarter of acre of land under where the Wagon Wheel Square Dance Hall is, and they did all the work except putting up the walls. This energetic group put in the floor. Flippo himself scraped part of the quarter of an acre for parking.

"Our main guy was Larken Drake. He was a carpenter, so you know, he was kind of the boss really."

The first night they had a dance, the floor buckled. Flippo told me it was really a good floor but when they put it down, they didn't know to leave any air space around the edges. They had to go back and cut a board out all the way around the floor, and it settled back down, "and by God, come out to be a pretty good floor. Anyway, we kind of got pissed off at Larken about that."

Larken admitted he just forgot to leave any air space there. Flippo added, "But we got along pretty good."

The four couples agreed they could either put up $1500 or they could put up like $1000 and work the next $500 out by going out there and working. "So that's what Neeca and I did (Verified by Neeca). We didn't have that kind of money to put up thar at that time. And so, we worked part of ours out."

"You know about our fence around our backyard. It's underneath that floor out thar at the Wagon Wheel. We took the ole picket fence down and put up a chain-link fence. With that lumber, I don't know how Larken put it under thar. He put it under thar for support. And then we had a patio out thar, and it would hold about probably nine squares. But it was outside."

§.

Because of Flippo's calling career taking off and their move to Kirkwood Lodge as staff caller and his touring, they sold their part to the other three couples. After a series of sales within these three couples, the Wagon Wheel was sold to the Abilene Square and Round Dance Association.

They enlarged the building and enclosed the patio, "and the outside looks the same as we had it, so they done a really good job when they added on to it."

"I called at it quite a bit before and after 'The Auctioneer.'"

Flippo's loyalty to the Wagon Wheel and Abilene continued throughout his whole career, and he had his last dance, "The Farewell to the Road," there.

---

1. **Right and Left Grand** — If necessary, men turn up to 90 degrees to face promenade direction and women turn up to 90 degrees to face reverse promenade direction. Dancers blend into a circular formation as they Right Pull By, Left Pull By, Right Pull By, Left Pull By.
2. **Tip** — A square dance session consisting of two parts, a patter call, and a singing call. See Glossary for more.
3. **Join hands, circle to the left** — Dancers join hands with adjacent dancers to form a circle and move the circle in the indicated direction, or to the left if no direction was given.
4. **Wash those clothes and wring them out** — Older unstandardized call with no definition.
5. **Hang them on the line, sunny side out** — Circle facing out.
6. **Caller(s)** — A person who prompts dance figures in such dances as line dance, square dance, and contra dance.
7. **Hash** — Same as Patter — A single tune, used by a caller as background for a series of calls, with no

lyrics accompanying the music. Couples are moved into a variety of formations, but brought back to their home positions before the next set of calls.

8. **Singing Calls** — The caller sings parts of the songs. See Glossary for more.

9. **Patter** — A single tune, used by a caller as background for a series of calls, with no lyrics accompanying the music. Couples are moved into a variety of formations, but brought back to their home positions before the next set of calls.

10. **Dip and Dive** — They dive through the first couple, arch over the next, then do a California Twirl on the outside to dive and arch across to the starting point. Each couple, when they reach the outside, do a California Twirl to dip and dive back through to starting point. See Glossary for more.

11. **Bow to your partners, corners all** — It is traditional at the beginning of a dance to honor your partner and corner by (men) bowing to your lady, and (ladies) curtsying to your man.

12. **Figures** — (Flippo's version: figers) — 48 beat group of calls that takes dancers from their home position to a Corner for a Swing and a 16 beat Promenade.

13. **Circle to the left, go around the hall** — Dancers join hands with adjacent dancers to form a circle and move the circle in the indicated direction, or to the left if no direction was give.

14. **Break with the left, pull the right hand lady under** — Older unstandardized call with no definition.

15. **Circle to the left and ya go like thunder** — Circle to the left.

BURMA-SHAVE JINGLES

Many years ago, we found various callers established their own brand of calling by the *patter*[1] rhymes they used during such calls as *right and left grand*[2] or *do paso*.[3] Some callers still use this technique. Listen to or go to a Flippo dance and see how this pro uses this technique to add his own brand of flavor to the dances he calls. Pappy Shaw used to refer to this as flavor, excitement, or that special quality that leads a caller to the pinnacle of calling. He used this to develop what he called 'bubble over,' that overall quality that sets the good apart from the mediocre and the great from the good.[4]

"Burma-Shave was an American brand of brushless shaving cream, famous for its advertising gimmick of posting humorous rhyming poems on small sequential highway roadside signs."[5]

One of my favorite memories of Flippo's calling was his use of the Burma-Shave jingles in his *patter* during a *right and left grand* or other similar count calls. They were catchy, silly phrases that rhymed. These jingles date from the 1920s to late 1960s, and Flippo began using them in the '60s and continued throughout his career.

J. C. Wilson, down at the Y in Abilene, helped Flippo a lot. "He had excellent, excellent rhythm, and he had all these thangs like, '*Chase that rabbit. Chase that squirrel.*' He'd say, '*Up the river, go down the bend.*' He had these jingles he got off of the Burma-Shave signs alongside the highway." Flippo started picking some of those up and some of that *hash*.[6]

J. C. wrote the jingles down for Flip, and he shared, "So I stole a lot of *patter* from him that he'd gotten off of the Burma-Shave signs."

Source: Larada Horner-Miller

Flippo sang his favorite jingle:

Ningo bingo, six penny high
A big pig, a little pig
A root hog or die!

Flip added, "I don't know of any others that could beat that. Thar're some that are really, really funny."

Here's another one:

If courting in autos
is your sport,
trade it off
for a davenport.

Flip talked about the Burma-Shave jingles often, but when he was trying to remember them, one time he stated, "Let see, they're not coming to me. If I was calling, they'd come to me!"

After a couple minutes, he remembered this one:

A car, a miss
A kiss, a curve
He kissed the miss

and missed the curve.

Then he continued, "Damn. That is so bad. The one that I used the most and I can't even thank of it. Almost came to me then. Oh, boy."

The next time we talked, Flippo had a list ready:

Ida Red, she ain't no fool,
She can put a saddle on
a humpback mule.

"I probably used that more than any of the others because it would just come out of me," Flippo told me.

Flippo shared a couple more and ended, "That's it," but in a following conversation continued, "And let me thank of another one."

He wanted to remember more because J. C. Wilson had a bunch of them. "And he wrote 'em down for me, and bless his heart, he just was one of those good guys, and so I used them all through my calling."

I asked Flippo if other *callers* "borrowed these from him."

He stated, "Stole it! I stole it from J. C., and other callers researched it from me."

He remembered J. C. telling him that it's fun to call on a *right and left grand* "or somethang like that or when you call a *dosido*[7], you could keep calling that *hash* in thar until you tell them to promenade."

Flippo added, "*Callers* liked that."

Flippo's dear friend, Ann Salwaechter, sent him at least a hundred Burma-Shave jingles she got off of the computer, but he didn't like them because they were only about shaving and not funny.

In the February 1987 issue of *American Square Dance* magazine, Joel (J. C.) Wilson wrote, "I taught Flippo all he knows—just ask him."

See more Burma-Shave jingles Flippo used in Appendix C.

---

1. **Patter** — A single tune, used by a caller as background for a series of calls, with no lyrics accompanying the music. Couples are moved into a variety of formations, but brought back to their home positions before the next set of calls.
2. **Right and Left Grand** — If necessary, men turn up to 90 degrees to face promenade direction and women turn up to 90 degrees to face reverse promenade direction. Dancers blend into a circular formation as they Right Pull By, Left Pull By, Right Pull By, Left Pull By.
3. **Do Paso** — Left Arm Turn with partner until facing corner and release armhold. Right Arm Turn with corner until facing partner and release armhold. If there is no further instruction, Courtesy Turn partner to end facing the center of the set.
4. John Kaltenthaler, *Sets in Order,* The Callers Notebook (November 1982): 40.
5. Wikipedia, "Burma-Shave," March 7, 2020, https://en.wikipedia.org/wiki/Burma-Shave
6. **Hash** — Same as Patter — A single tune, used by a caller as background for a series of calls, with no lyrics accompanying the music. Couples are moved into a variety of formations, but brought back to their home positions before the next set of calls.
7. **Dosido** — What has come to be called Do Paso except that in the Texas Dosido the arm turns continued for an indeterminate period until the caller gave the next call. "Partner left and corner right and keep on going if it takes all night."

"THE AUCTIONEER" AND BLUE STAR LABEL SKYROCKETED FLIPPO'S CAREER

"The Auctioneer" record label for first version. Source: http://www.
45cat.com/record/bs1517

Flippo had worked hard on his craft and mastered his timing problem. The turning point in his career happened in the Hayloft in Abilene. It was 1957, and Flippo was calling "The Auctioneer."

One night Flippo was at the Hayloft in Abilene, and he was calling "The Auctioneer" before it was recorded. Two *callers*[1] from Baytown near Houston had been to Colorado at some square dance and were going through town. They decided to come to Flippo's dance. One of them had a French name that Flippo couldn't remember, and the other one was Andy Lyons.

They came up after Flippo called "The Auctioneer" and congratulated him. "That's pretty damn good." They encouraged Flip to call Norman Merrbach in Houston, who was the producer of Blue Star records.

They repeated, "Call him."

Flippo responded, "I've never thought anythang about recording it."

"That's pretty good. You ought to do it."

After that, Flip forgot about it. Then he got a phone call from Norman.

Norman asked Flippo to send him the words to that song.

So, Flip sent him the words. "Thar's a lot of words."

If you're not familiar with this song, it does have a lot of words. Leroy Van Dyke released "The Auctioneer" in 1956, and Flippo released his singing call in 1958. Take a moment to listen to a fifty-second sound bite of Marshall Flippo's famous singing call.[2]

Here's the original hit by Leroy Van Dyke.[3]

Norman called Flippo up, "I believe I'm going to pass on that 'cause callers want one with not too many words, and they don't have to learn all the words."

So, Flippo understood that, and he continued calling for a couple months. Then Norman called him up again and asked him to come to Houston "and do that thang.'"

Flippo answered, "Well, I've got to work Monday. I've got a dance Saturday night in Abilene, here. How far is it?"

"It's three hundred and sixty-five miles."

He stalled a little, "I don't know."

Norman persisted, "Well, I'll tell you how you can do it. After that dance, start driving down here."

"What you mean—at night?"

"Yeah, drive down here and get here early morning and we'll do the thang. You can drive back and be ready to go to work Monday."

Flip's humor prevailed, "Wait a minute. You must be talking about my brother, and I don't have a brother."

Norman encouraged Flip to think about it.

So, Flippo asked Neeca, "You thank we could cut this? Go down?"

"Oooh," she exclaimed, "I bet Momma and Daddy would go with us, and they can both drive. I can drive. We'll take turns about sleeping."

There were three sitting up in the front seat, one in the back seat trying to sleep. They drove down to Houston and got there about nine in the morning, just in time for Flippo's appointment. "We had breakfast at a Sambo's, which they don't have anymore. I remember Fred trying to pay for it. Fred was Neeca's dad."

Flippo told his father-in-law, "No, you drove down here. Let me get it."

Fred answered, "You don't have any money. I have your billfold right here. You left it up on the table last night at the dance. Bless your heart!"

They went to Norman's place, Norman and Nadine Merrbach, the owners and producers of Blue Star Records. "He was really a good guy and a good engineer."

They did the recording in the studio, and "the studio acoustical stuff was egg crates." "I can see the studio from my mind right now. We went in and when they played it, I called it at the same time. Well, I remember one time we had trouble. I'd make a mistake and we'd have to start over, and then somebody else would make a mistake. It wasn't one of those days that everythang went well."

But now "The Auctioneer" went really well. Flippo hit it the first time, and course he had been calling it with a band for a long time, so he was lucky to get out of there, and they headed back to Abilene. They got back in time to get a little sleep and go to work the next day.

"Anyway, 'The Auctioneer' hit pretty good. Well, I'd say, you know, all of my career I just lucked out, being in the right place at the right time. I don't know what it was, and 'The Auctioneer' hit really good."

Flippo was pleased with the way it sounded, but he didn't realize it was anything big. He would think about it from time to time. Then the square dance magazine started praising it. "The only thang I can thank of is a lot of dancers bought records at that time, and learned the singing call that was on the record."

The records were only sixty-five or seventy cents apiece, and they were 78^4 records. You could take a pile of them into a dance and they'd just be gone in a minute. People were just hungry for some kind of records to play at home or listen to. And some *callers* started from listening to tape recorders and to records. "They picked up ideas, started calling, and some of them turned into really good."

Flippo remembered calling with a band in Houston one time. He turned around and asked them if they knew 'The Auctioneer.'"

Their response, "Oh, yeah, yeah. We done that. We can play it for you if you want to call it. Ohhhh, that's Norman's big one!"

They repeated, "Oh, that's Norman's big one, big one." Flip repeated their response and chuckled.

"Well, I thank I'll call it next the *tip*."[5]

So they did a good job on it, and they said this is "going to make ole Norman." After that, Flippo was recording quite a few songs through the late '50s and all the way through the '60s and all the way 'til now. He would come up with a tune and call Norman up and say, "Is this going to be alright?"

Norman would say, "Yeah, come on down and let's do it. I'll get you a dance down here. You can make a little money."

It went on that way for a long while.

How Flippo Choreographed "The Auctioneer"

When asked how Flippo choreographed "The Auctioneer," he chuckled. One person, all eight parts! He did it in the living room at 1918 Marshall in Abilene.

That shocked me, so I asked him, "So you danced all the parts?"

Flippo walked through the whole thing. "It's a terrible *figer* [figure],[6] the first one [in] the first Auctioneer. Of course, we didn't have a lot of *Basics*[7] they got now, so I had six *Basics*. It's not too good of a *figer* [figure]. Nowadays, you have to walk people through it two or three times before they get it, but back then, people, I don't know."

His laughter continued as I commented about the feat of him walking through it, one person doing all eight parts.

People tended to memorize singing calls because there weren't that many basic calls. Now, if Flippo went into their town and called "The Auctioneer," and changed the *figures*, "they flat-ass knew it. They knew it. They memorized that— they did better than you did!"

Flippo commented about square dancing today, "They don't do that anymore. No, but back then, you know, they'd practice. It was really a time of square dancing. It was different than it is today."

I asked Flip if it was unusual to take a pop song like Leroy Van Dyke's "The Auctioneer," and it became popular then in the square dance world. Was that going on or did he kind of pioneer that?

"No, I don't know what happened thar. I know I went to Houston after he had recorded it, about six months. I don't know how come it to hit. *Callers* bought it big."

Norman didn't think it would go. Flippo was surprised, and Norman was surprised, too, that it took off like it did, but the reason for that big sale back then was the dancers were buying records, too, and callers. So, callers were buying, and dancers were buying them. "I's putting 'em in the garage! Breaking 'em!"

Flippo chuckled. "No, I wouldn't [break 'em]."

Later, "The Auctioneer" was re-released, and Flippo put different *figures* (calls) to it, and it never did sell like the first one.

More about "The Auctioneer"

Flippo's first version was done by Earl and His Hoedowners from Houston. His name was Earl Caruthers. The second version was a different band, but Flippo couldn't think of the name of that band. "Oh, God! I'm going to have to write that down and getcha that name. I know it. 45s.[8] 45s. Oh, oh! It almost came to me then. I can see the guy, plays clarinet, but it was a different band. I thank Norman said it did good, but it wasn't even close to what the first one did."

Flippo found the name of the band that recorded the second "Auctioneer" but didn't know how to spell it. The ones that made the second "Auctioneer" was the 'Shannoneirs' and 'Rhythmaires.'[9] "And Dick Shannon was the leader of that band."

When asked if the band made a big difference. Flippo replied, "Larada, I just don't know."

Nadine and Norman Merrbach of Blue Star Record Label. Source:
Neeca Flippo

Blue Star and the Merrbachs

From an article entitled "It All Started as A Hobby" in one of Neeca's
albums/scrapbooks:

> By 1953, the Merrbachs were into the activity body and soul, going to square dance
> weekends at camps and taking their records with them. Their prime label, Blue Star,
> has had an enviable existence. For many years, featuring the calling of Marshall
> Flippo, sales records were set in this specialized field that have yet to be broken.

Blue Star Record label and Norman and Nadine Merrbach played an important
role in Flippo's success as a caller.

Flippo proudly stated, "It was Blue Star for twenty-eight years."

In one of the albums/scrapbooks, we found a write-up by Otto Warteman entitled, "Memory of Norman Merrbach." This is how Norman was described:

"If and when the history of square dancing in Houston is ever written, there
will be some names that will stand very prominent among the long list of workers
for square and round dancing. Norman Merrbach will be among those names.

"He had a very large bolo tie, and Marshall Flippo said, 'That's the only way to
keep Norman's feet on the floor.'"

The Switch from 78s to 45s

In the mid-'60s, Norman wanted to switch the 78^{10} records to 45s.

Flippo stated, "Well, I don't like the quality of the 45 records." Norman waited
a while.

Flippo explained, "And so, 45s got pretty good, so Norman switched. He took
'em all off that big ole [78] record, put it on 45s."

. . .

Square Dancing Back Then

In the later 1950s, after Flippo did "The Auctioneer," he was playing baseball, so Flip and Neeca didn't even square dance in the summer for a good while, and even after he started calling, they didn't. When Flip came back one time to call, Dick Van Hook introduced him, "Here's a guy who won't dance with us in the summer."

Square dancing in the '50s and '60s was different from today. At a dance, they had multiple *callers*. If you were a *caller* and went to a dance, then they'd ask you to call. They'd have three *callers* a *tip* then take a break, and it wasn't very long and two more *callers*. Every once in a while, a *caller* came in and called the whole dance, but as far as Abilene went, Flippo just went to a dance, and if somebody asked him to call, he'd call. The dances usually went from 8:00 to 11:00 p.m. Flip reflected, "We were all young. It seems like we were all young."

During this time, they didn't have *round dancing*[11] as we know it today, but they did have "Couple Dancing." This evolved into *round dancing,* and Flippo shared, "I don't remember when they started changing."

At this time, Flippo's calling career had taken off. He was the only *caller* for the longest time at Wagon Wheel, but sometimes, he'd have a *guest caller,* somebody that was dancing on the floor, come up and call, if he knew he wouldn't hurt someone else's feelings. If there happened to be just one caller there, Flippo would ask him to call one or two.

As Flippo matured as a caller, he noticed differences in how calls were done in different towns.

Whenever Flippo and Neeca traveled to Melton's, Cisco, Texas, fifty miles east of Abilene, at that time, they danced with their hands up, and they had never seen that. In Abilene, their hands were always down. So when they went back, Betty Casey instructed, 'Now if you go somewhere and they do it different than what we do, you do it their way and don't say a word about it.'

Melton said, "*Walk around your corner,*"[12] they did it opposite than what they did only fifty miles away in Abilene. In other words, you'd walk in front of the lady and go around and come back around and *seesaw your partner.*[13] "[It would be] a *dosado,*[14] really, what we call nowadays. And so, that was different. Some of the other stuff was different, so we would do that one when we were over thar because Betty said to! You dance like they danced. Don't try to change them 'cause that's their way of dancing."

Flippo remembered one time they danced to thirty-six callers at a festival over in Stanford, Texas, "Stanford Somethang." Shocked by the number of callers at the Stanford festival, I wish I could have experienced this!

Out of the thirty-six callers that called, the *middle break*[15] was '*Corn in the crib and wheat in a sack. When you meet your partner, turn right back. Turn right back and go the other way. Keep on going 'til you meet your own. Pass her by and do an allemande left,*[16] *and elbow swing.*'[17] "[*Elbow swing*] was one of the figures in 'The Auctioneer'—the first 'Auctioneer' I did. That figure was in thar—terrible figure."

Another difference from today's square dancing and the heyday of the '50s and

'6os, they printed a program identifying songs the callers would do for the evening. I had never seen one before looking in Flippo's albums/scrapbooks, so I asked about them.

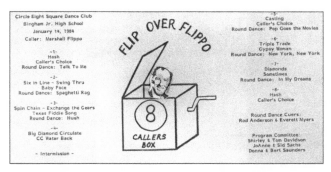

1984 Circle Eight Dance Program. Source: Neeca Flippo

He recalled, "It was usually a bigger dance when they had the programs. They'd have different callers calling different *tips*."

Flippo's calling career skyrocketed with the release of "The Auctioneer" and his association with Blue Star label, and another "piece of luck" was about to unfold.

Norman & Nadine Merrbach, Bob Fisk and Flippo. Source: Neeca
Flippo

1. **Callers** — A person who prompts dance figures in such dances as line dance, square dance, and contra dance.
2. "Square Dance History Project," 2017, Audio of Flippo's "The Auctioneer," https://squaredancehistory. org/items/show/160
3. blizzard 7500, "YouTube," November 2, 2011, Audio of Leroy Van Dyke's original hit: https://www. youtube.com/watch?v=WaVTxiPBJgM
4. 78 Records - an early type of shellac-based phonograph record that played at 78 revolutions per minute.
5. **Tip(s)** — A square dance session consisting of two parts, a patter call, and a singing call. See Glossary for more.
6. **Figure** (Flippo's version: figer) — 48 beat group of calls that takes dancers from their home position to a Corner for a Swing and a 16 beat Promenade.
7. **Basics** — The beginning CALLERLAB program with fifty-one calls.
8. **45s (Records)** — The most common form of the vinyl single is the "45" or "7-inch." The names are derived from its play speed, 45 rpm, and the standard diameter, 7 inches.
9. Buddy Weaver, "Blue Star Redefining Square Dance Music," December 13, 2019, http://www. buddyweavermusic.com/bluestar.php
10. **78 Records** — An early type of shellac-based phonograph record that played at 78 revolutions per minute.
11. **Round dancing** - Couple dancing in a circle formation, using choreographed routines to a definite arrangement of music.
12. **Walk Around Your Corner** — Dancers face their corners. Walking forward and around each other while keeping right shoulders adjacent, dancers return to their original position, with their backs toward their corner.
13. **Seesaw Your Partner** — Men face partner (usually returning to home position from doing an All Around the Left Hand Lady) and pass by left shoulders as ladies move into the center. Men loop to the left around partner and walk forward to starting position as ladies move back out to place.
14. **Dosado** — Walking a smooth circular path, dancers walk forward, passing right shoulders, slide sideways to the right, walk backward, passing left shoulders, and slide slightly to the left to return to their starting position.
15. **Middle Break** — The middle break in a singing call is the same as a break. See singing call definition.
16. **Allemande Left** — An Arm Turn by the left (plus a Step Thru as the dancers head toward their next dancer interaction).
17. **Elbow swing** — Like a right and left grand but you went around each person. You'd go around her all the way around her. Go to the next with a left and the way around her.

"THE AUCTIONEER" (BLUE STAR 1517)
CALL SHEET

CALLED BY: Marshall Flippo, Abilene, Texas
    Record: Blue Star 1517
    Music By Earl & His Hoedowners

FIGURE:
    First And Third You'll Bow And Swing
    Go Up The Middle And Back Again
    Go Forward Up And Swing That Opposite Gal
    Face To The Sides With A Right And Left Thru
    Turn 'Em Around Like You Always Do.
    And Duck To The Middle And Swing The Gal You Meet (Original Partner)
    Go Down That Centre, Crosstrail Thru
    Up The Outside Around Just Two
    Meet Your Girl And Swing Her Round So Neat
    Half Square Thru Across The Set
    With Your Corner Gal You Box The Gnat (Corner Becomes New Partner)
    Then Allemande Left (With New Corner) Meet Em All With An Elbow Swing

1st Time
    It's An Elbow Swing You're Doing Fine
    Now Swing The Next Gal Down The Live
    Then Swing That Pretty Gal In Calico
    Swing Em All With An Elbow Swing
    You Meet Your Own Coming Around The Ring
    And You Promenade This Gal Back Home You Know

2nd Time

25 Dollar Bidda Now 30 Dollar 30, Will You Gimma 30 Make It 30
Bid In Poem Of 30 Dollar, Will You
Who'll Make A 30 Dollar Bid
30 Dollar Bidda Now 35, Will You Give Me 35
Bid Me That 35 Dollar Bid

3rd Time

35 Dollar Bidda, Now 40 Dollar 401 Will You Gm Me 40, Make It 40
Bid In Form Of 40 Dollar Will You Give Me 40
Who'll Make A 40 Dollar Bid
40 Dollar Bidda Now 45, Will You Give Me 45, Make It 45, Biddle De 45
Who'll Bid Me, That 45 Dollar Bid

4th Time

45 Dollar Bidda Now 50 Dollar 501 Will You Give M 50, Make It 50
Bid In Form Of 50 Dollar, Will You Give Me 50
Who'll Make A 50 Dollar-Bid
50 Dollar Bidda Now 55, Will You Give Me 55, Make It 55, Bidde De 55
Sold To That Square For A 50 Dollar Bid

SEQUENCE:

Figure, Break, Figure, Break, Figure Break, Figure Break;
Note: Elbow Swing Can Be Used For The Break Each Time If Desired

FIRST CHANGE BID SUGGESTION IS AS FOLLOWS, IF DESIRED:

10 Dollar Bidda Now 20 Dollar 20, Will You Gimma 20, Make It 20
Bid In Form Of 20 Dollar, Will You Give Me 20
Who'll Bid A 20 Dollar Bid
20 Dollar Bidda Now 25, Will You Give.Me 25, Make It 25, Biddle De 25
Who'll Bid Me That 25 Dollar Bid

Go to my website: https://www.laradasbooks.com in the Private Membership Only section for the an original call sheet shared by Mark Newton.

"THE AUCTIONEER" (BLUE STAR 1825)
THE SECOND VERSION CALL SHEET

OPENER - MIDDLE BREAK - CLOSER

Now join up hands and make a ring,
    Then circle to the left like everything
    Then reverse trail along in single file
    The girls step out and take a back track
    And turn 'em with a right when you get back
    Left allemande and weave the ring awhile
    Now pretty soon he began to see how the auctioneer talked rapidly
    Dosado then promenade from here
    He said oh my, it's do or die, I've got to learn that auction cry
    Gotta make my mark and be an auctioneer

FIGURE

Now 1 & 3 1/2 square thru, then dosado that outside two
    Go once around and make a right hand star
    The heads star left inside the town, gotta turn that star go once around
    To the same old two then do the right & left thru
    Now dive thru, and pass thru, and swing thru
    And then those boys trade and promenade that Jane
    *Twenty five dollar bid, now thirty dollar thirty, will you give me thirty
    Make it thirty bid in form of thirty dollar will you give me thirty
    Who'll make a thirty dollar bid?

*Increase bid by five dollars each time through.[1]

---

1. Vic and Debbie Ceder, "ceder.net," March 17, 2020, https://www.ceder.net/recorddb/viewsingle.php?RecordId=8049&SqlId=283110

KIRKWOOD YEARS

Flippo's favorite picture: Flippo and Bob Fisk laughing at Bill Speidel's joke. Tommy
Lipscomb is to the left of Bob Fisk. Source: Neeca Flippo

9

KIRKWOOD LODGE

Kirkwood Lodge, Osage Beach, Missouri. Source: Neeca Flippo

During our interviews, Flippo returned to the topic of Kirkwood Lodge and Bill Hagadorn often. Kirkwood Lodge and Flippo's subsequent yearly tours shaped his life and calling career. For forty-two years, he called at Kirkwood, a vacation spot in the Lake of the Ozarks at Osage Beach, Missouri, then for six months, he traveled on the road with dance engagements booked from dancers he met at Kirkwood. Bill Hagadorn, the owner, hired him. As we talked one day, Flip requested, "Now we got to have a whole damn section about Kirkwood Lodge."

Aerial view of Kirkwood Lodge. Kirkwood Lodge, Osage Beach, Missouri. Source: Neeca Flippo

Bill Hagadorn saw in the young Flippo a potential star as a caller.

Bill Hagadorn, "The Best Boss I Ever Had in My Life"

To Flippo, Bill Hagadorn and Kirkwood were synonymous. When Flippo looked at a picture of Bill in one of his albums/scrapbooks, he repeated, "Thar's the best boss I ever had in my life. I worked for Bill for thirteen years 'til he sold out. One of the best guys, Mr. Bill Hagadorn, owner of Kirkwood Lodge. Him and Betty."

Bill sold clothes in the winter and needed somewhere to spend his summers, so he bought Kirkwood Lodge in 1946.

So, he was out on this boat with this guy, [Dr. Amick][1] and the guy said, "Well, hell, I've got a place in Missouri. Do you want to look it over and buy it? It's rundown. Hasn't had anythang done in a long time."

Bill found out it was on the Lake of the Ozarks, right on the water's edge. Without seeing it, Bill proclaimed, "I'll take it!"

Bill Hagadorn. Source: Neeca Flippo

Flippo added, "Whew, he's still in the boat."

Bill didn't care and bought it on the spot! So, that's the way Bill bought Kirkwood, and he came and was a little disappointed, but he saw somehow it could be fixed up, and fix it up he did!

In addition to Bill, Flippo saw Betty, Bill's wife, and Amy, his mother, as the main force behind the success of Kirkwood Lodge. They were good with names and had a system worked out on greeting their guests. This trio saw the guests arrive, with no badges or hints to their names. When the guests came down the hill to register, they would say to each other, "Who's that? Who's that?"

Amy (Bill's mother), Bill Hagadorn & Betty (Bill's wife). Source: Neeca Flippo

So, helping each other, one of the three would figure out who the returned guest was. When they'd come through the door, all three of them greeted the guests, calling them by name. "That means a lot to people. And I suppose that's why we had so many, so many come back every year."

Looking at the schedule, Bill wanted a longer summer season of six months, but he only had about three. He kept renovating and making improvements, and he wanted to fill up those other three months.

Then Bill heard about square dancing. Ed Gilmore was going to call over in a state park near, so he decided to go and check him out. So Bill went over there, and it wasn't Ed Gilmore. It was Les Gotcher, so Bill hired him. "I thank they started off with two weeks, and they kinda grew, and they got three weeks, four weeks, and then five weeks. They did five weeks a year. Five weeks—that's pretty good. So, Les was thar (calling) until 1958."

1957 – Burned Out

Looking at the pictures in Neeca's three photo albums/scrapbooks triggered lots of memories for Flippo. He remembered the first time they went to Kirkwood on vacation. A Greyhound bus driver and his wife who square danced in Wichita Falls, Texas came to Flip's regular Saturday night dance at the Hayloft in Abilene.

One night, he told Flippo about a place down in the Lake of the Ozarks in Missouri where he took high school seniors on their Senior Trip from the little towns around Wichita Falls and on up into Oklahoma, and they have square dancing. The bus driver said he always had a great time there, and it's run with an iron fist. And the kids are made to go to bed at one o'clock. If they're not in their rooms, a night watchman runs them in. They do a lot of skiing and swimming, and he had been taking them up to Kirkwood Lodge for two or three years.

The bus driver ended with, "Do you ever go on a square dance vacation?"

"No," Flippo stated. He wouldn't call or dance in the summertime because he played baseball, and "we were kind of thanking about getting out of square dancing in the late '50s."

Then Flip added with a laugh, "Well, wait a minute. That might be a good way to end our square dancing—go on a square dance vacation and then quit square dancing 'cause we was kind of burned out. They do have square dance weeks thar, so we looked up, and sure enough he got us a brochure. Les Gotcher and a *caller*[2] from Houston were the *callers*. We went and had the best time of our life, before or after."

So, in 1957, Flippo and Neeca went up there that week, and he remembered four couples from Texas were way back in the corner. They went through the first number. At that time, they had three numbers in a *tip*,[3] and the Texans went through the first number—perfect. They were good. Second number, they hit nothing. Third number, about halfway through, they were sitting on the floor and couldn't do anything.

Flippo remembered a man named Pete who only had two fingers on one hand. Him and his wife came by and said, "You Texans sure have a lot of fun, but you can't dance worth a shit."

Flippo accepted this good-hearted challenge! "So, we had, looking back on it, probably the best time that Neeca and I ever had. Well, we had not been on a vacation in a long time, so that was one thang."

Flip remembered waking up and Neeca had strung her petticoats on the line above the bed, and he looked up, thinking, "Where in the hell are we?'" Then he realized where they were.

When I asked Neeca about their first trip to Kirkwood, she said, "We had no idea how to dance *hot hash*[4] and did not know Les Gotcher. We tried to dance with three other couples from Texas on that first night, and they did not know much more than us. On Monday, we danced the workshops—nine hours. By mid-week I had blisters on the bottom of my feet. We had a great time and met really nice people."

It might be hard for a non-dancer to understand dancing nine hours, blisters on my feet, and having a good time all in the same sentence, but it works for me!

Flippo had just recorded "The Auctioneer" before they went there, and Les Gotcher, the staff caller, from 1952–58, called it, but before calling it, Les announced, "The author is in the house. Hold up your hand, Flippo."

Flippo explained, "So I was embarrassed as hell. But, anyway, that was the year we had such a good time. He didn't ask me to call or anythang, but he did recognize me."

Meeting Bill Hagadorn played a big part in Flip's life, and Flip liked how he ran Kirkwood Lodge. Bill would give a speech, and because his enunciation and diction were so clear, you heard every word. It came naturally for him. Bill was a good businessman. He was also good with people, but he put up with "no crap." He'd send people home if they started fooling around. Flip added, "He's the best boss I ever had, and one of the best people I ever knew—him and Betty. Now Betty just died about last year or the year before. I believe it was last year she died [2017]."

The Flippos had such a great time, they signed up for the next year.

1958 & 1959 – Returned Again and Again

The staff situation changed in 1958. Flip didn't know why, but Les Gotcher was out.

After, that Bill went to multiple *callers* in '58. He had heard about Frank Lane, so he talked to Frank, and Frank was ready to call there. Frank helped get up his staff, "and so that's the way that Bruce Johnson and Red Warrick got on thar." And so, Flip and Neeca went back.

Red Warrick, out of Kilgore, Texas, the owner and producer of Long Horn Labels, was really a good caller and had a lot of good records. They were all on *78s*,[5] and they're hard to find now.

Bruce Johnson was from Santa Barbara, California, and Flippo and Neeca had another really good time. But they met their friends from Illinois who kidded them about their dancing the year before and that rejuvenated Flippo again. When they got back after that first trip, having had so much fun, Flip thought, "Well, I'm going to keep on calling," and so he did and went back.

Neeca added, "In 1958, Hagadorn parted ways with Les. Les had moved to Eureka Springs, Arkansas when he contacted Flip to work a week." Obviously, Les identified Flip's talent immediately!

In 1959, Neeca shared, "Les lost that location [in Arkansas]. We had our vacation planned, so we were able to get in Kirkwood."

Joe Lewis and Jerry Helt were the callers that year, so they had an amazing time, even though Jerry never did get to call because he had laryngitis for the whole week.

1960 – The Staff Caller

Neeca shared about Les's offer to work in Arkansas, "Flip accepted and we had a great time being with many of the couples we had met at Kirkwood. Flip was supposed to be on the staff with Les again."

Source: Neeca Flippo

Jack Jackson was the staff *caller* at that time at Kirkwood. They had two different *callers* the next week and two the next week. Jack had about six weeks of square dancing at that time, and then they'd go into their regular fall season. So, the next time they went, Flip knew Jack Jackson had been the staff *caller*, so he was one of them, and Frank Lane was the other one. So, they went and had another good time.

After Flippo and Neeca vacationed there for several years, Bill called Flippo aside and asked him if he would like to be the staff *caller* there.

"Well, I don't know." Flippo added, "See here—it's another one of those lucky thangs that I just happened to be thar." Flippo always attributed any success to luck, not crediting his ability and personality for his success!

Bill explained that Jack said he's not coming back for the next year. The job consisted of six months working, and then you could do what you wanted the other six months.

"I gotta a job, and my wife's gotta a job. I mean, we're going to have to . . ."

Bill answered, "Think it over. I'll write you a letter if I want you."

Flippo emphasized, "If I want you . . . ?"

Neeca remembered, "When Flip came to our room—I was ironing. It was hard for us to fathom. Abilene was our home. Our parents lived there; we had jobs there."

Flippo figured Bill probably didn't want him. Anyway, they went home, and that was in 1960. Christmas passed, and January passed, and they hadn't heard anything from Bill.

Flippo stated with a chuckle, "Neeca, I don't thank he's going to write any letter, so I thank our jobs are safe."

But then they got a big letter from him telling Flip all the stuff that he was supposed to be doing, and Bill would pay Flip $25 a night, and he would call six nights when the square dancers were there.

Twenty-five dollars a night in 1960 translates to $217.04 in 2020,[6] which would be a lot per night in the square dance world even today. He was getting that pay per night for working six to seven nights a week at Kirkwood where normally *callers* call one night events or two- to three-day weekend festivals. Also, Kirkwood paid for the Flippos' housing, utilities, and groceries, and use of a boat, so they struck a gold mine!

The letter outlined Flippo's duties with the high school seniors, emphasizing that he would have to teach them because they would know nothing.

Flippo thought, "I'm not a very good teacher."

The letter stated, "We start with the [high school] seniors and they're here for anywhere from three to five weeks."

And so every night Flippo would call.

The letter continued, "We had different ones in. We'll have about two hundred head each night. Some of them leave, some of them coming in. So, you'll probably have to teach a little bit every night."

So Flippo exclaimed, "Ah, holy—what have I got. I don't thank I can do this." He added with a laugh, "Anyway, let me thank"—he repeated that phrase several times like a square dance *hot hash* call.

The letter added, "Then we have two weeks of square dancing in the summer. You'll have to do the Wednesday night. What we do is we start on Sunday night at 5:00 p.m. with a Beer Bust Introductions to everybody, and then we dance Sunday night, Monday night, and Tuesday night, and what you'll have to do is if the two *callers* that I hired want you to call a *tip*, they'll call you up, and you'll call a *tip*."

So Flippo fretted, "Oh, damn, Neeca, I don't thank I can handle this."

Neeca answered, "Read on." With a chuckle, he did.

"And after that we have our summer season, we call it, which is just regular guests. Now they're going to dance five nights a week: Sunday, Monday, Tuesday. Then on Wednesday, they go to the Opry. It's a show downtown called the 'Ozark Opry.'"

John Flippo added that they also danced on Friday. Later, the Opry night was moved from Wednesday to Tuesday, and they ended the week on Thursday instead Friday.

More explanation in the letter, "When they come back, you'll have to have *guest callers* up thar that are here for the vacation—not the staff *callers*, but the *guest caller*. You'll have to MC that. After they get back from the Opry, we'll have hot dogs for them, and we'll go dance for an hour or two. And the *guest callers* will call. You will MC it."

Flippo uttered, "Ooooh, God, what doin' here?"

The letter continued, "Now, after the summer season, which is about eight weeks, we go back into square dancing. Square dancing lasts from last week of August 'til the middle week of October. Now, at that time, when you're the staff *caller*, you will dance. When they go to the Opera on Wednesday nights, you can call on Wednesday night after they get back or you can introduce them. We have enough *guest callers*, introduce them, and if we don't, you can call and even if we have quite a few, you can still call."

Neeca shared her perspective, "Bill wrote us later to go more in detail what our jobs would be there." Bill expected Neeca to work in the gift shop when needed and handle the *after party*[7] snacks. "We decided to take a leave of absence from our jobs, keep our house. We had no children after ten years. We decided to take a chance, at least for one season. We were grateful for the opportunity, so we took the offer."

"Luck!" Flip said, becoming philosophical about life. "A lot of my success in calling and everythang has been luck more than talent. I just happened to be in the right place at the right time. Probably starting in Abilene, I was with some folks that really wanted to build a building. We did. So, I lucked out thar, and then two guys came before we ever built the building and told me about recording, and I was lucky they came by and told me ole Merrbach wanted to record. Well, I was lucky thar, and I happened to be lucky when I did 'The Auctioneer.' Lucked out! Lucked out at Kirkwood—just happened to be in the right place at the right time. Lucked out on my tours. Most everythang for my success I was just happened to be lucky, at the right time, at the right place."

With a chuckle, he added, "'The Auctioneer' got me in different places. I had no idea that it would turn out like it has turned out. I didn't plan it."

1961 – The Rest is History

In 1961, the Flippos started life at Kirkwood. Flippo liked being a staff *caller* there. He added, "When we went to Kirkwood, we's getting twenty-five dollars a night. Twenty-five dollars a night for calling—that was great pay for the time!

When Flip first went to Kirkwood, it was just two *calls* [*a singing call*[8] and *patter*[9]] a *tip* plus a *round*.[10] They wanted to do two *rounds* [two songs], so that was a big fight there, but finally it materialized into two. When he first went to Kirkwood, it was a *singing call* and a *hash* and a *round*.

Bill respected Flippo's opinion, so he regularly asked his advice about other callers. He'd give Flip the caller's name, and Flippo gave his pat response, "Oh, yeah, he's a pretty good, pretty good."

Bill added, "Thar's an ole boy over in Eldon," and he came around, and he said, "How's this guy?"

With a laugh, Flippo answered, "Bill, he's good." He added, "And ole Bill went somewhere, I thank out in the state park, where this guy was calling, and he come back and he says, 'I ain't gonna ask you about nobody else. The guy ain't worth a hoot!'"

Flippo's association with Kirkwood continued for four decades with a rich variety of national *callers* and *cuers*. He loved everything about Kirkwood: the dancers, the employees, and the *calling* and *cuing* staff he worked with over the years.

Source: Neeca Flippo

The Orbiting Squares Dance Club near Columbus, Ohio posted on their website: "In 1967, a group of couples began to caravan across Ohio, Indiana, Illinois, and into Missouri—down to central Missouri to the Kirkwood Lodge, Osage Beach, at the Lake of the Ozarks, for a week of square dancing, round dancing, and waterskiing; several of the club members towed boats. This began the association with caller, Marshall Flippo, from Abilene, Texas, who continued to call a special annual dance for the Orbiting Squares in March until 1999." [11]

For thirteen years, Kirkwood Lodge with Bill Hagadorn at the head and Flippo, the calling expert, succeeded and continued to grow. In one conversation, Flippo started, "So I might have already told you all I know about Kirkwood."

But as we continued to speak weekly, more and more details came to Flippo's mind. When Bill owned Kirkwood, he had the back cover of the annual National Square Dance Convention program, "which was a real big book, which was a really good advertisement." It had all the pictures of the callers that come to Kirkwood for the weeks that they came.

We proudly announce that MARSHALL FLIPPO of Abilene, Texas will be back again as our Assistant Host. And "Flip" will again be directing the EVENING ENTERTAINMENT for a barrel of fun and good fellowship for those who want to stay young and enjoy the time of their life!

Marshall Flippo back at Kirkwood. Source: Neeca Flippo

An Abundance of Dancing

Through the combined efforts of Bill and Flippo, Kirkwood Lodge grew the schedule into four seasons of dancing: high school senior weeks, summer square dancing, regular guests, and fall square dancing. The year started in April and ended in October.

Seniors Weeks

They started off with high school seniors on their senior trip. It was when Kirkwood first opened for the year, and they would have anywhere from eight to eleven weeks of high school seniors. They would have anywhere from 100 to 210 seniors, which is about twenty squares every night. Flippo exclaimed, "Every day was the fourth of July, and every night was New Year's Eve. It was fun because the kids were fun at that time. I had so much luck when I first started because the kids liked the square dancing, Larada, in that era from the '60s on 'til the '70s, and then it started changing quite a bit, but those kids just loved square dancing."

So the first bunch of kids that came in, Flip taught them just like callers do *one night stands*,[12] and those young kids caught on fast. Flip didn't know how many squares [mathematics: 100 kids=12.5 squares; 210 kids=26 squares; 220 kids=27.5 squares] he had that first time, "but I know I was well pleased, and I thought, 'Oh, my! These kids up thar, and I thank they'll stay one *tip* and go on,' and that's what eventually come out, but not then. They liked it. They really liked it, and I've thought about this a lot. If the lake had been vacant, you know, why was it so good at that time? Were kids at that time all over the country—were they the same way? And I thank that they were. If kids all over the country got a chance to take square dancing, and they liked it that much, that was the '80s and '90s boom of square dancing."

The first night Flippo called, the hall was full, and he was so glad. He slept a little late the next morning, and the phone rang.

Neeca got the phone, "It's ole Bill Hagadorn."

Bill asked, "Hey, Flip, can you come down here? They're still leaving, and they want to do one more square dance."

Flippo loved their enthusiasm and responded, "I'll be right down." He went down, and of course, they wanted one.

Then they questioned, "Can we have one more?"

"One more, and that's it. That's all you're going to get! The bus driver's waiting."

That happened the whole season, so Flippo asked Bill, "Should I just come down here?"

"No, no, no, no, no. Let 'em ask for it!" Flippo laughed at his response.

Bill added, "They might ought to ask."

So basically Flippo had to go back. They were all rural schools who came on their senior trips. One school had been there forty-eight times on their senior trips, so their grandpas had been there.

Kirkwood's mainstay was repeat generational guests. A girl came up to Flippo one night and asked, "How are you doing?" He added, "I's standing thar."

"Are you Flip?"

"Yeah."

"How are you doing?"

"I'm fine."

"Momma said hello. Momma said I was conceived here."

With a laugh, Flippo quizzed her, "What? What are you talking about?"

"Well, Momma met my Daddy."

Flippo explained, "Another school was here, and we usually had four or five schools at one time."

She added, "They had a little somethang going on, and so, they swore that I was conceived at Kirkwood. They got married. She got home, and he got home, and they got all up with their parents." He added, "I don't know which town they were from, but I thank one of 'em's mother was from Smithville, and I don't know where the boy was from."

The young dancer repeated her Kirkwood connection again, ending with, "Well, Momma said tell you hello."

These kinds of experiences were heartwarming to Flip. He enjoyed Kirkwood so much. "And my salary went up over the years. It really kept a-going up, and that's enjoyable."

Because of Flippo's expertise of working with young dancers, he was interviewed in *Sets in Order*, and wrote an article about working with young people.[13]

Summer Square Dance Weeks

When Flippo started at Kirkwood Lodge, he only had two square dance weeks in the summer, but because of its popularity, Bill finally doubled it to four weeks summer square dancing with different staff. He knocked off a couple regular guest weeks and added a couple more square dance weeks.

In 1963, the schedule increased from nine weeks to ten and the staff increased from nine to ten for the season.[14]

Over the years Flip worked at Kirkwood, they featured some of the top national *callers* at the time: Frank Lane, Arnie Kronenberger, Dave Taylor, Max Forsyth, Ray Smith, Bob Fisk, Red Warrick, Sam Mitchell, Zelmer Hovland, Ron Schneider, Jim Brower, Johnny LeClair, Ken Bower, Gary Shoemake, Jerry Haag, and Bob Yerington.

The *cuing*[15] staff also stood out in their profession: Nita and Manning Smith, Na and Jack Stapleton, Carolyn and Frank Hamilton, Naomi and Ernie Gross, Edna and Gene Arnfield, Wanda and John Winter, Midge and Jerry Washburn, and Darlene and Jack Chaffee.

Summer Guest Weeks

Then they went into their summer guest weeks with regular people that came just like the square dancers did for two and a half months.

These guests came back "year after year after year, and you know, I can remember their names better than I could a square dancer 'cause with square dancers" he would sneak a look at the badge. The summer guests didn't wear badges, so he had to remember them better. To prepare for each week, they found out who was coming the next week.

Flippo ended sadly, "It kind of dwindled down."

Fall Square Dance Weeks

Then Kirkwood went back to square dancing until October and then closed. So, they were only open six months a year, and Flippo traveled the other six months.

. . .

Weekly Schedule

Flippo kept up a rigorous weekly schedule but each season differed.

Neeca described his schedule, "Flip called six nights during square dance season, every night during high school seniors, and four nights during family season." He kept up that pace for the six months he was at Kirkwood for forty-two years!

Square dancing started on Monday night and from the *Basics*.[16] Before Flip started with the adults, he always had about forty minutes of pre-teens and little ones dancing. Those little ones have grown up now and have kids, and some of them are grandmas and grandpas, and they're the repeat visitors.

Two key people who contributed to the success of Kirkwood besides Bill were Betty, his wife, and Amy, his mother. Flippo had favorite stories about them.

Betty Hagadorn

"I haven't mentioned Betty Hagadorn, Bill's wife. Pretty woman. Beautiful, beautiful waterskier. She just look like she's born on skis, one ski especially."

Betty would come down to the boat dock ever once in a while. She would be making the rounds and check around because she missed the beach and the swimming pool.

So, two families came to Kirkwood as guests, and they had gone to a ski school the night before. Joe Hollandsworth, boat dock captain, taught guests to ski, and he taught a lot of people. He was sitting in the ski boat, and right off the ski boat was a place where you can sit down on the dock and leave on two skis.

The two families came down to the boat dock. "Boy, they was all 'hot up' about this skiing and they's talking, 'Gentleman, where can we rent a boat?'"

Joe asked them what kind of boat they wanted.

"We want a boat. We're going to ski. We went to ski school. That looks like fun."

They stayed for a week, "and it was like Abbott and Costello every day out at the dock, 'cause they were trying to teach theirselves, see." Flippo said these people were the best people on earth. They tried everything, and some of them got to ski pretty well. But they definitely didn't start off "pretty good."

So, this "ole boy" was standing there. Joe was in the boat, and the back of the boat was right even with the edge of the dock. And he was about a yard and a half back on the dock, but the bottom part of his skis should be in the water if he was going to sit down and take off on the dock.

He saw them take off at the water show, just standing up off of the dock, but they had their skis about halfway off the dock to start. When that rope played out, it would give a little jump, and they'd be in the water.

This "ole boy" was standing there, and his skis were about a yard and a half from the edge of the boat dock. He's standing there with the rope in his hands, and the boat was out there. "Well, thar ain't no way he's gonna make it."

Joe asked, "What are you doing?"

He answered, "Joe, Joe, hey Joe, can I get off the dock this way?"

"Well, sure you can."

Flippo laughed outright at this. Joe had the boat out there, and they had slack in the line, and finally, somebody came up behind Flip. He was over on the other side of the boat dock, standing next to a boat well. Here comes Betty.

"She very seldom come down thar."

Betty questioned, "What's going on?"

And Flippo answered, "I'm watchin' this guy goin' to take off the dock. I really don't know, but he just asked Joe if he could get off the dock." Flippo, in his caller's voice sang, "dock."

"Joe should stop him."

"Well, he's going to have to get the skis in the water," Flippo sang. "You know, he's going to have to sit on the edge of that dock, put the skis thar. Ah, he don't know that. And he just asked Joe if he could get off the dock and Joe had told him yes." Flippo laughed at this again.

"Well," Betty replied, "Joe shouldn't have done that. Well, he can't take off from thar."

"I know that. Joe knows that. He cannot make it."

Betty's standing there and exclaimed, "Oh my God!"

He had a lot of slack in the rope, which was way too much. About that time, that "ole boy" said, "Hit it!" The boat took off, and when that slack played out, you could have put a cup of coffee on each one of those skis and not spilled a drop. It just pulled him right out of them, right out into the lake.

Flippo had trouble getting his words out past his own laughter, he was laughing so hard. I couldn't help but join in, not just at the visual his story displayed, but at Flippo's contagious laughter, too!

When it hit, when that slack got out of that rope, that "ole boy" went flying out into the lake. "Skis were there. You couldn't imagine it! It just pulled him right out into the water."

The want-to-be skier yelled, "Joe, you said I could get off that way."

"Bull, where are you?"

"I'm in the lake."

Flippo exploded in laughter.

Joe continued, "That's what you asked me! Aren't you in the lake?"

"Oh, damn."

"You had your skis too far back."

Anyway, just pulled him right out of the skis. And so, Flip turned around and was going to say something to Betty.

Flippo sang, "And Betty wasn't thar." He looked up the dock to see where she'd gone—no Betty. He kept looking around.

He called out her name. Flip said, "She's down thar."

Betty yelled, "Flippo, Flippo, git me out of this water." She had backed up laughing and stepped in one of the boat wells and went off into the water. They had some canoes in the wells and then fishing boat wells and stuff that they all had a little edge of water around them. But she fell down and "looked like a wet hog. So, I got her out of thar. She wasn't that heavy—little, little woman."

But Flippo questioned, "What in the hell are you doing?"

"Well, when he come out of those skis, it looked like a perfect dive out into the lake." His retelling of her response was punctuated with laughter.

She continued, "You know, run off out that rope but flying through the air." At this point, Flippo's chuckles turned to belly laughs then a storm of coughs.

So, she explained, "I stepped back, Flippo, and thar was no more boat dock thar. It was just water. When he started to ski, I stepped back to git a better look, and I fell into the boat well."

Flippo stated, "Well, next time you come down here with us crows, you be sure and put on a . . . You know. Bill and Betty were always saying, 'When you're down around the boat dock, be sure to get on a ski belt or a life vest or somethang if you can't swim.'"

So Flippo added, "Next time you come down here, we'll find you a life vest."

"You son of a bitch!"

And Flippo added, "And just walked off!"

With a laugh, Flippo added her saying, "I don't like getting on board."

He continued, "But she's a good woman."

Amy Hagadorn

Amy, one of the trio that kept Kirkwood going, was Bill's mother and ran the Gift Shop. "And she was selling moccasins one or two years in a row. She always had lots and lots of moccasins on hand." Again, Flippo sang the word, "row." Those moccasins that she brought in were so good to dance in, and she sold lots and lots of them. "They were like ones the Indians wear and had a hard sole."

Gift Shop at Kirkwood Lodge ran by Amy Hagadorn. Source: John Flippo

On Sunday afternoon at five, Kirkwood had with a Beer Bust with free beer. Bill introduced everybody, and he would tell short stories. Then he'd talk about the Gift Shop, "I don't know whether Momma is a good salesman. Moccasins or not, but I do know that the moccasins salesman is one hell of a salesman, 'cause she always has so many."

His laughter continued, "Well, she did ask after everybody. Those were damn good moccasins. I wish I had a couple pair of them to last the rest of my life. Well, I guess one pair will last me the rest of my life, but very good moccasins."

Kirkwood and Bill Hagadorn contributed to Flippo's success, and Flip influenced Kirkwood's success. The dancing schedule grew, and life was good. From the very beginning, Flippo's move there and lengthy stay was a dream job for any *caller*, but he worked hard there, reaping the benefits for him and Bill.

---

1. *Lake Times,* (June 5, 1986): 7-9.
2. **Caller** — A person who prompts dance figures in such dances as line dance, square dance, and contra dance.
3. **Tip** — A square dance session consisting of two parts, a patter call, and a singing call. See Glossary for more.
4. **Hot Hash** — A special tip with no pauses between formations. The tempo of the music is increased, adding to the difficulty.
5. **78 Records** — an early type of shellac-based phonograph record that played at 78 revolutions per minute.
6. Comparison of $25 in 1960 to 2020. Ian Webster, "CPI Inflation Calculator," 2020, http://bit.ly/39kUVKC
7. **After Party** — The party after the square dance with skits and a variety of entertainment usually put on by the event staff of callers and cuers. Sometimes dancers participated in skits, too.
8. **Singing Call** — The caller sings parts of the songs. See Glossary for more.
9. **Patter** — A single tune, used by a caller as background for a series of calls, with no lyrics accompanying the music. Couples are moved into a variety of formations, but brought back to their home positions before the next set of calls.
10. **Round** — Couple dancing in a circle formation, using choreographed routines to a definite arrangement of music.
11. The Central Ohio Corporation of Dance Clubs, "The Orbiting Squares Square Dance Club," January 6, 2019, https://cocdc.cboh.org/Clubs/OS.html
12. **One Night Stands (One-Nighters)** — A one evening square dance that has a party atmosphere and a few *Basics* are taught. The objective is to get people up dancing and having a good time.
13. *Sets in Order,* (September 1967): 24-25, 70.
14. *Sets in Order* (February 1963): 58.
15. **Cuing Staff** — Leader at the front of the ballroom [hall] who tells the dancers, as they dance, what steps to do.
16. **Basics** — The beginning CALLERLAB program with fifty-one calls.

10

THE PRIDE OF FLIPPO'S LIFE, JOHN

Source: Neeca Flippo

Fathers and sons can be an interesting dynamic! Flippo and his son, John, shared a remarkably close relationship. That was obvious any time Flippo talked about him, because he couldn't say enough. "Of course, the pride of my life is John, my son. He's good, knock on wood."

Flippo relished the year they spent together touring when John graduated from high school before he went to college.

In talking about John, Flip mentioned in passing, "He had cancer when he was three. That's a story in itself."

Flippo and Neeca lived at Kirkwood when she got pregnant, and they worried about how that would affect their job there.

Neeca shared, "Jack Jackson was the caller who Flip replaced [at Kirkwood]. They had a child, and it was not working out. At the end of 1962 season, we found out that I was pregnant. We thought that they would not want us for the future at Kirkwood with a child, but they were satisfied with Flip, so we became permanent employees. They loved John. They purchased a plot next to Kirkwood property with a small house. They had it remodeled and furnished it and even provided a diaper service for John. We had free rent, free utilities, and no cooking. Free use of the Kirkwood boat. It was almost perfect."

John was born in Abilene, Texas on June 8, 1963. Neeca returned to Abilene to have him, "so he's a pure Texan. They're just thar a few days, and they came on back to the lake. He's not enough Texan to move down thar. He'll never leave that lake, I don't thank."

Flippo mischievously stated, "And John was conceived thar [Kirkwood] in a trailer. When we first went thar, Bill had a little trailer up at the top. The concrete slab the trailer sat on is still on the Kirkwood property. We'd go up thar, and sometimes in the afternoon have 'a nooner'—sex in the afternoon. Well, I know good and well that's where. As exactly, I just felt it at the time."

He thought, "Oh, I thank we've gone too far." And he added, "And sure enough, Neeca was pregnant—in Bill's trailer."

As he shared this, I wondered if that may be the reason John loves it there so much.

Flippo laughed out loud. "So Bill, bless his heart. Thar are two little houses down to the side of Kirkwood's land. They were vacant. That son of a gun heard that Neeca was pregnant, so he went down and bought that land and those two little houses, and he tore down the worst one and kept the better one and remodeled it, and we went from living in a trailer then to that little house, and I can see that little house where I'm sitting right now. It's just across the street over here from John."

With a chuckle, he added, "Any way I tell this, John says, 'Dad, you're making all this stuff up.'"

Flippo answered, "John, no, I'm not. I'm telling you that was the only time that I didn't use any protection 'cause we were in a hurry." To me, he said, "I always pull out first, but I didn't that time and didn't use protection, and I said [to John], 'That's where you were conceived.'"

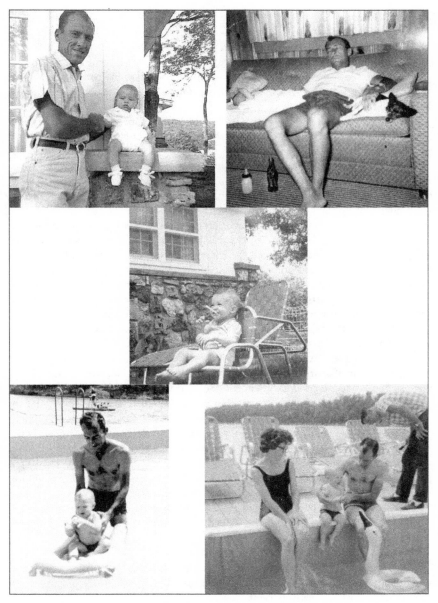

1st Row: L to R: Flippo & baby John, Flippo asleep on the couch with baby John.
2nd Row: L to R: Flippo's favorite picture of John with a cigarette and beer can. 3rd
Row L to R: Flippo in the pool with baby John, Neeca and Flippo sitting by edge of
pool with baby John. Source: John & Neeca Flippo

John's Cancer

At an early point during our interviews, I asked Flippo about John's cancer and if he wanted to share any more about that part of their lives.

Curtly Flippo answered, "Well, he recovered."

Then the seriousness of the topic set in. John had neuroblastoma, a cancer of the stomach, and they got it all out in the operation. Except the two percent, they killed it with radiation.

They were at Kirkwood, and little John was coming down a slide at the pool. That's when Flippo noticed. "I saw a little knot on the side of his navel, kind of pooched out."

First thing Flippo thought was he had ruptured himself. And so, the next morning, every time he'd come down, Flip would mash on it.

Flippo asked John if it hurt when he mashed it, and John responded, "No, no, it don't hurt."

John ran around, and he came down the slide again, and Flip could still see it. So, the next morning, before he got up, Flippo went into his room, and John was asleep on his back. When he pulled the covers back and kind of mashed on it with his hand, he noticed it was oblong.

And Flippo thought, "Oh, that's a tumor, I bet." So, they took him over to Camdenton. Two doctors sent them to the university hospital. "Thank the Lord they did! It was just a Godsend! And I will never forget those doctors. They thought it was a tumor, and we got over thar and Dr. Adams came out and told us that they were going to operate."

Flippo exclaimed, "And oh, we were about sick as dogs!"

In the midst of sharing this heart-wrenching story, Flip chuckled softly, "They were so good to us, so good to him at the Missouri University Hospital."

After John got out of the hospital, Flip took him over to Columbia every day to get radiation, and of course, his hair all came out, but the nurses were good to him. "They'd write little handy thangs where you put the needle, you know, so, he didn't mind going. It was eighty miles over thar, and so, we did that for a month, and after that is when they went home."

Then they thought the cancer was coming back because everything John ate came up, and Dr. Johnson agreed with them. Flippo was on tour in New York, so Neeca took John back to Abilene and got a second opinion from Dr. Schaeffer.

Dr. Schaeffer's gone now, but he helped them a lot. If he hadn't, Dr. Johnson would have just let John die.

Flippo punctuated this tale, "Scary. Very scary."

Dr. Schaeffer, after taking a look at the boy, proclaimed, "We're operating right now." Neeca demanded to get Flippo home first, but the doctor repeated, "Get him home, but we're operating right now!"

So, they found adhesions, that's all it was. When they did the radiation, they told us that it would kill all of the sperm cells. And it did, so he can't have kids. He's married to Shelly, "and they're like to two peas in a pod."

"Yeah, he turned out to be my best friend. We talk to each other every day, you know, mostly every day. But he's just one of those good guys. Well, he'll do anythang you want. If you need anythang else from him, just call him and he's very prompt about it."

During one of our last phone calls, Flip called John about his phone dying, and he announced, "Here comes John with the charger."

John was afraid the phone would die during our interview, so he interrupted his busy day, ran back to the house from his store and brought the charger.

Flippo ended, "Good kid! Good guy. I lucked out thar."

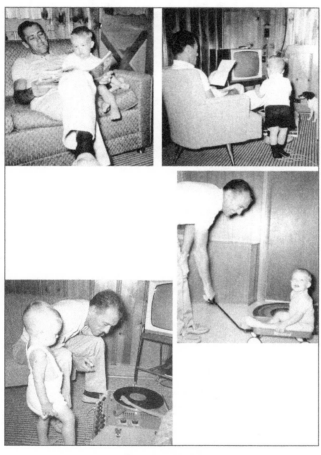

1st Row: L to R: Flippo and John looking at book, Flippo reading with John and dog. 2rd Row: Flippo pulling John in a wagon. 3rd Row: Flippo and John looking at record player. Source: John & Neeca Flippo

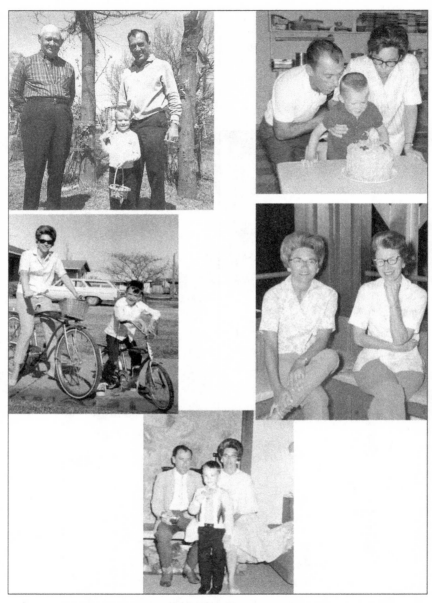

1st Row L to R: Three Generations: Roy Flippo, John and Flippo Easter in the 60s, Flippo and Neeca celebrating John's birthday. 2nd Row L to R: Neeca and John on bikes, Neeca & Hattie Bell, John's godmother. 3rd L to R: Flippo, John and Neeca.
Source: John & Neeca Flippo

Like father like son, John trying his hand at calling. Source: John & Neeca Flippo

1st Row: L to R: John & Flippo on the beach, Flippo throwing a snowball at John in Colorado. 2nd Row: Flippo and John. 3rd Row: L to R: John & Flippo resting after rollerskating, Flippo talking to John in trouble. Source: John & Neeca Flippo

11

LIFE AT KIRKWOOD & MORE

F lippo's life at Kirkwood Lodge buzzed with a hectic mixture of his family, dancing, Kirkwood employees, *after parties*,[1] and waterskiing, and he loved it all! Flippo's popularity soared during this time, and he was in high demand across the country, so he did weekend festivals during his six months at Kirkwood whenever he could squeeze them into his already busy schedule.

Kirkwood Employees

People, people, people were so important to Flippo, and he didn't distinguish the Kirkwood employees from the callers, the cuers, or the dancers. He loved them all. He specifically wanted to tell stories about Kirkwood employees who he worked with daily the forty-two years he was there.

Flippo stated, "I would like to include 'em in. I'd like to tell a story about 'em."

But Flippo had too many stories, so the Kirkwood employees' stories will be in the Private Membership's space.

Here are the people Flippo shared heartfelt stories about: Lillian Youngblood, Barbara Lindstrom, June Howser, Rabbit, Richard, Gladys and Dally and Susie, Mona Wilson, Dee Johnson, Leeman Wilson, Red Graham, Joe Hollandsworth, Lesley, and Harry Linden. John, Flippo's son identified two other employees, Richard and Colette Hicks, but Flip didn't have any stories for them.

Flip ended his storytelling about the employees, "Employees were kinda like family. I swear to God, it was good going to work because you know you's going to see the employees that you really did like."

Standing - L to R: June Howser, Richard Hicks, Harlene Langdon, Gloria Dampier and Jack Lindstrom. Seated: L to R: Unkown, Neeca Flippo. Source: Neeca Flippo

More pictures and Flippo's stories about individual employees are in the Private Membership Only page, using a membership code, on my website: https://www.laradasbooks.com

The Life of the *After Party*

Flippo shared that Ray and Harper Smith started this square dance tradition. An *after party* is the party after the square dance with skits and a variety of enter-tainment usually put on by the event staff of callers and cuers. Sometimes dancers participated in skits, too. This was also time that alcohol was allowed. I've included them here because most of the pictures in the three photo albums/scrap-books happened at Kirkwood.

After parties finished off almost every evening at Kirkwood with laughter and frivolity! When I asked Flippo about *after parties*, he laughed, "Oh, oh, oh, me! Ah." This tradition was done at Kirkwood, on Flippo's tours and his festivals.

"I remember quite a few of them, but where would you put that?" Always worrying about the organization of the book. I convinced him *after parties* had to be included, especially because of their uniqueness to the square dance world.

Flip continued with a laugh, "I can conjure up some of them, but the funniest thang is getting ready for them."

During a practice session, one time Flippo's second wife was down in the Terrace Room, which is the dance hall at Kirkwood with "ole Jerry Haag," and they had a green plastic tub from Walmart. She was going to do a skit that she loved. He was going to sit in the tub, and she was going to sing a love song while she was bathing him.

She instructed [Jerry], "Now sit in this tub."

So, he sat in the tub. When he tried to get out, he couldn't, and she was laughing, "and he's up walking around with that thang sticking out his ass [the tub]. She was down on the floor laughing."

She exclaimed, "I never laughed so hard in all my life."

Flippo couldn't help him because he was lying down on the floor laughing, but things like that happened a lot when they were getting ready. They also laughed a lot when they screwed up a skit.

As we continued talking, I asked Flip what was his favorite skit.

His response surprised me, "Oh, no, I won't say. I didn't have any favorite. I cringed when I had to do one."

I stated, "But you were so good at them."

"Well, I don't know whether I was or not. I was scared."

When asked about their frequency at Kirkwood, they did four nights a week in Kirkwood, which was a struggle. They did them Monday, Tuesday, Thursday, and Friday. Flip thought they finally cut it down to three nights. He felt they should have done just one night, but people seemed to like it. They always had *after party* snacks with the responsibility of putting out the skits.

Popular *After Party* Skits

In Flippo's era, skits dominated *after parties*. Jerry Haag, Ken Bower, Gary Shoemake, Scott Smith, Frank Lane, Flippo and many other callers entertained hundreds of enthusiastic dancers with skits. The following site some vintage skits Flippo remembered:

Jerry Haag did that Brenda Flea (Brenda Lee) for the longest time, singing that Louisiana song, "Jambalaya," when he was dressed up like a woman, and he got out on stage and pantomimed the song. Flip would always end with that one because it always brought the house down.

And then, Ken Bower did a couple of them for a while, but Flip couldn't remember the names of those.

Jerry Haag doing his
"Brenda Flea" pantomime.
Source: Neeca Flippo

L to R: The Boxer with Gary Shoemake, "I Just Don't Look Good Naked Anymore," The Golfer, and The Boxer with Frank Lane. Source: Neeca Flippo & Larada Horner-Miller

Flip's popular skits were "I Just Don't Look Good Naked Anymore"[2] and "Super Man." He did "The Boxer'" the most. Quite a few different callers interviewed him when he did that one. Gary Shoemake was one of the interviewers, and so was Frank Lane. Flip remembered Frank did it at Asilomar and other places that they had weekends. He also added "The Golfer."

Skits like "The Boxer" have too long of scripts to include here.

With a chuckle, he got fired up, "We got one off of that BBC. Two guys are sitting on a park bench. And also, we did 'Hey, Steve.'"

A guy goes to a ball game, and he sits in the stands, and he talks to the guy next to him and says, "I'm sorry ole George died. I hope we get a good guy next to us." Here comes a guy down with about five or six bags of potato chips, two or three drinks, and some candy.

He protested, "Oh, no, no, no."

Flippo continued with a laugh, "Sure enough, he sat right down beside him."

He observed, "Boy, a big crowd here today, isn't thar?"

"Yeah, very big crowd here" and Flippo laughed as he continued.

Somebody yelled, "Hey, Steve."

This guy asked, "Do you mind?" So he handed all this stuff to the guy next to him. The guy was shaking his head, and he stood up and looked back up the bleachers, shook his head, and sit back down. The guy handed him the rest of the stuff. He was fixing to open the package of potato chips.

And somebody else said, "Hey, Steve." Again, he hands all that stuff back to that guy again, and the guy's shaking his head. He finally gets it all to him. He stands up and he looks back over and sits back down, and, of course, the guy hands all the stuff back to him.

So, he shared, "I hope it's a good game today."

Again, someone yelled, "Hey, Steve." Once again, he hands all this stuff to him, and the punch line is he stands up, and he looks back up in the bleachers, and he says, "I wish you'd quit calling me Steve. My name is Bill."

Flippo continued, "Ole Scott Smith done that a long time. That was a good one. Thar's so many of them. I don't know how to explain some of them."

"Haag and Ken always done the 'Dumb Brothers': and that was really funny because they ad-libbed most all of it. Jerry was the farmer or whatever."

Flippo told another skit about "an ole mule," and you can find it on my website on the Private Membership Only page.

As Flippo thought about people he did skits with over the years, he recounted, "And thar's some damn people that could have been actors and actresses. They just had that knack, a lot of them, you know."

He felt "ole Bill Speidel" could have been on TV, easily. In fact, he was funnier than some of them were on TV at the time. They had people like Sam Mitchell that sang a song and just raise the hair on your neck. Flip thought he had "the best damn" voice that he ever heard. "I'm talking about on television, radio—pop singers or anythang. I thank ole Sam had the best voice to me that I have ever heard. He'd sing at *after parties* and just sing a regular song. He just had that voice that was unbelievable. And he could have made it. He could have made it like Jim Reeves. He's just as good."

Flippo added about current *callers*,[3] "Like ole [Johnny] Preston. Now he could be on Broadway. Thar's been a lot of really good talent that I've seen."

I asked Flippo if they found any of the *after party* skit material when he moved from Tucson to live with John. His response was sad to me in that they didn't find any. He thought there was a box that Jerry and Sherry Haag had given him when Jerry retired. Flip remembered getting into the boxes a couple times, but later he couldn't find them.

He never did find them, but his son, John, just found some, so we'll see what we can do. Jim Mayo, a caller and square dance historian, would love to get his hands on them to archive them.

Here's some pictures of those memorable skits to remind you of all the fun Flippo and his cohorts had:

L To R: John Flippo & Flippo horse racing, Flippo & John Winter. Source: Neeca Flippo

135

1st Row L to R: Flippo & Melton Luttrell, Flippo. 2nd Row L to R: Flippo & Bob Yerington. 3rd Row L to R: Flippo, Melton Luttrell & Flippo, Flippo. Source: Neeca Flippo

1st Row: Flippo & Gary Shoemake , Flippo & Gary Shoemake . 2nd Row: Flippo & Gary Shoemake , Flippo & Gary Shoemake . 3rd: Flippo & Made-up band. Source: Neeca Flippo

1st Row: Dee & Ken Bower, Ken Bower and Flippo. 2nd Row: Flippo, Ken Bower and Elmer Sheffield, Wanda and John Winter, Gary Shoemake and Flippo. Source: Neeca Flippo

Waterskiing

During our weekly talks, Flippo never mentioned his love for waterskiing or his amazing abilities until I saw a video that Elmer Sheffield and Darryl Lipscomb put together for his 90th birthday, featuring a great photo of him waterskiing. Then Dee Dee Dougherty-Lottie and Dana Schirmer mentioned his expertise. Flippo and I had this conversation a month or so before he died. I was surprised he had never brought up the topic, especially after I got him talking, and it was obvious how much he loved it.

When I asked Flippo how he got into waterskiing, his humorous reply was, "Well, I was on a lake."

Flip had learned to waterski before Kirkwood Lodge on Cisco Lake in Texas—Cisco, Texas. Then they took the job in Kirkwood, and he skied most every day at lunchtime. Whenever the boat captain got a little break, he and Flip skied.

He identified the callers he pulled. "Arnie Kronenberger I pulled skiing. I pulled Dee Dee Dougherty skiing. I thank I pulled Gary [Shoemake] skiing. I thank I pulled Ken [Bower] skiing and also Jerry Haag."

Any of the callers, if they skied, Flip would pull them skiing, "and it seemed like I taught a couple of 'em, but I cannot remember. I don't thank I taught anybody, but if they knew how to ski, I pulled 'em. I pulled Darlene Chaffee, Jack Chaffee's wife, skiing most every lunch when they worked at Kirkwood. Good skier. She loved to ski. Jack's still alive. I talked to him not too long ago [2018]. Darlene passed. It's about all I know about skiing."

When he said that, I was shocked because I knew better from stories I'd heard and pictures John had sent me, so I asked about skiing without skis.

"Yeah. barefooted, yeah, and I didn't teach him [John], but he learned how to waterski barefoot, too, so we'd go double. He's got a good picture of me that I have framed at Tucson. It's him and I both going barefooted."

I asked if Neeca waterskied. He added with a chuckle, "Neeca waterskied, yes on two skis, and she'd do the 'Fifty Yard Douche' before she stood up. In other words, she did squattin' on the skis, and we'd be a going a good piece, and finally she'd stand up a little and a little more, and she'd be standing up, but she always took off with a 'Fifty Yard Douche' 'fore she stood up. But she skied on two, and she skied very well on two. She never did go barefooted like John and I did, but she did pull us."

L to R: Neeca, Flippo and John. Neeca and Flippo in boat. Source: John Flippo

When Flip first learned how to ski barefooted, Neeca drove the boat, so they knew that they had to go a certain speed. At first, they thought it was really fast, so they went about forty miles an hour, and Flip wasn't doing too well. "When you fall when you're learning how and you fall trying to barefoot, your face is the first thang that hits the water." At that point, they were going about eight miles too fast, so they kept slowing it down and kept slowing it down. Finally, they got down around thirty-two. With Flippo's weight, that was about the right speed. John skied about the same speed.

Flippo waterskiing barefooted. Source: John Flippo

Flippo & John, his son, waterskiing barefooted! Source: John Flippo

John Flippo & Waterskiing

John became Flippo's skiing partner.

He added, "John's got big feet, which don't mean a thang. His feet are bigger than mine, but what happens when you're waterskiing—I's reading in a book—thar's a little bubble that forms under your arch, and when it burst, you're gone, I mean, you're down, but that little bubble's got to keep going. Thar's a little bubble under all's feet. I know he skied right behind the boat. I never did try that, but we had a platform that was at the back of the boat, and he'd stand on it, and he'd ski barefooted right behind the boat. He became quite a trick skier, too, and he does this air chair thang, you know, that you'd have to see it, too. It's kinda like a chair, but it's got a big ole lookin' like an anchor a-way down [under it], and it lifts you way up in the air and come down on that chair ski."

John Flippo trick skiing. Source: John Flippo

Flip had a little dog named Smokey they took with them skiing, and they'd ski on a disc, at a real slow speed, and they put him out on the disc.

We talked about funny stories that happened with waterskiing, and he responded, "Those are thangs you try to forget. I run John up on the beach one time. We'd go around in a circle, and he was on this, what we call a slip board, and go around the corner and he'd git outside the wake, and I thought, 'My God!' He's going really fast around that corner, and I thought, 'Oh, geez!' Run him up on the beach and hurt his ankle a little, but not enough for him to quit skiing that day."

Flippo told John, "Man, I'm sorry."

John answered, "Well, I's so far out I couldn't git myself back in. I knew I's going to hit the beach if I didn't git back in, and I didn't git back in and went right up on the beach."

They had this disc they skied on, and you could turn around on it really easy. It's just a big "ole round board" called a disc. And they put a step ladder on it, and then climbed up this step ladder and skied way up in the air on a step ladder. They had some big falls on it. "It's a wonder we hadn't killed ourselves, because we tried most everythang."

Flip and John both did shoe skis before Flip started skiing barefooted. He skied on shoe skis, which are just a little bigger than a shoe, but it's got a foot piece in it for your feet, and they call them foot skis.

Then they had trick skis where Flip turned around. The one Flippo learned on was called Banana Peels. "They were real long and had no runner on 'em, and you learned how to turn around and go backwards with 'em as you learned how to turn all the way around when you're skiing. And then, later on, John bought some regular trick skis, which was a later version of Banana Peels only they were wider and a lot easier to turn around on, and John could do everythang you did with the Banana Peels. So, you could do all kinds of tricks that you could thank of. You could turn around and go backwards or you could turn completely around and do all kinds of tricks." Flippo never did do many tricks, "but John got to where he could do pretty good—all the trickies, and the Air Chair, what he skied on the other day when I was out thar with 'em [in 2018]."

Flippo's favorite subject for waterskiing was his son, John. He taught John how to ski behind a fishing boat with a five and a half horsepower motor to it. And he was a little guy, maybe four or five years old. Flip finalized it was five. He would get John in one of the fishing wells and pull him around and tell him, "Now keep those feet up." So once he got behind this fishing boat, they took off and he got up, and he didn't weigh that much. The rope was sagging into the water, but he was holding on as he kept going. It looked funny to Flip, but that's where he learned to ski first on two skis.

And, of course, they continued to experiment, "and every time I learned somethang, he was, 'I want to do that.' You know, and so, he became quite a skier. I wanted him to go to the ski show, but he said, 'Dad, they would ruin all my days. They're over thar practicing all day long. I don't want to do that.' So, he never did. He's good enough to ski in the ski show, but he never did. He surpassed me. I got to where I'd learn somethang, then he'd go on all the slalom, which is just one ski. Well, I could ski on it, so he wanted, 'I want to learn how to on one [ski].' So, we learned how on one, then he'd get better than me on one, you know, so I'd have to find somethang else. So, I thought, 'I'll teach that sucker. I'll go barefooted.' Well, I got up barefooted finally without slapping my face too many times. It was a while before he learned, before he started trying to go barefooted. He got to where he could turn around backwards and everythang."

Top: Flippo & Rooster Tail. Bottom: Flippo waterskiing in 1970s. Source: John Flippo

Arnie Kronenberger & Waterskiing

Flippo continued with a throaty laugh, "Ahhhh, yeah a lot of funny thangs happened. Kronenberger gained a lot of weight one year, and he liked to ski, so we bought this damn ole Howitzer-type of rope to get him up 'cause he kept breaking the ropes. And so, we got a great big ole rope for him, and I remember going around a corner out by the main channel. And he's going way out thar, and you knew damn well he's fixin' to fall. When he fell, he looked like a big ole whale, you know, and he hit that damn water, splashed everywhere, but he hit the water about three or four times." Flip sang the word "times" like he did so often.

"He just skipped along like a rock, a big rock! And then a big splash."

After that incident, they nicknamed him, "Arnie Kronenberger, Puff's Magic Dragon." About eight of Arnie's friends bought coveralls and put on the back of it, "Puff's Magic Dragons."

Flippo ended, "Thar's a whole square of 'em that had those thangs on."

Joe Hollandsworth & Waterskiing

Flippo remembered one time that Joe was teaching a woman with a bikini on. "This little gal wanted to learn how to ski, so Joe's teaching her, and she goes right up. But when she did, her bikini came down below her ass, so he drives toward the main channel, and he makes a circle up thar, and he comes back by the boat dock and turns around, goes back out of the main channel. Well, her whole ass was showing all the way around, and she was too afraid of trying to pull 'em up or anythang, and so she went around Kirkwood."

When she returned, she was asked if she knew her pants were down.

Joe & Marie Hollandsworth.
Source: Connie
Hollandsworth-Stacy

"Yeah, but I was too scared to reach down thar and try to pull 'em up. I can't even ski. I had both hands on the handle. They were going to stay thar."

Another skiing incident happened. Joe and Flippo would ski and they both got hurt. Flip forgot his injury, but Joe hurt his foot.

Bill Hagadorn commanded, "Boys, no more skiing 'til you git Coast Guard licenses." Flippo explained, "You needed Coast Guard licenses to drive the boat and to pull anybody skiing on the lake thar."

They found out they could get the license in St. Louis and Bill offered the use of his car. So, Joe and Flippo used his Cadillac to go to St. Louis to get their Coast Guard licenses.

Flippo described Joe as a big man, "Probably 6'6", 250, somewhere in thar. When he leaned on a slalom ski, he could throw up a wall of water you would not believe it, just beautiful to watch."

When asked if Bill Hagadorn skied, Flippo said he could probably ski, but he didn't know. Betty skied, a beautiful skier, but all the time Flip was there with Bill, he never saw him ski, and Bill never did even talk to Flip about skiing, other than, "You guys are not skiing anymore 'til you get your Coast Guard licenses."

A lot of funny things happened waterskiing. They rode the inner tubes, too. The inner tube was a lot of fun. It had no runner on it, "just a big ole inner tube," and they'd go around that corner so fast, "it's unbelievable." They could go faster than the boat, and "it's a lot of fun on that damn inner tube." When they'd get two or three kids on the inner tube at the same time, they'd hit a big bump, and it'd throw them up in the air.

Flippo ended that he got burned out after many, many years. "I didn't care whether I went or not, and so, I guess, oh, when you're really interested in it, you want to go, you know, and you go, 'My turn next?'

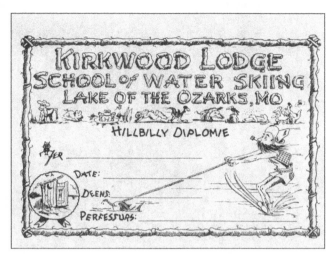

Source: John Flippo

Flippo waterskiing in the rain in the late 50s. Source: John Flippo

The Hagadorn Era at Kirkwood Ended

Flippo and Neeca and Pat and Joyce Munn bought Kirkwood in 1973 from Bill Hagadorn. One day after they bought Kirkwood, Pat called Flippo, and as they were talking, out the blue, Pat told him that he canceled the ad on the back of the National Square Dance Convention program because it cost too much.

Shocked, Flippo exclaimed, "God, Pat, that's really good advertisement. No telling how many square dancers that brought in."

Pat didn't realize the value of that ad then, but about six or seven years later before they sold Kirkwood, he admitted, "I done the wrong thang. I should never have canceled that."

Pat tried to get it back, but there was no getting it back. The line was like a hundred people.

Flippo ended with, "Been a good ad, you know. It was just a perfect ad."

1991 Kirkwood Lodge at in the National Square Dance Convention program book. Source: Neeca Flippo

They owned Kirkwood for twenty years. Pat and Joyce, his wife, were square dancers, and he was a contractor. Trouble arose for this partnership.

"Now when I heard about suing somebody, I thought, when I was a young kid, 'Well, I'll never do that. That's stupid!'"

Flippo continued with a chuckle, "Neeca, bless her heart! She found the goods on Pat. He was screwing around down at Kirkwood, and she had him by the short hair. She hired a lawyer in Abilene, Mr. Glen Heatherly, and we sued ole Pat and Joyce. Good friends and still good friends after we sued him."

When we talked about it, Flip didn't want to get into the specifics—his loyalty to his friend and partner continued all these years. Flippo and Neeca trusted Pat as a business partner, but he cheated the Flippos out of a large amount of money. How they stayed friends after this is beyond me, but that's Flippo!

They settled out of court, and Flippo got a new automobile and a four hundred dollar a week raise. He was getting eight hundred dollars, and Pat raised him up to twelve, and Neeca got $25,000 from the settlement which showed the kind of money that had been taken from the Flippos.

So, then she caught him again, and the same thang happened, but "it wasn't that bad of a deal."

After the suit Flippo described Pat "was the same. He never was down on us or anythang."

The Wall Street Journal published an article about Pat. "He's written up in that sucker, and it wasn't too good. Well, I 'member they called him a shyster and everythang. When we were suing, he never would show up in court, you know when we'd be thar. The first time we were all scared and everythang about showing up. We never had sued anybody or been around a court or anythang."

Remembering back to the suit, Flippo's lawyer came from Abilene to Kirkwood, and they went over to Camdenton, fourteen miles south of Kirkwood. The Flippos had done this before, but before they didn't meet with the judge. This time they were supposed to meet with the judge. "It had some kind of big word that we thought, 'Oh, this is getting serious now!' Well, hell, Pat didn't even show up! And I guess he'd been sued so many times, he knew he didn't have to. Heatherly presented our case to the judge, and the judge says, 'Hey, somebody's got to stop this son of a bitch.' But it was settled out of court, but anyway, he [Pat] was a big wheeler that didn't have the know-how to be a big wheeler."

Flippo corrected himself with a laugh, "Now I said that wrong. He's a big wheeler that knew how to be a big wheeler except he got caught!"

It's hard to believe that they ended up good friends after all of that. "And we'd sued him twice. I don't know whether I could have been that way or not. Somebody sued me twice, I don't know whether I'd like him or not! But his demeanor with me was the very same as it was before we sued him. But he's a good friend, and I thank we ended up just as good as friends as ever."

Later Years

As we talked about Kirkwood, Flippo lit up each time memories surfaced. He had so many stories and an amazing capacity to recall them. One story sparked another with no problem whatsoever. His mind was as sharp at ninety-one as it was the first time we met twenty-five years ago.

As he thought about Kirkwood, he reminisced about the changes it underwent. In my heart, I lamented because I had danced in the '70s during its heyday and returned twenty years later to see much smaller crowds.

In the later years, Kirkwood changed some. They had to start putting out *brochures* to promote Kirkwood. "And oh, hell, the first twelve or fourteen years I was thar, we didn't put out a *square dance brochure*.[4] We didn't have to. Lot of repeaters—lots and lots of repeaters, and then it started kinda changing, dropping off."

Flippo Sweeping the floor.
Source: Neeca Flippo

The high school seniors started changing and didn't want to square dance. "You just pulled your teeth trying to get 'em up for the first time. You thank, 'Well, maybe they'll try it once and then.' And some of 'em did still like it. They'd come back but the big majority of 'em said, 'I don't want to do that stuff.' I don't know—it just seemed like it wasn't as much fun as it was at one time, and maybe it was me."

With a chuckle, Flip recalled, "I's getting older. And they very seldom wanted to come back and dance the next morning, you know, and that all ended."

Flippo recalled why Neeca and he saved more money because they didn't have to buy groceries because they ate at Kirkwood Lodge. They didn't pay rent or utility bills.

He commented, "It was gravy."

"Well, you know, I don't know whether I've told you everythang about Kirkwood or not. Someday we'll get to talking, and we'll just have a session on Kirkwood, and we'll go over it, if you want to, and we'll go over the whole shebang. Kirkwood meant a lot to me, and of course, Blue Star did, too."

Neeca and Flippo. Source: Neeca Flippo

Neeca and Flippo dancing. Source: Neeca Flippo

Neeca and Flippo. Source: John Flippo

KIRKWOOD STAFF - Top: Flippo, Sue & Gary Shoemake, Wanda and John Winter
Bottom: Standing L to R: Flippo & Neeca, Bettye & Charlie Procter. Sitting L to R:
Ken & Dee Bower. Source: Neeca Flippo

KIRKWOOD STAFF - 1st L to R: Lovella & Max Forsyth, Flippo, Jack & Darlene
Chaffee. 2nd L to R: Frank Lane & Flippo, Gary Shoemake, John Winter & Flippo.
Source: Neeca Flippo

KIRKWOOD STAFF - Top: 1st R to L: Ken & Dee Bower, Flippo, Margie Sheffield, Barbara and Jerry Pierce, Elmer Sheffield. Kneeling: Matt Asanuma. Bottom 1st row L to R: Frank Lane, Flippo, Manning Smith. 2nd row L to R: Barbara Frank, Neeca Flippo, Nita Smith. Source: Neeca Flippo

Dick Jones, Flippo & John Hendron. Source: Neeca Flippo

Guy Davis, Flippo & Bob Fisk. Source: Neeca Flippo

Lee Kopman, Flippo & Dave Hodson. Source: Neeca Flippo

1962 Sets in Order Ad for Kirkwood Lodge. Source: Neeca Flippo

Festivals During Kirkwood Months

Even though Flip had a rigorous schedule during his six months at Kirkwood, he still squeezed in other festivals.

. . .

Lubbock Conclave

When Flippo saw an article about him doing the Lubbock Conclave, April, 1971, he commented with a laugh. "You know a funny thang—I called that Conclave quite a few times, and they'd always have another caller with me."

One time, they had a caller, and "I'm not going to say his name. I love him like a brother, but he came from one of those east coast states, and they flew in thar. So, Saturday morning, I told him he had a workshop."

He didn't know any better, so he started the workshop. There was "this ole boy in the front square."

The caller turned the music down and instructed, "Sir, now when I'm teaching you this movement, at that point right there, you go left. Don't you go right. You went right. You should have went left."

So, Flippo was seated behind the curtain and couldn't see who the caller was talking to.

He turned down the music again and repeated, "Sir, you did that again." They were at the old gym at Texas Tech University, and it could hold a lot of people, but it had very good acoustics.

The man continued, "Sir, I told you last time at this point right here you've got to go right. You went left again. At that point, you're gonna go right and so." Flippo was getting a little anxious, thinking, 'Who the hell is he talking to?'

So, after a while he turned the music down again, "Sir, that's the third time you did it."

Third time everybody got quiet.

And he scolded, "I said now you went left and you're supposed to go right there. Are you stupid?"

And then this voice comes out and said, "I must be. I come out to dance with you!" And people just roared. You could hear that all over that damn gym. So, Flippo looked around through the curtain to see who it was, and he thought, "Oh my God!" and then, he thought, "Oh shit!" He could have said that to anybody but who he said it to. He gets through and he comes back.

He said, "Hey, Flippo, who's that son of a bitch right over there?"

"He's the chairman of this convention."

He exclaimed, "NO!"

Flippo continued, "Yeah, he is."

"Oh my God," he concluded. He never did recover from it the whole weekend. Then Flippo repeated the distraught dancer's comeback with a final laugh, "I must be stupid. I come out to dance with you!"

National Square Dance Convention – Last Week of June

Flippo called at numerous National Square Dance Conventions. As he looked at a picture of the 1991 convention Kirkwood Lodge ad, after a moment of silence, all Flip could say was, "Gollllllly!"

His business side came out as he remembered they used to have an ad for Kirkwood on the back page of the National Convention program book. This was the ad Pat Man cancelled. Flippo repeated, "Yeah, yeah. Let me see, how many of them died? He's alive, he's alive, he's alive."

As he scanned the ad, Flippo repeated, "He's alive" several times. Then he repeated, "He's dead." Flip kept in contact with his caller and cuer friends to know if they were still alive or not—commitment to friendship, for sure. He continued the recitation of these two phrases as he named the callers down the page.

English Mountain Resort

In researching Flippo's affiliation with English Mountain Resort, he worked there from 1989 to 1996 and 1999 two separate events, a weekend in May or June and a five-day event in July. One event he called with all the Chaparral callers and one with Jerry Haag and Gary Shoemake.

English Mountain was Shoemake's place up in Tennessee, right up above Gatlinburg. It's up a windy road all the way around. Flippo worked there with Gary Shoemake, Ken Bower, and Jerry Haag. Dan and Linda Prosser came to English Mountain when he did a weekend, and Linda did the rounds for them. He remembered doing it most every year for a while. It's burned down now.

English Mountain had two square dance halls, a small one that would hold about five squares, and then the other one would hold twenty squares.

English Mountain Ad. Source: *American Square Dance*, June 1988

Dollywood Square Dance Festivals

Flip did the Dollywood Square Dance Festival August 28 to 30, 1987. He worked a dance at Dolly Parton's place, and they danced out on the parking lot. To him, it seemed like she showed up and walked around.

Three hundred and sixty-eight plus squares attended the first Dollywood Square Dance Festival in Sevierville, Tennessee.

This memory brought up a hilarious story for Flip because I know Gary Shoemake and Ken Bower and the amazing trickster relationship these three callers had over the years. A funny thing happened one time when they went to that "Dolly Parton thang."

In the early afternoon, Gary Shoemake and Flippo went to eat at a popular restaurant. Lots of people always mistook Gary for, "what's-his-face, Conway Twitty." They went into the restaurant, and Flippo was sitting across from Gary.

Thinking Gary was a star, the waitress looked at him and said, "My sister's your biggest fan."

Then Gary protested, "No, no, no. I'm not who you think I am."

"Oh, yes, you are."

Ornery Flippo added to conversation, "Yeah, he is, too!"

So, she went searching for a piece of paper and a pencil and returned. When she came back, she sat down next to Gary, and again requested an autograph for her sister.

Gary wondered who she thought he was, so he asked, "Who do you think I am?"

Knowingly she nodded at him like she knew the answer, "I know who you are."

Either Gary or Flip asked her if she thought he was Conway Twitty.

Indignant, she stood up with her hands on her hips and exclaimed, "I know you're not Conway. You're Mickey Gilley."

Again, Flip agreed, "That's right. You got it right."

So, he said, "I'm a sound Mickey Goodman, but I am really not Mickey Gilley."

She continued, "Oh, yeah, you are."

Flippo reassured, "Yeah, he is, too. He just does this everywhere he goes."

To end the debate, Gary signed it "Mickey Gilley," and she just went off, so as they walked out, she ran up to them, and asked Flippo, "That's Mickey Gilley, isn't it?"

He answered, "Sure is, you know!"

So they get back to the motel, and Ken and Dee Bower and four other people were headed to eat supper.

Flippo asked the group where they planned to go, and they named that same restaurant.

"Oh," Flippo instructed, "if you get a waitress named Rachel, say somethang about Mickey Gilley."

Dollywood Square Dance Festival from August 28 - 30, 1987 ad. Source: *American Square Dance*, June 1987

So Ken said he would. So that night at the dance, Flippo hadn't heard anything from Ken, but Flip got up on stage. Ken was already up there getting ready to start.

Flippo asked Ken, "Did ya'll go over to that restaurant?"

"Yeah."

"Did you have that waitress named Rachel?"

"We sure did. She thought I was that Charlie Rich, that white-headed guy who played the piano. She thought I was him."

Flippo asked Ken, "What did you tell her?"

"She wouldn't take no for an answer. I had to sign 'Charlie Rich.'"

"Did you say anythang about Mickey Gilley?"

"Yeah, I told her I'm not Charlie Rich, but I did play in a Mickey Gilley band."

She stated, "Hey, he was just in here."

Flippo's responded to this memory, "God, we had more fun!"

Oklahoma City Twirlers

The October 1988 *American Square Dance* magazine stated, "In Twirlers' 30 seasons, 75 callers from 28 states have pleased some 400 member couples and a large number of guests. Marshall Flippo and Frank Lane shared the record by having called for the club in each of 27 successive seasons."[5]

Flippo shared his deep love for everything connected with Kirkwood! He enjoyed the life he lived there, all the traveling to various festivals, and all the fun he had.

---

1. **After Parties** — The party after the square dance with skits and a variety of entertainment usually put on by the event staff of callers and cuers. Sometimes dancers participated in skits, too.
2. See the video of Flippo pantomiming to "I Just Don't Look Good Naked Anymore." Larada Horner-Miller, "YouTube," March 24, 2020, Flippo & "I Just Don't Look Good Naked Anymore," https://youtu.be/HTD_XHHFr5g
3. **Caller** — A person who prompts dance figures in such dances as line dance, square dance, and contra dance.
4. **Square Dance Brochure** — Advertisement for Kirkwood's schedule and calling and cuing staff.
5. Stan & Cathie Burdick, Best Club Trick, *American Square Dance* (October 1988): 33.

ANNUAL TOURS

Where Was Flippo Headed?

Source: Larada Horner-Miller

TOUR MAP

Flippo zigzagged across the United States from April to October in three tours.

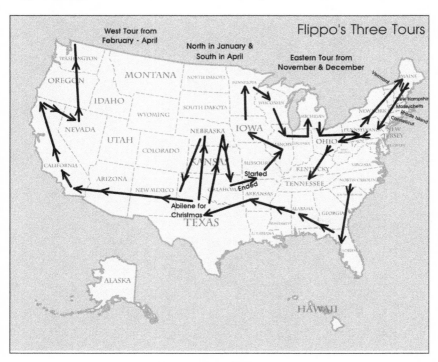

Source: Larada Horner-Miller

12

TOURS

Life on the Road

"... And lastly to Marshall Flippo for being so special and, unfortunately, so loved by everyone you can't get a date on his calendar."[1]

Flippo traveled a hectic pattern for his yearly tour: after six months at Kirkwood, he spent another six on the road fulfilling his regular engagements and then adding any festivals he could. When we talked about the tour, he thought geographically, rattling off directions and towns easily.

In the fall, he headed north, east toward New England, then south and west, home to Abilene for the holidays. He added a short trip north through the Midwest then back to Abilene, and then he headed to the west coast. Flip went north up the coast, east, and south, back to Kirkwood by April to start his season there again.

He never did describe what this gypsy life was like to him—sleeping in a different motel or host's house every night, eating repetitive restaurant food, driving millions of miles behind the steering wheel alone in the car, but because he never bemoaned it, it was obvious he loved it!

"I did the tour for forty-two years," Flippo shared. These tours grew out of his fan base at Kirkwood. Again, he attributed his success to being "lucky—to be in the right place, you know, somebody wanted me, and that really helped."

Repeated weekend events, annual club visitations, and special events became the backbone of his tour. Some of these events followed the tour as identified, but Flippo had to fly to some too far to drive.

He called it one tour, but actually it was several carefully stitched together by his tour director, Neeca. Flippo shared, "What happened was Neeca helped me a lot because guys would come to me [at Kirkwood Lodge] like from West Point, Iowa and Minneapolis, Minnesota and they'd say, 'Hey, can you call for us?'"

And he would say, "Well, I'd sure like to." And he added, "So, she'd fixed a little tour where I'd went up all over Iowa, Minnesota, and then I'd go over to Wisconsin. And she had a nice little tour going over to Illinois and all the way out to New England." Flippo had quite a few dances in Michigan.

Neeca remembered, "We had received several booking dates, mostly from guests at the Lodge. Some were several miles apart. We were made welcome in many homes; many of these people became dear friends. Word of mouth spread quickly and we kept getting more dates. We never in all my years found the need to write and ask for a booking. We soon received more request than we had dates open. It was difficult to write people back and tell them he could not make; we had to turn down more than we accepted. It took some time to accept dates that would make it easier to travel. In order to accept some dates, he would only go to that area every other year. Flip was always quick to refuse full pay when the crowd was small because of the weather or some other reason. He called many dances for no pay at all. He truly is a special one of a kind person. His scrap book is filled with thank you notes. He is loved by so many; there will probably never be another one quite like him. I am thankful for the good memories of our life together."

Flippo complimented Neeca on how she put this tour together. "Boy, I thought, I was hitting them every night and not having to travel too far. Every once in a while, I'd hit a four hundred mile, but she had it fixed up really good. I worked myself all the way back down through Tennessee, and Alabama, then over to Arkansas, back into Texas. And so, this went on for years and years, and I'd get new bookings, and I'd lose some. Anyway, she was very good at setting up that tour."

That initial tour grew to cover more and more of the USA. Flippo's tour covered these states:

- **NORTH** – Illinois, Iowa, Minnesota
- **EAST** – Wisconsin, Illinois, Indiana, Michigan, Maine, Vermont, New Hampshire, Massachusetts, Rhode Island, Connecticut, New Jersey, New York, District of Columbus, Delaware, Pennsylvania, Ohio
- **SOUTH** – Kentucky, Tennessee, North Carolina, Alabama, Arkansas, Texas, Florida, Georgia,
- **ABILENE FOR CHRISTMAS**
- **NORTH** – Oklahoma, Kansas, Nebraska
- **WEST** – New Mexico, Arizona, California
- **NORTH** – Nevada, Washington
- **SOUTH** – Oklahoma, Kansas, Nebraska again and back to Kirkwood lodge for the six-month season

Hearing about all of Flippo's constant traveling astounded me. I couldn't imagine all the wear and tear on Flippo's cars.

When I said as much to Flippo, he replied, "I'd get a new car every two years, and what was pretty good about the touring at that time when I first started, you'd get a motel for $6, or $8 or a night. So, it was pretty cheap."

Besides his yearly tour, Flip also called at weekend festivals in Colorado, Louisiana, Maryland, Mississippi, South Carolina, Virginia, and West Virginia for a total of forty-two states, but I possibly missed some!

During the 1960s, square dancing boomed. Here are four festivals worth noting from 1963: Flippo called at the Seventh Kross Roads Square-Rama in Fresno, California with two thousand dancers in attendance. He called the Eighth Annual Mississippi State Square Dance Festival in Jackson, Mississippi with seven hundred dancers. Two thousand dancers attended the Seventh Annual Iowa Square Dance Fall Festival in Des Moines, Iowa with Flip calling. Detroit, Michigan hosted the Michigan State Square Dance Convention with six thousand dancers and Flip calling.

As Flip looked at articles about these events, he observed solemnly, "People on thar that have gone bye-bye."

In an interview with Arnie Kronenberger in the April 1967 issue of *Sets in Order,* his response when asked who are those most sought-out traveling callers was "Frank Lane and Marshall Flippo."[2]

> J A N U A R Y   20,   1974
>
> ANNUAL C.K.S.D.A. SPRING MEETING/ELECTION
>
> I.O.O.F. REC. HALL 411 EAST WALNUT, SALINA
>
> P_R_O_G_R_A_M
>
> MEETING STARTS AT 1:00 P.M.
>
> POT LUCK SUPPER FOLLOWING MEETING
>
> SQUARE DANCE WITH MARSHALL FLIPPO
>
> FROM 5:00 TO 8:00 P.M.
>
> DANCE ADMISSION -- $3.09 COUPLE
>
> REMEMBER ? MUST SHOW YOUR C.K.S.D.A. MEM-
> BERSHIP CARD TO VOTE.

Source: Neeca Flippo

"SPRING FLING"

WEEK END

MARCH 15, 16, 17, 1974   BLOOMINGTON, IND.

FOR FURTHER INFORMATION WRITE:

FRANK & BARBARA LANE, P. O. Box 1382
ESTES PARK, COL.
80517

FRANK LANE
AND

MARSHALL FLIPPO

Source: Neeca Flippo

FRANK LANE'S
AND
MARSHALL FLIPPO'S

2ND ANNUAL

S_I_O_U_X_L_A_N_D   S_Q_U_A_R_E U_P

MARCH 22, 23, AND 24, 1974

SOUTH SIOUX CITY, NEBRASKA

A TRULY GREAT WEEK END OF FUN ....

FOR INFORMATION WRITE ....

FRANK AND BARBARA LANE
P. O. Box 1382
ESTES PARK, COLORADO
80517

Source: Neeca Flippo

1. Wendy Cuss, Sandy, Utah (Letter to the Editor), *Sets in Order* (November 1978): 61.
2. Bob Osgood, *Sets in Order,* (April 1967): 29.

13

NORTH AND THEN EAST, SOUTH, & HOME FOR CHRISTMAS

Chula Vista Resort, Wisconsin Dells, Wiscon. Source: https://www.chulavistaresort.com/

I n mid-October, Flippo headed north from Kirkwood, and two weekends at Chula Vista Resort in Wisconsin Dells, Wisconsin[1] stood as the highlight for him of the northern section of his tour.

When Flippo left Kirkwood Lodge on tour, he did "two or three little dances, then I'd get to Chula. I say little dances." On his way, he worked through Illinois,

Iowa, Minnesota, and over into Wisconsin. He worked Chula for years, two times a year by himself. They had a lot of dancers then, many from Chicago and Minneapolis.

How Flippo Started at Chula Vista

Vintage photo of Chula Vista Resorts, Wisconsin Dells, Wisconsin.
Source: Chula Vista Resort, Wisconsin Dells, Wisconsin. Source:
https://www.chulavistaresort.com/

Joe Kaminski, the owner, called Flip and asked, "You're a square dance *caller*[2]?"
"Well now, I don't know."
"We'd like for you to come up here and call. We'll do the advertising and everything."
Flip described his first year, "Now this was ole man Kaminski. I mean, ole Joe. Way back thar. And so, I went up thar, and they had a little ole dime-size dance floor, hold about three squares stretching it, but the rug was on the outside of it. So we danced maybe three or four squares for a couple weeks, then it hit and we danced about seven squares with four to five being on the rugs. Now our entertainment after each *tip*[3] was Vera Kaminski, Joe's wife. She'd play the piano, and she could play the piano. Anyway, she'd play two or three tunes, and we'd get up and square dance again."
Joe's routine each night was to look in at the end of the dance and announce he was going to bed.
Vera answered, "Well, glad to have you around."
After Flippo's success the first year, Joe vowed when Flip returned the next year, they would have a hall that you can dance in. Flip added, "And sure enough, they did." It would hold about fifteen to sixteen squares. It had a little balcony that

would hold three more. And ads in the *Sets in Order* magazine identified on October 29–31, 1963—SOLD OUT!

Flippo worked one weekend at Chula, then he toured around Indiana and Illinois and then returned to do another weekend there.

After awhile, the format at Chula changed, and they added two other callers, "Gary Shoemake and—what that's grey-haired guy's name, Ken Bower. So, we worked that way for a long time before square dancing started falling off, but it's a nice place."

"They had an ole wooden building, so I stayed in one you could hear anythang that somebody else in the next room was doing. You could hear it, but then they had gone really first class. And so, the others are uptown, uptown, uptown."

Flippo added, "But Chula meant a lot to me."

His popularity there continued. By April 1969, the ad in *Sets in Order* identified Flippo's weekend "SOLD OUT!" for October 24–26—six months out! October 23–25, 1970—SOLD OUT!

Today they are still in operation, and the facility has grown.

1977 Ad for Chula Vista Resorts 18 Great Weekends. Source: *Sets in Order*, January 1977

"I bet you I've been thar over one hundred times. Joe and Vera Kaminski are the ones who hired me. They're both died now. Then Fred took over when Joe died, and now he's been retired long time. Mike is the one now, so thar's three generations since I've been going thar."

From then on, Flippo was touring and heading east, going to Chicago, Illinois and Gary, Indiana. From there, he went into Michigan, alternating one year he had about six or seven cities and the next year he would just do maybe one or two dances and then go on east because Flip was going to New England. He went to New England every other year.

❧

Because Flip got paid in either check or cash on his tour, he devised unique ways to hide his money. Often the dances paid him in cash since they would pay him out of the money they collected at the door. He never mailed the money home to Neeca, so he would carry it all with him until he got home.

Flippo did a Sunday morning at Chula Vista Resort then hurried like heck to get over to Rockford, Illinois and had a dance Sunday afternoon at two o'clock. Then Flip had the next night off, but he always drove a little ways because he was going down into Indiana for Monday. So he usually drove to Chicago and stayed in "this motel in Chicago—nice hotel, nice motel. And I had stayed thar before.

"This time I had a lot of cash on me, and I was so tired when I got in thar. We went out to eat after the dance in Rockford—a bunch of us, then I drove on over to Chicago, and so I was quite tired when I pulled into the motel. With my clothes on, I just laid across the bed and went to sleep. I slept about three hours. I woke up. It was 11:30 at night, and I was hungry."

So Flippo thought, "Well, I'll go out and get a hamburger somewhere," but he had all this cash.

He thought, "I don't want to go out this late at night with all this cash." So, Flippo took the toilet paper off the spindle, wrapped all this cash money around it. Put the toilet paper back on, went out, and got himself a hamburger. The next day, he was going to Kokomo, Indiana, and got there about 4:00 p.m.

Flip decided to eat dinner, and he opened his billfold and there was no money.

He thought, "Oh, I left that money on that spindle." So Flippo called that motel. As we talked, he worried about not knowing the name of the motel and promised to find it somehow but never did.

He told the clerk, "I was in the room—I don't know what the number was now. I left some money on the spindle on the toilet paper in that room. Forgot it. Left it and I'm over in Kokomo, and I left that money in thar."

And the desk clerk asked, "You know, how big was the roll of toilet paper?"

"Ah, about a quarter of it had been used."

He stated, "Well, that's pretty good. When it gets down pretty low, they usually take it off and put a new roll on thar."

So Flippo thought, "Oh."

The clerk commented, "I'll go over and check. Give me about two minutes."

"Well, after a while, he came back."

"I got sixty-five twenty dollar bills here." That was $1300! Today that would be over $11,000![4]

"Glory me. Take one of those twenties for yourself and send the rest to that address. You got my address when I checked in." Can you imagine sending that amount of cash in the mail today!

He stated, "I'll do that," and Flippo added with a flair, "He did."

That's unbelievable!

Flippo repeated, "It's amazing! It's not the end of the story. The next year, same motel, same situation—God, I didn't thank I'd ever forget the name of that motel. Same motel. Same type of situation—tired, laid out across the bed, went to sleep, woke up hungry."

He thought, "I ain't going to put that toilet paper around that dang gum money, so I put it under the floor mat of the car. I'll be in that car. I'll know where my money is."

Next day, while Flip was driving toward Kokomo, before he got out of Chicago, he saw a car wash.

Flippo went on, "Oh, thar's a car wash, pulled in thar. It was a full service. Pulled up to the vacuum, and the ole boy stopped me thar."

The attendant directed him to go through that tunnel, go down to the cashier, and pay out.

"Okay." Flippo added, "It's a young black guy. So, I'm walking down that tunnel, and I hear the door open behind me."

And that guy stated, "Hey, sir. This money almost went down the vacuum."

"He had it in his hand, so I give him five dollars."

Flippo told him, "Oh, thank you very much. I forgot it. I 'member putting it under thar last night."

Flippo concluded these stories, "They talk about, you know, the crime in Chicago and everythang. Thar was two incidents that the guys could have said, 'No, haven't seen no money,' and anyway, end of the story."

And he added as he finished, "I need to go smoke."

Then East

Flippo had two major places in the East he loved to visit: Bay Path Barn in Boylston, Massachusetts and Ranchland in Mechanicsburg, Pennsylvania.

New England

The connection this Texas *caller* had with New England is amazing. He would go to New England every other year calling in Maine, Vermont, New Hampshire, Massachusetts, Rhode Island, and Connecticut.

According to Jim Mayo, a renowned square dance historian,

> During the 1950s many of the traveling callers who came through New England from California were associated in some way with Bob Osgood and the *Sets in Order* magazine.
>
> Callers who were not, particularly, associated with *Sets in Order* also traveled the country regularly. Among those who visited New England were Marshall Flippo from Texas . . . [5]

Flippo worked about a week and a half or two weeks in New England. The first time he went to New England, Neeca was with him, and they flew into Connecticut.

Earl and Marian Johnston had written him a letter, so Flippo called with him. They had eighty-eight squares.

So that was Flippo's first joint to New England. He got some good bookings out of that, but he remembered "those little books you sign." They're called Century Club Books and are small books that dancers had callers sign. Once you had the autographs of one hundred different callers, you were eligible to order a special Century Club badge.

"This ole boy from Massachusetts was the one who started those damn books."

Because Earl lived in the area, he'd already signed all of the dancers' books, but when Flippo went out in the hall after he called his first *tip,* he signed books all the

Earl Johnston. Source: http://www.
sdfne.org/

way through the rounds and all the way through Earl's calling which was his break. This repeated during his next break after his *tip,* and Flippo ended up signing books all evening.

Then Chet and Barbara Smith were the next ones that hired Flippo, and then he got a few more dates out of that.

Chet and Barbara Smith owned Bay Path Barn in Boylston, Massachusetts, a little city, and they were out in the country. They had a big barn with a beautiful floor, and it would hold anywhere from twenty to twenty-five squares. Chet was a caller, and Barbara was a *cuer.*[6]

Flip was intrigued with Barbara because she was totally deaf. It was unbelievable how she could play a piano so beautifully. He couldn't understand how she cued. "Somebody said it's the vibration or somethang, but she was a very good cuer —anyway, just a sweet, sweet woman. I'm sure she's passed away by now, they were older than Neeca and I."

Flippo remembered they stayed with them in their farmhouse, "and she could cook—whoa-wow! She was a good cook and probably the best seafood I ever ate was at their house at that time. Every time I go to Red Lobster, I thank, 'Maybe I'll get somethang that's like Barbara,' but I haven't found anythang yet."

During this visit, they were sitting around one day and Chet was giving Flippo some material to call, "and by the way, I was still using some of that stuff. I still remember those, but it was good and so he had a big ole cabinet thar. You know."

Chet stated, "Now I've got 'the patent' on this," and Flippo added, "He really had a New England accent, I mean really, and he kept a-saying it."

Later Neeca peppered Flip with questions, "Do you mean to tell me that what he showed, all those thangs he said he had the patent on. Did he have the patent on them? Did you hear patent on it?"

With a laugh, Flippo replied, "Neeca, no, he said, 'pattern.'" He added, "So anyway, just a beautiful, beautiful couple. They were just so, so nice, and he booked people into Bay Path for other callers, and he really had a nice thang going thar for him."

Flippo did two nights—Friday and Saturday—at the Bay Path Barn, which, by the way, is still operating. Tom and Mary Rinker bought it from Barbara after Chet died. [From Ken Ritucci in May, 2019: "Tom calls there once a week and Mary uses it for line dancing, but there are no dances there anymore."] After Bay Path, Flippo would work Connecticut and Massachusetts. "People were so nice, they were just unbelievably nice, and so I enjoyed it up thar."

Zigzag South of New England

From there, Flippo went to Atlantic City, New Jersey with Al Brundage and worked the Thanksgiving weekend that started on Thursday [Thanksgiving] and went to noon Sunday, so it was long, long weekend. Flip worked that with Al for about twenty years, and then the casinos came in and tore down all of "our old hotels down. All of them had beautiful ballrooms."

PUT A TIGER IN YOUR TANKSGIVING AT THE FABULOUS

AL BRUNDAGE
MARSHALL FLIPPO
JACK JACKSON
JULES & BILLARD
DOTTIE

HOTEL/MOTEL

Dennis
ATLANTIC CITY, N. J.

NOVEMBER
24 · 25 · 26 · 27
1966

WRITE TO: AL BRUNDAGE   83 Michael Rd. — Stamford, Conn. 06903

Thanksgiving Weekend Dance Ad in Sets in Order magazine with Al Brundage 1966.
Source: *Sets in Order*, September 1966

At this time, they didn't even have to put out a *flyer*.[7] The *cuers* were the Easter-days, Irv and Betty. "She's really good—one of those couples you never forget. I looked forward to it. It would hold about anywhere from thirty-five to forty squares, and we'd usually sell out every year."

Flippo remembered one time Al got "ole Dave Taylor" to come in. Dave was from Detroit, Michigan, and then he moved over around Chicago, Illinois but beautiful caller—a really good caller. He was recording on Winter Records.

So one time he looked at "ole Al" and said, 'Hey, Al. Have you heard my last recording?'"

Al replied, "I sure hope so." Flippo laughed at Al's comment.

"But we had so much fun thar, and then they tore all the ole hotels down."

Al vowed to find a place for next year, same time.

"So, I don't know—about a week or two later, I had a letter from Brundage."

It said, "I found a place. It's at West Point. So, it's at the Thayer Hotel. They got a ballroom that's a real long ballroom, and it danced about three apart and about ten down. And the sound's good."

The hotel was right on the grounds of West Point. In fact, if a parent went to visit their child, they'd put them at that hotel. They used it for a long time.

After the weekend with Al, Flippo headed down south into New Jersey. "It was down to me—I am sure that West Point was above New Jersey. I'd head south down into New Jersey, and I would call—it was about twenty minutes from New York City—in Caldwell, New Jersey, Sunday afternoon, 2:00–5:00 p.m. dance. Tom and Mary Rinker were avid square dancers thar, and they booked *callers* in, so they booked me in thar. They had a hell of a crowd each year. They'd get anywhere from forty-five to fifty-five squares."

From Caldwell, Flippo went to Trenton, New Jersey and spent a Sunday night with Whitey and Gladys Puerling. They put up a lot of callers that came through, so, they asked Flip to stay with them. He had met them earlier when they came to Kirkwood Lodge.

Monday Flippo went to Dover, Delaware for one dance, "but thar was always— kind of like Albuquerque—nice people."

Flippo used Whitey and Gladys's house in New Jersey for headquarters and went into Philadelphia and Pennsylvania, and back into Trenton to stay with them because it wasn't too far for calling a dance at night. "Whitey is gone now, but Gladys is still alive. I just talked to her about a month ago [December 18, 2017]."

It used to be people would record callers at the special dances to take home to listen to them and practice. One time, in New Jersey, sixty recorders lined the edge of the stage, and there were a lot of people at that time. One guy operated them all and started them all, but the *caller* could hardly walk on the stage because there were so many recorders.

Flippo had strong connections with New Jersey and Whitey and Gladys. With a laugh, Flippo added, "Thar's funny stories that goes on with them."

Marshall Flippo Fan Club

Looking through the albums/scrapbooks, I found the Marshall Flippo Fan Club.

Flippo laughed, "Yeah, what'd they charge a year—sixty-five cents or somethang? Yeah, Whitey and Gladys Puerling, old friends, started this thang. I thought they called it 'Fan Flub,' but it's 'Fan Club.' Gold Square Stamp Savings Book—interchangeable [exchangeable] when filled for one membership in the Trenton, New Jersey Chapter of the Marshall Flippo Fan Club."

"Only had one member."

As we looked down the page, I saw another one, Marshall Flippo Fan Club, Los Angeles, California Chapter. Joe Le Broce.

So in the summer of 2018, I created a Marshall Flippo Fan Club group on Facebook,[8] and it all stemmed from Whitey and Gladys' fan club Puerling. I post favorite pictures of Flippo, and pose questions I have about facts in this book. This group has been so supportive!

Source: Neeca Flippo

Buick Day

Flippo enjoyed life and Whitey; here's one of his favorite stories that involved his co-conspirator.

After calling down in Atlantic City, Flip stayed with Whitey and Gladys in Trenton. When the dance was over, Whitey and Gladys were with him, and they were going to drive back up to Trenton.

Another couple said, "Hey, hear you're calling in New York City tomorrow. Would you mind if we go along? I got a brand-new Buick I kind of want to test it out. We can take three couples up there."

Flip welcomed them, and they decided on the time to leave.

So, Whitey told them, "Well, I'll fall in behind you and just follow you up there." So, when they hit the Lincoln Tunnel, Whitey paid for the toll.

Whitey told the toll booth worker, "You see—about three cars back there. Can you see that new Buick? Toll master, can you see that Buick?"

"Yeah, I see it, a brand-new Buick."

"We're going to pay for it."

"Alright. That'll be okay."

"Just tell them it's Buick Day."

So they got to the dance, and Flip was taking the sound out and putting it up, and Whitey was helping. "Here that couple come in with those other two couples. Boy, that ole boy come up thar."

"Got a brand-new Buick. The first time I go through the tunnel, it was Buick Day. How sweet can it be?"

After the dance, Flippo and Whitey decided they'd stop at a little restaurant at the corner of the Garden State Parkway on the way back to Trenton. So, the Buick was ahead of them, and they're getting close to the Lincoln Tunnel.

And Whitey proclaimed, "God, I hope he stops."

"He was so happy—good day, you know, telling everybody, 'Buick Day. I got in thar free.' I don't know what the fine is now, but at the time, the fine for running that thang was $90. It's probably two hundred now, but anyway, he's up ahead of us."

Whitey exclaimed, "God, please stop this time."

Whitey and Flippo watched him. "He slowed down and waved, went right on through."

Whitey moaned, "Oh my God!"

Two miles down the road, the police had him pulled over.

Whitey asked, "Are you going to stop?"

"No, I ain't going to stop. I'm going to the restaurant." Flippo continued, "We get up to the restaurant. We're waiting for them to show up, just kind of talking thar at the car. Here they come. He whips in thar and whips into a parking place."

As soon as that door opened, he jumped out of the damn car and exclaimed, "Buick Day, my ass!"

"Oh my God! Did he give you a ticket?"

He answered, "No, he asked me why did you run that toll booth?"

He said to the policeman, "Well, ah, was it Buick Day? It was Buick Day going in."

The guy asked, "'Have you fallen for that old joke? Lord Have Mercy. Go ahead.' So, he didn't give me a ticket."

Flippo added, "Thank the Lord 'cause I knew I'd have to pay the ticket if he got one."

❧

This story continued. Thirty-some years later, Flippo was calling at Rincon West RV Resort in Tucson, Arizona, where he was [2017]. Way back in the back, he saw this couple come into a dance.

Flippo thought, "Who is that couple? I know them from somewhere. I kind of recognized her face."

He went back and introduced himself, and they said they were from the East Coast. They said they'd only danced to him a couple times when he was back there. So, the guy had a pretty good haircut.

Flip asked him where he got his haircut.

"It was cut real good around the ears and really nice and really neat, but he had a full head of hair. Of course, I was bald headed. I like the way the barber had went around his ears."

He shared, "Oh, down at that Mexican barbershop right out the gate down there on Mission."

"The Mexican barbershop? Well, I go over thar, but I never had that kind of haircut."

Flippo continued quizzing him, "What did you tell him?"

"Oh, I asked for number three."

Flip added, "Ask for a number three?"

"Yep, number three."

Flippo went down to the Mexican barbershop the next day and told the barber he wanted a number three, "and I seen hair flying all over my head. I mean, it was awful. The guy is shaving my damn head. Well, a number three is like this—and so I got back in the car, and I looked."

And Flippo thought, "God, he took all that hair off, and I had never had it cut that short." Two nights later, Flip had a dance again and the couple come in.

He went over, and Flippo stated, "Man, you'll look familiar, and the name is familiar, but I cannot really place you."

And Flip added, "Look at my hair. This is what they did."

He answered, "Yeah, that's a number three," and added, "Remember the Lincoln Tunnel?"

Flippo concluded, "He kept that grudge for a long, long time, but that was funny as hell. Yeah, he said, 'member the Lincoln Tunnel.'"

His Tour Continued

After Trenton, Flip went to Wilmington, Delaware and through Pennsylvania. He would go to Mechanicsburg, a suburb of Harrisburg. Tom Hoffman had a hall there in Mechanicsburg named Ranchland, and it held about fifteen squares. Flippo called there one night. Dan and Linda Prosser took over Ranchland after Tom Hoffman. She was a *cuer*,[9] and he was a *caller*, and they still call and cue.

Dan Prosser shared in an email, "Flip Called at Ranchland from the early 1960s through the early 1990s. He was there every Tuesday the week following Thanksgiving and packed the house."

From Mechanicsburg Flippo traveled to State College, and then he went down to Greensburg, Pennsylvania and stayed with a *caller* that booked him there, Vic Miller. He was about six feet eight inches tall and went around with the name 'Taller Caller' on his license plate [Help from Tom Miller].

"We were close. Vic and his wife, Doris, were just really nice."

From Pittsburgh, Pennsylvania, he'd go to Meadville, Pennsylvania when he called in Ohio. Flip went over into Cleveland and called at the Berea Fairgrounds for years. It held about thirty-forty squares and had a really good floor and sound.

While there, he stayed with "a beautiful couple that were florists, Gil and Marian Deverney. I thank they're both gone now. But I went in thar for years and years. I called two nights thar—one night in a school and one night out at the fairgrounds in this hall they had. They lived right out of Cleveland." Rob Schneider, a *caller* up in Cleveland, used it all the time. From Berea in Cleveland, Flippo went down to Columbus, Ohio and called for the Orbiting Squares for years.

Flip thought geographically and having just talked about Ohio, he had a Neeca story from that area, "I'll skip over here just a minute and tell you how good she was. I had a Califone player, and they had booked me in Pinkington, Illinois. That was another one of those quick trips—drive from Pinkington, Illinois, and then drive back to Abilene to go to work. It was colder than hell. Boy, I was cold. I put the needle on thar, and the damn needle broke. Oh, boy, thar was a bunch of guys coming up thar and some of them were callers."

Flippo exclaimed, "Oh, no! We don't have any extra needles." He added, "So that dad-gum Neeca come up thar."

She asked, "Will these needles work?"

"Where did you get that?"

"I put it in the car about two or three days ago."

Flip exclaimed, "Bless your heart, boy!" and added, "I stuck that needle on, and we took off."

South

With a cough and gaps of silence, Flippo continued to sketch out this tour he did so many years ago. The next night Flip went to Jackson, Ohio, then Clarksburg, West Virginia, and the next night he ventured to Ironton, Ohio. From there, Flip went on "down to that place I can't thank." From that city, he went on to Corbin, Kentucky, then Knoxville. Then Flip called Sunday afternoon in Chattanooga in the Allemande Hall that they built just for square dancing.

Georgia Story

When we were going through all the different *callers* that Flippo thought he would tell stories about, he asked me to specifically remind him about Georgia.

"Well, I have a story about a Macon, Georgia nudist camp."

I giggled, and he asked, "You want it now?"

Flippo had a letter from Macon wanting him to call down there. "This is hard to tell because you need to—I don't know if you can tell it or not. I suppose I can."

I encouraged him to continue.

So, Flip got down there and went to the address. It was way out in the country, the gate was locked, and the mailbox was right there. A couple had written Flip. Pretty soon, he looked up, and a girl in a really small bikini went over and unlocked the gate and opened it up. She came and sat in his car.

So she instructed him to drive through the gate, but she stopped him with this explanation.

"Now, Marshall, we wouldn't tell you this in the letter because we were afraid you wouldn't come, but this is a nudist camp."

Again, I had a surprise laugh because I'd never heard of nudist square dancing! And Flippo asked, "A nudist camp?"

"Yeah."

"Do you dance in the nude and everythang?"

"Oh, yeah, we get in thar, and we take off our clothes. The only time we put them on is when we have to go to the gate or somethang."

Flip observed she was really built and had a tiny bikini on. So, they drove through that gate.

And Flippo asked, "Wait a minute. Do I have to take off my clothes?"

"Yeah, you've got to take off your clothes, too."

"I thank we'll just turn around right now. I'll take you wherever you want to go."

"We got cabins and everythang on down here in the little camp."

"Well, I thank I'll just take you down thar, and then turn this son of a bitch around and get out of here."

She exclaimed, "No, no, no, no, no, no! I'll guarantee you after the first, I'll say, three or four minutes, you won't even pay any attention to it. I guarantee you that."

"No, I don't thank you're right thar."

"Well, it won't even bother you about being naked 'cause everybody's naked."

Trying to figure how he could do this, Flippo asked, "Well, can I stand behind a table?"

"Yeah, you can do that."

"Does it got a tablecloth on it?"

"Yeah."

"Well, I'll just stand behind thar."

"Well, that'll be alright."

So anyway, they drove on, and here they are playing volleyball on the volleyball court—men against the women, "so I snuggled down real good."

She stated, "We got to get going here."

Flippo answered, "Ah, yeah, okay, okay."

Flippo drove on, "and sure enough, thar's little houses, little cabins and everythang, and thar was a big . . ."

She explained, "Now that big hall will hold about eighty squares, and it'll be full tonight."

"Well, ah, ah, and they dance naked?"

"Yeah, that's right."

". . . and I'm naked?"

"Yeah, that's right."

She pointed over to a little cabin.

"You'll be staying over thar. Go on over thar and take your clothes off and come on over here, and we'll check out the sound."

I couldn't quit laughing through this.

And Flippo thought, "Gollyyy."

Then he observed, "Well, you got your clothes on."

She commented, "Oh, they'll be off. I'll take them off."

He thought, "Yeah, wouldn't be bad seeing the rest of her."

And so, Flip went into the cabin, took a shower, took off his clothes, and walked towards the front door, passing by a full-length mirror.

Flip thought, "No, I ain't going out thar." So he sat on the side of the bed, thinking, "Surely I could step out on the porch," so he stepped out on the porch, looked all around, and saw a woman sitting underneath a tree. "She was nude, but she had her arms crossed and her legs crossed, and she had her arms across her breasts."

He observed, "That looks like maybe it's her first time, too."

So, Flip walked on over there.

Flippo asked, "Hey, how you doing?"

She replied, "I'm fine."

"You know that lady that picked me up at the gate. I'm calling here tonight. I'm a square dance caller."

"Oh, yeah, we're going to the square dance."

"Well, you look like it might be your first time."

"Yeah."

Flippo continued, "Well, she told me where the hall was. I was supposed to check out the sound. Do you know where it is?"

And she just nodded and explained, "It's right over thar."

Flippo look over there, and he had "my hands across my privates like I did when I come out on the porch. I put my hands down thar, and they were still down thar."

So, Flip looked over, and he couldn't see, so he asked, "Where's the hall?"

"Right over thar," and she nodded her head in that directions

"I don't see anythang."

"Well, it's right over thar."

She nodded her head again, and he couldn't see any building.

So, Flip claimed, "Well, I cannot see it," and added, "She uncrossed her legs, with one foot she pointed. Of course, her legs were wide open. She pointed toward the square dance hall."

With a master storyteller's flair, Flippo exclaimed, "IT'S JUST A STORY! So, you can put that in or put it out—whatever."

After a round of laughter, Flip explained, "It's easier to tell when you can make motions or whatever. I told it a long time, you know. People believed it up to when she pointed with her foot."

We vacillated whether to put it in the book. He suggested, "I'd say not put it in thar." I decided to keep it because it's classic Flippo, the master storyteller!

November, 1989

MARSHALL FLIPPO
Feature Caller For GMS&RDA's
Annual Christmas Special, Dec. 13th.

The annual winter tour of the world's most popular square dance caller, MARSHALL FLIPPO, will bring him thru Memphis and a stopover on Wednesday, December 13th, at Conrad Central Hall, 5530 Shady Grove Rd. at Yates.

The dance, sponsored by GMS&RDA for its membership, will begin at 8 p.m. and Gordon & Mary Brower will °cue the °tween tip 2X2 rounds. Admission is free to GMS&RDA members, non-members admission, $3.00 per person. Usual refreshments will be served.

Flippo's annual Christmas Dance in Memphis Tennessee. Source: Neeca Flippo

West and Home for Christmas

Flippo's tour began to head west with a stop in Birmingham. Then his fast-paced schedule had him in Memphis, Tennessee one night, where he called the Annual Christmas special on December 13. The next night Flip was in Little Rock, Arkansas and called their Christmas dance and did them "for a good many years."

In looking at Flippo's photo albums/scrapbooks, we saw a hand-drawn map of Arkansas. The artist's name was Billy Webbs from Magnolia, Arkansas. The map stated "Magnolia, Arkansas is the square dancing capital of the world."

"He was always saying Magnolia, Arkansas was the center of—Square Dance Capital of the World. Yeah, you want to know that smart ass capital of the world—Magnolia, Arkansas. He's died now."

"His wife's name was Bobbie, B-O-B-B-I-E. Billy and Bobbie, and she's still alive and still dancing. No, was she dancing? I seen her in Mesa."

We both laughed. Down at the bottom of the map, it says "Population eight squares."

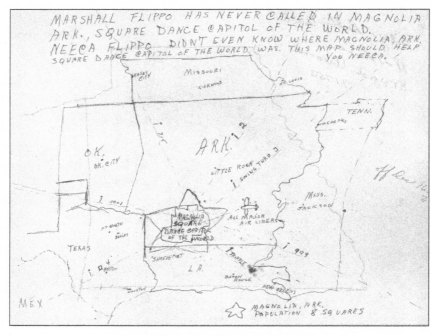

Map of Arkansas Billy Web drew. Source: Neeca Flippo

As we talked, Flip stopped me, "Wait a minute. I'm leaving a lot of stuff out."

My response to his vigorous schedule was, "Wow, wow, wow! What a schedule!"

"Well, I hope you don't take it like I'm egotistical. I'm not that way! Neeca really made this schedule out for me, and some towns quit, and some towns added on. Stuff like that, but she's originally made the tour for me. Pretty good, isn't she?"

I agreed wholeheartedly! "I thought Neeca was good that way."

Flippo headed west toward home and the holidays, calling in Dallas. "It's 180 miles down to Abilene, so I went home, spent Christmas. I was calling basically every night. I was usually home around one or two weeks. Then after Christmas back to tour again."

---

1. Chula Vista Resort in Wisconsin Dells, Wisconsin Web Site: https://www.chulavistaresort.com/
2. **Caller** - A person who prompts dance figures in such dances as line dance, square dance, and contra dance.
3. **Tip** — A square dance session consisting of two parts, a patter call, and a singing call. See Glossary for more.
4. Comparison of $1300 in 1960 to 2020. Ian Webster, "CPI Inflation Calculator," 2020, https://www.in2013dollars.com/us/inflation/1960?amount=1300
5. *Step by Step Through Modern Square Dance History*, p21.
6. **Cuer** — Leader at the front of the ballroom [hall] who tells the dancers, as they dance, what steps to do

7. **Flyer** — (same as Square Dance Brochure) — Advertisement for Kirkwood's schedule and calling and cuing staff.
8. Marshall Flippo Fan Club group on Facebook — https://www.facebook.com/groups/328325644382769/?ref=bookmarks
9. **Cuer** — For definition, see Footnote above: #9.

14

NORTH AFTER CHRISTMAS THEN WEST

F lippo went north after Christmas going to Sherman-Denison, Texas. "I know I called for old Harper Smith over thar in the Dallas area, but I can't remember when that was—whether it was after Christmas or before. Well, I thank it had to be after."

Then he went up in Oklahoma, Nebraska, and Kansas, specifically to Wichita Falls, Oklahoma City, Tulsa, and then to Wichita, Kansas. From Wichita, he drove a long trip to Frank Lane's old home town, Atchison, towards Kansas City.

On January 17 & 18, 1969, Flippo and Ken Bower called at the opening of the Century Two Building in Wichita, Kansas with two hundred squares dancing.

Claude Wiley, a *caller*,[1] stated, "I've got the *Grand March*.[2] We're going to have a double *Grand March*. I've got it all figured out."

Flippo laughed. "Well, one side did so good. The other side—hell, they don't know. They're so damn late."

Twenty-five years later, Ken and Flippo called their twenty-fifth anniversary of the opening of the Century Two building. They called the first opening and then the twenty-five years later opening, too.

As his tour continued, Flippo went to Manhattan where Kansas State is, and from Laurence, he drove to Kansas City and flew

Ad for Mid America Fun Fest, January 17 & 18, 1969. Staff: Flippo, Nita and Manning Smith and Ken Bower. Source: *Sets In Order*, December 1968

185

out to Omaha, Nebraska, and he stayed with the Bolts.

They took Flippo to the airport and picked him up. He was just there one night to call at the Livestock Exchange on the tenth floor. The Bolts ran the dance. They had a hall there that would hold "a good forty-five squares." It was a beautiful hall that had good sound and a great floor. The most squares Flippo ever saw there was sixty squares. From Omaha, he flew back to Kansas City and picked up his car and drove to Salina, Kansas.

Source: Neeca Flippo

As we went through Flip's photo albums/scrapbooks, we saw "Annual Flippo Square Dance—25 years of calling for Buttons and Bows—Washington, Missouri."

Before they went to 45^3 records, they took a 78^4 record of "The Auctioneer," made a clock out of it and presented it to Flippo. He had so much fun there. They danced in a Pavilion out in the fairgrounds that held about thirty squares, and if they were lucky, a train didn't come by. He had to wait until it went by before he could say another word. They had to fight the mosquitoes some years, and some years they didn't bother, but the people were nice, and they had such a great time. A lot of St. Louis folks would be there, because they were just twenty to twenty-five miles from St. Louis.

We saw a nice note from Dick and Bette Barker that shared, "Hope to continue to have you call on the third Saturday in September for many years to come."

He reacted, "Yeah. Dick and Bette—I hadn't thought of them in years. They had a good teacher over thar and a good *caller*. She's still alive, but he's gone. Ah, damn, but '86—that hasn't been that far back, has it?"

We both laughed when we calculated it had been thirty-two years.

Flippo responded, "Damn while." He had trouble remembering the names of a couple who were instrumental in the Washington, Missouri square dance and the Buttons and Bows. He told me that Jerry Junck would know, and he did—Dobby and Betty Dobsch. They would come to Kirkwood on vacation.

Then he added in reference to his photo albums/scrapbooks, "I should go over all of them again. I make it as one of my Bucket List. Go through the albums and read all those letters again."

Flippo recalled that he called two Super Bowl Sundays in Salina, Kansas. "I know they had a TV up on the stage for me, 'cause Dallas was playing and won the Super Bowl."

Remembering the specifics about his tour, Flippo recalled going north from Abilene twice—once right after Christmas and once after the western tour. He remembered calling in Stillwater after the west coast tour. "Damn. I know Durant, Oklahoma was in thar. I went back to Abilene, and I was just in Abilene for two days. Now I went back thar from, I guess, say Stillwater, Oklahoma."

Flippo remembered a really special New Year's Eve dance. "The one big thang in my mind about New Year's Eve in Odessa-Midland at the airport, somebody went out thar and turned the heat on at the hangar we were going to use, and we's going to have, I believe, we ended up with over a hundred squares. In the meantime, some guy went out thar that evidently worked at the airport. He thought, 'Well, what's these heaters on?' He turned them off and opened the doors."

It was seventeen degrees, and people were dancing with their overcoats on, "and we decided to hell with this. So, we moved that dance, and we moved it over to Midland Square Dance Center, Square Dance Hall they had built, and we got over thar with twenty-seven squares. The rest of 'em, I'm sure, went home. It was colder than hell."

Inaugural Ball

L to R: Mack Henson, daughter of the Winters, Wanda & John Winter, Gary Shoemake and wife, Neeca & Flippo. Source: Neeca Flippo

Preston Smith, then governor of Texas, personally invited Flippo and Gary

Shoemake to call at one of his Inaugural Balls on January 19, 1971, a Texas size party. The *cuers*[5] were John and Wanda Winter, and their daughter, Jonna, joined them. Mack Henson of Fun Valley, Colorado was the MC.

With a chuckle, Flippo identified a letter from the governor of Texas, Preston Smith in one of the scrapbook/photo albums. At that Inaugural Ball, they had two hundred squares. "You know, they have dances, and the governor and his wife visit each dance. They came over and said a few words."

STATE OF TEXAS
EXECUTIVE DEPARTMENT
AUSTIN

PRESTON SMITH
GOVERNOR

A Special Message to Square Dancers:

You are invited to attend the Governor's Inaugural Festival. Of particular interest to you, will be the Square Dance Inaugural Ball to be held at Gregory Gym on the University of Texas campus. This ball will be Tuesday night, January 19, 1971, at 8:00 P. M.

The Square Dance callers will be Marshall Flippo and Gary Shoemake. The Round Dance leaders will be John and Wanda Winters.

All Square Dancers are invited. Reservations are not necessary, and there will be no charge. I think this will be one of the best square dances ever held. I certainly hope you will come and dance with us, and help make our Texas Inaugural Festival a continuing success.

Sincerely,

Preston

Preston Smith
Governor of Texas

Mack Henson, Chairman
Square Dance
Inaugural Ball

PS/mjw

Invitation to square dancers to the Inaugural Ball. Source: Neeca Flippo

Gary Shoemake shared his memory of that amazing night:

"That was a week night, and we had dinner before the dance. I asked Flip,

'How many squares do you thank we will have?' Since this was the first time this had ever happened, Flip was skeptical and said we'll be lucky to have twenty squares. Back in those days that was a small crowd. I disagreed and said I thought we would have at least forty squares. As it turned out, we were dancing on the floor of the University of Texas basketball court and thar were two hundred squares. Dancers showed up in bus loads.

"When the Governor and his entourage arrived at our dance, the back doors opened and as they entered, the music stopped. Flippo said, 'Ladies & gentlemen, welcome the new governor of Texas,' and it was like the parting of the seas. Those two hundred squares parted to make room for the group to come to the stage, to thundering applause.

"Governor Smith was an ol' time square dancer, and after a few remarks he asked if we could call the 'Texas Star,' and Flip said he could do it. So, we got him a partner and Flip called the 'Texas Star' routine for him to dance. When he danced to Flip's calling, the dancers went wild with applause.

"While this was going on, I was on the stage with the Lieutenant Governor, Ben Barnes, and the head of the highway patrol. They mentioned to me that this was the best reception of all the balls, because everyone was so attentive and polite to Mr. Smith. He went on to tell me that ours was the best to listen to his comments and applaud often during his remarks. I guess some of the other balls drinking was allowed, and it took them quite a bit of effort to keep people from crowding the governor for hand shakes, pats on the backs and other attempts to get close to the governor.

"Ken Bower was traveling in the area and had the night off. He joined us on stage for a couple of tips.

"This was made possible by Mack Henson, the owner of Fun Valley, who was a personal friend of the governor. I was working for him at the time, at the resort, and Flip, who was his favorite caller, lived in the same town [Abilene]. So, Flip was a shoe-in, and I just happened to be at the right place at the right time. At that time of my life it was the biggest group I had ever called for, and it was all due to Mack Henson's efforts to get it organized."

Gary ended, "That's my memories of that great evening."

Flippo had a history with Preston Smith that he wasn't aware of. He didn't know whether this happened about the same time or not, but a bunch of square dancers went to visit the governor, trying to make square dancing the dance of Texas, like the flower is the blue bonnet, but when they went, Preston said, "Well, Momma and Dad used to square dance in Lubbock, and thar was a guy. I remember they took me out thar to the Lubbock Dance Federation dance, and the *caller* was a guy from Abilene named Flippo," and they said, "Yeah, that's right."

Preston asked if he was still calling.

Flippo added, "And that was in '71."

STATE OF TEXAS
EXECUTIVE DEPARTMENT
AUSTIN

PRESTON SMITH
GOVERNOR

February 1, 1971

Mr. Marshall Flippo
c/o The Lubbock Area Square and Round
Dance Federation
2826 - 63rd
Lubbock, Texas

Dear Marshall:

I wanted to take this opportunity to express my personal
appreciation to you for your part in making the Inaugural
celebration in Austin this year a great success.

We are very glad you could be a part of the festivities,
and we would like to welcome you back to Austin any time.

Very best regards,

Sincerely

Preston Smith
Governor of Texas

PSgmh

An appreciation letter from Governor Preston Smith to Flippo. Source: Neeca Flippo

200 Dancers at the Inaugural Ball. Source: Neeca Flippo

Headed West Now

New Mexico

Flippo was home for just a couple days after the side trips to the Midwest and then started his West Coast tour, starting in Roswell, New Mexico on a Saturday night. Sunday afternoon at 2:00, he was in Silver City, New Mexico "That was a pretty good to drive through thar—a good seven-hour drive, and I made it every year."

He worried about the year when the speed limit went down to 55 miles. Flippo went through that pass, and he'd always worry about it being snow. And then when the gas shortage came in the '70s, all those clubs along the way had gas for him, so he didn't have to worry about running out of gas. Flip had been touring "down in thar in the '60s, but the gas shortage was in the '70s though."

On February 19, 1977, Flippo called at Silver City, with eighty-eight couples in attendance.

Sunday night Flip was off, and then he had the scenic drive the next day, "route 25 that goes through the mountains and through Devil's—Devil's somethang, whatever it was. It was a very nice scenic route. I usually tried to take it, unless it was snow. I was able to go that way most every year, and it took about the same time to go that—across that I-25, I thank it is—through the mountains as it did to go back to Deming."

Then he would come out south of Truth or Consequences on that scenic drive, drive up and have breakfast at Truth or Consequences, and then drive on in to Albuquerque on a Monday night. He never had to go back toward Deming and take that cut-across.

Traditionally Flippo came in February to Albuquerque for his annual visit for many years, but because of snow storms, which caused cancellations, it was moved to March.

Flippo in Silver City, New Mexico Thursday, February 10, 1977 with 88 couples on the floor. Source: Neeca Flippo

Urban legend in Albuquerque is that Flippo financially helped build the new square dance hall in 1978, the Albuquerque Square Dance Center, so when I asked him if this were true, he responded, "No, I'd give them a little each time I called. They had my name up thar [on a plaque in the hall]. Yeah, but now the place I called before that [hall] was on a Monday night, too. It was The Barn. That hall that was split down the middle. You couldn't see the dancers on the right side thar. It was kind of a split hall with a wall down the middle. It was out in the park."

Edris Davis, who planned many square dance events, remembered Flippo tearing up his paychecks, so the legend may be truer than Flip wanted to admit.

Flippo recalled he stayed with the Scotts most every time he was in Albuquerque.

Another person Flip remembered from Albuquerque was his dear friend, Bob Brundage who was Al Brundage's brother. When Bob was healthier, they would have dinner together, and he'd go to the dance with Flip. If Flip flew in to Albuquerque, he'd usually pick him up.

"We had quite a few dinners together. Bob got to where he couldn't drive at night. He was the best thang—really a super person."

And very early the next morning, before the dawn because Flippo wanted to look back at the lights of Albuquerque, he would head west on I-40. He'd get out somewhere where there was a pull-off, turn off the car, and get out and look at that city. "You could look back and see what a beautiful sight it was—that whole town down thar with the lights on and everythang. It is gorgeous with all those lights."

California

When Flippo left Albuquerque, he drove to either Barstow, California, or Las Vegas, Nevada and had a night off. He'd usually get in late evening, have a dinner, and then go to bed. He stated he didn't go to Las Vegas to gamble. "I did gamble some but not that much, but I just walked around. I wanted to look at the red lights." Tuesday would be the night off. Wednesday night, Flip called in Ridgecrest, California "which is China Lake anyway and then go to Santa Maria, California." For thirty-five straight years, he called for the Curly-Q's and later Squaws and Paws.[6]

"You know, you thank of some of these towns, and some of them were so damn good to you, you get a catch in your throat thanking about it."

They always had a good dinner at Shaw's Restaurant before the dance, so Flip tried to get in there so he could get a little nap before dinnertime. It seemed like it was the whole club for dinner but just the officers of the club, and they had a good bunch going that filled "that ole hall up. I still got a friend over thar. I'd like to see her. We correspond still. She's older than I am, so she's up in her 90s. Anyway, someday."

From Santa Maria, Flippo did a weekend and a week at Asilomar, California, which is going to be the next chapter about his favorite venue to work.

Flippo's memory astonished me, but he had a hard time remembering where he went after Asilomar. He knew it was west, farming country, and the name possibly began with an M.

Merced, and it wasn't a very big city. Flip remembered caravanning over there from Asilomar with anywhere from four to ten cars because he called over there. "From thar I have no earthly idea where I went. Yeah, I do, too. From thar, I went up to San Francisco."

Flippo had two different possible destinations from San Francisco. He went from San Francisco to Stockton and worked with Dick Houlton on Monday night. He weighed about almost 400. Flippo could stand behind him and nobody would see him. Dick was an excellent *caller*[7] and lived in Stockton with his sister. He never did marry. And his mother was always with them, and she was quite an old lady. Flip worked with him in Stockton and Concord. Flippo would pick up Mary Sheehan Johnson, a square dance friend, and she'd go with him across the Bay Bridge to Concord. Then he went back, taking Mary back over that night. That night was always Monday night. "I'd take her back over. What did I do after I called with Dick now? Jesus, that week is a blank."

DICK HOULTON

Source: *Sets in Order*, March 1966

His memory revived. That's when Flip went up to Yuba City, and Marysville's right there close by.

This memory brought up a story. Flippo broke down one time and "ole Frank Lane" passed him when he was in a gray Dodge and had a flat tire.

Barbara, Frank's wife, commented, "You know, Frank, that car back there had clothes in it like Flippo's car—hanger across the back."

Frank replied, "I didn't notice."

"Yeah, it's on the side of road there."

Flippo explained, "So ole Frank, he turned that thang."

Frank asked Flip how he was.

Flippo answered, "I need help."

Frank stated, "Well, I'll see you later." Flippo added with a laugh, "No, he helped me. I'm trying to thank where I went that night. Let me see. We fixed the flat tire, got back in the car . . . Now I'm on I-5. From Yuba City, I always went over to Reno, Nevada." His itinerary sent him out of San Francisco a couple different directions.

Washington

Gary Shoemake, Ken Bower, Scott Smith, and Flippo had a weekend north of Seattle, Washington, in Marysville, right off of I-5. They had a lot of Canadians come down for their weekend, but then the Canadians couldn't come over because the money exchange was too bad. "Thar's a good place thar to eat, too. We'd go for breakfast then. It was a nice place. It was an old building but a good restaurant."

Nevada

From Yuba City, Flippo went to Reno, Nevada, and then he had to come back over Donner Pass to Fresno, California, and he called for Ernie Kinney, a caller. Ernie had a festival going on there, and "I believe I was only snowbound one time at Donner Pass, and that's when Neeca was with me. It was still snowing like hell up on Donner Pass. Traffic stopped, you know." So, Flip called Ernie and said, "Ernie, we're up here, and they've got us stopped. And it's just snowing like hell. I can't hardly see my—I had to use one of those pay phones.' I said, 'I don't know if I'll be thar tonight or not.'"

Ernie assured him, "Don't worry about it, Flippo. You will be here."

Flippo shared, "Well, I don't know. I can't even see ahead of me."

Ernie commented, "Flippo, I've been over that mountain a hundred times, and if you're stopped, you will not be stopped long because they're so good about tearing everythang up."

Flippo ended the story, "And sure enough, about thirty minutes later, they let us go."

At this point, Flippo got confused about the direction of his tour and I told him how amazed I was that he remembered what he did. His response: "I'm an old man trying to make it through today."

On a serious note, Flippo shocked me when he stated, "I had a heart attack in Las Vegas, Nevada in 1996. It's one of those times I wanted to die. I believe I missed that whole weekend and the whole week at Asilomar, so I put ole Frank ahead of me going to Asilomar and everythang."

Larry Letson was the first one to visit Flip.

Flip asked Larry, "What are you doing here?"

Larry replied, "I come to see you."

Flippo stated, "Ah, you got a weekend here or somethang."

He added, "No, I haven't. I had to tell them that I was your son to get in."

Flippo continued, "And after a while, the black guy caller, Johnny Preston, come in before Larry left. Now, he was having a weekend in Las Vegas, but he came up to the hospital to see me."

Letson asked Johnny, "How did ya git in?"

Johnny answered, "I told 'em I's his son."

Letson agreed, "That's what I told 'em."

Flippo exclaimed, "Golllyyy! I bet they're down thar saying, 'Ah, that guy has some funny lookin' sons."

With a deep laugh, he added, "One of 'em black; one of 'em red-headed."

Then Flippo described his heart attack, "[My second wife], bless her heart, probably saved my life. We were going to bed, and I just slammed back on my back. I said, 'I've got a hurting up here that I've never had. It was right on my chest.'"

She stated, "We're going to the hospital." She checked out of the motel, got all of their clothes back in the car—they always took their clothes in with them because Flip had them stolen a couple times. She called the office and found out where the hospital was and took off. "She was fumbling over thar by herself."

Flippo thought, "She's never going to find the hospital." He was just sitting on the other side because she wouldn't let him drive.

So, she shouted, "There it is!" It was the Trauma Center, so she pulled in the first drive she could, and it was in the back of the hospital, and she pulled back there. A policeman came and said, "Ma'am, you cannot park here."

She proclaimed, "I damn sure can. My husband's having a heart attack."

"Oh, I'll get a wheelchair."

So they got a wheelchair and wheeled Flip in. He hadn't had the attack yet, but it was hurting. They put him up on that "ole steel table," and nobody was around. "I mean nobody come back to see me or nothing. And so, I thought, 'Well, I believe . . .' and it kept a-getting worse. It kept a-getting worse, so evidently they had a monitor somewhere."

Finally, a nurse came in and asked, "How do you feel?"

Flippo responded, "Goddamn! I'm hurting pretty bad."

The nurse stated, "Well, you're right in the middle of a heart attack right now."

They give Flippo two stents, and he hasn't even had much of "a heart even hurt since then, so evidently, they treated people with heart attacks. I benefitted. Good practice."

In late December or early January, Flippo did the Holiday Hop with Ken Bower and Gary Shoemake in Laughlin, Nevada many years, but he had no idea how many years.

Flippo remembered, "I remember once thar he kicked me off and said, 'Next year you don't come back.' No, he didn't say that."

Gary couldn't remember how many years Flip called with them at the Holiday Hop and shared, "I really can't remember how many years. It seems like a long time, maybe five or ten years. He was like an old pair of socks; he just fit and was comfortable, so it didn't matter."

❧

Zigzagged Back to California

Flippo returned to California where Ernie Kinney, a caller, had a festival and booked him at the Saguaro—like the tree—not far from Fresno.

After that he went to on down into Los Angeles, and Arnie Kronenberger's clubs hired him. One time they had a hundred squares, because they were trying to send an Asian boy to college. It was billed as helping the boy out, so a lot of that money went to him.

Another time with Arnie Kronenberger, Flippo called at Anaheim, a suburb of LA. And they'd always have "big ole crowds," and the treasurer was back by the door, and a guy came in and took off with the cash box, but they'd already got all the money out of it. The only thing in it was a check from Pat Munn, Flippo's partner at Kirkwood, for his entrance fee, and he just canceled the check, "so the guy didn't get anythang, but if it had been full of money, he'd made off with a lot."

After working in the LA area, Flippo would go to Yucaipa, California and called for "an ole student, Pete Smith." From Yucaipa, Flip went over to Palm Springs, met up with Bill and Betty Hagadorn, who went there each year for about almost six months. Neeca would fly in and also Frank and Barbara Lane. Arnie, another caller, who lived in LA would drive over.

The group had dinner the first night—tell ole stories and laugh a lot. They stayed almost a week and played golf at all those courses they used for "the Bob Hope Clambake or whatever they called it—big tournament. We'd play at Bermuda Dunes, Indian Wells, and thar's two more, but we'd play them all. Anyway, we'd stay thar with ole Bill." He especially enjoyed the golfing.

After time in Palm Springs with Bill and Betty, Flippo drove down to Chula Vista, California, south of San Diego. He called for Bill Berry's club, the Snaparoo's. Flippo made a note here to mark the difference for the Snaparoo story coming up!

Arizona

Flippo left Chula Vista around 5:00 or 6:00 in the morning because Tucson was a seven-hour drive, and then you'd lose an hour. "You got your ass on the ball. So I'd try to get in thar in time to get a little nap in the afternoon. And most of the time, I could. I'd call them and tell them I was in town." He warned them that he was taking "a little nap. Will you give me a call back?"

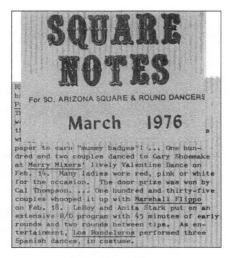

Source: Neeca Flippo

That ended the western tour. After Tucson, Flippo left early the next morning because he wanted to get to Odessa for the Permian Basin festival in February.

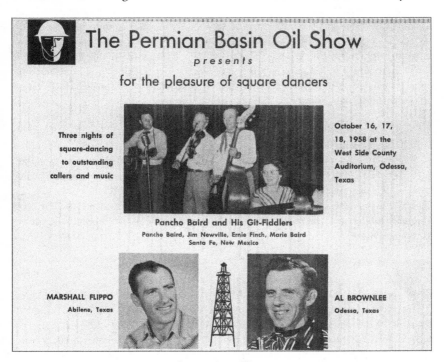

Source: Neeca Flippo

"I done it [Permian Basin festival], I thank, for thirty-two years. The 34th was the last one I called thar, and I called with another caller, and that's Jerry Haag, and that's Don and Pete Hickman from, I believe, 'San Antone'—that's where they finally ended up. Her name is Pete. It would draw anywhere from seventy-five to a hundred squares each year."

After that festival, Flippo drove back home to Abilene, "and that's basically— I'm going to have to go over some stuff—my whole tour. Neeca might have a copy because she's the one that set the whole thang up in the first place. People would write her and if we could take a dance, we'd take it, and if we couldn't, we'd just tell them we couldn't take it."

End of the Tour

Flippo's tour ended in the spring, and then he would head back up north, into Kansas and Oklahoma again. He revisited some of the same towns, then it was back to Abilene, which was getting close to Kirkwood time.

As he thought about the end of his yearly tour, Flippo added with a chuckle, "It seemed like I went out again. Oh, boy! Seemed like I went out again before Abilene. My mind is just like a mouse trap, a closed mouse trap."

Flippo gave credit to Neeca for the creation of his successful tour schedule. "Neeca was the cause of me having such a great tour, and then I was asked back each year, so that helped. She set the first one up with the guests that were at Kirkwood Lodge, and then they would say, 'Can you call for our city or club or whatever?' I know that I'm leaving some thangs out. I know I'm sitting here thanking right now I'm leaving Cincinnati. I'm leaving some thangs out that I don't know how I got thar or when I got thar." It is possible that Flippo left out some stops along the way, but his recall of this six month adventure, in its variations and duration of forty-two years is astonishing!

Still More Commitments

Flip had a major tour lined up six months of the year with annual weekend festivals, club visits and special events, but he even added more to this already grueling schedule with other events. He called at WASCA in Washington, D.C. in March. During the last weekend in March/first weekend in April, he did the Alabama Jubilee two or three times in Birmingham. Flip even took a jaunt to Alaska and more!

WASCA[8]

Flippo talked at length about WASCA, the Washington Area Square Dance Cooperative Association, held the second weekend of March but couldn't remember how many times he called it. Through research, Jeff and Bobbi Fuhr, the current WASCA historians, found Flippo called at WASCA for fifteen years from 1963–1980: 1963–1971, 1973, 1975, 1976, and 1978–1980, and also sent me the old WASCA program books.

WASCA was held at the Sheraton Park Hotel, Washington, D. C. from 1960–1991. It moved a couple times and presently is at Hilton Alexandria Mark Center Hotel.

Flippo commented, "It's not like it was. It was a huge thang. We'd have anywhere between four and five thousand dancers for that weekend, and it was a long weekend, starting on Thursday went to Sunday morning—Saturday night it was over."

WASCA Calling Staff Sitting on Steps March 6–8, 1969. Source: Neeca Flippo

One specific picture from WASCA intrigued me with nine well-known callers sitting on the stage, but Flip couldn't remember when the picture was taken.

While we looked at this picture, he named all the *caller* icons in the picture: "Bob Van Antwerp up at the top. Lee Helsel next to Bob, Les Gotcher sitting down with the big hat on, and thar I am, next to Bob Fisk, and up here at the top is Sam Mitchell with his head almost to the board, Singing Sam Mitchell, Johnny LeClair next to him, looking right at him, Dick Jones and Max Forsyth."

With the programs and flyers Jeff provided, we narrowed down when the photo was taken. It was March 6–8, 1969. Les Gotcher was there, but he died March 6, 1974.

Flippo enjoyed WASCA because he worked with a lot of callers. He couldn't remember the exact number—"nine or maybe ten or eleven, but anyway, it was a good, good festival—a lot of people."

Flyer for the WASCA Festival in 1969. Goes with above picture.
Source: Jeff and Bobbi Fuhr

❧

In April, Flippo did the Spring Festival in Ardmore, Oklahoma and stayed with a couple who had a little girl.

When he walked in, the little girl said, "Where's your guns?"

Flip answered, "I don't have any."

She stated, "Well, most marshalls have a gun."

Flippo added, "And so, anyway . . ."

❧

Flippo did the Alaska State Square Dance Festival in Juneau, Alaska, April 11–13, 1975 and, then he did Santa's Swingers Spring Fling in 2012 and the state festival in 2013 in Fairbanks.

SQUARE DANCE
WITH
MARSHALL FLIPPO

Swinging in the rain

ALASKA STATE
SQUARE DANCE FESTIVAL
APRIL 11-13, 1975
JUNEAU, ALASKA

ROUND DANCE
WITH
ART & JIMMIE KEBORT

For Information write: Stan & Connie Constantine, P.O. Box 207, Douglas, Alaska 99824

Source: Neeca Flippo

When asked about the festivals in Alaska, he answered, "Yeah, in Juneau. I did it again later on—hell's bells, I can't thank of that. It starts with an F. Fairbanks. I did it later like it was twenty years between the two of them. Yeah, I'm sure that's at least twenty years."

When Alaska came up, Flippo thought of Roger and Kandie Christian and he spelled her name, "K-A-N-D-I-E, I thank, Christian. Really, really, really top of the line people. Really nice folk. I went over two days early for their club dance, and ole Roger took me all over. I mean, I voted him number one tour guide of Alaska. We went to pipeline. We went to a gold mine. We went to a—what the hell do ya'll want to call it—some other kind of mine, but he was very good. He was very patient with an old fellow, you know, so I enjoyed Roger. I enjoyed Kandie, too. They were both just good people."

Reminiscing about his Alaskan trips, Flip laughed, "I cannot ever thank of that, dad-gum. I can thank of Fairbanks ever' once in a while but Juneau, I don't know why I never can thank of that name. Yeah, that's right, Juneau and then we went over to the Red Slipper [Dog] Bar afterwards. We just walked over thar. It was cold and snowy, I mean, not snowy, but snow on the ground and cold, and we walked from the hall. I remember that walk from the hall over to the, I believe it was the Red Slipper [Dog] or Red Somethang, and had a few, and let's see. That was in Juneau. Fairbanks—I still correspond with Fairbanks people. And I enjoyed Alaska. They were just as good as gold to ya. They just treated you so nice, good people."

Read Roger and Kandie's experience with Flippo in Alaska in their story in Chapter 30, Stories About Flippo.

❦

Flippo called at the Gulf Coast Square Dance Festival in Biloxi, Mississippi for years. He did the Friday night by himself, and then Saturday somebody else would come in. That Gulf Coast Festival was pretty big.

One year when Flippo was at Kirkwood, he had plans to call this festival, and one of the summer guest heard about it. The guest needed to go to New Orleans and was flying down and offered Flip a free flight. Flippo took him up on the offer.

The guest was an ex-pilot of Southern airlines, "so he took me down thar and flew me over to Biloxi, come back, and got me. We was up in the sky, up in those fleecy white clouds, you know, flying around, and come to find out he didn't have any flight plans or nothing. He'd just get in a plane and took off. So, I didn't know that until after I got home, but anyway, I had a good free flight."

❦

Flippo talked about a variety of clubs and repeat dates, but the one he referenced the most was Grand Squares Square Dance Club located in San Antonio, Texas. They created a photo album for him with individual pictures of the member couples.

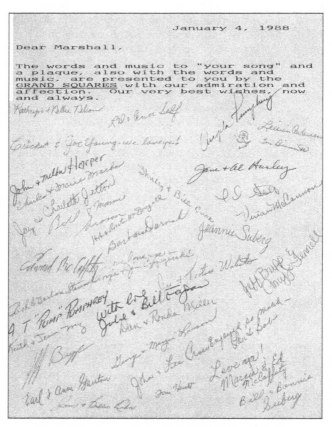

Grand Squares Thank you January 4, 1988. Source: Neeca Flippo

He reminisced, "They were one of those clubs, kind of like people around your town up thar—Albuquerque. They were that kind of people. I called thar I don't know how many anniversaries—over forty-five of them. But Joe Young was the *caller* for Grand Squares, a very good friend, very good *caller* thar in San Antone. Bill Wright's still alive. In fact, I was going to call him yesterday [2018]."

Joe Young started it, and Flip always stayed with Joe and Cricket. They started the Grand Squares, and then they had him call an anniversary dance, and then they hired him back for the next anniversary dance, and it just kept going like that for forty-four years, even after Joe and Cricket died.

Cricket died first, and Joe was lost without her. He never did recover from Cricket dying. He met her when he was in the service, and she was just a young girl, "fifteen or somethang like when they were married. So, they'd been together all those years, and they were just a close couple. They have a daughter who lives in San Antone. She married ole John Thompson."

The club now is fifty some odd years old. "I will call Don Winkler, W-I-N-K-L-E-R. I spent many a night with 'em after Joe and Cricket died. I started staying with Don and Barbara."

Flippo remembered the last one. It was just not too long ago, and they were always so nice to him, "kind of like the Albuquerque folk!" His reference to Albuquerque folks always made me laugh because I'm from Albuquerque.

Flippo added, "Most of them were ole farmers."

Flip labored over how many years he called Grand Squares's anniversary dance, so he called his friend, Don Winkler, and found out, "Forty-four years! He'd been president eleven years. Very, very good president, and for eleven years of those fifty-four, and he's president again this year. Oh God, it was really a good club. They had good leadership in that club—that's why it kept going so long, I suppose. They're still dancing."

After Joe died, Chris Crisler called for them quite a while until he died, and Allene, his wife, is still alive. They were very close friends, and he was a good *caller*.

Flippo spent six months on the road, calling so many dances and seeing so many people during his regular tour engagements and the many added festivals. The tour would end, and he headed back to Kirkwood for his six months there to start all over again!

But we have one more stop on his tour, Asilomar, California, his favorite venue which warranted its own chapter.

---

1. **Caller** — A person who prompts dance figures in such dances as line dance, square dance, and contra dance.
2. **Grand March** — An opening ceremony at a ball that consists of a march participated in by all the guests.
3. **45 Records** — The most common form of the vinyl single is the "45" or "7-inch." The names are derived from its play speed, 45 rpm, and the standard diameter, 7 inches.
4. **78 Records** — An early type of shellac-based phonograph record that played at 78 revolutions per minute.
5. **Cuers** — Leader at the front of the ballroom [hall] who tells the dancers, as they dance, what steps to do.
6. Ron and Linda Mineau, Houston Photo Album.
7. **Caller** — For definition, see Footnote above: #1.
8. **WASCA** (the Washington Area Square Dance Cooperative Association) Web Site: http://wascaclubs.com/

15

ASILOMAR

Asilomar Sign. Source: https://www.visitasilomar.com/

Early in our interviews, I asked Flip what his favorite festival or weekend was, and without hesitation, he replied, "Asilomar."[1] Bob Osgood, the publisher of *Sets in Order* magazine, saw a name appear repeatedly in his magazine with song after song being reviewed and lauded—Marshall Flippo! Did this play a part in his asking Flippo to join the staff at Asilomar once a year for one week and one weekend, starting in 1964? This partnership lasted for thirty-six years!

Bob Osgood provided dancers a beautiful square dance vacation with two choices at Asilomar: *Sets in Order* Summer Institute in July or Winter Asilomar in February. The Winter Asilomar consisted of two consecutive events: a weekend event from Friday until Sunday morning and immediately following with a week-long event from Monday until Saturday morning. As publisher and editor of *Sets in Order* magazine and the chairperson of the Asilomar events, Bob advertised heavily for these events in his magazine and attracted a lot of dancers. He also hired the top national *callers*[2] at the time.

Bob Osgood. Source: http://www.sdfne.org/bob-becky-osgood/

Flippo's west tour continued into February to his favorite weekend and week at Asilomar.

Right after Santa Maria, Flippo went up to Asilomar. It's Monterey and Pacific Grove, two little towns that had pretty good restaurants in them.

"It was run by Bob and Becky Osgood—my favorite weekend 'cause they run it with an iron fist, and you got different thangs thar that you didn't elsewhere."

Bob would have contras and town hall meetings. Flippo worked a weekend with Bob Page and a week with Frank Lane. Flip did the weekend about three to four years, and then Bob Page died. And from then on, they had different *callers* in for the weekend, like Bob Van Antwerp, Lee Helsel, Bruce Johnson, and Arnie Kronenberger. Also, they had Daryl Clendenin in one or two years. They would work with Flip on

Bob and Becky Osgood. Source: Neeca Flippo

the weekend, but Frank and he did the week, and they never did change. Frank and Flippo did the week for thirty-six years at Asilomar.

Source: Neeca Flippo

206

For Flippo, Asilomar was lots of fun, and they would sell out. For the weekend, they'd sell out two hundred people—twenty-five squares, and then they'd break for Sunday—but then Monday they started the week and had two hundred different people for the week. They had twenty-five squares for the weekend and a brand new twenty-five for the week. Some of the dancers stayed over the weekend and the week, too.

Asilomar is a state-owned lodge right on the Pacific Ocean where you can walk about a block, "and you're on that Seventeen Mile Drive, which is real beautiful. Thar's a lot of golf tournaments in thar, too. It was a Bing Crosby thang for the longest and then after he died, they changed the name of the golf tournament thar." It was changed to AT&T Pro Am.

Merrill Hall, Asilomar, California. Source: https://www. visitasilomar.com/

When I asked Flippo why Asilomar was his favorite, Flippo responded, "It was different from any other weekend I ever worked. It was run in a way that no other weekend was ever run and never has been run since then. Of course, you learned so much from Osgood 'cause him and Becky went to Colorado Springs where ole Pappy Shaw was. I thought of Bob Osgood as the 'Pappy Shaw' of our time."

"Shaw was an educator and is generally credited with bringing about the broad revival of square dancing in America."[3]

Bob and Becky and Flippo's teacher, Betty Casey, and her husband, John went to Pappy Shaw. "So, I was lucky to have a teacher like that, and I was lucky ever to meet Bob Osgood, I swear to God." Again, Flippo created "luck!"

Crocker Dining Hall — 1920s. Merrill Hall, Asilomar, California. Source: https://www. visitasilomar.com/

How Flippo Was Hired

When Osgood hired Flippo, he said, 'Now, on the weekend thar'll be a fellow named Bob Page working with you.'"

Flippo knew him.

Bob added, "On the week Frank Lane will be thar to work with you."

Flip knew him real well!

After Bob and Becky gave it up, Frank Lane ran it one year after that, and then Flippo and his second wife ran it one year after that, "and it was just too much damn trouble to run, and it wasn't anythang. It was just a normal weekend like you worked anywhere else after Bob and Becky gave it up. But when they were thar, it was so different."

One thing about Asilomar was everyone dressed for every session—workshops and all. You had to have square dance clothes on. That was during the day and night time, and then you had to be clean. Flip witnessed Bob Osgood run one couple off that had BO [body odor], and he asked another guy to leave because of kicking and twirls. He didn't believe in that. "You'd dance real smooth thar—no kicking or double dishrags or anything like that, and it was just a different weekend. I still thank of it as my favorite place, but now I've had some real good weekends—don't get me wrong."

Flippo shared the weekends he worked with Shoemake and Bower were a lot of fun, and he enjoyed them. But Asilomar was just different atmosphere and everything. "I don't know how to put it. You had to be thar

Flippo & Bob Page. Source: Neeca Flippo

to see it. It had a beautiful setting, right thar on the Pacific Ocean." Flippo's room was up in the Tide Inn building—great architecture, beautiful fireplace. Each building had a fireplace, and each building had a living room. "I could open my windows and just hear that ocean coming in the middle of the night. Rock you to sleep."

Osgood started off the day with contras at nine o'clock. Flippo tried to go because he liked to do the contras. Bob called the contras, and he was very good at it. Most nights they'd go down, and Bob had somebody in from the area that was maybe a chorus or a quartet for entertainment before the square dance, and then he'd get different groups from the Monterey area, and they'd come in and perform.

Bob and Becky took lot of trips, and during a town hall meetings he'd tell about some of the trips they'd been on overseas or some of the square dancing, or how *Sets in Order* started.

They ate about 6:00 p. m. and then went directly to the hall, and from 7 till 8 they either had entertainment or Bob talked about keeping your feet on the floor or styling. "You'd be calling a singing call, and if you turned the music way off, you could hear those feet going 'Swish, swish, swish, swish, swish.' And we danced a lot slower pace, even we dance nowadays. I say we dance about 120, 121 [a] minute, and part of that time, when you left Asilomar, you'd be up thar around 130-some odd. I mean moving on, but the ones that signed up for Asilomar—thar's a lot of repeaters [every year]."

. . .

Flippo's Schedule at Asilomar
Weekend

The weekend started on Friday, so they danced Friday and all day Saturday, Saturday night and up until 10 or 11 on Sunday morning. "People were great. I enjoyed calling thar as much as I enjoyed calling anywhere, I guess, and I looked forward to it every year."

Sunday Off

The weekend at Asilomar was over about 10:30 or 11:00 of a morning on Sunday, and the staff had the rest of the day off. For Sunday noon, they gave them box lunches. They didn't have anything to do that night, so a lot of them would go down on the beach and eat lunch down on the beach. "And of course, you're eating some kind of food, thar's gooney birds all around, you know."

He continued, "Oh, I said gooney birds. I meant, I'm talking about seagulls. We called them gooney birds when I was in the Navy, yeah. But they were a fun bird."

They put an apple, a good sandwich, and the leg and the thigh of a chicken in their lunches. "Well, ole Procter, he was over thar, and we's all eating. I believe it was Charlie. It was one of us anyway. He was fixing to eat that damn leg, and that damn gooney bird come, seagull come by, and grabbed that thang and flew off with it."

After a while, Charlie exclaimed, "There's the damn bird. There's that bird. He got my damn chicken."

He threw a rock at it, and Flippo said, "Charlie, thar's birds all over. How do you know which one?"

He pointed, "Well, look at that bird."

They looked at that bird, and he had swallowed that chicken thang whole, and it was sticking out. It didn't break the skin or not, but it was poked way out thar.

Week

Then the week-long event started on Monday, they danced every night, but it was slower paced than the weekend. The evening format was similar to the weekend with entertainment, and Bob and Becky told interesting stories about their travels. It would finish on Saturday. "And then I would go over and call Saturday night at this place I'm trying to thank of."

With a laugh, his sense of humor snuck out. "It was my favorite place after Albuquerque! No, it was my favorite weekend and my favorite week. But anyway, it was wonderful. I was sick when it was over."

After Parties[4] at Asilomar

After the dancing for the evening was over, it was time to relax. Traditionally dancers sat back and loosen up at the *after party*. Because of their popularity and the dancers' enjoyment, Flippo participated in *after parties* at Asilomar.

1st L to R: Becky Osgood, Flippo and Frank Lane. 2nd L to R: Becky Osgood,
Flippo ducks and Frank Lane gets it. Source: Neeca Flippo

As Flip looked at a favorite *after party* picture, he described the skit portrayed: "Looks like Becky Osgood with the pie. The guy on the right could be Frank [Lane], but I can't tell with that hat on. And is that me behind the podium? Standing thar? In the middle."

I answered, "Yeah, it looks like you."

Flip chuckled about the skit they did. "What happens is Frank wanted her to hit me with that pie. And she's thrown that pie and smacked him right in the face —that was the way it was supposed to be. Frank kept saying, 'Hit him, hit him.' And she said, 'Okay.' She threw the pie, and it hit Frank right in the face. I duck, and Frank gets it."

The Asilomar *after parties* had a reputation, and Becky Osgood played a game that was a legend. All the staff would have a different object in their hand, and people from the audience were supposed to guess what it was and then tell what it was, and she didn't tell them what to say. Once, Bettye Procter had a round ball and green glass.

Bettye stated, "This is a little unborn baby soda pop bottle."

Flip added with a laugh, "And do you know— that's what it really was. She guessed right. She didn't open it. Anyway, then the people would vote to see if she was correct or not, and every one of them had a different type of object." Flippo forgot what kind of game she called that.

His go-to person for that information about Asilomar was Mary Sheehan Johnson, and she said, "It was the Liar's Club."

Bob Page was a good *after party* skit guy, and the best one he ever did he had some little ole horses out in front of him and regular string for their reins, "and he'd sing—oh, shoot! He'd sing a damn song about—what the hell was the name of it? And he'd whip those horses with a little ole whip he'd made out of leather. Ah, what the hell? God, that tune is right on my tongue." After asking for help, we think the song was "Mule Train."

1st Row L to R: Frank Lane & Flippo, Flippo & Frank Lane doing Superman. 2nd Row L to R: Flippo & Charlie Procter doing Rocky, Flippo. Source: Mary Sheehan Johnson

Flippo as The Boxer with Frank Lane, Source: Neeca Flippo

The Beautiful Setting

Flip loved the way the Osgoods ran the program, but he also loved the Pacific Ocean setting. "We had some beautiful times thar. Merrill Hall—you can open doors on each side—full doors and that breeze comes through thar, and the wooden floor is great. The architect for the buildings thar was a lady. It was beautiful architecture. It was wooden."

Flip by the ocean. Source: Mary Sheehan Johnson

He continued his description, "And a big stage. I mooned ole Frank Lane up on that stage one time. The curtains were pulled. Anyway, nobody could see back thar. Thar's a wall. Well, it happens you could go up on the stage. You went through the door straight up some steps, turn left, and walked around where the electric box was and everythang on the wall, and then you walked out on the stage. Well, I was back thar. I had just called, and I was back thar, and they'd played the *round*.[5] I believe they played two *rounds*,[6] and then Frank was calling. So, I got up to go back and down to the dance floor. Nobody could see me, and I could see him, and he could see me. But I was around behind that wall, and I whistled, and he turned around and looked, and I mooned him."

With a chuckle, Frank added, "Folks, you're not going to believe what's going on up here."

Funny Stories

As always, Flippo related funny stories to places, so he had another one with Frank Lane and Asilomar. "Well, at Kirkwood, Frank called this new call, and it just come out called 'Ring Those Bells' or 'Won't you ring those bells!' I had a couple ole cowbells in the stick [broom] closet. So, he called it one time first of the week, and I thought, 'If he ever calls that son of a bitch again, I ought to get that cowbell out,' so he did, man, about halfway through, somehow that damn cowbell rescued it."

Flippo and Frank Lane in Merrill Hall 1978. Source: Mary Sheehan Johnson

With a chuckle, Flippo thought, "I ought to take that to Asilomar." So he took it to Asilomar and hid it backstage, and he was dancing when Frank started calling the call.

In Flippo's view, at one time Frank and Carolyn Hamilton and Manning and Nita Smith were two of the best known *round dance cuers*[7] there were.

Flippo explained who the two Franks were in this story: Frank Hamilton and Frank Lane.

"Ole Frank Hamilton was kind of a staid type of person, you know. Straight as a board. Tall. Gray haired, good-looking fellow. He was sitting over on the sidelines, and I was dancing, and Frank [Lane] started calling 'Ring Those Bells.'"

So, Flip exclaimed, "Hell, I motioned for an ole boy to come, and he came over."

And Flippo told him, "Go tell Frank [Hamilton] to cut me out of the square."

Flippo told him, "Tell Frank [Hamilton] to cut me out. I've got to go up and get that damn bell." He added, "Well, he went on and told Frank [Hamilton], 'Cut him out.'"

"He thought I meant cut Frank Lane out of calling, so, he's walking up toward the stage, and I's thinking, "Where in the hell is he going? Come over here, Frank [Hamilton], cut me out." He wouldn't turn around. He was going right toward the stage, went up there where the amplifier was plugged, and he unplugged "ole Frank [Lane]."

Frank looked at him. "What have I ever done to you?"

Anyway, he got that all straightened, and Flippo finally got somebody to come down, and he went up there and rang the cowbell. "The funniest part was Frank cut Frank out. Anyhow, we had fun all through that thang."

Flippo loved Asilomar, Becky and Bob and how they ran it, and the fun times he had at that beautiful Pacific coast setting —years of memories with callers and dancers.

Ad for Winter Asilomar, 1967. Source: Neeca Flippo

1978 Attendees at Winter Asilomar. Source: Neeca Flippo

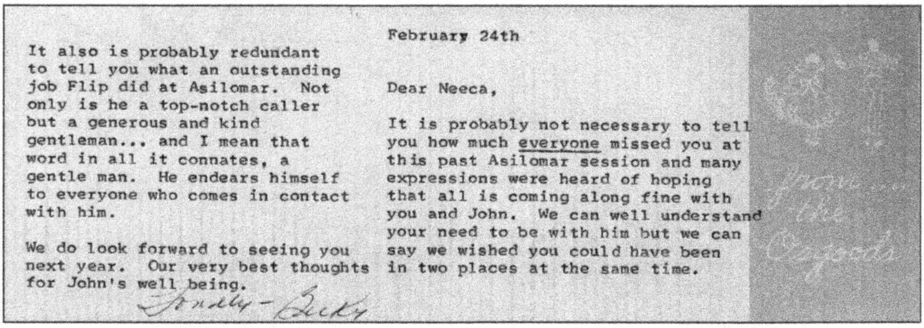

February 24th

It also is probably redundant to tell you what an outstanding job Flip did at Asilomar. Not only is he a top-notch caller but a generous and kind gentleman... and I mean that word in all it connates, a gentle man. He endears himself to everyone who comes in contact with him.

We do look forward to seeing you next year. Our very best thoughts for John's well being.

Dear Neeca,

It is probably not necessary to tell you how much everyone missed you at this past Asilomar session and many expressions were heard of hoping that all is coming along fine with you and John. We can well understand your need to be with him but we can say we wished you could have been in two places at the same time.

Fondly - Becky

Note from Becky to Neeca about missing Asilomar when John was sick. Source: Neeca Flippo

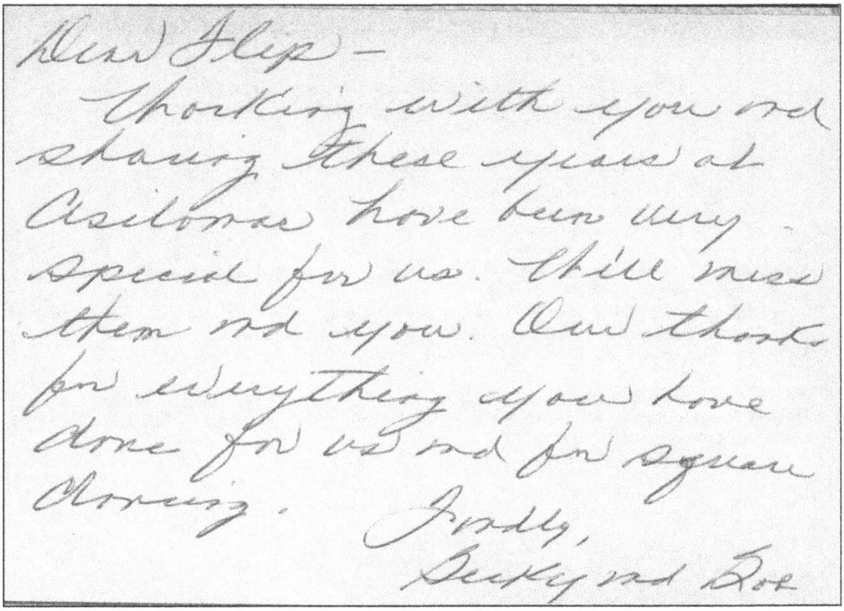

Dear Flip -

Thinking with you and sharing these years at Asilomar have been very special for us. Will miss them and you. Our thanks for everything you have done for us and for square dancing.

Fondly,
Becky and Bob

Note to Flippo from Becky and Bob Osgood when they retired. Source: Neeca Flippo

215

1981 Asilomar Staff: Barbara and Frank Lane, Charlie and Bettye Procter, Becky Osgood, Flippo and Bob Osgood. Source: Mary Sheehan Johnson

1. Asilomar Web Site: https://www.visitasilomar.com/
2. **Callers** — A person who prompts dance figures in such dances as line dance, square dance, and contra dance.
3. Wikipedia, "Lloyd Shaw (educator)," June 17, 2019, https://en.wikipedia.org/wiki/Lloyd_Shaw_(educator)
4. **After Party** — The party after the square dance with skits and a variety of entertainment usually put on by the event staff of callers and cuers. Sometimes dancers participated in skits, too.
5. **Round** — Couple dancing in a circle formation, using choreographed routines to a definite arrangement of music.
6. **Two Rounds** — Two different round dance songs.
7. **Round dance cuers** — Leader at the front of the ballroom [hall] who tells the dancers, as they dance, what steps to do.

CALLERLAB, INTERNATIONAL TRIPS, & CRUISES

The founding fathers of CALLERLAB. Source: Neeca Flippo

16

CALLERLAB

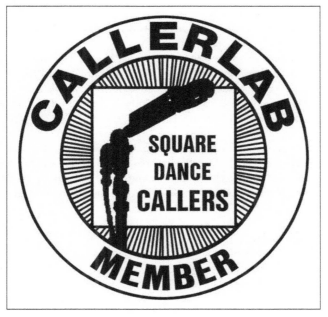

Source: Dana Schirmer

To most square dancer in the world, the term, "CALLERLAB"[1] is a familiar one:

We are an international organization of square dance callers. Our mission statement is 'To foster the art of square dance calling, and improve caller skills.' We fulfill this mission by providing guidance and education, certifying caller coaches, maintaining standardized lists of calls and definitions, and generally promoting the square dance activity.[2]

Marshall Flippo was one of the eleven founding members of CALLERLAB.

Flippo was also an active member of the American Callers Association, another caller organization and was identified at the fiftieth anniversary: "The American Callers Association is very proud to recognize and thank the following callers for their dedicated service regardless of their caller affiliation."[3] Marshall Flippo was listed with twenty-nine other callers and recognized for fifty-seven years of service.

During our conversations, Flippo returned to the topic of CALLERLAB, often vacillating in his opinion about the success of the endeavors of this organization, but he loved CALLERLAB to the end.

In July 1964, Bob Osgood organized a Leadership Conference at the University of California at Los Angeles (UCLA) before the National Square Dance Convention held that year in Long Beach, California. Osgood gathered together fifty of the most active and respected callers throughout the country. Jim Mayo wrote, "Most of those present at that meeting would also be present at the first CALLERLAB Convention a decade later."[4]

Jim Mayo, the first Chairman of the CALLERLAB board, wrote,

> The thirteen callers, who were members of the *Sets in Order* Hall of Fame in 1971, were: Lee Helsel, Arnie Kronenberger, Bob Van Antwerp, Marshall Flippo, Bruce Johnson, Frank Lane, Joe Lewis, Bob Page, Dave Taylor, Don Armstrong, Al Brundage, Earl Johnston, and Johnny LeClair. The first ten callers on that list and Bob Osgood attended the meeting in February of 1971 . . .[5]

That February meeting became the start of CALLERLAB's planning.

For more than three years, Flippo participated in the Gold Ribbon committee, "our own miniature think tanks,"[6] and this committee had "fifty square dance leaders."[7] This committee attempted to encourage some good solid guidelines in fifteen areas of square dance interest:

1. One Night Stands
2. The Basic Program of American Square Dancing
3. Extend Program of American Square Dancing
4. Caller/Teacher Leadership
5. Square Dance Caller Associations
6. Dancer Associations
7. Round Dance Leaders Associations
8. The Exploratory/Experimental Program of American Square Dancing
9. Research and Tradition
10. Square Dancing in Recreation
11. Square Dancing in the Schools
12. Getting the Word Out: Public Relations-Publicity-Promotion-

Advertising
13. Square Dance Publications
14. Square Dancing's Big Event
15. The Commercial Side of Square Dancing[8]

Bob Osgood published in *Sets in Order* a monthly report for each area, starting in December 1968, then the committee's final report was published in November 1969. The scope of the success and influence of this committee's work was gigantic. In fact, CALLERLAB was a by-product of this committee—both would change the future of square dancing around the world.

Flippo recalled, "In 1971, thar was eleven of us that kind of started it. They're all gone now except for Frank Lane and myself. [Frank and Flippo passed in 2018.] Dave Taylor just died here a while back. I kind of thank Bob Osgood was the main guy on this. I felt like he was the Pappy Shaw of our generation of our square dance life."

HALL OF FAMErs GATHER: In a unique celebration held February 7th, ten of the fourteen members of The American Square Dance Society's Hall of Fame gathered together at California's Asilomar Conference Grounds for a banquet and get-together. Present at the unusual session (and shown in the picture at the right) were Bob Page, Marshall Flippo, Ed Gilmore, Lee Helsel, Arnie Kronenberger, Bruce Johnson, Joe Lewis, Bob Van Antwerp, Dave Taylor, and Bob Osgood (for S.I.O.A.S.D.S). Also present but not shown - Frank Lane.

Hall of Famers met and become the original eleven callers who help form CALLERLAB. Source: Neeca Flippo

According to Jim Mayo,

Bob Osgood had believed for many years that a national organization of callers could exercise leadership that would benefit the square dance activity. Bob had also started a 'Hall of Fame' in his magazine. He had oil portraits painted by Gene Anthony of callers he felt were deserving of recognition for their contributions to square dancing. He then used the portraits as covers for his magazine. By 1970, he had inducted fourteen of the callers he respected most into his hall of fame. Many of the members of this group had also served on the staff of the square dance vacation institutes that Bob ran at the Asilomar conference facility near Monterey, California. It was this group that joined him in the initial stages of the formation of CALLERLAB.[9]

Flippo's association with Bob Osgood set him up to be a part of this pioneering group of callers.

They'd all talked about getting the *calls* standardized, but it was three or four years before it ever happened. They had caller's meetings at Asilomar and talk about it. This group of callers felt they had to do something, so Bob invited all those *callers*.[10]

CALLERLAB described the process, "It was decided that initial growth of the organization would be on a gradual basis and that each person selected for membership would be personally invited to attend one of the meetings and, having attended, would be included as a member."[11]

So, organizational meetings occurred in 1972 and 1973, and because Flippo attended one or more of these, he became one of twenty-five on the Board of Governors.

> Those twenty-five became the first CALLERLAB Board of Governors. They were: Don Armstrong, Al Brundage, Stan Burdick, Marshall Flippo, Cal Golden, C. O. Guest, Jerry Haag, Lee Helsel, Jerry Helt, Bruce Johnson, Earl Johnston, Arnie Kronenberger, Frank Lane, Jack Lasry, Johnny LeClair, Joe Lewis, Melton Luttrell, Jim Mayo, Angus McMorran, Bob Osgood, Bob Page, Vaughn Parrish, Bill Peters, Dave Taylor, and Bob Van Antwerp.[12]

Flippo was on the Board of Governors for ten years, "but I got off it and decided I'd never get back on it. I had enough. I wasn't much of a leader, Larada. I was just in thar, and I'd be real quiet. Sometimes I wouldn't say anythang the whole meeting." Flippo never envisioned himself as a leader—he helped get this organization off the ground and running but didn't want to participate in the governing anymore; however, he was a regular attendee right up until the 2018 CALLERLAB Convention, the year he died.

Note from Bob Van Antwerp about the Board of Governors. Source: Neeca Flippo

The Sets in Order AMERICAN SQUARE DANCE SOCIETY
462 NORTH ROBERTSON BLVD. • LOS ANGELES, CALIFORNIA 90048 • TELEPHONE: (213) 652-7434

publishers of SQUARE DANCING *magazine*

April 20, 1978

Mr. and Mrs. Marshall Flippo
1918 Marshall
Abilene, Texas 79605

Dear Marshall and Neeca,

Has anyone circulated a petition for your reelection to the
Board of Governors? In the event that they haven't, I would
indeed like the privilege. A good reason for the success to
this point of CALLERLAB has been its leadership. Each one of
the members of our Board of Governors is a different type of
individual. Some command respect because of their years in the
activity. Some are excellent speakers and others do a great
deal of work in teaching new callers. There are others, such
as yourself, who command so much respect simply because of the
continuing excellent work you do with your calling and with
your total involvement in the square dance activity. You would
be surprised at the great number of callers who are most impressed by a person such as yourself and what you do.

Over the years it has become more and more obvious to me that
the continued success of our group depends upon the versatility
and strength of our Board of Governors. You don't have to be
anything but Marshall Flippo and you will be contributing to
the credibility of our group. I think that you should run,
and, if for any reason a petition has not been submitted let me
know and I would consider it a distinct honor to handle it.
Whatever happens, do run for the office. If for any reason you
wouldn't be elected (and I can't see this happening) that would
be one thing. However, I feel that the members of CALLERLAB
need and want you. Let's give them that opportunity to vote.

Fondest regards to you both. You are very important people.

Bob Osgood

BO/bs

Letter from Bob Osgood. Source: Neeca Flippo

Why was CALLERLAB Formed?

CALLERLAB was to standardize square dancing across the country. "In a way,
I thank it was good and in a way, I thank it didn't happen the way I thought it
would."

Because a caller could go fifty miles, and call "Double the goose's neck," and
they'd be just perfect doing it. "Next town, they don't even know what the hell
you're talking about, so it was to standardize. I thank that came up probably more
than anythang. If it was only standardized."

Flippo wondered about CALLERLAB, "See, we were getting great, huge,
humungous classes at that time. I wonder if CALLERLAB hurt it, or did it? I
believe it might have. It could have made the longevity longer, you know. Anyway,
I thank, but it might have hurt it in a way like I go into a town and the guy
following me, he called the same type of dance. So now you went in, at that time,
you went in as a person, but now you go in as 'He's a *Mainstream*[13] *caller* or *Plus*[14]
caller or, at best, *caller*.' They still used your name, but it's just incidental."

Flippo referred to going to Cisco, Texas, to dance to Melton. At Cisco, when
they would walk around their corner, they'd go in front of her and come back, and

it would be like a now days *dosado*[15] your partner. In other words, they'd go in front of the corner, not around behind her like a *seesaw*.[16] "Thangs like that, little thangs like that. Hand holds—hands up and hands down. We talked a lot about styling in square dancing. What was in the book or what was in CALLERLAB never did catch on. You'd go someplace and the hands would be down, and some places hands would be up. It's still that way. Some *callers* used it, and you could tell their dancers had some styling. If I knew enough about it, we could do a chapter on styling. I'm not the guy to do that, though."

"I really don't know how to word it. Nowadays you can go most anywhere and call a dance, but at one time, *callers* were hired for their name and the way they did thangs. Now they kind of evolved into they would hire them for what level they taught. And still, the name meant somethang, but it didn't."

When Flippo hired *callers* into Abilene before CALLERLAB, he did it because of their name. After they finished Beginner class, Betty Casey hired Joe Lewis to come down and call a new dancers' dance. They did most of the stuff he did because she gave him a list of what they could do. This was before CALLERLAB. He called something, and Flippo remembered the square he was in but he couldn't remember the call. The dancers were all trying to *figure*[17]—"well, do you go this way? No, no, no, you go the other way. You go two hands and then you turn back." So they were trying to get that figured out, and some of the floor did it, and he walked through it, and they couldn't even walk through it from what he said. Other than Flippo's class, there were a bunch of other people there because of Joe Lewis's name and popularity.

During a *caller*'s meeting at Asilomar in 1972, a negotiation happened over a dispute in some square dance vocabulary. Frank Lane worried about how the new call, *Star Thru*,[18] which had been invented in 1962, would affect the familiar *Star figures*.[19] Because of his concern, he called the same move, *Snaparoo*.[20] Another new call had been introduced, *Barge Thru*, which Flippo described as "*square thru*[21] *four and then you'd pass through in the middle.*"

By 1969, the *Trade By*[22] call had been deemed a useful piece of choreography and named, but doing this eliminated the use of the call, *Barge Thru*,[23] for most *callers*; however, Marshall Flippo stuck with it.

According to Jim Mayo,

> At this 1972 meeting, there was considerable discussion of the need for standardization. In the heat of the discussion, Marshall asked Frank Lane when he was going to quit calling *Snaparoo*. His response was 'As soon as you quit calling *Barge Thru*.' Marshall said 'Deal!' and they both lived by the agreement thereafter.[24]

Flippo told his side of this story about the *caller*'s meeting at Asilomar, "At that, we had all types of meetings. Osgood would have a town hall meeting. *Callers* would have meetings. Seamstresses would have meetings, so it was kind of like that at Asilomar. So, we had a *caller* meeting one time. Frank Lane and I were doing the week, and he was, of course, the leader."

With a chuckle, Flip added, "He was a born leader. At that time, thar's a thang come out called a *Barge Thru*. If you said, *Barge Thru*, it's kinda like *square thru four and then Trade By*. So, at that time, you said, *Barge Thru*, then you sung the words of the song as they were doing the *Barge Thru*. Jerry Haag had a call, I don't have an idee what the name of this call was, but he had a call out at that time that had *Barge Thru* in it.

"*Star Thru* came out at the same Nationals as *Snaparoo* in one hall. At the same time, somebody was calling, I thank it was Les Gotcher, and he called it *Star Thru* in the other room. I thank it might have been Red Warrick, introduced it as *Snaparoo*. So thar became a good big ole debate about that, and finally we all decided we'd stick with *Star Thru*."

Frank Lane commented, 'That's ruining all your *Star figures* when you call it *Star Thru*."

Flip felt Frank was absolutely a hundred percent correct. And so, he stayed with *Snaparoo*. He'd tell people at the dance, "Now when I say *Snaparoo*, it's the same as a *Star Thru*. Don't let it bother you."

So they're having this meeting and Frank was the leader of the meeting. "If you know Frank Lane, it's hard to beat him. I've got a couple other funny stories. I worked with him a long time. Anyway, Frank was the oldest biddy, looked right at me."

And Frank added, "Now, we got *Trade By*."

That was just when *Trade By* came out. So, in other words, *Barge Thru*—you'd *square through four and then you'd pass through the middle,* which is a *Trade By*, basically.

Flippo laughed, "And anyway, I called him, '*Barge Thru!*'"

Frank continued, "Now folks, we've got the *Trade By* down. I don't suppose we ever use that 1/2 *Barge Thru*, 3/4 *Barge Thru*, *Barge Thru* again. Most of us have stopped."

Flip added, "And he looked right at me."

Frank stated, "Some people are still calling it!"

"Yeah, some people are still calling it *Snaparoo*," Flippo responded. To me, he said, "Well, Jesus! I only got him two times that I know of. No, three times, but that was one of them."

Frank stated, "My God, I'll quit if you will."

So Flippo cheated a little. "I still called that call a little bit 'cause I liked to say, 'Bar that fellow.'" Not sure what that meant!

So, Frank came to Kirkwood back in the fall. The *Caller* meeting was in February at Asilomar, and he came there in June, and Flippo watched him close to see if he called *Snaparoo*, but he didn't. He called *Star Thru* all week long. So, he came back in September, and he called *Star Thru* again. So, Flippo took him aside.

Flippo asked, "Frank, haven't you ever called a *Snaparoo*?"

"One time I fouled up. I called it, apologized to people."

He asked Flip, "What about your *Barge Thru*?"

"Well, I can tell you I continued on."

Frank exclaimed, "You continued on! I spent all my time not trying to call *Snaparoo*."

Flippo and Frank continued to have fun with *Snaparoo*. "So precisely was the calling, so definite the instructions, that even Lane's *Snaparoo* immediately translates itself into a *Star Thru* and Flippo's *Flip-Flop*[25] becomes a double *Star Thru*. We liked it!"[26]

Flippo returned to the topic of *Snaparoo* and a *caller* named Zelmer Hovland. I was so excited to hear his name because I knew him when I was growing up. Zelmer married Marvin Schilling's widow, Ada Mae [Corky], and became a family friend.

Zelmer and Frank had a week at Kirkwood with Flippo, and they agreed that they might lose their *Star Figures*, using the name, *Star Thru*, instead of *Snaparoo*.

This controversy existed in the wider square dance world outside of CALLER-LAB, and so Frank called it *Snaparoo*. Six months later, their paths crossed on tour, and Zelmer was calling *Star Thru*.

First CALLERLAB Convention

Source: Neeca Flippo

Bob Osgood's dream came true! The first CALLERLAB convention was held in 1974. Their first meeting—when everybody was invited—was in St. Louis, Missouri. Callers were invited to join, so at one time, CALLERLAB had a lot of *callers* in it.

"It didn't go the way I thought that it would, hoped it would, but I just don't know if it was a good thang for square dancing or square dancing would still be alive. I mean—would we have a lot more people than what we got now if we had not had CALLERLAB? That's been discussed over the years, I thank. Did CALLERLAB help or did it hinder? And I thank it helped really in a great way, and in a somewhat smaller way, it hindered square dancing because, you know, when we took lessons, we took ten lessons, and we were square dancers. And we could go out and dance most anywhere fairly good."

Today it takes twenty to twenty-five weeks to learn the *Basic*[27] level of square dancing.

In reference to the first CALLERLAB Convention, Flippo was probably biased. Pappy Shaw had died, but Dorothy Shaw was there, and she gave a speech.

He said that she talked on for about an hour and half, but it was good. Dave Taylor was up on the stage. They had the Board of Governors all seated up there, and "ole Dorothy" goes into this long speech. Dave Taylor had to go to the bathroom, and so he thought, 'Well, I hate to get up and all sitting up thar. Everyone is going to see me get up and leave,' so he kind of slipped out of his chair and was crawling, and he got around and turned around the corner, and he ran head-on into somebody else. Flippo couldn't remember who that was. They were both headed to the restroom. "She talked and talked and talked. Bless her heart, but we were proud! This bunch that showed up thar—thar's quite a few for our first convention."

So, they had some *callers* that were really smart about square dancing. Flippo was on the Board of Governors and was amazed at the ability and the know-how of some of the *callers*.

Flippo wrestled with the CALLERLAB's value several times during our conversation. "I really thank CALLERLAB was good for square dancing or maybe it wasn't that good. Or maybe it shouldn't have been so standardized or whatever. We had weekends of stuff like that at that time and we'd have lots of people, like I worked with Brundage before CALLERLAB and, of course, with Frank Lane before CALLERLAB, and we got by alright."

Flippo laughed, "I don't know now looking back on it."

The Lists

CALLERLAB'S standardization divided the square dance *calls* into separate lists at five different levels, with each level becoming more difficult. It started with *Basic* and then *Mainstream*. Originally, they had *Plus 1* and *Plus 2* but consolidated into *Plus*.[28] Then they had *A1* and *A2* with the A standing for *Advanced*.[29] The last level was *Challenge*[30] divided into five levels. Today we still dance and teach these levels.

This topic was hard for Flip. "Geez, this is tedious." So, when the list came out and everybody was teaching the same things, it became easier for a *caller* to go someplace and they say, "Now we want *Mainstream*." Then he knew they could probably dance *Mainstream* pretty well.

Pretty soon they were hiring *callers* for the level they could call, and a lot of the festival were all *Mainstream*, and then *Plus* got in there and most of them now are *Plus*. "So, damn, I can't say it the way I want to say it."

But once the list came out, it seemed all the *callers* began to call the exact same things. "Basically, if you hired one *caller*, the next *caller* you hired would call basically what the other *caller* called. Do you see what I mean? Before . . . it seems like they hired *callers* for their name and how they called . . . so pretty soon, they were hiring them for their level instead of for their name."

After the lists came out, Flippo remembered that he was to call over in Lubbock, Texas. "Man, I knew those guys over thar were good dancers, so I made up a whole dance of stuff that I wanted to call. Well, when I got over thar, I started calling. Well, I thought they could do what I had written down, but every time I'd try somethang, it would go under. I knew the first tip that they weren't going to be able to dance what I had written down and what I thought they could dance, so I had to kind of fall back on really what I thought they could do. It was tedious for a *caller* in a way to go somewhere without the list."

How the Standardization Progressed

"They've [*Callers* in CALLERLAB] fought over these lists all these years and changed them and changed them. Took some [*calls*] off and put some on. We used to have quarterlies [specific calls]. Some of them hung around, and some of them didn't. It seems like if we had one list, you could have took the *Mainstream* list, and if *callers* would have worked on it, you could have called a just umpteen different variations of some of the figures in the *Mainstream* that would be hard, so I'm not as sure.

Maybe, I thank, maybe the lists were a good thang. At times, I thank, and at times I thank, 'Oh, maybe the lists what screwed it up.' But I don't thank it would have stayed without CALLERLAB. I don't thank that it had a whip to do with square dancing falling off. I thank this society and the thangs that come. People with different interests. I thank that's what really knocked it down."

Looking Back Before CALLERLAB

"In fact, back in the early '50s when bowling came in, everybody and their dog were bowling, and we were so sad. I thought it, and we all thought it; that square dancing would go on forever 'cause everybody was bowling, you know."

So, square dancing survived that, and then there was a big dip, but it came back pretty good through the '60s, '70s, and '80s. Then it started dropping again in the '90s when the computers, cell phones, and smartphones came out. People rushed home to get to their computers to check email, connect on Facebook, shop, or send messages to somebody instead of square dancing.

Flippo didn't believe CALLERLAB had anything to do "with the way that square dancing is now. In fact, I feel like it's just survived this big ole dip that it's been in for twenty years. I thank it's going to survive it. Somebody once told me, 'Flippo, it's not going to go away. It'll end up just like folk dancing. You'll see little splotches here, little splotches thar like folk dancing. That's the way that square dancing will eventually end up.' But I don't thank so. Just look at Indio, California. Thar's some big festivals. Now, you know, we had big ones. Washington, D.C. Spring Festival for seventeen years. And at that time, we'd have anywhere from 4500 to 5000 dancers for the weekend."

The sad part is we have nothing that big now, not even the Nationals, "but you still got—good Lord—you got the hundred and some odd squares at Indio. What gets me now is some of the festivals are well attended." Flip wondered where the dancers come from, and guessed they came from small towns that have just one or two squares. "God, I don't know. I wish I knew; I'd be rich! But I believe square dancing is going to live. I don't thank it will die out like the guy told me that it would die out like folk dancing, but it might. It's funny."

Flippo recalled he had two squares in the class in Tucson, Arizona about three or four years ago in a Beginner Class. Every one of them showed up every time, and they seemed so exuberant about it. He graduated them and never saw "a-one of them again! Not one! I just wish I knew what the problem was and how to beat it."

Flippo's statement, "We took ten lessons, and we were square dancers" demonstrated the evolution in square dancing. Today's weekly lessons average four and a half months—a far cry from ten weeks.

He responded, "Yeah, that's about all you had to do. You know, Betty taught four or five classes a year because if you just did ten lessons, you had two and a half months. She could teach another class, and that's what I did when I first started calling. I'd teach a class, and two weeks later, I would start a new class. So that way, I thank, we got too uppity, uppity or somethang."

Looking back, CALLERLAB came up in fourteen interviews with Flippo, a topic he loved to talk about yet wrestled with often. No matter what, he loved it!

Banquets are a major part of the CALLERLAB Convention. 1st: L to R: Neeca and Flippo. 2nd: L to R Jon Jones and Neeca. Source: Neeca Flippo

Flippo and Neeca at a CALLERLAB banquet. Source: Neeca Flippo

ALL WAS NOT SERIOUS BUSINESS as you can see from the head table shot of Neeca and Marshall Flippo and Dave Taylor. —All Photos by Haines

4th CALLERLAB Convention. Neeca, Flippo and Dave Taylor enjoying a moment. Source: *Sets in Order*, June 1977

OVER 800 — COUNT 'EM, 800 — CALLERS/SPOUSES AT CALLERLAB CONVENTION
The biggest event of its kind, held at the Marriott Motor Inn in Chicago in April, produced history-making decisions, all of which will be reported in the following story and in issues to come. "Professional Responsibility" was the theme.

600 Husbands and wives attended CALLERLAB in Chicago, Illinois. Source: Neeca Flippo

Board of Governors & wives, CALLERLAB convention. Source: Neeca Flippo

Incoming and Outgoing Board of Governors and wives. Source: Neeca Flippo

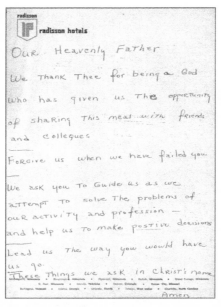

Flippo said grace for one of the CALLERLAB Convention banquets.
Source: Neeca Flippo

Flippo and Keiko Hirago at the CALLERLAB Convention in Los
Angeles, California 2008. Source: Masaharu "Doc" Hiraga

1. CALLERLAB Web Site: http://www.callerlab.org/
2. International Association of Square Dance Callers, 2020, http://www.callerlab.org/
3. Patrick Demerath, *American Square Dance,* (July 2008): 19-20.
4. Jim Mayo, *Step by Step Through Modern Square Dance History* (2003): 75-76.
5. Jim Mayo, *Step by Step Through Modern Square Dance History* (2003): 98.
6. Bob Osgood, *As I Saw It* (2017): 2808 E-book version
7. Bob Osgood, *As I Saw It* (2017): 2808 E-book version
8. Bob Osgood, *Sets in Order* (November, 1969): 12-30.
9. Jim Mayo, *Step by Step Through Modern Square Dance History* (2003): 95.

10. **Caller** — A person who prompts dance figures in such dances as line dance, square dance, and contra dance.
11. International Association of Square Dance Callers, 2020, http://www.callerlab.org/For-The-Public
12. Jim Mayo, *Step by Step Through Modern Square Dance History* (2003): 100.
13. **Mainstream** — The CALLERLAB program after Basic, adding seventeen new calls.
14. **Plus** — The CALLERLAB program after Mainstream, adding twenty-nine new calls.
15. **Dosado** — Walking a smooth circular path, dancers walk forward, passing right shoulders, slide sideways to the right, walk backward, passing left shoulders, and slide slightly to the left to return to their starting position.
16. **Seesaw** — Men face partner (usually returning to home position from doing an All Around the Left Hand Lady) and pass by left shoulders as ladies move into the center. Men loop to the left around partner and walk forward to starting position as ladies move back out to place.
17. **Figure** — almost always causes each woman to progress to a new man. Once this has happened, she temporarily takes on the Head/Side identity and home position of that man.
18. **Star Thru** — Man places his right hand against woman's left hand, palm to palm with fingers up, to make an arch. As the dancers move forward, the woman does a one quarter (90 degrees) left face turn under the arch, while the man does a one quarter (90 degrees) turn to the right moving past the woman.
19. **Star Figures** — The designated dancers form a star by stepping forward if necessary and placing the appropriate hand in the center of the formation. Forming the star may require a dancer to individually turn in place up to 3/8 of a turn. Dancers turn the star by walking forward in a circle around the center of the star. The distance traveled may be specified in fractions of a star full around, or until some condition is met (e.g., Men Center Left Hand Star, Pick Up Your Partner with an Arm Around, Star Promenade).
20. **Snaparoo** — What Frank Lane called a *Star Thru*. Man places his right hand against woman's left hand, palm to palm with fingers up, to make an arch. As the dancers move forward, the woman does a one quarter (90 degrees) left face turn under the arch, while the man does a one quarter (90 degrees) turn to the right moving past the woman.
21. **Square Thru Four** — Right Pull By (Square Thru 1 has been completed); Face partner and Left Pull By (Square Thru 2 has been completed); Face partner and Right Pull By (Square Thru 3 has been completed); and Face partner and Left Pull By (Square Thru 4 has been completed). Ending formation: Back-to-Back Couples.
22. **Trade By** — The couples facing each other pass thru, the couples facing out do a partner trade to face in.
23. **Barge Thru** — Square through four and then you'd pass through in the middle.
24. Jim Mayo, *Step by Step Through Modern Square Dance History* (2003): 101.
25. **Flip-flop** — Unknown call.
26. Bob Osgood, *Sets in Order* (April 1966): 12.
27. **Basic** — The beginning CALLERLAB program with fifty-one calls.
28. **Plus** — The CALLERLAB program after Mainstream, adding twenty-nine new calls.
29. **Advanced** - The next CALLERLAB program of square dancing after the Plus Program. In addition to the Mainstream and Plus calls, Advanced dancers and callers are responsible for knowing an additional group of calls divided in A1 and A2 lists.
30. **Challenge** — The CALLERLAB program after Advanced which has five levels, the most difficult level of square dancing ranging from C1 (easiest) to C2, C3A, C3B (also called just C3 or full C3) and C4 (most difficult).

FLIPPO'S INTERNATIONAL CALLING EXPERIENCES

M arshall Flippo became a worldwide hit as a square dance *caller*[1] and enjoyed memorable experiences on international trips and cruises. He traveled to Japan and Germany several times. He trekked to Spain, Morocco, and Majorca on one trip and also England. He also took numerous cruises with a variety of callers. Even though Flip saw the world through these trips, he was calling and working.

See a list of international travel and cruises in Appendix D.

Japan

"I kind of had a love affair with Japan. When I started going over thar as a *caller*, I had stood over a year down at Yokosuka after the war, and they treated you like their kinfolk. I mean, they just treated you so good, it was unbelievable."

After two trips to Japan after the war as occupational forces, Flippo returned to Japan as a square dance *caller* and continued a long love affair with the Japanese. When asked how many times he called in Japan, he remembered a trip right after the war in the Navy. Then he made another trip after the war to the same place, but he couldn't recall how many square dance trips. Flip did remember going with Neeca once "'cause I remember us getting sick on the way back—yeah, food poisoning." He went over

Flippo calling in Japan. Source: Neeca Flippo

there with Gary and Ken. Flip finally settled on four or five times total and as far as square dancing goes, three or four times.

Matt Asanuma, a Japanese *caller*, first booked Flippo in Japan. "He's dead now."

That was Flippo's first trip with square dancing. The Japanese dancers understood "our lingo," because they were taught to dance in English, and so Flip had no trouble calling, but he had to use square dance *calls*. "I couldn't say, 'Walk by somebody.' I'd have to say, '*Pass by somebody*,' 'cause they didn't understand the word, 'Walk.' Very seldom they would not understand me."

The first day Flippo arrived in Japan, they danced in the afternoon. They had a bunch of square dancers at that time.

Matt announced to Flip the Prince would be there in about thirty minutes, and the Prince only knew about twenty *Basics*.[2] "The Prince is NOT going to break down. Do not let him falter. You stay within those twenty *Basics*."

Matt added, "We'll all dance what he wants. He won't stay but about twenty minutes. Call a tip, and he'll probably be out of there, but don't call anything so damn hard that he can't do it."

And his wife at that time could not be seen in public. Flippo didn't know why, but it's changed since then. "I 'member that afternoon almost like it was today. I called to them, and he came in."

Matt stressed to Flippo, "Don't call anything that he can't do. We'll put him in our best square, and he will NOT BREAK DOWN. He'll probably be here only one tip."

1st L to R: Flippo, Neeca and the late Prince Mikasa. 2nd: Neeca dancing with the late Prince Mikasa. Source: Masaharu "Doc" Hiraga & Neeca Flippo

Well, he stayed two hours, and all these really, really good dancers just smiled about it. They didn't mind. "Boy, they just danced along with twenty *Basics* for two damn hours. And they came after he left and said, 'We're sorry about that.'"

Flippo answered, "Well, I betcha you are, too."

"Oh, no, no, no. We had fun. We had fun. We like to dance."

Flip and Matt both thought the Prince would leave earlier, but Matt said, "He is having a good time."

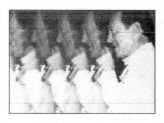

10 hours of non-stop calling. Flippo said, "I should have been quintuplets! Source: Neeca Flippo

PROGRAM SCHEDULE   No.

	MC	Feb-11		MC	Feb-12	
11:00	Moto	Moto		Matt	Matt	
		Marshall			Marshall	
12:00		Marshall			Marshall	
		Marshall			Marshall	
13:00	Okada	Okada	Lunch for Marshall & Neeca (with Moto & Matt)	Okada	Suzuki Kazuo	Lunch for Marshall & Neeca (with Tokuko & Kumada)
		Watanuki			Kawaguchi	
		Ogura			Hosokawa	
		Ito			Nakajima	
14:00		Tajima		Moto	Marshall	
	Matt	Marshall			Wada	Prince Mikasa joins
		Marshall			Tac	
15:00		Marshall			Marshall	
	Moto	Lofty		Matt	CEREMONY	
		Marshall			"	
16:00		Marshall			Marshall	
		Ojima			Marshall	
		Marshall			Marshall	
17:00		Marshall			Marshall	
	Matt	Matt	Supper for Marshall & Neeca (with Kumada & Moto)	Moto	Moto	Supper for Marshall & Neeca (with Matt & Tokuko)
		Tanaka			Ando	
18:00		Suzuki Tsuneo			Kurosu	
		Mitchell			Hara	
		Sakai			Horie	
19:00		Marshall			Marshall	
	Moto	Marshall		Matt	Marshall	
		Marshall			Marshall	
20:00		Moto with Matt			Matt with Moto	
		Marshall			Marshall	
		Marshall			Marshall	
21:00		Marshall				

(Subject to change with prior notice)

Caller's Schedule for Flippo's trip to Japan 1983. Source: Neeca Flippo

Look at the rigorous schedule Flippo followed when he called in Japan and note when the Prince was supposed to be there. Flippo added, "It's the Japanese *callers* on thar, too. It looked like they called during the lunch break."

The next morning, Flip met with the Prince at "a big shot affair anyway. The mayor, the equivalent of a mayor, and I knew we were in this big hall. A lot of people thar. And so, they started questioning me, you know, about square dancing and everythang."

Then they asked Flip if he had ever been to Japan before.

Flippo avoided their question because he had been there twice but hated to say anything about the war. "So anyway, they were very, very, very nice and polite, you know. They were bowing and smiling and bowing and smiling. They are really nice people, and they treated us like we were long lost friends, so it was nice."

Flippo and Neeca with a Japanese family. Source: Neeca Flippo

While in Japan, Neeca and Flip enjoyed meals with different hosts each meal.

❧

Neeca and Flippo were on the way home out of Tokyo and were the only Americans on the plane. They had put them in Business Class—in-between regular and First Class—in two real nice seats together. "Nobody around us. We could look back and looked like a million Japanese all sitting thar and a great big ole plane. So, someone asked us if we wanted Japanese food or American."

They decided on American.

So, they brought Neeca and Flippo a filet with brown gravy on it. Flip planned to watch a movie after they ate, "'cause the screen was right thar ahead of me. I had earphones and everythang they'd given me. And so did Neeca."

Neeca went to sleep.

Then Flip put the earphones on, and they were in the air. "And all of a sudden, man, I tell you, I was sick as a horse."

238

And he didn't know where any restroom was, so Flip walked all the way to the back, went to the restroom there, and vomited. When he returned to his seat, he still felt bad. So, he got up again and looked for a closer restroom and found one right around the corner.

It was night time, and most people were asleep. He ended up going four or five times before Neeca woke up.

Then she asked about the movie.

"I don't know. I haven't been watching."

And she questioned, "What's wrong?"

Flippo answered, "I believe if it's the food, you're going find out." Then she had it worse than Flip. They had left their car in San Francisco with Mary Sheehan at the time, and she met them at the airport. By then, Flippo was starting to get over his sickness, and Neeca was still really sick.

Neeca asked, "Mary, if you see a convenience store, be sure to pull into it. I don't think . . ."

So, they stopped two or three times before "Mary had us to a motel."

Flippo asked for a room with two bathrooms—but they didn't have one!

That was a Monday morning, and Flippo was to call with Dick Houlton that night. He was well enough to go call, but Neeca was still sick. Mary got them to the motel, and it was more dangerous than what they knew. They should have called a doctor because it was probably food poisoning. Neeca started getting over it Tuesday morning, and it was a trip to Japan they never forgot.

Flippo felt the Japanese just treated him like he was family. They went out at night after one dance. "They don't ever sit on a chair, and there were three rings deep around a pretty big hall." Flippo and Neeca were up in the front ring and it went around all the way around, with everyone sitting on the floor.

They were eating raw fish, and Flippo got a piece of "a big ole crab meat, you know, uncooked. He asked a guy which one he should take. "He's kinda funny guy anyway."

He directed, "Take that piece right there. Get that piece right there."

Flip took that piece, put it in my mouth, "and pretty soon, that thang got so damn big, and all the Japanese seemed to get it, so they're all looking at me. And they started laughing like hell, and I finally take it and spit it out. It's as big as a baseball."

It was just some kind of "octopus thang. But it's part of an octopus. But instead of getting smaller, it got bigger, and they were laughing, but we had a lot of fun with it."

He ended this story, "Oh, they accepted us so well. It was just a wonderful trip, and that was the first time that I went back over thar after I'd been over thar, you know, a long while at Yokosuka on a ship."

Letter to the editor of *Sets in Order*

Dear Editor:

Thank you for the article in the April magazine about our trip to Japan. Everyone there was great to us. We especially wish to thank Mrs. Sekiko Yamaguchi and Mr. Mitchell Osawa, contacts for the Kyoto club, also the Tokyo Fukyukai Square Dance Club and Motohiro Yoshimura and Matt Asanuma for the dance in Tokyo and Miss Tokuko Yasuraoka our translator.

Neeca and Marshall Flippo
Abilene, Texas

Sets In Order Cover, Japan Diary, April 1983 about Flippo and Neeca's trip & Letter to Editor, *Sets in Order*. Source: Neeca Flippo

Flippo and Neeca's trip to Japan 1983. Source: Neeca Flippo

Two escorts, Neeca and Flippo preparing to ride the Bullet. What
surprised Flippo? Source: Neeca Flippo

241

10 hours of non-stop calling. Flippo said, "I should have been quintuplets! Source: Neeca Flippo

Neeca and Flippo with group. Source: Neeca Flippo

April 1, 1986

To: Mr. and Mrs. Marshall Flippo

Kon Ni Chi Wa!!
Go Ki Gen Ika Ga De Su Ka?

The cherry blossoms are in full bloom and it is the beautiful
spring season here in Japan. How is it for you at Kirkwood?

In February Mr. Bronc Wise of Hi-Hat records came to Japan and
treated us to some great calling before returning to the U.S.
He told us that that are many callers in the world, but there
are none better than Marshall Flippo!!

In February 1987 Mr. Gary Shoemake will be coming to Japan with
a tour group, and will be calling for our club's 30th
Anniversary Jamboree. As you may recall, he was among the four
or five callers you recommended to us as being exciting callers
when you were here in Japan. On this basis we contacted Gary
and arranged for him to come in 1987. On our advertising for
this jamboree we have included the following:

                    Gary Shoemake
The man who was highly recommended by the great Marshall Flippo!

Letter about Gary Shoemake. Source: Neeca Flippo

Flippo returned a couple times with the Chaparral Record Label "boys," Gary Shoemake, Ken Bower, and Jerry Haag, but he couldn't remember if Beryl Main ever went with them before he died. Gary said Beryl had already died before they traveled to Japan.

There's a lady now who books *callers* to come to Japan, Martha Ogasawara, who is fluent in Japanese. She was American, but she now lives in Japan.

Flippo loved his experiences with "The Boys" in Japan. One trip started with Ken having a broken leg. Dee told Ken, "Now, you've got that beautiful motorcycle, and you've been riding it around and around. They're having a motorcycle safety class. I want you to go out there and find out about the safety when you're riding a motorcycle," so he went, and the first thing he did was lay his bike over on his leg—it broke his leg.

So, they were headed to Japan in a couple days, and Ken was in a cast. They were seated in business class for the flight. Flippo was sitting next to Ken, and Gary was sitting over next to Jerry Haag, and Ken was really in pain. Flip felt so sorry for him.

Ken exclaimed, "Flippo, I don't know if I can stand this or not."

So they stopped the stewardess as she came by, and she was really helpful to him. She did everything she thought she could do, but he was still in pain, so she came up with a possible solution— "I'm going to put some ice down his cast. Can we get the cast far enough apart to drop some ice down in there?" And so, they worked around and slipped some ice down, and it relieved the pain. "Boy, he was glad of that."

When they got to Japan, Gary and Flip roomed together, and Jerry was with Ken. Flippo thought they stayed at a Radisson, but he wasn't sure because they stayed in different hotels each trip.

Of course, Ken had to have a wheelchair, so Jerry was pushing him everywhere. Ken would take a crutch with him so he could hobble along when he got out of the wheelchair. So, sitting in the chair, he'd point with that crutch, say, "Take me over there. Take me over there. Take me over there. Take me over there.'"

Jerry shared, "At times, I get so tired of that guy, I don't know what to do. He's making me push him everywhere." So one morning, they were going downstairs, "and—yep, Jerry and Ken were ahead of us, Gary and me."

So, Jerry came into our room.

He stated, "I fixed that son of a gun."

With a laugh, Flippo asked him what he did.

"Well, Ken pointed over and said, 'Let's get out this door,' and he pointed over to the elevator and said, 'Take me over to the elevator.' So, a little while later, I just pushed him where he's facing the back wall, and I stepped out of the elevator and pushed every button I could on the way out."

Later on, they found out that some Japanese dancers were getting on the elevator to go downstairs. They talked a little English, and so Ken thought Jerry was still behind him, so he's still talking to Jerry, and finally one of the little Japanese says, "Ah, Mr. Bower, I don't think Mr. Haag is on here."

So they helped Ken out of the elevator and got him down to the bottom of the steps. There was a ramp that they could push him up, so "four of those little

Japanese got behind him. Big ole boy, anyway, so they get almost to the top, and then they couldn't get it any farther. They'd go back down to the bottom, so they finally got enough Japanese on thar, they'd get him all the way up."

Another time on this trip they went in to eat and were seated at a big round table, and so, "of course, they eat a lot of rice over thar, so everybody had a bowl of rice in front of them, and Ken started putting sugar on his."

The Japanese exclaimed, "No! No, no, no!"

Later on, they had some coffee, and the Japanese dancers with them ordered coffee at the end of the table. They started putting sugar in the coffee, "and that's when ole Ken got 'em back."

He protested, "Oh, no! No!"

Flippo recalled a breakfast one morning but couldn't remember if it was Tokyo or where it was. "I'll have to try to find out about that."

He sang the word hotel, "We's at a little ole hotel, and the guys got up early and had breakfast, and the waitress couldn't understand them, and they couldn't understand her. And so they ordered. Everyone of 'em got eggs and bacon, I thank."

But they all had ordered different things. So Flip went down for breakfast by himself, and a lady came by and couldn't understand him, and so he got eggs and bacon, too.

Then, the guys came back and Flippo was sitting in the lobby of "this little ole hotel, and I's reading the Japanese paper."

One of the guys asked, "What the hell are you reading?"

Flippo answered, "Japanese paper."

He explained, "Well, they didn't know anythang else."

But he stated, "Well, you dumb shit. You've got it upside down."

Flip ended his Japanese memories with a deep laugh and shared in our last conversation, "But anyway, little ole thangs like that I'll try to remember."

The Love Affair Was Mutual

In 1994 Martha Ogasawara wrote in an article, "Out of the American callers popular then, Marshall Flippo probably had the most influence on Japanese *callers*. Everyone slavishly imitated his style of calling, and to this day, many older callers call with a Japanese/Texan accent."[3]

The Japanese people loved Flippo. I connected with one of Flippo's friends, a Japanese caller named Masaharu Hiraga, for information and mementos from Flippo's times in Japan. He was incredibly helpful, contacting several people who knew Flippo throughout Japan and sending me their photos and stories of Flippo.

"I talked to Mitchell Osawa, one of the top callers in Japan. He remembered before the Fukyuukai's [One of the oldest square dancing clubs in Japan. "Square Stars" is its other name.] thirtieth [anniversary] party, Marshall did go to Kyoto to call to the West Japan dancers. Mr. Osawa is one of the Japanese callers who appeared in the *Sets in Order* Magazine's Premium LP in 1980. He, with one of his supporters, Sekiko Yamaguchi, had a lunch together before the afternoon dance. There, Marshall's jokes made the whole dances up!

"One of his [Flippo's] funny actions [was] to give a kiss on the back of his hand [when shaking hands]. The male caller, Mitchell, was a little twisted. He [Flippo] didn't kiss Mitchell's but on his own hand. That joke was used over and over since then. Marshall was a guy who loved to makes the dancers laugh. I understand he and his wife went back to Tokyo to call the night by the bullet train."

Masaharu added a note about the prince Flippo called to: "The Prince Mikasa is a short name of Takahito Mikasa as one of the members of the Imperial family. He was one of the Emperor Hirohito's brothers who was in charge of the Recreational activities of the nation."

"He [Marshall] grabbed the Japanese dancers' mind in the later half of the 1980s because of his great calls with his talented ability to make people (even Japanese dancers who understand his English only five percent) laugh."

1st Row L to R: Special Flippo memorabilia from Ms. Fukuyo Asaga, Flippo, Neeca and the Prince Mikasa. 2nd Row L to r: The CALLERLAB Milestone Award recipient Masaru Wada and Mitchell Osawa were well known Japanese callers who also joined the party to enjoy the dance with the Prince Mikasa, note from Flippo. 3rd Row: More memorabilia. Source: Masaharu "Doc" Hiraga.

Fun badge created for Flippo in 1983. Source: Masaharu "Doc" Hiraga

Germany

Flippo traveled three times to Germany with Tom and Gina Crisp as one of the calling staff. Once when he was still married to his second wife and two by himself. Flip couldn't remember which city they flew into, "basically the trips were the same all three times. They really were well-planned. Tom had married a German girl. He was over in Germany a long time, and so he's still calling here in Tucson."

The first time Flippo went over, they only had one bus, and the next two times he went, they had two buses. He knew he went with the Chaparral boys once, but he wasn't sure about the other trips. "They're a lot of fun, well-planned."

Tom Crisp clarified Flippo's trips to Germany. "We took Flip three times to Germany, first in 2002. We were scheduled for 2001 but had to cancel because of 9/11. He went again in 2007 with Jerry Haag, Ken Bower, and Gary Shoemake. We took them all again the next year in 2008. All three were sell-outs."

Spain, Morocco, & Majorca

Spain, Morocco, Majorca trip with Marshall & Neeca Page and Bob & Nita Page. Source: Neeca Flippo

Neeca and Flippo went to Spain, Morocco, and Majorca with Bob and Nita Page, and the Pages put them on as secondary, so they didn't have to pay anything. The trip lasted about eight days, and they stayed in Madrid. "Oh, yeah, I had to go back. I had to fly all by myself out of Spain to New York City, and our car was thar. I had to drive somewhere because I had to be back because I had some dates that I had to be thar on."

But Neeca stayed with the tour, and they took a ferry to Africa where Neeca rode a camel.

They were in Spain during the Easter weekend, and these travelers heard about an Easter parade. Now Whitey and Gladys Puerling from Trenton, very close friends of Flippo's, joined him on this trip, and they palled around with them. So the group decided they wanted to go to the Easter parade. A bunch of them went where they thought it would be and didn't see anybody lined up ready for a parade.

It didn't look like the parade was going to be there because five streets came into this one intersection, and a cop stood on a pedestal out in the middle of it, like a five-point star, directing traffic for all those streets.

So, Whitey stated, "I'll go out there and ask that guy where the parade is."

And Gladys disagreed, "Whitey, you can't go out there. He's out there directing traffic."

"I don't care. He'll probably know where it is."

Flippo chuckled as he remembered this scene.

So, Whitey directed, "Come on, Flippo. Let's f**k your luck."

"I thank I'll stay here."

Then Flippo added, "You can't ask that policeman. He don't talk English and you don't talk Spanish."

He commented, "I bet he'll understand me."

So, Whitey and Flippo went out there, and the policeman kept looking at them, finally he took a little break and he asked them how he could help them.

Whitey said, "Want to see," and Whitey pointed at his eyes.

"Want to see," and Whitey did his fingers like somebody was walking. "Want to see parade," so he wiggled his fingers along. "I don't know how you will word that, but the policeman said, 'No compriende' or whatever."

And so, the policeman stated, "Just a minute, I'm busy."

So, he continued directing the traffic.

Then he said, "Okay. Now—say again."

So, Whitey pointed at his eyes like he wanted to see the parade. He made his fingers moving like people walking.

"Want to see parade."

"Oh," the policeman said, "Ah, ah."

The policeman put his hand up, and he pointed right at a street, then he held up two fingers.

Whitey interpreted this, "Two blocks, two blocks, two blocks."

"Si, si."

So Flippo's out there with Whitey. Then he went to the right with his hand and held up two more and said, "Two more blocks to the right."

"Two more blocks."

"Si."

Whitey and Flip went back to the anxious group and stated, "Ah well, we found out where the parade is. Come on."

"Where is it?"

"Two blocks down that way and two blocks that way, and there's the parade."

So they took off—"a whole mess of us—just like a herd of cattle down the sidewalk. Everybody's 'grumble, grumble.' We're going down to see the Easter parade. So, we get down thar, and hell, thar's nothing going on at all. I mean, no people on the curb. We're looking around and looking around."

Bob Page commented, "I don't believe the parade's going to come along here. There'd be people waiting for them."

"Well, that's what I understood him to tell me. Flippo was there."

And Flip added, "Yeah, that's what he said—go two blocks and turn right two more blocks, and you could see the parade."

Flippo continued singing the word "around" and laughing. "So, they're looking around. 'Oh,' one lady started laughing like hell. And she was almost in tears, she was laughing so hard."

And she pointed, "Look at the sign."

The sign on this building said, "Optical Company." They never did get to see the parade.

Flippo ended this story about this trip with an emotional statement about Bob Page, "I don't know much more about Bob except I loved that ole boy. It was good!"

One truly memorable moment going through Flippo's three albums/scrapbooks was finding a little tiny piece of paper with this typed message, "I'm not sure you remember us but maybe so. You and Bob Page visited Madrid, Spain in April 1973 at Torrejon Air Base when we were club callers there. Mary Ann and I can truthfully say that that was one of the high spots in our Square Dancing life."

Flippo responded, "Well, that's a nice little piece. I can't 'member the people but—sad. Memory's shot."

England

Flippo and his second wife went to England with Dave Taylor, flying into London. They rented a car, and he remembered Dave asking, "Have you driven over here?"

"No."

Dave stated, "I drove over here for about a mile."

When they got into the car and Dave turned on the key, the windshield wipers came on, and they couldn't figure how to turn them off. At this point, they were still in the parking lot. And they were headed to Exeter, England to call.

Finally, they got out of the rental car parking lot, after about ten minutes. They finally found out how to turn "that damn windshield wipers off."

But Dave was going the wrong way, and Flippo remembered a cop there, and he stopped all the traffic. He motioned to them to U-turn—go the other way. They knew he was saying to himself, "Those damn Americans driving."

Then Dave moved over into what he thought was the slow lane. Flippo thought he was going 82 miles an hour, and that was the slow lane. Cars were passing them like they were sitting still.

Eventually they got down to Exeter, and Flip was sitting on the driver's side, the left side of the car where Americans usually have a steering wheel. Dave was pulling in, and they saw their hotel, so they found a good parking space up alongside of this big stucco type fence, and Dave was pulling in.

So Flippo exclaimed, "Dave, Dave, you're getting too close over here."

And he stated, "Shut up. I'm parking the car."

So, Flippo's left-side rearview mirror was knocked off.

Dave asked, "What was that?"

"I told you you were getting too close. The mirror is gone."

Flippo continued, "Anyway, boy, Dave is gone now. He's dead. I can't thank of that couples' name that booked us over thar, but they had like sixty to seventy squares."

Dave warned him, "You'd better hold on. These people can dance." Dave knew because he had been over there before.

When Flippo starting calling at the dance that night, right off the bat, he called an *Arky (Left) Relay the Deucey*[4] and *Crossfire*[5] from lines facing out, and he watched the floor, and they were doing it. "I mean, the whole floor. And so, I thought, 'Well, Boy Hidey!'"

So, they had a really good night of square dancing. From there, they went back and called in London and somewhere else they called, "and I can't ask Dave 'cause he's not thar."

Flip remembered staying with this couple in London, and before the dance they called, the couple had some friends over.

"Well," Dave stated, "I'll take the upstairs room."

Flippo added, "So I can still see him trying to get that big ole bag up those stairs, way up in thar like he was going up into the attic."

Flippo decided to take a nap, and then they met the friends of the people they were staying with. They were all in the living room.

[Flippo's second wife] told him that after the host got ready, he came out in just his jockey shorts. Nobody said anything; it's just like it was normal. So Flip went back into the bedroom. This behavior shocked [his second wife].

New Zealand

Flippo finished up his discussion about his international travels with, "And let's see. I never did get to go to New Zealand. I guess I was asked a couple of times, and it always . . . Thar was somethang holding me back—somethang."

PRIME MINISTER

October 9, 1989

Kirkwood Lodge
P O Box 37
Osage Beach
Usa M0 65065

Dear Marshal

Next year, 1990, will be a very special and exciting year in New Zealand. It's our anniversary year and I'm delighted to be able to write to you personally and, on behalf of Art Shepherd of Christchurch , invite you to visit New Zealand during 1990.

The invitation in 1989 from the Prime Minister to celebrate their anniversary in 1990.
Source: Neeca Flippo

Cruises

Flippo went on several cruises, so here's a couple he highlighted.

Flip remembered going quite a few times down south into the Caribbean, and he specifically recalled going on one cruise with Bill and Phyllis Speidel to the Caribbean.

"We went on one cruise with a slew of callers." They had over six hundred people with them. It was "Ken Bower, Scott Smith, and Gary Shoemake, and myself as far as the Chaparral [Recording Label] goes."

And then Flip went with Jerry Story, Tony Oxendine, and Larry Letson. He remembered Wade Driver and Mike Seastrom were on that one. "That was our biggest one down thar. I'll try to find a brochure on that and see how many callers. I left somebody out, I know. I thank we had nine or ten callers."

As you can see, Flippo's popularity spanned the world—he had become an international sensation!

170 **DANCERS AND CALLERS** from more than fifteen states participated in a recent cruise on Carnival Cruiser Lines' M.S. Holiday. Informal dances were held every day, with the highlight being a gala evening under the stars in Cozumel. Pictured are callers Marshall and Neeca Flippo, Bill and Phyllis Speidel and Chris and Rita Vear, along with most of the participants. Organizers Bob and Debbie Meaut accompanied the group and worked tirelessly all week to ensure that everything ran smoothly. The cooperation of Captain Gavino and his staff made the week a memorable event for all who participated.

Linear Cycle Around the Globe Tour. Source: Neeca Flippo

Ad for Top of the Line cruise in 1994. Source: *American Square Dance*, June 1993

1. **Caller** — A person who prompts dance figures in such dances as line dance, square dance, and contra dance.
2. **Basics** — The beginning CALLERLAB program with fifty-one calls.
3. Martha Ogasawara, *American Square Dance* (November 1994): 8.
4. **Relay the Deucey** — Plus Call — From Parallel Waves or Eight Chain Thru (in which case dancers first step to Parallel Waves). It can be done left-handed and is called Arky
    Arm Turn 1/2;
    Center 4 Arm Turn 3/4 as Others 1/2 Circulate;
    Wave Of 6 Arm Turn 1/2;
    Center Wave Of 4 Arm Turn 1/2 as Others (do a Big) Diamond Circulate;
    Wave Of 6 Arm Turn 1/2;
    Center Wave Of 4 Arm Turn 3/4 as Others move up.
5. **Crossfire** — Plus Call — As the centers begin to Trade, the ends Cross Fold. Upon completing their Trade, the centers release hands and step straight forward, forming an ocean wave or mini-wave with the dancers they are facing.

CAREER CHANGE AND PROMOTIONS

Source: Chaparral Records Logo. Source: https://www.ceder.net/
callerdb/viewsingle.php?RecordId=927

18

MOVE TO THE CHAPARRAL RECORD LABEL

Chaparral Records Logo. Source: https://www.ceder.net/callerdb/
viewsingle.php?RecordId=927

F lippo's loyalty to Blue Star records and Norman and Nadine Merrbach kept him there for twenty-seven years, but times changed. The move to Chaparral welded lifelong friendships for Flip with the callers at that record label: Gary Shoemake, Ken or Kenny Bower, Jerry Haag, Beryl Main, and Scott Smith.

Gary Shoemake had told Flip before, "If you want to change labels—I'm not begging you to or anythang. I'm just telling you. If you want to change labels, we want you to come over on Chaparral."

After talking with Neeca about some royalty issues with Blue Star Records, Flip decided to make the big move.

Flippo's big concern was for the Merrbachs. He lamented, "I don't want to hurt Nadine and Norman Merrbach. I don't want to hurt them. They were owners and producers of Blue Star Records."

Neeca suggested, "Write them a nice letter if you want to change."

Flip replied, "Well, I'd kind of like to call with those guys."

So Flippo wrote Norman Merrbach a long letter. He remembered doing that and told him he was set to go over to Chaparral. "This is one thang I know; I hurt Nadine and Norman and wished I hadn't've ever done that. But of course, they were great friends. I always stayed with them when I was in Houston, but I don't know whether we just tolerated each other after that or not. I felt like we were still friends, but thar was a coolness, you know, between us.

"I don't know, and I look back on it and I thank, 'If I'd stayed with Blue Star, would I . . . ? I really did love the weekends with the Chaparrals, you know, and all those weekends and the trips to Japan and the stuff like that. I don't thank I'd have had that experience if I'd stayed with Blue Star."

"So, I thank back. Well, you know. Deep down, I thank I should have stayed with Blue Star, no matter what, but I don't know. I don't regret going with the Chaparral 'cause I really, really did have a lot of fun that I probably would have never had at Blue Star. But it was always a fun stay with Blue Star. It might have been altogether different. I don't know. But I did hate it. In my soul, I hated it that I hurt Nadine and Norman."

He ended, "So, I changed and I had really second thoughts about it."

Chaparral Weekends

Chaparral Boys on stage. L to R: Gary Shoemake, Marshall Flippo, Scott Smith, Beryl Main, Jerry Haag, and Ken Bower.

Flippo cherished the relationships he had with the "Chaparral Boys." He truly enjoyed the weekends they did together. When I asked if he did a lot of weekends with the Chaparral label, he replied, "Yes, we had quite a few." For several years, they did five weekends a year.[1] Then his stories began.

Welcomes

MARSHALL FLIPPO
Abilene, Texas

CHAPARRAL RECORDS is honored to produce the music for MARSHALL FLIPPO and offer him as one of the premier callers in the world. Many have been amazed to experience Marshall's polished flow and timing which enables him to easily guide dancers through unfamiliar choreography. And we feel you will agree.

=C-702 "Welcome to—(Lake of the Ozarks)". A great tune to open any special dance. With a little imagination, you can change the lyrics to fit any occasion.

=C-703 "If you're gonna play in Texas, you gotta have a fiddle in the band".

Born and raised in West Texas, Marshall started calling in 1952. Nine years later, he became associated with the Kirkwood Lodge in Osage Beach, Missouri, launching his full time career. Now one of the owners, Marshall travels each year from Abilene to kick off the square dancing season at the lodge.

Throughout his career, Marshall has been instrumental in guiding beginning callers and, in the same way, has added his special touch to the recording industry. In 1981, his peers at Callerlab recognized Marshall's talent with the distinguished Milestone Award, the highest accolade given by the organization.

Marshall and his lovely wife Neeca make their home in Abilene, Texas when they are not at the Kirkwood Lodge. Their 21-year-old son John is a junior at Central Missouri State College.

We feel that the combination of the number one caller with the number one square dance recording company will bring exciting results. Welcome, Marshall and family!

arral
RDS
X 75075 • (214) 423-7389

Source: Neeca Flippo

Their first weekend was in Kansas City, Missouri, and they lost the hotel, so they moved to Oklahoma City, Oklahoma. Eventually, that same weekend became Paris, Texas, which is still thriving today. They moved because of the prices of the motels.

They also had a weekend in Branson, Missouri, and a weekend at Chula Vista Resort in Wisconsin Dells, Wisconsin. Flip thought they had four "for a good while," but he wasn't counting Indio, California. Then he remembered it wasn't one of our Chaparral weekends. "Thar was somethang before Branson. What the hell was it? I'll try to remember. But we did three or four together every year for many years, so I'm going to miss it."

In thinking about his joy in working with these callers, Flip lamented in his retirement, "What I'm going to miss a lot is the guys that I worked with. I won't get to see them. I'll try to see them, just go to one of their dances sometime to see them, but I'll miss seeing those guys I worked with so long."

When I asked about the callers on the Chaparral label, I listed Ken and Gary and Jerry Haag.

He added, "Scott Smith, Flippo, and Beryl Main."

❧

A funny story happened in Kansas City. Beryl Main was still alive at this time, so there were the four original Chaparral boys, which was Gary, Kenny, Beryl, and Jerry. They needed to add two more people. Beryl was sick, and eventually died of cancer, and they knew they were going to lose him.

He continued with a chuckle, "I thank what they thought was we'll get two guys to take his place because Beryl was so good." They added Scott Smith and Flippo.

But when Beryl was on chemo and farted, it would knock you out. "I mean terrible." So, they're up thar on the stage, "and we're fixing to start the dance and somebody did. Beryl said it wasn't him this time. So [on stage], it was Beryl, and then it was Gary, and then it was Kenny, and then it was Jerry, and then it was [me], and then it was Scott Smith. Scott Smith is a real devout Mormon. So anyway, up on the stage before we started, somebody passed gas which sounds worst to me than fart. We were all looking at each other, and we looked at Beryl 'cause he's usually the culprit."

Beryl claimed, "It wasn't me this time, boys. It was NOT ME."

Individually Gary, Ken, and Jerry chimed in, "It wasn't me."

Jerry Haag was standing next to Flippo, and he said, "I bet you Jerry . . ."

Jerry protested, "No, no, it wasn't me."

Flippo asserted, "By golly, it wasn't me. It's got to be Scott Smith."

Scott Smith stated, "Mormons do not fart!"

Flippo added, "So coming from a devout Mormon . . . We always watched ourselves. We wouldn't curse around him, or we wouldn't tell dirty jokes around him."

So, Flippo stated, "My God, that's the worst word I've ever heard you say, Scott."

Scott repeated, "Well, Mormons do not fart."

Flippo suggested, "Here's the culprit down here. I thank he's the one who started."

Scott interjected, "No, no. It wasn't me. I tell you. Mormons do not fart." The perpetrator never confessed.

Another time they were doing a weekend in Gatlinburg, and Gary was taking

260

them all back to the airport because Beryl was going to fly out, so they were all together.

So, they took off and they're in this car, air conditioning on. Beryl was sitting up front with Josh, Gary's ten or eleven-year-old son. Kenny, Jerry, Scott, and Flip were in the back. "I don't know how that was. Four of us sitting? Ken, Jerry, and Scott being so big. I believe it was one of these wagons that had an extra seat."

They turned the corner toward the terminal, already in the airport grounds, and turned in for departing passengers. Beryl let them have it. "And I want to tell you—you would not believe the hands that were trying to roll down the windows. And we were all laughing like heck. That dang-gum Beryl. He could have gone out of here and done nothing."

He apologized, "I'm sorry, boys. Sorry, boys!"

Because of the effect the chemotherapy had, Beryl's farts were lethal. As soon as they could get stopped, all four doors flew open so they could jump out. And Josh was still in the front seat, down on the floorboard laughing! And Flippo remembered him saying, "Beryl, you're the king!"

Flippo had special relationships with each of these men, and after all the musings over his move to Chaparral, the rewards with these friendships and fun certainly outweighed the pain of leaving Blue Star. Flippo told stories about many of these callers, so look for them in his stories chapter, Chapter 31.

L to R: Flippo, Flippo, Neeca and Flippo applauding. Source: Neeca Flippo

1st: Gary Shoemake and Flippo. 2nd: Flippo greeting the ladies.
Source: Neeca Flippo

Top: L to R: Gary Shoemake, Marshall Flippo, Beryl Main, Jerry Haag, and Ken Bower. Bottom: L to R: Ken Bower, Gary Shoemake, Beryl Main, Jerry Haag, Marshall Flippo, and Scott Smith. Source: Neeca Flippo

> An agreement has been made with the Chaparral recording group to have two of their callers on each year. As most of you know, the Chaparral group consists of Ken Bower, Gary Shoemake, Marshall Flippo, Beryl Main, Jerry Haig, and the newest (and best looking) Scott Smith. Gary Shoemake and Scott Smith, along with the Pierces, will be the first two on the March festival. At any time Marshall Flippo is available, there is a standing request to have him as one of the two.

Source: Neeca Flippo

1. *American Square Dance*, (March 1985): 10.

19

TWO SQUARE DANCE MAGAZINES
PROMOTED FLIPPO

D uring the heyday of square dancing, two square dance magazines promoted the up-and-coming Marshall Flippo: *Sets in Order* and *American Squares*. Bob and Becky Osgood published *Sets in Order*, and several editors and publishers before and after Stan Burdick published *American Square Dance*. Flip only spoke of Stan.

Sets in Order magazine

Bob Osgood published *Sets in Order* from 1948–1985: 444 consecutive issues[1] where he masterfully helped shape square dancing.

This magazine played an instrumental role in Flippo's career. During the thirty-seven years Bob Osgood published it, Flippo was featured on the cover of *Sets in Orders* four times: July 1963 where the reader matched baby pictures with current *callers'* pictures, October 1964 had a collage of thirty-five pictures of *callers*,[2] May 1970 featured Flippo's Hall of Fame portrait, and April 1983 featured Flippo's Japanese trip and dancing with royalty.

Bob Osgood's Cartoon Banner at the typewriter from Sets in Order monthly article, "As I See It."
Source: *Sets In Order*, January 1965

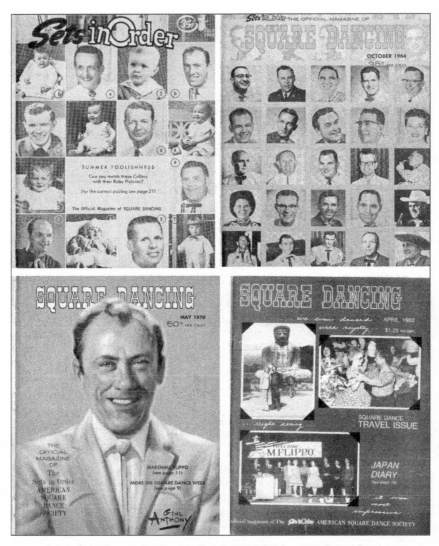

Sets in Order Covers - Top Row L to R: July 1963 & October 1964. Bottom Row L to R: May 1970 & April 1983. Source: *Sets in Order*

Marshall Flippo's name first appeared in *Sets in Order* November 1958 in the "Round the Outside Ring" article for the Permian Basin Festival. "The Auctioneer" also first appeared in the same issue in the "On the Record" section, listed as a new release. From then on, *Sets in Order* featured Flip's records and calling engagements often.

In 1970 many of the *Sets in Order* covers showcased the *callers* from the *Sets in Order* Square Dance Society's Hall of Fame's portraits. The original oil portrait was painted by Gene Anthony. Flippo's portrait was on the May cover of 1970.

266

Every year, Bob Osgood highlighted the popular national *callers* in his December issue starting in 1964 with a holiday greeting from the couples at the bottom of each page in the footer. This tradition continued until 1985, the end of the magazine.

The April 1983 cover featured Flippo and Neeca's trip to Japan and dancing with a Prince.

Here are the Flippos' holiday greetings:

- 1964: Flippo and Neeca said, "Yuletide Greetings"
- 1965: "Happiness Always and at This Holiday Season — Marshall & Neeca Flippo"
- 1966 and 1967: "Merriest of Holidays — Marshall & Neeca Flippo"
- 1968: "Gay Holiday Season — Marshall and Neeca Flippo"
- 1969: "Joyous Seasons Greeting — Marshall & Neeca Flippo"
- 1970: "Merriest Season Greetings — Marshall & Neeca Flippo"
- 1971: "Jolly Christmas Greetings — Marshall and Neeca Flippo"
- 1972: "Joy to all — Marshall and Neeca Flippo"
- 1973: "Gay Holiday Season — Marshall and Neeca Flippo"
- 1974: "Happiness to Your House — Marshall and Neeca Flippo"
- 1975: "Happy Holidays — Marshall and Neeca Flippo"
- 1975: "Happy Holidays — Marshall and Neeca Flippo"
- 1976: "Happy Square Dancing Christmas — Marshall and Neeca Flippo"
- 1977: "Good Wishes for the Holidays — Marshall and Neeca Flippo"
- 1978: "Peace this Holiday Season — Marshall and Neeca Flippo"
- 1979: "Have a fun holiday — Marshall and Neeca Flippo"
- 1980: "May Your Holiday be filled with Happiness — Marshall and Neeca Flippo"
- 1981: "Wishing You a Joyous Season — Marshall and Neeca Flippo"
- 1982: "Have a Fun Filled Year — Marshall and Neeca Flippo"
- 1983: "Warm Greetings and Yuletide Cheer — Marshall and Neeca Flippo"
- 1984: "Good Cheer and Happiness be Yours — Marshall and Neeca Flippo"
- 1985: "May Fun and Laughter Ring Out — Marshall and Neeca Flippo"

❧

Bob also promoted his big dance events at Asilomar with a quote from Flippo, "Marshal Flippo says, 'Join me at Asilomar.'"

Flippo shared his knowledge about calling in several interviews in Bob's magazine. His interview, "Working with Young People and Other Traumatic Experiences" showed not only his clever side but also his knowledge of his craft.[3]

In the May and June 1968 issues, Flippo was interviewed with two other *callers:* Frank Lane and Arnie Kronenberger for two articles in the DIALOG series focused on readers who might want to be a *caller.*

In "DIALOG: How Does One Go About Learning Calling?" Flip referenced his problem with keeping a beat and disclosed, "When I started calling, I had trouble staying on the beat. I could feel it, but I didn't know what to do about it. My wife suggested I pat my foot to the music and call to the rhythm of patting my foot. I almost wore a hole in the floor, but it sure did help."[4]

This trio continued their interviews with "DIALOG: How Does One Go About Learning Calling?" addressing some provocative questions that still apply today.[5]

In the April and June 1969 issues, Flippo joined Frank Lane and Bob Page for two interviews titled "DIALOG: Leadership in Square Dancing"[6] and "DIALOG: Building Dancer Retention."[7]

Flippo wrote an article for the "Workshop" section of *Sets in Order* titled, "Updating Memory Patterns."[8]

Bob Osgood's vision for square dancing included a textbook, *The Caller Text,* and Flippo was one of the contributing *callers*.[9] He wrote chapter 24: "Building and Maintaining a Repertoire."[10]

In *Sets in Order*, there was a monthly section called "Current Best Sellers." Thirty-five to sixty-three "dealers and distributors of Square and Round Dance records in key cities throughout the United States and Canada were canvassed to find out just what records were selling in their individual area."[11] They featured Flippo's records regularly and this increased his popularity.

🐚

Flip and I had a delightful conversation about a collage of baby pictures of *callers* featured on the July 1963 cover of *Sets in Order*. Flip wouldn't tell me which one was his. I missed it a couple times.

Flip's encouragement, "I believe you can pick it out," and I did finally.

"Number 3 is you!"

"Yeah," he chuckled. "That was on the front of *Sets in Order* that month, July, 1963."

Looking at the cover, Flippo really laughed at the price. "Thirty-five cents."

Then Flip tried to name all the *callers* who had their baby pictures on the cover with him. He had trouble at first but ended up naming many of them.

Sets in Order magazine cover. Source: *Sets in Order*, July 1963

In 1981, in "The Callers Notebook" section in *Sets in Order*, 300 Callers Voice Their Opinion, this tidbit was shared, "There are not enough Gilmores, Frank Lanes, Bob Dawsons, or Flippos."[12]

After thirty-seven successful years Bob and Becky retired and sent Flippo a note thanking him. They took their *Sets in Order* magazine off the market. He wouldn't sell it to anybody because he was afraid they wouldn't keep up with his ideas, so he just took it completely off. "And that's when square dancing, I thank, started kind of faltering a little after that. I don't know whether the magazine had anythang at all to do with it or not, but I know he had a large audience."

When Bob and Becky Osgood decided to retire from publishing *Sets in Order,* Flippo wrote them, "Will miss the magazine very much. Thanks for all you've done over the years—without backing from you two, I would have gotten nowhere."[13]

Kirkwood Lodge thanks Bob and Becky Osgood for years of publishing Sets in Order magazine. Source: *Sets in Order,* December 1985

American Squares/Square Dance/American Square Dance magazine

This magazine started publication in 1945 and continues promoting square dancing today. In January 1966, the magazine's name changed from *American Squares* to *Square Dance* and changed again January 1972 to *American Square Dance,* which is its name today.

. . .

History

On the twenty-fifth anniversary of the release of "The Auctioneer," *American Square Dance* remembered back to a November 1958 comment, "The Record Reviews: Marshall Flippo's 'The Auctioneer' is a beautifully executed lyric call with lots of song value."[14]

The chronology of *American Squares* magazine's change in leadership:

- The *American Squares* magazine began in 1945 with Charles (Charley) Crabbe Thomas as editor and was published in Woodbury, New Jersey.
- In April 1952, Rickey Holden became the editor, and he lived in San Antonio, Texas. Part of the operations stayed in New Jersey and part moved to Texas.
- Frank Kaltman became the publisher in July 1956.
- Rod LaFarge became the Managing Editor, and Rickey became a Roving Editor in 1956.
- In October 1959, Arvid Olson became the Editor, and Rickey remained the Roving Editor until February 1960.
- Frank Kaltman became the "Record Review" Editor in October 1959.
- Stan Burdick started doing a monthly cartoon April 1960 named "Do-Ci-Do Dolores" and had a long-term relationship with *American Squares* going into the late '90s.
- In October 1962, Frank Kaltman stopped being the "Record Review" editor.
- In January 1966, Stan became one of the Associate Editors.
- In October 1968, Stan and Cathie Burdick became the editors and headed this magazine until December 1991—twenty-three years. Stan and Cathie stayed on as "Editorial Assistants" when Jon and Susan Sanborn became publishers and editors. Stan and Cathie changed their role in January 1993 and became "Featured Writers," and later, Stan and Cathie became "Contributing Editors," ending this role in February 1999.
- In December 1997, Ed and Pat Juaire became the publishers and editors and stopped May 2003. Corben Geis became one of the cartoonists for the magazine in March 1999.
- The new publishers and editors, William and Randy Boyd, took over June 2003. In July 2003, Jean Ferrin joined William and Randy as publishers and editors. Stan Burdick came back as cartoonist in June 2003. Corben Geis joined Stan as a cartoonist in July 2003. Corben became the only cartoonist in October 2003 and continued through the end of 2010.
- In February 2004, Jean Ferrin left the magazine as one of the editors and publishers, leaving William and Randy Boyd in charge.
- On December 15, 2019, I received an email from SusanElaine Packer, the new editor, and they are still going strong today.

Flippo Promoted

This magazine promoted Flippo, too. In the "News" section, "ILLINOIS —
Marshall Flippo will conduct the 1962 Illinois Square Dance Callers Association
Workshop at the YWCA, Decatur, on September 8 and 9. All callers are invited to
attend this annual leadership training session."[15]

Cover, May 1965. Source: *American Squares*, May 1965

Marshall Flippo was on the cover of the May 1965 issue of *American Squares*.

Flippo wrote an article for this magazine entitled, "ONE NIGHTERS! Golden
Opportunities to Recruit New Square Dancers" in the May 1965 issue. He stressed
three ideas: Atmosphere, Program and *Singing Calls*.[16]

Stan Burdick wore many different hats in the square dance world: an accomplished *caller*, cartoonist, and magazine publisher. In *American Squares* magazine, he
used a variety of tricks to grab the dancers' interest every month and promote the
popular *callers*.Flip and I spent quite a while looking at this collage of pictures in
one of the photo albums, and he named a lot of the *callers*.

CHEK-A-KALLER KONTEST. Source: *Square Dance*, June 1971

Here's one of the promotional ideas, which was in the magazine: CHEK-A-KALLER KONTEST. "Test your memory for *callers* you've seen (or whose photos you've seen) and win a free renewal subscription for two years to Square Dance magazine."

Flippo exclaimed, "Thar, I'm over thar."

I answered, "There you are. You're number 33."

Then Flippo listed the ones he easily recognized but not in numerical order. He named thirty-five of them with "39 – Thar's Tex Brownlee" being the first name he called.

Flip and I returned to this collection of pictures a second time, and he really wanted to identify more of the *callers* than he did the first time. He had trouble, so we both wondered if there was a legend on the back of the picture.

When I asked him about it, he answered, "I'm fixing to look. No, it's pasted in thar. Wait a minute. It's going to all come off when I unpaste it."

I found the CHEK-A-KALLER KONTEST in *Square Dance,* June 1971, and the legend in August 1971. See the legend to this in Appendix E.

Both of these magazines helped shape Flippo's career and future with their generous promotion of his records, events, and knowledge.

Stan Burdick on cover. Source: *American Squares*, June 1965.

Cartoon by Stan Burdick, New England Caller, January 1970. Source:
Neeca Flippo

1. Bob Osgood, *Sets in Order,* (December 1985): 2.
2. **Caller** — A person who prompts dance figures in such dances as line dance, square dance, and contra
   dance.
3. Bob Osgood, *Sets in Order,* (September 1967): 24-25, 70.
4. Bob Osgood, *Set in Order* (May 1968): 19-21, 50.
5. Bob Osgood, *Sets in Order* (June, 1968): 18-20.

6. Bob Osgood, *Sets in Order,* (April 1969): 18-20
7. Bob Osgood, *Sets in Order,* (June 1969): 25-27.
8. Marshall Flippo, *Sets in Order* (September 1977): 37-39
9. Bob Osgood, *Sets in Order* (July 1970): 12
10. Bob Osgood, *Sets in Order* (March 1973): 23-28.
11. Bob Osgood, *Sets in Order* (April 1964): 60.
12. Bob Osgood, *Sets in Order*, (February 1981): 35.
13. Marshall Flippo, *Sets in Order,* (November 1985): 25.
14. Mary Fabik, *American Square Dance*, (September 1983): 25.
15. Arvid Olson, *American Squares,* (September 1962): 43.
16. **Singing Calls** — A singing call is most often done to a recognizable song with known lyrics. The caller mixes in the dance calls between sections of song lyrics. Generally a singing call uses a pattern where each person dances a portion of the song with each of the other dancers in the square before returning to their original partner at the end. The purpose of singing calls is to relax, dance as a group, and enjoy the song and the caller's performance

THE DANCE, THE CALLS
AND THE SONGS

Source: http://www.45cat.com/record/bs1517

20

FLIPPO'S CHOREOGRAPHY

When I think of square dancing, choreography does not come to mind—I'm a dancer, so I just enjoy it and do it. It took a non-dancer in my writing group to ask the question, "ask Flippo how he choreographed his songs?" So I did and acquired a new respect for choreography. The intricate design of each *figure*[1] and then the melodic match of *figures* to the music in a *singing call*[2] require a creative mind. Flippo excelled at this.

Always offering his expertise to new callers, in *Sets in Order,* September 1977 issue, Flippo shared a lot of ideas in an article, "Updating Memory Patterns," that appeared in a regular column called "Workshop for Leaders in Square and Round Dancing."[3]

Bob Osgood commented, "ABOUT THE 'FLIP'—Dancers for years have been delighted with the comfortable, free flow of Marshall Flippo's choreography. Callers have envied and attempted to imitate his programming, but the fact is — most of what Flippo does 'just comes naturally.'"[4]

In the "Records Singing Calls" section of *American Squares*, Stan Burdick pointed out, "We believe that good choreography is about 70% of a record. Most of our callers have good voices, but the good choreographer with ideas is about as scarce as hen's teeth. If the labels can show us a lot of good choreographers like Bob Van Antwerp and Marshall Flippo, then we are sure that we can tell you about a lot of good records that will be coming out."[5]

Stan Burdick cover. Source: *American Squares*, June 1965

When asked if Flippo did the choreography for all of his records, he answered, "We did some to the figers [*figures*] [6] that I stole. Yes."

After a time of silence, Flippo shared how he worked out his choreography. He called a lot around Abilene at the YMCA, the KC Barn, and then the Wagon Wheel. So, after a dance a lot of times, he would get a square to stay after the dance, and "I'd have this figer [*figure*] in mind," and they'd work on it. If it did not work okay, he'd have to change it. Usually he and the dancers would change it right then, and they'd have it the way they wanted before he let the square go home. Amazing that he included the dancers in the changes of his choreography!

He added with a chuckle about those who helped out after a dance, "Nice people stayed over, you know."

Flip explained the process with the volunteer dancers. If he had a call to "Alice Blue Gown," he'd have it in his mind, and they'd try it, and if something didn't work, they'd change it. That would be the square after the dance. "Sometimes I wrote some terrible figers [*figures*]." But when callers started getting calls like *Star Thru*,[7] then the choreography became easier to write a *singing call* because they had more *Basics*.[8]

Flippo added another hint about his mastery of his craft. Sometimes just listening to the tune over and over and over, things would come into his mind and almost tell him what to put where. He didn't how that happened like that. "After 'The Auctioneer,' I wrote a lot other figers [*figures*] and stuff over the years, but sometimes I repeated a figer [*figure*] that I put in another *singing call*. I'd put it to a newer *singing call*."

He had a different technique if Norman Merrbach wanted the record produced quickly. He would just use "a figer [*figure*]" that he had used before. One of "the figers [*figures*] that I had used before a long way back I'd use for that call that he wanted in a hurry."

Many callers use eight little dolls representing each dancer and move them around on a board to create their choreography. When asked if he ever used dolls, Flippo replied, "No, no. No, I never did use the dolls. Frank Lane did."

Frank Lane was sitting on an airplane with a guy with a real neat New Yorker suit, a tie, and hat, and he probably was some kind of a Wall Street guy. They talked a while.

Frank shared, "I believe I'll get my dolls out and work out some figers [*figures*] here."

Frank told Flippo "The guy got up and went and found another seat and wouldn't come back."

That guy probably said, "There's a guy back there playing with dolls."

Frank Lane on cover. Source:
Square Dancing, December 1970

So, the reality was that Flippo did a lot his choreography in his mind and then practiced that with the people after dances.

Flippo had another technique. He danced "in here in the living room at 1918 Marshall, my Abilene home." He remembered dancing a couple show tunes that they planned to record, and Flip recalled dancing them with no music, just the song in his head, "and I'd walk through that figer [*figure*] in the living room, and then I'd get it up to square dance tempo and call it and just walk it."

Flip knew *Square Thru*[9] took ten beats, so if he wanted to put *Square Thru*, then he knew he would be facing his corner after he called *Square Thru*.

Flip tried to remember the name of another call and chuckled. "I am 'retired-ite.' I just got square dancing out of my mind."

Let's end this with some of Flippo's humor! Mac MacCaller wrote in an article, "Notes From A Veteran Caller," "Then I thought of what the great Marshall Flippo said when asked in a meeting at CALLERLAB, what do you do when you use up all your planned material? He answered, 'I . . . I . . . I . . . just start over.'"[10]

Evolution in Square Dancing and the Changes

This west Texan's repertoire of recordings spanned country music to show tunes. Flippo responded with a laugh, "Well, you know, it's an identity. It just evolved. I knew if I wanted to record a number, Norman was so good. One time, I was riding along on the highway, down in south Texas somewhere, and I heard this song, 'Johnny Jingo.'"

He thought, "Boy, that'd make a good square dance." So Flippo just stopped alongside that highway and wrote down, "Johnny Jingo," and he wrote down the people who sung it. Next convenience store, Flip stopped and called Norman.

He responded, "Okay, well, I'll look it up."

Flippo had two or three more dances before he got back to Abilene. When he got home, he had the record there. Norman had already dubbed the music, and so Flip would work on it. What he would do is send Flip what he called "a dub," so he could work on "figers [*figures*] with that dub," and he'd have all the regular music. Then Flip kept a square after a dance and went through "the figer [*figure*] I had on my mind." They called it "Jingo," so, then next time he hit Houston, they'd go add to it with a band at the same time in a recording session.

"Well, what really gets me is all those songs we did, we very seldom had to do them again because we had that damn band, Earl and His Hoedowners." They had the kind of music Flippo loved, and they only had four pieces: a fiddle, a piano, a bass fiddle, and a rhythm guitar.

"So, it's amazing that we would have had so many times with the band and got through that at the same time 'cause sometimes I'd make a mistake, and we'd have to start over. Sometimes somebody in the band would do a clunker, and then we'd start over, but I'd say eighty percent of the time, we never did have to start over. We just went right through it—just unbelievable. Unbelievable! But they were musicians first class. They were good. They sounded good. I love to hear them play. I loved to hear 'em play on that first 'Auctioneer.' They just did a wonderful job. And they did it the same time I did it."

When asked if he worked with Earl and His Hoedowners on several records, he responded, "Ah, the first part of my recording—yeah, a lot of 'em, a lot of 'em." Some *callers*[11] would notice. They'd do the instrumental side with nobody calling, and then they'd go in, and Flip would do the *singing call* at the same time they played it over again. Sometimes they'd switch leads, and *callers* would notice that when he called it on the *caller's* side of the record, the *flip side*,[12] it would be different than the instrumental side, and it would change a little. The guitar would be playing where it wasn't playing on the record of the singing call that Flip did. It would be a little different, and *callers* would notice that. "I don't reckon square dancers would," but *callers* said, "Hey, that instrumental's a little different than the call side. It's got a piano here, and it didn't have the piano over in the calling side." It would still be the same song, but they'd switch leads sometimes. That *caller* would notice that the piano took a lead here while on the *caller's* side it was the guitar that had the lead. Those different things didn't happen often, but they'd try to play it the same way, the same instruments doing the same thing.

When asked what Earl's last name was, Flippo couldn't remember and I found Caruthers.[13]

Finally, when asked about his choreography, Flippo admitted, "Yeah, I stole it all! Research."

He ended with, "I never did write anythang down."

Dance Speed

The speed of square dancing has fluctuated over the years. It was anywhere from 121 to 124 beats a minute, and now it's really gotten up there a little higher, and then it really went up high. Sometimes through the '60s, they were calling up and around 134. People were moving, all of them.

But people were a lot younger then than they are now. They got older, and Flippo did, too. So, the music eventually slowed down a little bit, and Flippo thought most callers now are down around now 125, 126 and then sometimes a little slower, "but I like the slower pace 'cause I always felt when we's up thar really high that we were just running the hell out of 'em [the dancers]. So, now it's come down and some records back thar, Larada, were recorded real fast. You had to slow 'em a-way down. But I don't know why the tempo kept going up so high. I have no idee. But I remember I recorded some then, and John was playing one on his car."

John, Flippo's son, called him and remarked, "Dad, this record's going fast!"

Flip asked, "How fast is it?"

He answered, "136 beats a minute."

Flippo responded with a laugh, "Well, John, it must have been recorded back thar in the '60s to '70s when we were dancing at top speed. I tried walking it. That's pretty fast! You know, some people really like it at that tempo, but I'm glad it's slowed back down. I like the slower tempo."

Around Asilomar, it was 120 to 124, and Flip thought it was one of the reasons he liked it so much. "One reason I liked it, but I'm so glad, I'm sure glad it slowed down."

Phrase Calling

When Flippo talked about Ed Gilmore, he talked about "phrase calling," so I asked him what that meant.

With his mischievous laugh, he answered, "That means calling on phrase."

Ed Gilmore tried to teach Flippo to call on phrase. He couldn't do it, but Ed was a master at it. The beat of the music is what most *callers* call. Sometimes, they're on phrase, and sometimes they're not. That's the way Flip was.

Now on a phrase means you're going along exactly with the music. In other words, one, two, three, four. One, two, three, four, and you stay right on those phrase beats. Flip felt the need to talk to a musician about this topic, "but the phrase, I think, is eight beats and I'm not sure."

Ed Gilmore on the cover. Source: *Sets in Order*, November 1961

But they stay right on. In other words, Ed would call right on phrase, and Flip might call on phrase for a minute, but then he would get off and just call on the beat, and so there's a difference if you can call on phrase. The way our activity turned, it was very hard to call on phrase because of the length of some of the *figures*. "But Ed Gilmore, he had a way about him and he could call on phrase and keep you going."

Flippo ended with a laugh, "When I called on phrase, I couldn't keep them going all the time because I'd try to call on phrase, and pretty soon, I'd have to go with the beat. Phrase calling is about gone."

When Flippo talked about phrase calling, he shared this about a Burma-Shave jingle. "The one I just gave you [the Ida Red jingle] is a phrase when you're calling. When you're calling, it's okay that it's off period when you're calling and trying to phrase. You say like: Ida Red, she ain't no fool. She can put a saddle on a humpback mule. *Heads square through four hands around, go all the way 'til your corner.*[14] You're still on the phrase, and then this is where it starts getting off because *dosado*[15] only has six beats. And so, to *dosado your corner*—well, you have to get off of your phrasing because of the square dancing nowadays."

Flippo then asked, "Do you understand that a little?" I do now, a little. This shows the mathematical side of square dance calling. Flippo juxtaposed the mathematical with the whimsical side using the Burma-Shave jingles.

As I listened to Flippo describe his methods of choreography, I realized he was truly the master!

---

1. **Figure** — 48 beat group of calls that takes dancers from their home position to a Corner for a Swing and a 16 beat Promenade.
2. **Singing Calls** — The caller sings parts of the songs. See Glossary for more.
3. Marshall Flippo, *Sets in Order*, "Updating Memory Patterns," (September 1977): 37-38.
4. Bob Osgood, *Sets in Order* (January 1969): 38.
5. Stan Burdick, *American Squares* (February 1970): 48.
6. **Figures** (Flippo's version: figer) — 48 beat group of calls that takes dancers from their home position to a Corner for a Swing and a 16 beat Promenade.
7. **Star Thru** — Man places his right hand against woman's left hand, palm to palm with fingers up, to make an arch. As the dancers move forward, the woman does a one quarter (90 degrees) left face turn under the arch, while the man does a one quarter (90 degrees) turn to the right moving past the woman.
8. **Basics** — The beginning CALLERLAB program with fifty-one calls.
9. **Square Thru** — Right Pull By (Square Thru 1 has been completed); Face partner and Left Pull By (Square Thru 2 has been completed); Face partner and Right Pull By (Square Thru 3 has been completed); and Face partner and Left Pull By (Square Thru 4 has been completed). Ending formation: Back-to-Back Couples.
10. Mac MacCaller, *American Square Dance* (September 1995): 72.
11. **Caller** — A person who prompts dance figures in such dances as line dance, square dance, and contra dance.
12. **Flip side** — One side of a record had the caller singing the singing call and the other side had only the instrumental.
13. "Square Dance History Project," 2017, https://squaredancehistory.org/items/show/162
14. **Heads square through four hands around, go all the way 'til your corner** — Right Pull By (Square Thru 1 has been completed); Face partner and Left Pull By (Square Thru 2 has been completed); Face partner and Right Pull By (Square Thru 3 has been completed); and Face partner and Left Pull By (Square Thru 4 has been completed). Ending formation: Back-to-Back Couples.
15. **Dosado** — Walking a smooth circular path, dancers walk forward, passing right shoulders, slide sideways to the right, walk backward, passing left shoulders, and slide slightly to the left to return to their starting position.

21

FLIPPO'S RECORDING EXPERIENCES

When asked how many recordings Flippo did, he responded, "Exact number of songs I called, I have no earthly idee how many."

He instructed me to "look in the back of one of those albums. Neeca had put out the blurbs that came from *Sets in Order*. I don't thank the number is important."

He continued, "The listings go on forever and ever. Neeca'd put the ones I had recorded over in the back, but that was just up to a certain point—to a divorce point."

Flippo recorded for more than Blue Star and Chaparral. Rhythm Records is Wade Driver's company, and Flip did a few here and there. Also, he did one on River Records. "I believe I just done one or two for Chinook out of Knoxville, for ole Ted Frye." The Internet showed that Ted Frye was owner of Square Tunes and Pioneer Records.

When I listed the number of record labels he recorded with, he replied, "Holy mackerel! Good Lord a Mercy, some of them I don't even remember. A bunch of old records. Well, the one from Knoxville—Ted Frye's ole one. They'd call you up and say, 'Hey, can you do this number for me? Will you do it?' Of course, I usually did somethang. Some of 'em were terrible, but I did. I did one for Riverboat, I thank was. I hated for anybody ever to hear any. I don't know whether he released 'em or not. But it was God-awful!"

Flippo did quite a few long plays for Blue Star.

Then Flip did albums with *Sets in Order* with Bob and Becky Osgood. Flip never did do a single for Bob. He was always on an album with a bunch of other callers where each caller did one song. He was on quite a few of his long plays that he put out.

We had several conversations about the number of recordings Flippo did, but the specific number was much more important to me than him. Because Bob Osgood did multiple callers on an album, it made it impossible to count.

He pondered, "I don't know whether Seastrom knows much about that—the way that Bob Osgood did those recordings."

Finally Flip added, "Okay, okay. Anyway, I know I done as many as three," which made me laugh! Then he chuckled at my laughter.

I did contact Mike Seastrom, and he referred me to Masaharu "Doc" Hiraga, who sent me several pictures of the album covers Flippo did for *Sets in Order*.

2 Sets in Order Album Covers: 18 & Lucky 13th Jamboree.
Source: Masaharu "Doc" Hiraga

2 Sets in Order Album Covers: 1967 & 1969. Source: Masaharu
"Doc" Hiraga

2 Sets in Order Album Covers: 1971 & 1975. Source: Masaharu "Doc" Hiraga

2 Sets in Order Album Covers: 1978 & 1983. Source: Ted & Karen Clements

2 Blue Star Label Album Covers: Marshall Flippo Calling in Stereo & Marshall Flippo Calls the Basic 50. Source: Ted & Karen Clements

1 Sets in Order Album Cover & 1 Blue Star Label: Lucky 13
Jamboree & The Best Collection of New Squares Yet (Marvin
Fishman gave me this album, October 2019). Source: *Sets in
Order*, August 1964 & Larada Horner-Miller

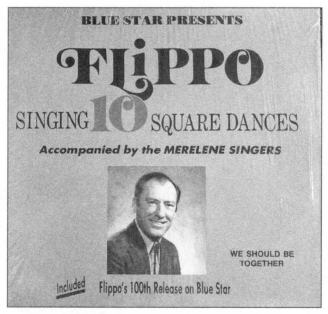

Blue Star Label Album Cover: Flippo Singing 10 Square Dances,
Accompanied by the Merelene Singers. Source: https://www.
podbean.com/site/EpisodeDownload/PB9E9CF6RRE6I

In the end, Flippo did twelve *Sets in Order* albums.

Flippo did a couple for "ole Jerry Story's label, Royal Label." He did a couple for them, and it was Jerry Story, Oxendine, and Letson until he quit.

Out of Tucson, Arizona, Flippo used to do some records—square dance calls—from Sun Records. It had a couple really good callers on that label. Way back in the '50s, they had a band, then starting in the '60s, they started getting records. "Let me thank—Pancho and Marie Baird was their name. They were real popular.

The band was Pancho Baird's Git-fiddlers. It might be on that list, but we recorded quite a few songs out of here."

"I recorded my first version here in Tucson, and I say, 'Version.' Larada, I always did it in Houston in the studio with a band playing at the same time I did my call. I was in thar with them. Now, this was about halfway through my west coast tour, and Norman [Merrbach] called me."

He stated, "I'm sending you a big master tape."

Flippo asked, "What?"

Norman repeated, "A master tape."

Flip responded, "Uh oh!"

He explained, "It's a tape of 'Blue Moon of Kentucky' that you're going to do."

And Flippo wondered, "Yeah. Do I look up a band out here or what?"

His response, "No, I'm sending you a master tape. Just go to a studio, give it to the technician there. He'll know exactly what to do with you. He'll put you in a little place with earphones on and a microphone. That's what he'll do, and he's going to pipe that music in to you. And, therefore, you are going to make a record."

To Flippo, this was scary because he never had anything like this happen to him. It was the first time he recorded like that, and from then on, it was nearly every time, they'd send him a tape. "So, yeah. It just continued being different from then on. I'd go to Houston a couple times, and we'd do some tunes then, but yeah, Tucson was a pretty good hub for thangs."

In the photo albums/scrapbooks, Neeca collected any time *Sets in Order* identified one of Flippo's songs—there are pages and pages of the short description or critique of his songs.

Flippo's Favorite Recording

When asked about his favorite recording, Flippo responded, "Oh, geez! I have no idee. 'Every Street's a Boulevard' is probably—you know."

For whatever reason, after Flippo recorded some of his songs, he never called them again. "I don't know why that was. But thar's a few that I called. Of course, I called 'em now and again, but probably I called 'Every Street's a Boulevard' more than anythang I ever recorded, probably." Obviously, he had his favorites, and those are the ones he returned to often.

Flippo continued, "I don't know what set my mind or body or makeup or psyche or whatever. After I recorded 'em, most of 'em I felt were worthy of calling, so I did call them [his favorites]."

Some of those show tunes "a way back," Flip still liked to listen to. He didn't call many of them, but Flippo liked to listen to the music and the song.

He returned to his repeated theme, "But as far as I know, luck played a whole lot of stuff with my calling and my journey and all that. I was just so lucky. It was unbelievable. You look back on it, and thank, 'Ah, boy, you were lucky thar. Yeah, be at the right place at the right time.' And thangs like that happen to you that didn't concern talent."

Flippo chuckled. "It just happened at the right spot at the right time."

289

When asked if Flip had a favorite *figure*[1] that he depended upon, that he used a lot, he emphasized, "NO! NO, I don't thank so. I remember calling lots of different figers [*figures*][2] to 'Every Street's a Boulevard.' I recorded songs that I'd call at a dance later on, but later on I'd be calling the figer [*figure*] that I put with it and realized, 'they're not getting it,' you know, so I'd switch over to a standard. What I call a standard figer [*figure*], one that I knew would work, and I'd fit it to the *singing call*[3] instead of the figer [*figure*] that I had recorded on the record, so I didn't have any standard, but I did have quite a few that I could fall back on in case the figers [*figures*] didn't work too hot with the one that we recorded on thar."

❧

Marshall Flippo's calling expertise sold his records and made him a success. Bob Osgood described the calling profession,

> A large part of the square dance recording industry is not a profitable business. Why then does it exist? A few of the well-established labels have protected themselves by building up a roster of calling artists who have, over the years, developed a proven sales popularity. In the case of prolific recording ace Marshall Flippo, whose first release was produced over twenty years ago, a large number of callers have said, "From past performance, I know that almost any record Flip releases, I can use. This takes away much of the *guess work* for me, and I automatically purchase each Flippo release that comes along.[4]

Then Bob laid out the steps in making a recording,

> Marshall will pay particular attention to the country western hits on the radio. Discovering one that rings a bell, he will tape it, listen to it several times, and possibly develop an idea or a call that might work with it. Sending the suggested tune to his producer, Norm Merrbach, Blue Star records in Houston, Texas, the tune will be checked against the releases of other [square dance] labels and, if it appears to be 'clear,' it will be turned over to the company's musicians for arranging. Then at a recording session the instrumental will be produced. A dub of the completed accompaniment will be sent to Flippo, who works with it as he perfects his call. At his first opportunity, he will go into the studio and record the calls over the prerecorded music.[5]

Funny Experiences Recording

In August 2018, I asked Flippo if he had any funny things ever happen when he was recording.

One time, they got through recording. "We's fixin' to leave the studio, and [Houghford, the Blue Star engineer] said in conversation, 'You know, back a few years ago, I did a commercial for a radio station, and I breathed in different spots. I did it twice. The second time I breathed different spots than I breathed in the first one. Then we took all the breath out of it.' Now he said, 'We can do a square dance that way.'"

So, the band and everybody went back in the studio and they played, "Take Me Back to Tulsa."

Flip called *figures* to "Take Me Back to Tulsa," breathed in different spots. Second time through, Flip breathed at a spot in the song he didn't breathe at first, and they went right through "the damn thang;" however, the timing for the dancers wasn't too hot, because Flip went along, didn't even take a breath, and it sounded like he took a big deep breath on the front of it and called that whole thing with no breath.

Always ready to improve himself and his craft, Flippo experimented with where he took a breath in a *singing call*. I wonder if he ever used this concept again.

This story led to another. Flippo was in Seattle, and a young kid started calling. He'd been calling awhile and was pretty good.

The young *caller*[6] observed, "I see every *tip* you go outside and smoke. How in the hell? The record lasted three minutes and twenty seconds. How in the hell did you do that without breathing?"

Flippo started to tell him what he did, and he stated, "You know, I've gone almost to three minutes on it, but I can't get it any further. I can't do it."

Flippo answered, "You kidding? Wait a minute. You called that with no breath for three?"

"Well, almost three minutes, about two and a half minutes with no breath."

Flip's belly laugh made me laugh.

Flip exclaimed, "God! Let me tell you how we did that."

Flippo thought he was going to kill him after it was over.

But he came over and said, "I wanted to see you smoking and everythang."

Flippo thought, "That guy must have lungs the size of a blimp."

Flip summarized, "Down thar smoking, and he called that damn record with three minutes and twenty seconds without breathing. And I got up to almost two and a half. Anyhow, lots of fun, lots of fun."

Mary Sheehan Johnson offered some explanation for this. "The record was 'The Caper' Blue Star #1617. And I believe that at the end, there was a big exhale (to match the big inhale that the start of the record), so this is an example of Flippo's sense of humor and trickery!

Magazine Reviews of Some of Flippo's Songs

The two square dance magazines played a critical role in Flippo's success with their reviews of current releases. Here's a few of his:

"Every Street's a Boulevard"

"A show time musical number with a good action pattern and good instrumental to back it up. Can be a real pleaser."[7]

❧

"If the World Keeps on Turning"

"Our 'Auctioneer' friend does it again with a dance that we predict will be a hit. First of all, it's a good clear record with excellent separation of the music (played here by the Texans). The pattern, with an interesting star figure included, is not difficult and moves quite naturally. Our first impression was that the figures were a bit crammed for good timing . . . . "You can forgive anything when you hear Flippo's deep mellow calling."[8]

"Square Dances with Calls by Marshall Flippo" — "Swinging With You" & "Somebody Else's Date"

"Marsh[all] has done it again. Two original singing calls, written and delivered perfectly. Excellent musical background recorded with perfect recording technique. 'Swinging' is bound to be a hit. Don't miss it. 'Date' is a simpler dance, beautifully done and useful in anyone's program who likes a well-done singing call. With no further comment we recommend this pair to all of you. What's the use of talking—we just like this Flippo's stuff."[9]

"Walk Right Back"

"Marshall Flippo, who has become unquestionably the undisputed hot-shot caller from Texas, beautifully delivers another one. We highly recommend that everybody hear this record."[10]

"Swing That Girl Tonight"

"A fast moving dance with Flippo's usual excellent timing."[11]

"Dixie Bell"

"A typical Flippo smoothie and a good tune."[12]

"So This Is Love"

"This has just got to be the greatest record since Kalox came out with Grand Colonel Spin. The dance is Flippo smooth, the figure is fantastic, and the music is great. Get it. FIGURE: Head couples right and left thru, pass on thru and cloverleaf, stand behind the sides. Double pass thru, cloverleaf again, square thru three hands, left allemande, do-sa-do your own, corner swing and promenade that lady home."[13]

❧

"I Love You Most of All"
"A different kind of singing call for Flip with a drum background. It comes out as a fine release. You can always depend on Flip's timing being danceable. The melody line is well established and dancers will recall the tune."[14]

❧

"Old Side of Town"
"A nice bit of choreography on this record. One can always depend upon Flip to offer something a little bit different."[15]

After all my research, Flippo had recorded over 224 records for fourteen different recording labels. He recorded twelve *Sets in Order* albums and twenty-five Blue Star Long Play Albums, and he enjoyed every minute of it!

Sets in Order Album Covers: L to R: Marshall Flippo Calling New Dances and Old Favorites, Fun Level Square Dances by Marshall Flippo. Source: Neeca Flippo

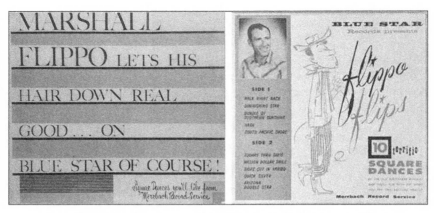

Sets in Order Album Covers: L to R: Marshall Flippo Lets His Hair Done Real Good, Flippo Flips. Source: Neeca Flippo

Sets in Order Album Covers: L to R: More Dances for Fun Level Dancing, Everybody Dances when the Great Marshall Flippo Calls. Source: Neeca Flippo

---

1. **Figure** — 48 beat group of calls that takes dancers from their home position to a Corner for a Swing and a 16 beat Promenade.
2. **Figure** (Flippo's version: figer) — 48 beat group of calls that takes dancers from their home position to a Corner for a Swing and a 16 beat Promenade.
3. **Singing Call** — The caller sings parts of the songs. See Glossary for more.
4. Bob Osgood, *Sets In Order,* (January 1979): 9-10.
5. Bob Osgood, *Sets in Order,* (January 1979): 9-10.
6. **Caller** — A person who prompts dance figures in such dances as line dance, square dance, and contra dance.
7. Bob Osgood, *Sets in Order,* "On The Record and Record Release, (February 1972): 73.
8. Bob Osgood, *Sets in Order,* "On The Record," (December 1959): 62.
9. Frank Kaltman, *American Squares,* "Record Reviews," (October 1960): 12.
10. Frank Kaltman, *American Squares,* "Records Reviews," (May 1961): 33.
11. Bob Osgood, *Sets in Order,* "On The Record and Record Reports," (March 1969): 84.
12. Bob Osgood, *Sets in Order,* "On The Record and Record Reports," (June 1971): 78.
13. Frank Kaltman, *The New Square Dance,* "Records Singing Calls," (July 1971): 23.
14. Bob Osgood, *Sets in Order,* "On the Record and Record Reports," (June 1980): 69.
15. Bob Osgood, *Sets in Order,* "On the Record and Record Reports," (September 1980): 76-77.

THE END OF ONE
MARRIAGE AND THE
START OF ANOTHER

22

DIVORCE

In January 2017, Lin and I stopped in Tucson, Arizona to have breakfast with Flippo and give him a photo album I made of his last calling event for the Albuquerque Square Dance Center. In that conversation, his divorce from Neeca came up, and he shook his head and admitted, "That was the dumbest thang I ever did in my life."

During our interviews, Flippo avoided the topic of his divorce from Neeca for several months before he was willing to talk. When he was finally willing, his heartfelt conversation broke my heart. At times, he was evasive about the date— he just didn't want to go there, but he always stated, "I'll ask Neeca. I wrote that down, and I'll ask Neeca." We did figure that they divorced in 1991 after forty-two years of marriage.

Then he decided to talk one afternoon. When he started talking, I thought he said they married twice.

They weren't married twice. They renewed their marriage vows, "so I don't know whether you'd say that was twice or not. We just renewed our vows. I don't know whether you call that the second marriage or not."

Neeca shared they renewed their vows on April 26, 1991. After renewing his marriage vows with Neeca, he faced what happened, "But it didn't take it too long. I was running around. I knew I was."

Renewing their marriage vows didn't help. He had decided he wanted a divorce.

Flippo recalled Neeca's statement, "Flippo, this is not your personality. It's not even close to it. You're hurting a lot of people."

Flippo added, "And I was too dumb, and you know, I had some other friends told me the same thang: 'It don't sound like you.'"

Flippo had it in his mind. He felt like he was in a trance. "I was dead and determined to marry [my second wife], and looking back on it, I know I made a big mistake; however, she and I got along. We had lots of fun together. She's a good ole gal. I'm lucky that both of 'em are still friends [of mine], really. So, it was terrible; it was one of those terrible times. I thank back on it, and you know, my son . . ."

Again, he recalled a comment by Neeca, "You're hurting John. You're hurting a lot of folks."

Then Flip added, "And I was too dumb to realize that. John never . . ."

Flippo remembered what John said, "Whatever you do, Dad, I'm with you, but I still love my momma."

Flippo shared, "So, anyway, I did. I hurt a lot of folks, and of course, and I don't know whether they knew it or not, but Neeca's mother and dad were on thar. I had a couple of little nieces that wouldn't talk to me for a long time, and finally they saw that Neeca and I were going to be friends again. Us being friends again didn't happen right off. It just happened later on. But when they found out that Neeca had forgiven me, they come around. I SHOULDN'T HAVE DONE IT, Larada! I shouldn't have done it!"

He concluded with, "Shit happens! So anyway."

Flippo love Neeca deeply, but his involvement with his second wife prior to their divorce hurt Neeca deeply. Time heals wounds such as these if the people are forgiving, and Neeca was. Later in their lives, Flippo and Neeca resumed a relationship and became good friends, calling and visiting each other often.

What a hard conversation to have and to own the fact Flippo was in the wrong. He chose to handle a touchy subject, so that it wasn't hurtful, and explained his mindset at the time.

23

THE TUCSON YEARS

Flippo's Second Marriage

When asked when did he marry [his second wife], Flippo had trouble with dates and answered, "I remember us getting married, and I remember thanking, 'What am I doing?'"

And also he had trouble with how long they were married. "I don't know how long I was married to her. I'm a pretty dumb ole fart. I thank it was twelve years, but I'm not sure."

In our last conversation, Flippo asked me if I had talked to his second wife.

"No," I replied.

Flip gave me permission to talk to her to see what she had to say. "In a way, I don't want to even mention her, but—you know—I still like the ole gal, and she was good. I guess we were pretty good together for a while, and then thangs started festering. And you know, I haven't heard anythang from any of [her] kids, and I just loved those kids, and now last year. Last year Christmas time [2017], I got one of those—what do they call 'em? Ahh, they type 'em out. Oh, it's on the phone. Text, yeah. I got a text from her [his second wife]—just said 'Merry Christmas, Marshall,' and that was it. She never did call me 'Flip.' And that's all I've heard from her in all these years, and none of the kids except Gary. He's the one that had cancer of the brain, and they got it. He come back. Boy, he really looks good now—real tall, and he sent a picture, and I heard from him after he'd went into college or somethang or graduated from college, and I sent all the other kids money that graduated."

Flippo didn't expect anything, but Gary wrote him back and thanked him profusely, "so that was nice, and I's probably closer to—well, I don't know. I's closer to those two children [of my second wife]. I thought they liked me, and whatever happened, I don't know. They all had the same grandma, grandpa, and they lived in Lubbock. I called them, oh, I guess about a year after my ex left, and they seemed kinda cool. They'd always been really—Boom, boom 'How you doin'? How you doin'? Glad ya call,' and all that stuff, but it wasn't any of that all, so whether my [second wife] told 'em somethang or what, I don't know." He sang the "what" in usual Flippo calling style.

After searching for her phone number, Flip did find it and shared it with me. I assured him I would try to connect with her. I did call a couple times and never heard back from her.

With a heavy breath, Flippo stated, "Whatever she says determines what I'll probably say about it. You know, Larada, she's good. I 'member us laughing so hard at different thangs that we's afraid we were gonna die. We'd be on the floor laughing at the other stuff, but we were good together for a good eight or nine years, I guess, and then it started falling apart."

With a chuckle, he concluded, "I still like the ole gal, but I'm over her as far as that goes, but God, it hurt thar at first."

How Flip Ended up in Tucson

Flippo's life took a turn out west with him living and calling the last sixteen years of his career in Tucson, Arizona, during the winter months and continuing his tour travels the rest of the year.

Flippo moved to Tucson, Arizona in 2000. He came out there to stay two years, and that became eighteen years. "I know a couple that was at my first class. It's their nineteenth year, so I thank they were here before I was." He was still living in Tucson when we started our interviews in 2017.

John Flippo, Flip's son, added details about Flip's move, "Dad owned Kirkwood '72 to '94, sold it to the Links in '94, who owned it until 2000. Dad stayed on and worked for the Links while they owned it and for the Buchheits and Landau for the first year they owned it, which was 2000, and I believe moved to Arizona the winter of 2000."

After Flippo and Pat sold Kirkwood to a new owner, the Links, and it resold again, Flippo only worked with the new owner one year because it wasn't the same.

So, Flippo was looking for something to replace Kirkwood. Shane Greer was the resident staff caller at Rincon West RV Resort in Tucson, and he wanted to raise his kids somewhere else, so he was giving up being this position.

Gary or Ken suggested Flippo take that position.

Flippo answered, "Well, I don't know." With a laugh, he added, "I don't want to get involved with all that stuff out thar."

Then [his second wife] got into it and agreed, "We ought to take that job."

So the activity director called them up and said, "We'll send you a plane ticket. You and your wife come on out here." So, she did, and they took them out to dinner, put them up for a night, and she showed them all around Rincon West RV Park Resort. And they stayed in an RV.

[Flippo's second wife] observed, "Well, you know, this ain't too bad. It's an RV."

Then Flippo corrected her, "No, it was a park model."

So, they decided to take it "'cause I didn't like the guy who had eventually bought Kirkwood. I didn't say I didn't like him, but I like a lot other people a lot better."

She told them about their activities. "I was just going to come for a couple years, but that didn't work that way. Now here's the thang I did for one year or maybe two: I still toured. I stayed here [Tucson] six months and then I'd tour the other six months. Wait a minute, hold it, hold it, hold it. I don't thank it's that important, but I called here for six months, and I know I worked one summer at Kirkwood, so I must have stayed two years with that old fart [Kirkwood's new owner]. I don't know."

To verify dates, I asked Shane Greer, and he replied, "I left Tucson in 1998, I believe he took over in 1999 or 2000. He was still working at Kirkwood, too, when he took over. If he said 2000, that is probably correct."

Flippo knew he was going to work six months in Tucson and six months at Kirkwood when they were opened. The six months in Tucson, they didn't dance anyway. He wandered that way, and from then on, Flip just kept touring. He toured during the summer, then Flip worked in Tucson in the winter, and he did that for a couple years.

As he remembered, he laughed with some sarcastic humor, "At that time we had a lot of dancers. You know, I built this sucker up out here after I got out here. I built it up from twenty-four squares to five squares. So, square dancing kept a falling off more."

Flippo described his [second wife]'s involvement at Rincon West. She worked in the office, and then they put her in charge of East Park, which is East Rincon. It's over on the east side, so, she stayed there for a while.

Then one day she warned Flippo, "I'm going back to Texas to be closer to the grandchildren."

Her desire to move bothered Flippo, and he was confused. Where she moved to in Texas was about twice as far from the grandkids as it was from Tucson.

Anyway, one day, Flippo's [second wife] warned him again, "I'm going to move back to Texas."

He never said she wanted a divorce at this time, but that's what happened!

Flip recalled they were carrying stuff in from the car. They'd been to the grocery store. "So, she took care of all the divorce proceedings and all that 'cause I had no idee how to do it. So, she'd bring thangs home for me to sign. Anyway, she moved on back. She stayed here for about six months, I believe, after she told me that."

She asked Flip if she could stay with him until the divorce was final.

"Sure."

She stayed a year. Flippo's generous spirit allowed her to stay for a year after the divorce!

So, she moved out by Galveston. "I thank she had a friend down thar that I didn't know of. I don't know how long she worked over at East Park."

But Flippo learned to live by himself. "It ain't too bad 'cause I go to the grocery store or whatever when I want to. Don't have to tell nobody nothing. So, it ain't too bad, but it's lonely."

. . .

Later Years

During Flippo's advancing years, a special couple, Bill and Linda Musson, drove him to his calling engagements from 2006–2016. At this time, he would doze off in the back seat often—things were changing for him. I enjoyed seeing them at different festivals, knowing that they were taking such good care of him.

Thinking back over the years in Tucson, Flippo ended with, "I had a hundred squares thar at one time. This wasn't the time, but that's a long time ago."

Flippo faced big changes during the years in Tucson, reinventing himself once more, but he kept calling half the year in Tucson, half on the road, and living his life!

AWARDS

2 Gold Records: 1st for selling 500,000 September 11, 1967 and 2nd for selling
1,000,000 records September 1972. Source: John Flippo

24

A CALLING LIFE REVERED!

I n Flippo's long and prolific career, he received awards and acknowledgment for his expertise:

- 1967 — Gold Record for 500,000 Records Recorded
- 1970 — *Sets in Order* Square Dance Society's Hall of Fame
- 1972 — Gold Record for one million records sold
- 2007 — Texas State Callers' Hall of Fame
- Texas State Archives

CALLERLAB Awards

- 1977 — Quarter Century Award
- 1981 — Milestone Award with Frank Lane and Cal Golden
- 1984 — Award of Excellence
- 2004 — Half-Century Award
- 2011 — Gold Card Membership
- 2016 — Lifetime Achievement Award

Sets in Order **American Square Dance Society's Hall of Fame**
"From 1961 to the present (1983), 34 leaders (including five couples) have been inducted into the Square Dance Hall of Fame.

Sets in Order Hall of Fame portrait of Marshall Flippo. Source: Neeca
Flippo

"Each inductee into the Hall of Fame had an oil portrait painted, which was hung in the *Sets in Order* Hall. Upon closing the magazine, the portraits are all sent to the Lloyd Shaw Foundation archive and dance center in Albuquerque, New Mexico, where they still hang."[1]

Sets in Order magazine featured these portraits on the cover with Flippo's portrait on the May 1970 issue.

Two Gold Records

Source: John Flippo

306

Flippo received his first Gold Record in 1967 for selling five hundred thousand records of "The Auctioneer." Flippo's voice lit up when he saw the picture of him and Norman with the plaque of "The Auctioneer" when it sold 500,000 records. He was the first square dance caller to receive a gold record.

Norman Merrbach congratulates Flippo at Kirkwood Lodge.
Source: Neeca Flippo

In 1972, Flippo received another Gold Record for selling one million records of "Every Street's a Boulevard."

From where Flip was sitting, he pointed out, "It's right up thar. I can see it right up thar now." He was describing the gold record in the room he was sitting in at the time we talked on the phone.

Norman Merrbach presents a Gold Record to Marshall Flippo as Bill Hagadorn of Kirkwood Lodge looks on.

Norman Merrbach, Flippo and Bill Hagadorn at Kirkwood Lodge. Source: Neeca Flippo

As he looked at the picture of Norman Merrbach, him, and Bill Hagadorn, he added,

"Wait a minute. On the right, far right is Bill Hagadorn, one of the best bosses, best bosses—smartest guy I guess I ever knew. He was the owner of Kirkwood. And that's up on a little podium up thar."

Flippo ended with, "God, we were young then. God!"

One Hundred Records Recorded

Flippo received a plaque from Norman Merrbach at Kirkwood honoring a hundred records recorded. When I asked where the plaque was, Flippo answered, "I guess it's out in the shed, yeah."

Flippo receiving a plaque for recording 100 records from Norman
Merrbach at Kirkwood Lodge. Source: Neeca Flippo

Texas State Archives

Flippo is in the Archives at the state capitol of Texas next to Willie Nelson.
With a chuckle, he added, "You can leave that out."

Flip added, "Well, I had a little niece that worked thar. I thank that's what
happened."

Texas Callers Hall of Fame

In 2005, Marshall Flippo joined the team that created the Texas Callers Hall of
Fame. The first three callers inducted into the Texas Callers Hall of Fame on
September 1, 2007 at the Chaparral weekend in Paris, Texas were Marshall Flippo,
Jim Brower and Al "Tex" Brownlee.[2]

A wonderful article about Flippo is available here:[3]

Here's a lively quote describing Flippo from this article: "A dancer, trying to
explain how Flippo manages to keep so busy throughout the year explains, 'He
wears well!'" [4]

CALLERLAB Awards

During his calling career of sixty-four years, Flippo received every award that
CALLERLAB awards its members!

· · ·

25 Years of Calling

At the 1977 CALLERLAB Convention in Chicago, the organization he helped start, recognized Flippo's twenty-five years of calling, as it does all its members.

Milestone Award

CALLERLAB'S Milestone Award, a prestigious award, recognizes callers who have exceptional leadership achievements.

1981 CALLERLAB Milestone Award Winners: Marshall & Neeca Flippo, Cal & Sharon Golden, Frank & Barbara Lane. Source: Neeca Flippo

In 1981, Frank Lane, Cal Golden, and Marshall Flippo received this award together.

When these pictures came up in our album wanderings, Flippo exclaimed, "This is when we got the damn Milestone Award. Looky here. And I guessed it all. I guessed all three of them. And they had us sitting down, all kind of down front—all three couples of us, and they had the Milestones. You could tell it was the Milestone. They had sheets over all three of 'em. They were all covered. But you could tell what they were."

1981 CALLERLAB Milestone Winners: Frank & Barbara Lane, Cal & Sharon Golden, Flippo. Source: Neeca Flippo

Flippo told the group seated at the table, "Ah damn, thar's a Milestone for you, Frank, one for you, Cal, and one for me."

They all just laughed because none of them thought that was going to be the case, but, when they called it out, it was called out in the exact order Flippo had guessed: Frank Lane first, and then Cal Golden, and then Flippo!

As he looked at the picture, he added, "Damn, we was young then."

Shirley Jones, Neeca Flippo, Jon Jones, Flippo and Melton Luttrell. Source: Neeca Flippo

He added, "Melton Luttrell—he's been my best friend—presented me with the Milestone award."

Flip and Neeca received a congratulatory letter from Al and Bea Brundage saying, "Bea and I would like to congratulate you on receiving the CALLERLAB Milestone Award. In my opinion, long overdue! Guess it's as close as we come to the 'Oscars' or 'Emmy' awards."

After looking at the letter, Flippo's responded, "Ain't that nice! That is nice. Very nice!"

As he looked at the letter, he added with strong emotions, "Yeah. God, it's been a long time."

Congratulatory notes: 1st from Joanie & Dale Cochran. 2nd from Max Forsyth.
Source: Neeca Flippo

Flippo also received notes celebrating his award from longtime dear friends. Joanie and Dale Cochran from Champaign, Illinois and Max Forsyth, a *caller*.

At the 1986 CALLERLAB Convention, Flip presented Melton with the Milestone Award—dear friends for years and the opportunity to honor each other!

Award of Excellence

Flippo continued to receive awards from CALLERLAB. In 1984, he received the Award of Excellence. As we were looking at this picture, he added, "And that is Bob Van Antwerp giving me—damn, I look pretty good."

Before I asked what award he received in this picture, Flip stated, "Don't ask me what that is."

Then he added, "I've got it out in the shed somewhere."

We couldn't read the name on the award, so I magnified the picture on my computer and it said "Award of Excellence."

Bob Van Antwerp giving Flippo the CALLERLAB Award of Excellence.
Source: Neeca Flippo

Gold Card Membership

Melton Luttrell presented Flippo with his Gold Card Membership.
Source: Neeca Flippo

On April 19, 2011, Flippo received the Gold Card Membership for calling fifty years at the 38th Annual CALLERLAB Convention in Las Vegas, Nevada, and again, his lifelong friend, Melton Luttrell, presented him with this award. Visit the video of the event.[5]

. . .

Lifetime Achievement Award

Flippo holding his Lifetime Achievement Award & his hilarious
acceptance speech. Source: Neeca Flippo

In 2016, Flippo received an award no one else had ever received, the Lifetime Achievement Award, and CALLERLAB had not yet prepared criteria for this new award. The day before the award's ceremony, he was hospitalized. Vernon Jones gave him this prestigious award. Visit the video to see Flippo's award and his hilarious acceptance speech.[6]

Flippo never bragged about his accomplishments but took a humble stance. These awards, respect, and honor lauded on a man confirmed he deserved each one!

---

1. Bob Osgood, *Sets in Order*, Loc 10429
2. Deborah Carroll-Jones, *American Square Dance*, (January 2008): 20-22.
3. "Texas State Callers Association," September 1, 2007. Texas Callers Hall of Fame article: https://9c4ae55c-9b62-4fa9-86b7-8f4deae14ee9.filesusr.com/ugd/7b8491_a5fc535dda974b3382b5a0460cfc1a5b.pdf
4. "Texas State Callers Association," September 1, 2007. https://9c4ae55c-9b62-4fa9-86b7-8f4deae14ee9.filesusr.com/ugd/7b8491_a5fc535dda974b3382b5a0460cfc1a5b.pdf
5. Dennis Farrar, "YouTube," May 7, 2011, Video of Flippo receiving his Gold Card Membership award: https://www.youtube.com/watch?v=ms4fb3PnQkg
6. CALLERLAB, April 27, 2016, Video of Flippo receiving the Lifetime Achievement Award: https://www.youtube.com/watch?v=eNAxdsZq16A

END OF FLIPPO'S CAREER

Marshall Flippo calling at his last Chaparral Weekend in Paris, Texas.
Source: Larada Horner-Miller

25

THE END OF A MARVELOUS CAREER

W ord got out to the dance community across the United State that 2016 would be "Farewell to the Road" for Flip, the end of touring. He would honor the remaining contracts he had signed but no more traveling. He would live in Tucson, Arizona, year-round.

So many cities across the United States scheduled events to honor the 60+ year calling career of Marshall Flippo. We had a delightful celebration in Albuquerque, New Mexico, on March 19, 2016. Wade Driver in Houston, Texas organized a big one in Houston in May. Other cities followed. Over Labor Day weekend in September, a big celebration started in Paris, Texas over Flip's birthday and ended in Abilene where his career started.

Albuquerque Square Dance Center's Last Dance with Flip—March 19, 2016

The Albuquerque square dance community honored Flippo at his last event sponsored by the dance hall board on March 19, 2016 with a potluck, festive decorations, a short program and lots of dancing. The dancers flocked to dance once more to one of their longtime favorites.

During the program, we surprised Flip with a 50 second sound-byte of "The Auctioneer" which brought tears to his eyes. I stood beside him seeing his emotion, then he signaled to cut it off.[1]

I also put together a video celebrating Flip[2] which we showed that night during the dance. What a night to remember!

Top: L to R: Flippo calling, Flippo and Bob Brundage. Bottom L to R:
Flippo with Larada Horner-Miller. Source: Larada Horner-Miller

Houston, Texas—May 23, 2016

On May 23, 2016, Wade Driver and Dee Dee Dougherty-Lottie joined Flippo on stage to call for his retirement party after a festive potluck, hosted by Bluebonnet Squares. They had in attendees: sixty-four Bluebonnet Squares' members, eighty-five visiting dancers, twenty non-dancers, fifteen callers and wives for a total of one hundred eighty-four. They created a beautiful photo album for Flippo with photos from the event, historical photos throughout his career and notes from friends, commemorating Flip's strong connection to the Houston dance community.

1st Row L to R: Thank you banner, Opening to Houston Album.
2nd Row L to R: Wade Driver, Flippo & Dee Dee Dougherty-Lottie,
Flipping greeting woman. Source: Bluebonnet's Album

Paris, Texas Festival—September 2016

THE FLAG
OF THE
UNITED STATES
OF AMERICA

This is to certify the accompanying flag was flown over the
United States Capitol at the request of the Honorable John Ratcliffe, Member
of Congress, in honor of Marshall Flippo's
exceptional contribution to the square dancing community

John Ratcliffe, Member of Congress
4th District of Texas

Certificate of flag given to Flippo flown over United States Capitol.
Source: Marshall Flippo

An extended weekend of celebration ended Flippo's career at the annual Labor Day Chaparral Square Dance Festival in Paris, Texas, with him calling September 2–4, 2016 with Ken Bower, Gary Shoemake, Mike Bramlett, Hunter Keller and Justin Russell. To top it off, it was Flip's eighty-ninth birthday on September 2. Before the dance stated Saturday night, Bob Hall presented Flippo with a flag and certificate that it had flown over the United States Capitol. He also gave Flippo an official document of resolutions honoring his contribution to the square dancing community.

After the dance and several skits at the After Party that Flippo participated in, we viewed a DVD presentation of Flippo's life created by Stan Jeffus and enjoyed an amazing *after party*[3] with Flippo participating in several of skits. One was with Mike Bramlett and another was with Mike and D' Bramlett and Justin Russell. The other was his famous "I Don't Look Good Naked Anymore."[4]

Flippo wasn't feeling well that weekend, but he called and did a fabulous job, calling and participating in the *after party* skits!

Calling Staff: Gary Shoemake, Marshall Flippo, Mike Bramlett, Justin Russell, Hunter Keller and Ken Bower. Source: Larada Horner-Miller

Flippo calling his last time at the Chaparral weekend in Paris, Texas, 2016. Source: Larada Horner-Miller

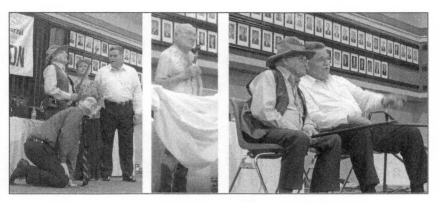

After Party Skits - L to R: Justin Russell, Flippo, D' and Mike Bramlett, Flippo, and
Flippo and Mike Bramlett. Source: Larada Horner-Miller

Abilene, Texas – September 2016

Flippo greeted people as the came in the door. 1st Row L to R:
Dee Bower, Flippo, and Ken Bower, Lin Miller, Flippo and Larada
Horner-Miller. 2nd Row L to R: Harue Swift, Flippo and Juanita
Portz, Flippo getting kissed, Mary Sheehan Johnson, Flippo and J.
J. Johnson. Source: Larada Horner-Miller & Mary Sheehan
Johnson

The celebration moved on to Abilene, Texas, to the Wagon Wheel, the dance hall Flippo and Neeca and three other couples built in 1958. Several dancers and *callers* drove from Paris to Abilene for "Flippo's Farewell to the Road" celebration on Labor Day, Monday, September 5, 2016. The day's celebration began with a Get Together/Welcome time from 2:00–4:00 p.m. ASARDA (Abilene Square and Round Dance Association) served a delicious Texas-style dinner at 5:30 p.m. The evening's festivities started with *round dancing*[5] at 6:30 p.m. with Kathy Stevens cuing. Square dancing began at 7:00 p.m., featuring Marshall Flippo and friends.

L to R: Gary Shoemake calling Flippo and Ken Bower, Gary
Shoemake, Flippo, Ken Bower and Jerry Junck. Source: Larada
Horner-Miller

Flippo, Neeca Flippo, Shelly & John Flippo. Source: John Flippo

The atmosphere in Abilene was celebratory with a tinge of reluctance and
sadness. Neeca, their son, John, and John's wife, Shelly, were in attendance. Melton
and Sue Luttrell were there, along with many lifetime friends like Gary Shoemake
and Ken and Dee Bower.

Life-Long friend, Melton & Sue Luttrell with Flippo. Source: John
Flippo

Later, Flippo shared Bob Sumrall's son and family were there to honor him that night. Flippo considered Bob Sumrall "the granddaddy of square dancing in Abilene."

Flippo remembered that evening, "You know the night ya'll come out to the birthday thang or whatever that was. A bunch of Bob Sumrall's kids were out thar. He's passed, but I got to talk to one big guy who was his son and his wife and a bunch of little kids, but they came up and said, 'Hey, I'm Bob Sumrall's son.' I was glad to talk with him."

Flip asked the young Sumrall if he ever tried calling.

He answered, "I tried it, but I was no good. I just quit."

Flippo added, "So anyway, it was good seeing them. I don't remember when they was little, but it was good of them to come out. And we mentioned somethang about Sumrall and I kind of introduced the kids, and they were so appreciative. It pleased me to learn they were thar."

The evening ended with one of Flippo's signature songs, "Another Square Dance Caller."

Through tears, I looked around the dance hall seeing I wasn't the only one feeling emotions. My husband, Lin had tears in his eyes, and I saw many others dabbing at their eyes, too.

That evening ended an era! It was a moment in square dance history I will never forget. When the song stopped, a solemn aura hung over the dance hall—Flippo's days of traveling as a caller were over!

Group of callers and cuers at Flippo's Farewell to the Road Dance, Abilene, Texas, 2016. Source: Larada Horner-Miller

Flippo and Gary Shoemake. Source: John Flippo

New Mexico Square and Round Dance Festival – May 2017

After this farewell event, Flip honored contracts he had: one being the New Mexico State Square and Round Dance Festival in Albuquerque, New Mexico, May 12 -14, 2017.

Flippo & Greg Tillery, the chairman of the New Mexico State Festival.
Source: Lynn Tillery

In 2008, Flippo had been hired to be the featured caller at the fiftieth anniversary of the Albuquerque Square Dance Club but ended up in the hospital. The next year at the annual March 2009 Flippo dance, a couple dancers put together a little remembrance of Flippo's hospital stay the year before. Joey Solis, a local caller, dressed up in cowboy boots and a hospital gown, hooked up to an IV pole attached to a whiskey bottle. I dressed up as a nurse, and we waited until the third tip and came into the hall.

L to R: Flippo, Joey Solis and Larada Horner-Miller in
Albuquerque, NM in 2008. Larada Horner-Miller, Flippo and Joey
Solis, 2017 skit revisited! Source: Larada Horner-Miller

When Flippo saw us, he stopped calling and exclaimed, "What the hell?" We wove our way through the crowd with lots of hooting and hollering by the dancers. Seeing Flip speechless and shocked was priceless.

At the 2017 New Mexico State Square and Round Dance Festival, we repeated our skit again and dressed up on Saturday night. We surprised Flip one more time and ended our long history together with a laugh!

Green Valley, Arizona – New Year's Eve, December 31, 2017

At the end of November 2017, Jerry Junck asked me in a phone conversation if we were going to Flippo's New Year's Eve dance in Green Valley, Arizona. Lin and I weren't sure.

He added, "I think Gary and I are going to drive down."

I had heard that this would be Flippo's very last calling.

"That's what he claims."

I added, "It sounds to me like it might be the place to be on New Year's Eve."

Flippo was asked four years earlier to sign a contract to do the Green Valley New Year's Eve dance, and he refused a couple times. Dean Capes, a member of the club, finally arrived with a contract in hand, so Flip couldn't refuse any longer.

As Flippo signed it, he stated, "I doubt if I will be here in four years!" But he was, and what a wonderful celebration it was.

Ann Salwaechter, a dear friend, called him the Sunday afternoon of the big event to see how he was feeling.

Flippo told her, "I'm nervous with all these professional callers coming tonight."

Ann exclaimed, "Flippo, you taught them all to call!"

When we arrived, Flippo met me at the door with a kiss, as usual. He always had a kiss for the ladies. He was greeting all the dancers as they came in and let me know about a man in attendance who wanted to talk to me about this book.

Numerous callers came from all over the USA, as well as many local callers. Larry Letson, a dear friend and caller from Indiana who had stopped calling, came in the door right after the announcements. It felt like a family reunion!

During the festive evening, the Green Valley square dance club gave Flippo a plaque thanking him for all his years of support.

Flippo called a memorable dance to faithful dancers and callers. Groups of callers gathered around the dance hall. Ken Bower, Gary Shoemake, and Wade Driver huddled together and shared a story (possibly a favorite Flippo), and belly laughs and deep laughter came from each of them.

Another time I saw Jerry Junck leaning up against a wall with eyes riveted on Flippo on stage. His expression stated everything—admiration and love for his mentor for decades, mixed with deep sadness. Often throughout the evening, the callers' eyes were glued to Flippo on stage with admiring expressions. Their teacher was done.

During the evening, he announced this book from the stage and asked a question he'd wondered about often in our interviews, "Who would want to buy a book about me?" In no way did he ask this question in a solicitous manner—he could not imagine anyone wanted to read a book about him. The crowd roared!

Several people came up to me after his announcement, querying when it would be done, wanting a copy.

Patty Greene, then chairperson of CALLLERLAB, exclaimed, "How are you going to edit out the X-rated stuff?"

During the amazing night, Flippo handpicked his music. He sang, "Another Square Dance Caller." He shared a heartfelt thank you to everyone in attendance and ended his final dance with the song, "I'm Leaving Here a Better Man." I'm sure that's how he felt that night!

Here's the chorus to his last song with a profound message:

> *Still, I'm leavin' here a better man*
> *For knowin' you this way*
> *Things I couldn't do before now I think I can*
> *And I'm leavin' here a better man*[6]

Flippo receives an award from Kay Hill, Vice President, Green Valley Square and Round Dance Club, Flippo and Dean Capes, MC. Source: Larada Horner-Miller

Callers from all over the United States in attendance to Flippo's Last Night. Source: Larada Horner-Miller

When Flippo stopped calling and the music ended, people gathered around him after the traditional big thank you circle. So many wanted to thank him personally with a final hug and kiss. Flippo and his fans lingered, exchanging stories. No one wanted the evening to end.

I'm sure that a sizable group of callers and friends took Flippo to a local drinking establishment to end the night with drinks, camaraderie, and stories to mark the end of an era in the square dance world.

To see the caller list of attendees for Flippo's last night, see Appendix G.

Kim Oxendine gives Flippo a hug with Gina and Tom Crisp waiting in line. Source: Larada Horner-Miller

Flippo calling his last contract New Year's Eve, Green Valley, Arizona 2017. Source: Larada Horner-Miller

---

1. Larada Horner-Miller, "YouTube," March 24, 2020, Flip signaling to cut off the sound-byte, https://youtu.be/CGpQKk9MLSc
2. Larada Horner-Miller, "YouTube," March 20, 2016, Celebrating Flippo, https://www.youtube.com/watch?v=m92CcYxnmBA
3. **After Party** — The party after the square dance with skits and a variety of entertainment usually put on by the event staff of callers and cuers. Sometimes dancers participated in skits, too.
4. Larada Horner-Miller, "YouTube," March 24, 2020, Flippo & "I Just Don't Look Good Naked Anymore," https://youtu.be/HTD_XHHFr5g

5. **Round Dancing** — Couple dancing in a circle formation, using choreographed routines to a definite arrangement of music.
6. genius.com, 2020, https://genius.com/Clint-black-a-better-man-lyrics

26

FOUR SPECIAL "ONCE MORES"

D id Flippo somehow know the end was near? He died in 2018 and connected in four very special ways with people and places he loved, once more!

Once More to CALLERLAB – March, 2108

Flippo's last CALLERLAB was in Albuquerque, New Mexico, March 26–28, 2018 so we arranged to have extended time together to work on this book.

He let me know that Bob and Cinda Asp were bringing him, and Bob had a Board of Governors meeting Wednesday afternoon until 3:00 p.m.

"I'll have that 12:00 to about 3:00 then. And any other time. You know, I don't do anythang at CALLERLAB anymore."

In preparation to come to CALLERLAB, I asked him if he was ready to come to Albuquerque.

Flippo responded, "No, not really. I haven't packed anythang. I got to wash clothes tomorrow. My laundry is . . . My whites and the darks are running over."

I reminded him of a couple things that he needed to bring: his war book and any pictures that he wanted me to scan. I promised to scan them and get them right back to him the next day.

He added, "I've got the war book packed and the manila envelope with some other stuff."

This was my first CALLERLAB, and I saw Flippo often during the three days talking to his friends. Tuesday night, they had a "Duos" time during the evening square dance, and he called a *tip*[1] with Elmer Sheffield and Dana Schirmer to his favorite song, "Every Streets a Boulevard."[2]

On Wednesday, we met in a restaurant at the host hotel and started to go through one of the three albums/scrapbooks Neeca made. We stopped for lunch and cigarette breaks for him. Several callers passing by wanted to say goodbye to him. It was a very profitable work time because we finished going through one album/scrapbook.

Then Flippo strategically took the three albums/scrapbooks back with him, and they became the focus for many of our interviews.

Flippo's last comment about the convention was he had the room next to his lifelong friend, Melton Luttrell. "He told me to turn my TV down."

During CALLERLAB 2018, he lost a dear friend, Bob Brundage, who lived in Albuquerque. Flip had looked forward to time with Bob, so I saw this dampen his spirit during the convention—another loss!

L to R: Melton Luttrell, Royce Dent, & Flippo, Melton Luttrell, Tom Miller & Flippo at CALLERLAB in Albuquerque 2018. Source: Donna Schirmer & Tom Miller

Once More to Asilomar, Flippo's Favorite Venue – April, 2018

A dream came true for Flippo. He was trying to find a cheap ticket to San Jose, California because Mary Sheehan Johnson and her husband, J.J., live in Morgan Hill, which is twenty miles south of San Jose and close to Asilomar. Flippo met Mary in 1973 when she was seventeen and in college preparing to be a teacher. He met her folks and her sister.

Mary and Flippo had talked about a return trip to Asilomar, "and I'd better get it done because I might not have enough time to see it. I thought, 'Well, I don't know whether I'll ever get to go or not,' and so one day, she called me."

Flippo answered, "Fine. By the way, Mary, I tried to get tickets down to San Jose. I asked Barbara about it. She's the one that does my plane tickets. The only thang she can find was $360, so I'm going to have to wait awhile to go to Asilomar, I guess."

Excited, she stated, "Flippo, our minds must run together. I have been worried about your plane ticket and how much it's going to cost us to spend a couple nights at Asilomar. For the last week, I've been on the damn computer trying to find a good flight for you."

They were doing it at the same time but didn't know it.

And she mentioned, "Well, I've already contacted Asilomar. They said as many times as we were there they're going to give us a break on the rooms."

Flippo clarified, "J. J., her, and me."

Flippo and Mary Sheehan Johnson at the Asilomar Sign. The gate
leading into Asilomar. Source: J. J. Johnson

As Mary reminisced she revealed, "I want to go to those old buildings and smell the familiar Asilomar mixture of smoke from the fireplaces and the scent of the ocean and old wood. But we've got to find your ticket."

Two days later, Mary called back with the price of $177, round trip from Tucson to San Jose, no stops.

"Boy, that's good!"

"Well, they've got this special on, and I've got a hold on it if you want it."

Flippo planned to fly out, and they would pick him up. Then they would spend two nights in Morgan Hill—Saturday and Sunday night, and then Monday and Tuesday go to Asilomar.

Mary proudly announced, "I've got your old room for you."

Flippo & Mary Sheehan Johnson &
Merrill Hall sign. Merrill Hall is the
building where the square dances
were held. Source: J. J. Johnson

It was the room Flippo stayed in for thirty-six years, and he could open the window and hear that ocean coming in. "You wonder what the poor folks are doing."

Then Mary called a few days before time to leave and asked, "Now, is everything firm on this?"

He answered, "As far as I know, unless I die, and if I die I might even take the hearse over to your house, and we can go down in it."

Flip continued, "But I'm looking forward to that, you know. I hope you can still open the windows and hear that roar of the surf coming in."

He added with a laugh, "It was one of those good thangs that happen."

Flippo added about Mary, "I thank she likes Asilomar as well as I did."

He recalled Mary saying, "I lived from Asilomar to Asilomar." It was just a gorgeous place, and Flippo told me they had so much fun there. "It was unbelievable."

❧

Again, Flippo's thoughtful nature came out, "Anyhow, thangs changed a lot, too, but basically it's still the same. I have so many fond memories thar. I thank it's unbelievable. I remember thangs, then I'll go through and thank, 'Now, what the hell was that I was remembering?' If I don't write it down, I'm screwed."

During the week of April 21–28, 2018 Flippo flew out to California. On Monday, April 23, they drove forty miles from San Jose to Asilomar once more with his dear friend, Mary and J. J. Flippo slept in his old room and noticed some specific remodeling done to this favorite spot. He wanted to hear the sound of the Pacific Ocean once more out that window.

Flippo's response after the trip was, "I'm trying to get recovered from our trip down to Asilomar. It was wonderful."

He emphasized, "I shall never forget it."

Flip got to stay in the same room he stayed in for thirty-six years. They had renamed it to "'Pirate's Den,' pirates like out on the sea." It was 'Tide Inn' all the time he used it, but Flip got to stay in the same room, and it was basically the same; however, they had remodeled the bathroom. They'd changed it, but it was much better.

When he stayed there before, Flip moved the mirror to above the sink, "And so that stayed thar ALL the time. I don't know how many people lived thar other than me for a weekend and a week each year, but that ole mirror stayed thar 'til I left."

With a chuckle, he acknowledged the renovations made. Now they had a real nice mirror and a place to put his shaving kit. Before Flip didn't have much place "'cause they had an ole table over thar where I put

Flippo & Mary standing by Pirates' Den sign (which used to be called "Tide Inn"). Source: J. J. Johnson

my shaving kit and everythang. [Now] thar's a real good tile on a counter, and underneath thar is storage and they even had a hair dryer in thar. I was surprised. Didn't need it but I was surprised."

Flippo enjoying his old room. Source: J. J. Johnson

Flippo & Mary Sheehan Johnson —the windows of his room are
just behind Mary's head. Source: J. J. Johnson

When he got to thinking about his room at Asilomar, a funny story came up. Flip was talking to Wade Driver one time about Asilomar. Wade did the summer Asilomar, and Flippo always did the spring or the winter.

Flippo mentioned Tide Inn, and Wade stated, "Don't say that. I want to get that out of my mind."

Surprised, Flippo asked, "What's wrong? You can open that window and hear the surf come in. Man, it is somethang."

Wade answered, "Open that window, my ass. I was freezing to death. I had every blanket in that room on me, and it had three beds, so . . ."

Flippo added, "He had three blankets on."

He complained, "I nearly froze."

Flip asked, "Why didn't you turn the thermostat up?"

Wade stated, "There was no thermostat."

Flippo suggested, "Wade, you should have walked out your room, turn left, go to the hallway, turn left. Right thar is the thermostat for the whole building."

"Ohhhh, now you tell me! Why didn't you tell me that before?"

Flippo ended the story, "Anyway, that's just one of the funny thangs. He liked to froze to death." It was an old building, but Asilomar had come a long way. Across the road from Asilomar they were building condos. It's state-owned, "but they're awful sticky about the fee they charged for staying thar. Yeah, Mary got us a rate that was pretty good, but she told them all about how many times we's thar and everythang. So, they give us a break."

Flippo's friends, Mary and J. J. stayed across the hall from him. Afterwards, they drove down to Cannery Row and all around and went down 17-Mile Drive, just having a good time. They went through downtown Salinas and had lunch. Flippo thought he had never been downtown. "I thought it just an ole burg, just where I turned left [to go to Asilomar], you know? But it's a pretty big town. It's really a farming community, and they really had a good town—nice buildings, good clean town, and we eat at some diner, some ole restaurant."

2nd Sunday Afternoon .. February 10th .. 2 to 5 P.

The *TAW TWIRLERS* of Monterey Peninsul

Proudly Present For Your Dancing Pleasure

MARSHAL FLIPPO

Direct From Winter Asilomar

SALINA NATIONAL GUARD ARMORY
on Howard St. between Salinas & Lincoln Ave.
.... In Downtown Salinas ....

Source: Neeca Flippo

He realized he had called in Salinas when we were going through the albums/scrapbooks, "So I guess I did call thar 'cause it says it right here. 'Salinas

National Guard Armory'—'Direct from Asilomar.' So, I guess I did call in Salinas. Well, now—golllly boy. What memories!!!"

Flippo described Mary's husband, "J. J. Johnson, Mary's husband. We've known each other a long time, and he is a picture fool. In fact, he's getting up some pictures we took on this trip, and he hopes to make an album out of them."

So Flippo enjoyed his last time at Asilomar, a step back into the past to his favorite place!

Once More to the 67th National Square Dance Convention with John – June, 2018

John, Flippo's son, helped Flippo get to the National Square Dance Convention in Kansas City, Missouri, June 27–30, 2018. For Flip, this was like a big family reunion where he connected with his friends from all over the world.

We were talking the week of the convention, and Flippo remarked, "Now I am going to go to the Nationals on Friday. I'll probably just go to the motel and go to sleep 'cause my plane don't get in until around four o'clock, and I have a three-hour layover in Dallas. So, I'm going to be tired as hell. John's coming."

The plan was John would come in from the lake and they would go to the convention on Saturday, and then they would leave early Sunday morning and head back to the lake.

Concerned about our interviews, Flip added, "I guess we could talk from thar. I'm going to spend six weeks with him and Shelly."

He added about the convention, "I'm trying to finagle a way in thar other than a spectator, and I thank CALLERLAB's getting us a pass, but I can't dance and I retired from calling, so all I want to do is get in and see ole friends that are thar."

After the convention, Flippo shared, "Thought I'd get to see Jerry Junck at the Nationals, but he's last calling assignment was, I thank, 7:30 or 8:00 on Saturday night, and then he took off driving home because it was his mother's birthday, so he drove on home. He got home, I thank he told me, at one o'clock at night."

Flippo added with a laugh, "And he said, 'if I'd a stayed, I'd a probably wouldn't left 'til eight or nine in the morning and miss half of her birthday.' So, anyway he went on home. I didn't get to see him at the National. I did see Shoemake though and Bower at Nationals."

Flip spent Saturday threading his way through the crowds of people who wanted to greet him. He hugged and kissed as many women as possible and shook as many hands and gathered as many hugs. This was his tribe, his people. He loved being with them, one last time.

Once More to Tucson with John and Shelly – September, 2018

Flippo spent six weeks in at Osage Beach, Missouri, with John and Shelly, as planned—right across the street from Kirkwood Lodge—had visits from many callers and enjoyed their availability to him. He then planned to return to Tucson to his home and friends, but his plans changed. Flip ended up in the hospital twice with pneumonia in July and August. During the last hospital stay, his doctor advised him that he could no longer live alone. So Flippo started the adjustment he knew he would eventually have to face—giving up his independence and moving in with John, but he wasn't ready. He loved being with John and Shelly, but this signaled such a major life adjustment.

During one of our interviews before they left, he talked about his home in Tucson, saying that the saleswoman said it would be a hard sale because it didn't have an Arizona Room.

Flip had an answer for her, "Well, somebody can git it pretty cheap because I'll sell cheap, and then they can put one on thar, you know, cheaper than they can buy one with it already on thar. Hopefully I can sell it before the October date. I'm supposed to pay my rent for the whole year, so if I can save that, it would really help a lot."

He also planned to talk to George O'Leary because he used to buy RVs and

John, Shelly Flippo and Flippo on the Lake. Source: John Flippo

redo them, and Flip heard that he quit doing that. He didn't want to talk to him on the phone but face-to-face. George had been a good friend to Flip. Flip thought he might buy it. "I don't know, but she put a 'For Sale' sign up today on it, and so, I hope it sells before the first of October."

So, on September 15, 2018, John, Shelly, and Flippo flew back to Tucson, Arizona to pack up his belongings and to sell his park model home and car.

They had to spend the night in Dallas on the way out because the airplane didn't arrive in time to make connections. So, they put them up in a 250-dollar room.

They moved everything out in pretty good shape. "I tell ya—ole John and Shelly—they did somein' else. I couldn't believe it, and I sold my unit. I sold my car."

He continued, "Sold both of 'em, so we're out of thar, I guess, and of course, we're on the phone back and forth, but as far as I know, everythang's going off pretty good."

They shipped sixteen boxes of his belongings from Tucson to Missouri.

On September 18, 2018, the square dancers in the Tucson area held a nice going-away party for Flip, even though he wondered about it.

"Ah, I didn't know—you know—half wanted to do that thang, and I said, 'Thar's nobody here, Ann! They're all gone. If we have ten people, we're gonna be lucky.'"

Ann Salwaechter, a dear friend of Flip's, assured him, "No, no, no. We'll have more than that." He also shared his doubts about the party with Harue Okazaki Swift.

They had friends from Sierra Vista and Mesa, and so Flippo was quite surprised and saw a lot of old friends. They had about sixty people at the party, which surprised Flip. Winter dancing in Tucson usually starts in mid-October, so this was a good turn out for this time of the year. This ended an era for Flippo, his life in Tucson.

1st L to R: : Rick Gittelman, Dave Walker, Don Haney, Ron Koehler, Ron Hunter. Flippo & Harue Okazaki Swift 2nd: Trying to get a little of his CALLING MOJO and blessing Flippo! Source: Harue Okazaki Swift

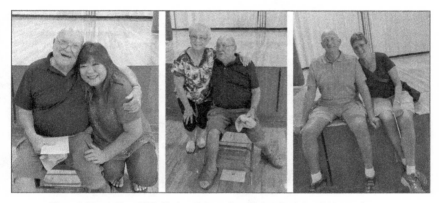

Flippo & Harue Okazaki Swift, Ann Salwaechter, Bob & Patti Ann Jackson. Source: Harue Okazaki Swift

More friends, Flippo is serenaded. Source: Harue Okazaki Swift

1st Row L to R: Harue Okazaki Swift & John Flippo, Harue Okazaki Swift kissing Flippo, Flippo talking to Ron Hunter. 2nd Row: Circle of Flippo's friends. Source: Harue Okazaki Swift

John & Shelly Flippo and Patti Ann Jackson and Harue Okazaki Swift giving Flippo a kiss. Source: Harue Okazaki Swift

Flip filled his last year with four memorable "Once Mores," events that he

cherished! Each of these had such a major significance to him as he looked back at his life!

---

1. **Tip** - A square dance session consisting of two parts, a patter call, and a singing call. See Glossary for more.
2. Horner-Miller, Larada. "Marshall Flippo, Elmer Sheffield, Dana Schirmer Calling to 'Every Streets a Boulevard'" March 27, 2018. https://youtu.be/_Qw6VNTKugk

27

MUSINGS ABOUT FLIPPO'S CAREER, HIS LIFE AND THIS BOOK

W e don't often have the chance to hear our elders speak about their lives, careers, and end of life. I did with Flip. I loved the times Flippo sat back and pondered his life, "I had many, many good memories thar [Asilomar]. And— you know—Larada, it just seemed like I never did ride anybody for a badge or anythang. It seemed like it all just kinda happened, like with Blue Star. The way I recorded was he called me. But I hadn't even thought about recording until all that happened. I told you before—at Kirkwood, Bill asked me if I'd come and be a staff caller. Well, I know I'd have to give up my job. Neeca'd have to give up her job, and I told him all that. And then Osgood from California called me and asked me if I'd work at Asilomar. So, it seemed like I just kinda lucked out on thangs."

He added with a laugh, "I never really pushed myself toward anythang, but I was glad to get it, whatever comes. I don't know how they explained it. I know one thang is is that I dearly do love people, and I thank that friendship goes a long way! Just happened to be at the right place at the right time. Whatever it was was good. I look back on it and thank, 'Well, wish I could do it all again!'"

Flippo added, "I see thangs that I dearly loved to do when I was younger, and I know that I'll never do again. That's the hard part about getting old. I'll see somebody waterskiing. I thought, 'Oh God,' and I'll never do it again, and the same with calling. Dad burn! I'll never call again, and it bothers me more than anythang. However, I am enjoying retirement. Like I said, I thank I'd be glad to start all over again! I'd change a few thangs, but I've been lucky through a life, so I gotta bitch about it."

He continued, "I was lucky to have a good momma and dad, I know that, and sisters. So anyway, thar's another thang I thought of the other day that I ought to —now I can't 'member it, but I know I wrote it down somewhere. So, I'll find that note somewhere."

He ended this walk down memory lane with, "I really didn't sell all those records. I have a garage full of them somewhere." He kept his humor alive!

Flippo's relationships with so many people continued throughout his lifetime. He related a story after I shut off the recorder one day about an old friend coming by and it "blew my mind. It shook my day up! The person came at noon and left at two o'clock."

Hospital Stories

With a laugh, Flippo shared, "I was in the hospital two days."

Flip thought he could have come home in one day, but the doctor demanded, "No, you're not going home today. You could, but I want to see you in the morning, so you're staying over."

So he stayed over, and the doctor came early the next day, and they talked a while.

Then Flip sang this sentence in his best calling voice, "He examined me a while."

He took Flippo's oxygen level with "that thang they put on your finger, you know? Yeah, it was good. It was up in the 90s. That's where it's supposed to be."

"Oh," the doctor stated, "boy, it's a lot better than when you came in. It was 82."

When Flippo checked into the clinic, a nurse responded, "If it was 82, he couldn't talk," and added, "Well, wait a minute." She checked it later and said, "It's down to 80 now and he's still talking."

With a laugh, he added, "So anyway, they got that sucker up pretty good. They give me some inhalers and stuff like that, and I know they are helping it, and I really feel good after I use it, but, no, I survived okay, and I feel really, really good. So, I'm glad of that."

When I asked him when he went to the hospital, he responded, "Oh, God! All these days! When you retired, you don't know what day it is." He went over Friday and stayed Friday night, and then on Saturday the doctor said, "Nay, you'll have to stay over." So, Flip stayed over on a Sunday and got out Sunday. "And so, I'm doing well."

ᔥ

Flippo had a flip phone until almost the end of his life, and often during our conversations he'd struggle to hear me. At one point, when he was in the hospital, the doctor started laughing at Flippo's flip phone. When the doctor took it, it rang, and so he answered it.

He stated, "It's for you," and handed it back to Flip.

When Flippo finished the call, the doctor added, "Your volume is way down."

Flippo agreed, "Tell me about it! We're fixed to go to Verizon in a couple days, see if they can fix it."

The doctor offered to look at it, so he turned it over and did something.

And he stated, "You can hear now."

344

Flippo laughed. "What the hell'd you do?"

He answered, "On the outside thar's two black buttons, and it's usually above your thumb but sometimes when you're holding your phone, your fingers right on it, and you probably hit by accident, and you hit the lower volume."

Flippo ended, "And so, within about a minute, he had my phone fixed right up and the reception is so good 'cause I can hear now!"

Later on, Flippo was talking to a nurse, and that same doctor remarked, "Hell, you're a square dance caller."

Flip looked at him and realized, "He had googled me up in his computer he's carrying around."

The doctor continued, "Hey, thar's a lady right there writing a book about you."

Flippo agreed, then the doctor commented, "I might even read that damn thang, and it's kind of interesting to me. I worked on a square dance caller."

Flippo promoted, "Well, by golly, it's available. Lady in Albuquerque's doing it, and it will be available, and it's $20-25."

The doctor added, "Oh, I'll be a little older than this."

Flippo laughed and added, "No, it'll be out, probably next year."

❧

Talking about the book, Flippo looked to the future and made a stark statement, "Larada, tell me. You're sitting right thar thanking that this book will sell."

I assured him it would, and I had already enough pre-orders to cover the cost of editing and printing the initial batch. He was so worried about my expenses, so I guaranteed him that I would be okay.

Flip responded, "Oh, well, that's good. I'll relax a little then, 'cause I's afraid you wouldn't gonna get no money out of this."

Overhearing our conversation, Lin jumped in, "Flip, right now we're looking for a Japanese translator."

"Are you? Wait a minute. God Almighty!"

I shared with Flip that one of the pre-orders was for Doc [Masaharu Hiraga] from Japan.

Flippo & Larada talking about this book in Green Valley, New Year's Eve, 2017. Source: Harue Okazaki Swift

He replied, "Oh well, you know, if those other callers see that Doc bought it, they're going to buy it, too, 'cause Doc is the main guy over thar [Japan]. And they'll say, 'Well, we follow ole Doc like people over here follow Jerry Story.' So, Jerry buys somethang, all the rest buy somethang, so well, he'll pass the word around Japan over thar. I used to do a lot of Japanese. I don't know whether they still square dancing, but I went over two or three times."

345

ॐ

Another time, out of the blue, Flippo stated, "Oh, I don't want a Fan Club or t-shirts or my picture on it."

I was confused then realized what he was talking about. I had created a Marshall Flippo Fan Club Group on my author's Facebook page to promote his biography. Also, Lin and I had worn t-shirts with his picture on them at the Fun Valley Resort in Colorado as a promotion and posted our picture in our t-shirts on Facebook.

I assured Flip that the only ones that would have the t-shirts with his pictures on it was Lin and me. That's it—nobody else. I used Whitey and Gladys Puerling's idea and made a group on Facebook, just to promote this book and post some of his pictures there.

He agreed to those limitations. "But I thought maybe you were selling 'em."

"No, no, no, no. Lin and I are the only ones that have those shirts. Nobody else gets one."

"Okay, okay."

ॐ

On October 20, 2018, we had scheduled an interview, but Flippo was sick with pneumonia, so we had to cancel it and reschedule for the next week. We did chat for a little while, and he lamented on "that dang pneumonia again."

He explained, "It's the second time, but wasn't too bad. I'm gittin' to know the doctors so. Ahhh, yeah, she [Neeca] came down, and she's here about three days that week before I had this. Okay, I'm gonna quit. I'm very sorry about it."

He ended with his usual greeting to Lin. "We'll see you later. Okay, hon, love you."

"You bet, love you!"

"I love you!!!"

Through all the ups and downs, Flippo kept his sense of humor. I loved his interest in the intricacies of this book, thinking we had ample time ahead of us to continue the interviews and that ultimately, he would live to help edit and see this book published. It didn't work that way.

Taken on October 13, 2018 — Flippo, Neeca, John and Shelly. Source: John Flippo

28

OUR LAST CONVERSATION

At the time, I had no idea this would be our last conversation. Yes, Flippo had been sick again with pneumonia for the third time in four months, but he seemed better than our previous talk.

The interview began with Flippo clearing up some name spellings and miscellaneous questions that he had written down on scraps of paper and found—specifics like the band who played for the second recording of "The Auctioneer."

When he finished those, he focused on this book project. I had sent him some of the beginning chapters to read and a preliminary outline of the book.

Breathing heavy, Flip whispered, "I haven't gotten done hardly at all, but I's reading this outline."

With a chuckle, he added, "Ah, I'm not too sure of the name, yet."

His labored breathing continued.

After some discussion about the title, he responded, "I don't know. I'm still dickerin' with it. I thank that's still pretty good title, though."

Flip continued to ask about having a hard back book and demanded, "Ah, I don't want it to be too big!" Remembering the size of Bob Osgood's biography, he stated, "It is monstrous. I don't want it to be that big! It's summin."

We talked about the picture placement, and I shared that I thought it would be good to have pictures throughout relating to chapter, and then maybe a little photo album at the back."

Flippo whispered, "I thank I like that, too." Then we discussed the number of pictures available. There were so many!

Flip asked an interesting question, "Is it gonna be slick pictures?"

I told him it would probably be pictures within the page, which won't be slick. Amazing that he would think of a specific like that!

Then he asked, "Did you get that picture of me calling with the band behind us?"

"Yes."

Flip added, "John's got that. He got that blew up and I don't know why. I don't know where we're gonna put it, but it might be pretty good on the fly page thar in front or somethang."

His humor continued, ". . . or in the back. It don't matter."

The conversation continued about the organization of the book.

Flippo stated, "Ah, I'm gonna have summin' to say, I guess, after your Dedication," then we talked about the possible location of the Acknowledgment page. I had listed a possible Prologue for both of us, and he really wanted to write his.

As we talked, Flippo laughed, "Just a minute. My hearing aid fell out. I gotta git it back in. I can't hear. I was looking forward, and I blew it." I waited for three to four minutes.

When he returned, he apologized and said, "I need new earrings," and we laughed at his statement.

As we continued down the book outline, Flippo added, "Another thang, too, is I really wanta get Neeca in thar 'cause she's the one that really got me, you know, took care of my tours and my bookings and all that stuff and took care of the money. She's a frugal gal. I wouldn't have a cent now if it wasn't for her."

We continued to wrestle with the organization of chapters. He emphasized that Blue Star was really what changed things. Then Flip went back and forth on the importance of Blue Star and Kirkwood. He finally settled with, "Blue Star changed everythang, and then a bigger change came when I went to Kirkwood."

Going over the outline encouraged him to reminisce. Flippo retold his trip to Houston to record "The Auctioneer" and made sure I had Norman Merrbach's name spelled correctly, "Merrbach—M-E-R-R-B-A-C-H. Norman and Nadine." He still spelled out names so I would get them correct.

When we got to his tour section, Flippo summarized, "Went east. I went north, east, south, and then home for Christmas. I went north and west then." Then Flippo retold how he ended up at Kirkwood.

When we got to the CALLERLAB chapter, Flip talked about the picture of the original eleven. "They're all gone now except Frank and I." Frank Lane died October 31 and Flippo soon followed.

We discussed the placement of the CALLERLAB chapter, and Flippo reminded me that Asilomar had to go first. He couldn't remember where the CALLERLAB name came from but added, "I don't know who coined the phrase CALLERLAB, but one of those guys did, and I'll try to find that out, too, and we finally all decided on that'd be a good, a good name for it."

As our interview drew near an end, Flippo promised, "I'll try to get through the rest of this outline before next week. I'm sorry I haven't gotten any further than I have. Thangs have been happening terrible around here. Not terrible, but . . ."

I assured him, "Well, you were sick."

He remarked, "Fast, fast! Well, we had to move and all that stuff."

I asked about a story about Dave Hodson that Flippo had talked about in connection with an ad Kirkwood did annually in the National Square Dance Convention program book. He asked if I had the ad, and I did.

He responded "Oh, you're super-duper!"

As he reflected, Flippo shared with a laugh, "So many funny thangs! When they come to me, they come to me at night, and the next morning, 'What the hell was that?'"

I looked at the clock and realized our hour had ended.

Flippo stated, "Talking to you time passes fast!" I wholeheartedly agreed.

Flippo interrupted me and then laughed, "You said summin' and I jumped on top of ya. What was it?" I repeated my agreement. We set up the next week to talk on Wednesday at our normal time. "Three o'clock my time, two o'clock yours."

My heart ached as I listened to him during this interview. He had trouble breathing and seem exhausted, so I said, "I hope you're feeling better, and hopefully, you're getting over that pneumonia."

Flip replied, "The last few days I've felt really, really good, so I'm hopin' I'm gettin' over it, anyway, I thank you for the call, pretty girl. Tell ole Lin I said hello."

As we ended, I assured him that the book was coming together.

"Okay, sugar. I hope so."

Flippo ended our conversation, "Okay, hon, will see ya next week!"

I responded, "Okay, love you!"

"I love you, hon!"

And, in unison, we chorused, "Bye, Bye!"

Flippo sounded weak but lucid during our talk. It thrilled me that he took such an interest in the specifics of this book. He had bounced back before, so I had no doubt he would again.

&.

As I looked back, the last six months of our conversations took an interesting twist. We didn't talk from June 21 to July 11, 2018. We both had commitments for a couple weeks and decided to take a break.

We made plans to talk on Wednesday, July 17, but Flip confused our time and thought it was the next day, so we talked on Thursday, July 18.

During our interviews, he repeated retirement was hard because he missed his friends.

My last interview with Flippo was October 24, 2018, but he called me the weekend after when I was in Walla Walla, Washington at a writing conference asking me if I had talked to [his second wife] yet. I told him I had called and left a message but hadn't heard back.

On October 31, 2018, one of Flippo's best friends, Frank Lane, died. I was supposed to talk with Flip that day, but John texted me to postpone our interview. After that, I followed John's posts on Facebook to get reports on Flip: good one day, then down the next.

Sunday afternoon, I got a text from Sharon McCafferty that Ann Salwaechter had told her that Flip's body was shutting down. I checked my email, and Ann sent more info from Shelly, John's wife.

I cried in Lin's arms before I left to go to Albuquerque to have dinner with a girlfriend, knowing somehow that this was the end for Flippo. On my drive to town, I checked my iPhone the whole way, dreading a report.

Flippo passed away Sunday, November 4, 2018 about 6:00 p.m.—Bryan Swift, Harue's husband, texted me, asking if I had seen the news on Facebook about Flip. Harue was in Japan and got the news first.

Thankfully, my girlfriend understood my pain, and I sobbed and sobbed, then I got a text from Mike Bramlett to call him. I tried but got a busy signal so I texted him. He called me immediately, and we comforted each other with D', Mike's wife, on speaker phone.

Flippo's death rocked the square dance world. When I got home, I went to Facebook to share my pain, and condolences and reminisces flooded my newsfeed.

Later, I emailed Neeca my condolences and she sent a lovely response. I had trouble sleeping that night—Flippo talked to me in my dreams all night. Monday morning, I called Jerry Junck, and we cried together.

On November 13, Lee Kopman, another national *caller* who greatly influenced our activity, died—three giants in the square dance world gone within three weeks.

Cartoon by CORBEN GEIS. Source: CORBEN GEIS

29

MARSHALL FLIPPO'S MEMORIAL
SERVICE & OBITUARY

A *Celebration of Marshall Flippo*

On November 26, 2018, loved ones gathered at Elliott-Hamil Funeral Home in Abilene, Texas to celebrate the life of Marshall Flippo. And what a celebration it was!

Thinking about the possible crowd, Lin and I arrived at the funeral home forty-five minutes early, and the reception area already overflowed with *callers* and dancer friends. We greeted close friends from all over the country who had come to honor a true legend. We were ushered into the chapel early. The majority of the people present were professional *callers* from all over the United States—the cream of the crop, for sure. We continued greeting each other with hugs and subdued smiles.

I looked for Mary Sheehan Johnson, a treasured friend of Flip's who took him to Asilomar, the site of his absolute favorite festival, in April for his last visit. We found each other and felt like we were old friends because of our common denominator, Flippo.

Kayla Jones began the service with beautiful soft music. Reverend David Hargrove officially opened with a warm greeting, Flippo's obituary and a prayer.

Then Jon and Deborah Carroll Jones and Vernon and Kayla Jones sang a beloved hymn, "The Old Rugged Cross." With the majority of attendees being *callers* and singers, many joined in. What a beautiful start!

Gary Shoemake gave the first eulogy with heartfelt stories. His longtime friendship with Flippo shined through his words and tears. We laughed and cried in response to his stories. I cried with my grieving friend and his raw emotion. Afterward, we recited the familiar Twenty-Third Psalms.

Then Wade Driver, Mike Seastrom, and Gary Shoemake sang "Amazing Grace," another beautiful hymn that many in the audience sang. What a delight to have of these *callers* sing!

Melton Luttrell, Flippo's longtime best friend, did a second eulogy with stories of Flippo's early years. Melton's deep love for Flippo grabbed my heart—they were best friends for decades. Then Reverend Hargrove shared several Scripture verses and a message of hope, personalized with Flippo stories—many that highlighted the precious father-son relationship that Flippo had with his son, John. He ended this part with us saying "The Lord's Prayer."

Source: Larada Horner-Miller

Then Ken Bower, Tony Oxendine, and Melton Luttrell sang the last song of the service, "Just A Closer Walk with Thee," another song that made me cry. I loved hearing all of Flip's cherished friends give tribute to him through music and song.

Stan Jeffus shared a beautiful video presentation honoring "Precious Memories" of Flippo that had us laughing one minute and crying the next. Stan had Flippo's songs playing in the background with photos of Flippo with so many friends through the years. The highlight was videos of many of the skits that Flippo was famous for: "The Boxer" and "I Just Don't Look Good Naked Anymore." Again, we laughed and cried.

Reverend Hargrove ended the service with the Benediction, then we drove to the Wagon Wheel Hall, the square dance hall that Flippo and Neeca helped build many years ago. The Abilene Square/Round Dancers provided a delicious dinner.

Larada Horner-Miller, John & Shelly Flippo at Flippo's Celebration of Life at the Wagon Wheel, Abilene, Texas, November 26, 2018. Source: Larada Horner-Miller

Then friends spent a couple hours telling Flippo stories—full of love and admiration for Flip and lots of humor. Jon Jones started the sharing with playing Flippo's first recorded song, "The Auctioneer," and a square tried to dance it but had trouble with the *figures* because we don't do some of them in square dancing anymore. Jay Henderson played Jerry Story's tribute to the three legends in square dancing that died in the last month: Frank Lane, Marshall Flippo, and Lee Kopman. Lin and I danced that time, and it was so heartwarming.

Then the end came; people lingered. Stories continued out the door. It was hard to leave this festive day. To me, this was the best celebration of someone's life I've ever attended—lots of stories, laughter, and tears about a man we all loved dearly. John and Shelly and Neeca—you did a great job in honoring Flip. I will never forget this day!

Paul Cote recorded Flippo's Memorial Service using Facebook Live. Go and watch this awesome service celebrating Flippo:[1]

Marshall Flippo's Obituary

Marshall Doyle "Flip" Flippo, 91, passed away November 4, 2018, at Lake Regional Hospital in Osage Beach, Missouri. Flip was born September 2, 1927 in Tuscola, Texas. He was the son of Roy and Gertrude Flippo. Preceded in death by his sisters, Helen June Moore and Onita Shelton.

Flip attended school in Wylie, Texas, where he was class president and played football and baseball. After school, he joined the Navy during World War II, where he served on the USS *Piedmont*, USS *Lander* and USS *Dixie* and played baseball for them after the war was over.

After serving, he returned to Abilene in 1949 and married Neeca Lee Redus. They started taking square dance lessons in 1951, and he started calling dances in 1952. After vacationing at Kirkwood Lodge in 1959, he was hired in 1962 as entertainment director leading to a forty-year history at the lodge, including being a part owner. In 1963, he and Neeca gave birth to their only son, John. Flip would work six months at the lodge when it was open and spend the other six months touring the world calling square dances in the US, Japan, and Germany.

He recorded for Blue Star and Chaparral as well as guest recordings for several other companies. He sold over a million square dance records, receiving gold records for "The Auctioneer" and "Every Street's A Boulevard." He has received just about every award there is in square dancing, including the prestigious Milestone Award and a Lifetime Achievement Award in 2016. Flip was also a founding member of CALLERLAB, the governing body of square dancing.

In 2000, Flip moved to Tucson, Arizona, to be the resident caller at the Rincon West RV Park, where he stayed until 2018. Then he moved back to Osage Beach to live with his son, John, and his wife, Shelly.

Flip was an avid golfer and waterskier and loved to watch the Dallas Cowboys play. Flip was world famous for his sense of humor and love for people. He is survived by his son, John, and daughter-in-law, Shelly.

Memorial service will be held at 1:00 p.m. on Monday, November 26, 2018, at Elliott-Hamil Funeral Home, 5701 Highway 277 South, Abilene, Texas 79606. There will also be a graveside service at 3:30 p.m. on Monday, November 26, 2018 at Elmwood Memorial Park, 5726 Hwy 277 South, Abilene, Texas.

---

1. Paul Cote, "Facebook," November 26, 2018Video of Flippo's Memorial: https://www.facebook.com/paul.cote.104/videos/10215219947390187/

EPILOGUE

W orking with Flip on this project has been the gift of a lifetime. We wandered through his memories and life to try to sketch out the highlights. I relished his side stories, enjoying every one of them. Some of them were not printable—I'm sure that some of you have heard those stories and know what I mean. Some of you were the topic of those "unprintable" tales.

Marshall continued to feel, "the Lord has blessed me. I was at the right place at the right time for so much of my life."

Flippo never forgot his roots, sharing so many stories set in his beloved Texas!

Jerry Junck offered closure to this book, "Flippo's longevity has to do with a lot of things. One of them was he loved everybody. He didn't like everybody, he loved them. He remembered all their names, but a bigger issue—so many of the guys fell out of popularity because they couldn't adjust to the activity. Flip's claim to fame is, as the activity changed, he was able to adjust to the changes, and he was always current, no matter what happened with the activity—how it changed. He was able to adjust."

This made me think about the major adjustment Flippo had to make in exchanging his $45s$[1] for a laptop, and he did it.

Jerry added more to how Flip adjusted,

Well, what it means is he went from the days of using live music and calling, to going to records, but the bigger adjustment was back in '58, they were using *Visiting Couple*[2] dances yet, and he adjusted from that to the modern-day choreography that began in the early '60s, and he was able to incorporate that choreography into his.

He's recorded 'The Auctioneer,' I think two times, and changed the choreography all two times to fit today's choreography. The first one that he did, you and Lin couldn't dance to it, literally. You couldn't dance to it, but he was able to adjust.

357

Some of our young callers have no idea what these legendary callers have been to us. They came along late enough, they didn't see them in their prime. I remember standing in Reno, and they had the recording artists do a dance on Sunday or Monday night. I don't remember which, but Mike Seastrom was the MC, and we made sure that we got Flippo on about 9:00 or 9:30. I was talking to some younger guys standing there over on the side. When Flip got up, I said, 'You guys, you've never really heard Flippo, have you?' They said, 'Well, no.' I said, 'You need to pay attention to this.' And for one *tip*,[3] Flip was like he was there in Abilene [Farewell to the Road dance, 2016] that night—Vintage Flippo. It was jaw-dropping! And those guys were just stunned! I remember that night in Abilene. That *tip* he did. It was jaw-dropping.

Jerry ended with, "It was vintage Flippo. And again, he didn't know."

Some ending words from Neeca about the three priceless scrapbook/albums she created for Flippo,

I put the first scrapbook together as a Christmas gift, then as time went on, I had enough for the second one and then later enough for the third one. I do not know if the clippings were kept after we divorced. It always amazed me how word of mouth spread with square dancers during the time we were together. He never had to ask for a date. He always had more requests than he could fill. Requests came from just about every state. He loved going to Alaska. The fact is he loved to call everywhere he was invited. He looked forward to seeing friends that he had met on previous trips. He really enjoyed his life. The good Lord was good to him. Still miss him.

We do, too!

The work put into this document has been a journey of pure joy. I've admired Marshall Flippo for years, but after our year and a half of talking and working collaboratively on this project, I see a man who savored a successful career he built on much more than luck. This talented man worked hard, loved his life, his family, and his friends—and had no idea who he was in the history of square dancing—a quiet legend, yet just another square dance caller.

---

1. **45s (Records)** — The most common form of the vinyl single is the "45" or "7-inch." The names are derived from its play speed, 45 rpm, and the standard diameter, 7 inches.
2. **Visiting Couples** — One couple would go to another couple in the square and would do the calls directed. Popular calls during the '50s.
3. **Tip** — A square dance session consisting of two parts, a patter call, and a singing call. See Glossary for more.

STORIES

Source: Neeca Flippo

30

REMEMBERING FLIPPO!

Because Flippo wanted to tell his favorite stories about *callers*[1] and *cuers*,[2] I asked *callers*, *cuers* and dancers for their favorite Flippo story. Some said theirs were not printable, but many were eager to share theirs.

The following stories are told by the individual in their own words. Let's start with John Flippo, Flip's son.

~John Flippo, Flippo's Son

I don't know if I have a favorite memory. You know, he was my best friend. Dad was always great to me in every way and always took me skiing when I was a kid. I played baseball. When he was here, we'd always go eat breakfast together, talk sports.

Touring with his Dad

Going on tour with him was a great memory. That was great. I didn't know what I wanted to do when I got out of high school, so Mom suggested it, and it really worked out good. I don't know what he expected, but he had to make room for all my t-shirts and playing my music in the car and what not, but he didn't complain at all. We had a blast! He still worked; it was basically six months. We would come home for Christmas, but other than that, we were on the road.

He'd introduce me right away at the dances, and I was a shy kid who had a time having to talk to adults, so it really helped me get over my shyness, learning how to talk to people better, because once they found out that I was his son, there was no stopping them. They were going to come talk to me.

When I was little kid, I would pretend I was calling. I don't think he ever plugged my microphone in 'cause he knew I couldn't sing. I don't really have any memory of it, but I did that for a good while, I guess.

Kirkwood, Waterskiing & Flippo's Athletic Abilities

Flippo and John Flippo, October 13, 2018. Source: John Flippo

Dad was always so good about coming down after a workshop [at Kirkwood] and pull me skiing. I can't tell you how many hours we spent out there on the water. [We] pulled the Kirkwood guests. He taught me when I was five years old, so he had a lot of patience, putting up with me, trying to learn how to do stuff.

Dad was great. He learned how to barefoot when he was in his 40s. Those falls hurt, and he was out there with Mom. He'd go like 45 miles an hour. He took some bad falls, but Dad was a good athlete, but I couldn't imagine. I'm 55 now, and I know how much those falls hurt. But he learned how to do it. Yeah, he was a great waterskier.

He really was quite an athlete. He wanted me to play baseball. He'd play left-handed against us when we were kids just to kind of make it somewhat more even. He never like turned around and showed us what he could do. He always played left-handed. He could do anything—good golfer. He loved to play golf. They'd set his golf cart out for him [at Kirkwood]. As soon as the sun come up, he'd be out there with a Kirkwood guest at 5:00-5:30 in the morning 'cause he didn't want to wait behind anybody, and then get back for breakfast and the workshop.

He'd do that probably four or five times a week, and he'd always pick up the tab. He never let anybody else pay.

Kirkwood was a big part of my life. I guess until I was 40; it was in my family. I got to hang out with my Dad 'cause in the winter time, he was mostly gone, so he was traveling all through my childhood, so come Kirkwood time, that's when we got to hang out.

High school seniors are the first part of the season. That's the first part they did, and you'd have to play music for the kids, and I helped him with that for years and years and years. He taught them how to square dance, too, and that was every night of the week for probably a month. I'd always help him since I was a kid, but he didn't know what songs were being played on the radio. He wasn't that familiar with the music, so I could help him with that. So, we would do that every night of the week for a good month to start the season.

We had it all. At the time, that's how your life is, but looking back on it, it was great.

I can do the very basic stuff in square dancing, the stuff he would teach in the summers. Real basic. I think the grand square was as far as I got, but people always thought I could [dance]. People always were trying to get me, but I'd say, "I'm sorry. I never learned." I never knew Dad to have a club or teach lessons, so it wasn't anything that ever came up. Looking back on it, I wish I would have learned, but I never did.

Family

I knew Onita June [one of Flippo's sisters]. In the wintertime, Dad wasn't home much, and June didn't live in town. So, we didn't get to see a lot of them, but boy, when they'd get together, there'd be smoking and telling stories and laughing. You could tell very much they were all related, and they sure enjoyed each other's company, and they all were just as funny as could be. Onita had a laugh that just get everybody going, but I didn't know them all that well. I would see them maybe once a year, even less than that.

My granddad died when I was probably in junior high, maybe elementary school, but they lived down the street. Dad's parents especially were really quiet. I remember he made ambrosia for the holidays. And then, of course, Dad wasn't in town a lot in the winter time, I didn't spend a lot of time with his parents. I don't have any strong memories of them.

I'm sure he told you that they wouldn't come to see him dance or call. I think they came to one of his dances but sit out in the parking lot and looked through the door. I don't know that they ever came in to one of his dances. They never came to his dances. Something with their religion. I know they were proud of him, and he got along with his folks, but yeah, they never came to his dances.

I spent more time with my Mom's parents, if they needed a babysitter. They [his mother's parents] were the ones that drove them to Houston. My Granddad Redus worked for the utility company in Abilene and fell off of a pole and got electrocuted, but I guess he was different after that. And then my grandmother never met a stranger. She would just talk your ear off. They loved my dad—through the roof about my dad, thought he'd hung the moon, and if Dad was in town, we'd always go over there and eat dinner. They thought the world of my dad.

Ties to Abilene

My Mom is still there. The school there was a whole lot bigger than the one here [in Osage Beach, Missouri]. Until I was a senior, I would start school here [Osage Beach, Missouri], transfer there and then transfer back to end the season. So, when I was a kid in elementary school and junior high, it was fine, but you get to high school and you're the new kid every year, so, Mom—even though she hated the cold—she stayed here my senior year, so I could go all year for my senior year here in Camdenton which is right outside of Osage Beach.

John's Illness

I have no memory at all, but Mom's best friend, Hattie Bell Martin, kept a diary that I read after I got older, and of course, Mom and Dad tell stories, but yeah, it's like it happened to somebody else almost but turned Mom gray, and I guess it was a pretty scary time.

They never treated me differently or tried to protect me or anything after that. It was just something we never really talked about. You went on with it, but it must have been something awful for them.

Hattie Bell was my godmother, and she did a lot with my parents. I know she went to Eureka Springs with them. She'd come up here to Kirkwood. She knew how to square dance and lived next door to my Mom in Abilene for years.

Neeca's Tour Knowhow

I remember, as a kid, Mom did all of Dad's bookings. The phone would ring four or five times a night for people wanting bookings all through the winter, and she always kept his calendars right there by the phone, and she had him booked out like four or five years in advance. That's just what people would do. They would just call for dates, and Dad basically had his schedule fairly set, so people were really having to struggle to try and find a date that he could call for them.

Back in the day in the 70s and 80s when square dancing was so popular, it was definitely hard for a new club to get him booked in.

Flippo's Navy Experience

As he got older, he talked about it more, but as a kid growing up, he never talked about it. Not that it was a bad experience, but it wasn't something that he talked about.

He had a couple close calls in the Navy that he hardly ever talked about or wanted anybody to know. He was on a ship and for whatever reason they transferred him to another ship, and the ship he'd been on ended up getting attacked. He'd talk about his friends in the Navy and what not, but other than that, I'm learning a lot about the Navy stuff just listening to the interviews [with Larada].

Flippo, the Storyteller

He was such a great storyteller. I'd be the security guard at Kirkwood Lodge. Basically, there was no security to it. They just needed somebody there overnight, but Dad had a very distinctive voice and laugh, so, you could hear him right along at the *after parties* after the dance telling a story or laughing. He was just amazing. It was just his timing. I didn't inherit that from him, but he was just an amazing storyteller.

This Book
I told him, "Pop, you can't do the book about you and not talk about you." And I think he came around more on that once you guys kind of got into it. He got more comfortable with it.

I never heard my Dad brag! I think deep down; he had to know a long time [about his place in square dance history]. So many people have told him, but I never heard him brag about it or even talk about it.

Flippo's Behavior as a Caller
I've seen Dad if there's this little turnout or weather affected dance or something he wouldn't take the money. I've seen him refuse the money several times, and wouldn't think a thing about it.

Dad didn't really care about money, really. He'd come home from touring. He'd have all his receipts in the glove box for my Mom, but he never really cared much. He wasn't good with money, much to my Mom's chagrin, I guess, but it was never a big deal to him.

His Parent's Divorce
They got divorced after 44 years. I think they both went through a tough time with it, but it really ended up being the best thing for both of them. They became much better friends afterwards. It's weird, but it was good they got divorced.

Flippo's Second Wife
After Pop died, I know he wanted me to call her, so I called her just to let her know, but that's the first time I talked to her since she left Tucson. I think he worried—knowing Dad—about what Mom would think. But he loved her, truly loved her, and there was no talking him out of it. He really cared for her, and I know it hurt him more than he ever let on when she left.

Flippo & Neeca Together in Their Later Lives
It was amazing when they'd get together. They got together recently in Abilene and drove around and discussing friends and family, and it was weird what happened there. Yeah, both of their memories are so good.

Mom came to visit fairly soon after Dad got his stuff back from Tucson, and they sat here one day when me and Shelly were at work, and threw away a bunch of stuff that I'd just as soon not got thrown away, but to them it was just you're never going to do these *after parties*[3] again or you don't need this calendar, so they threw a lot of stuff away that I wasn't really planning on them throwing away. I still have some stuff, obviously, but I don't know if the *after party* skits made it through there or not.

Talk to Stan Jeffus about the skits 'cause he was one of those guys that recorded everything, and I wish they had recording equipment back then, but still there were several people who recorded his *after parties*, night after night at Kirkwood, and Stan was one of them. He truly recorded every *after party*, and they came for years and years to Kirkwood.

Some of those were—Good Lord—so funny. I would love to have some of them on video, but back then, people were doing reel-to-reel to record the dances. I know people were recording those *after parties*, but they never put them up on YouTube or you never see them anywhere, but I know they're out there.

Dad couldn't care less [about the video on YouTube]. He wouldn't care at all.

If you think of anything, don't hesitate to call 'cause you're not bothering me at all. I love talking about my Dad.

~Gary Shoemake, Caller

There are so many things I could say about Flippo, but not many need to go into print.

I would just say in my early career of calling, Flippo was very helpful in getting me on the road. He passed my name to many, many people around the country who were looking for someone new to book. It was so helpful in my success in making it on the tour at that time.

Jokingly, I like to tell the dancers a story about that. I would tell the people that, in those days, that I had asked Flippo to help me in getting more dates on the road. Since he was so popular, you had to wait years to be able to get on his schedule. Knowing this, I asked him to recommend me for these

Gary Shoemake. Source: https://
www.ceder.net/callerdb/viewsingle.
php?RecordId=894

dates he was turning down. He replied that 'he would be glad to help me out.' Sure enough, I received inquiries and was able to book four nights in a row. (I had never experienced that.) These dates were 400 miles apart, but I took them just the same. After the third night, I called home and Flippo answered the phone and my question was "Why are you answering my phone at home?"

His answer: "Still just trying to help you out, Gary."

☙

I just remembered another saying of Flip's. When he would call me on the phone, he would talk for a while with trivial banter, and finally I would ask if he had called for any particular reason and he would always say, "No, I was just sitting on the crapper, and your name came to mind."

☙

He left Fun Valley, and he drove back to Tucson in his car. The air conditioner went out. He had a guy that kept his cars up, so he called him from his mobile phone and told him what was going on, and the guy said, "Well, great! Bring it in Monday when you get here, and I'll take care of it."

So, Monday morning, he got up, got in the car and rolled all the windows down because there was no air conditioning, and that was in August. He was driving down to the repair shop, pulled up to a stop sign and was waiting for the signal to change. A Tucson policeman on a motorcycle pulled up beside him and looked over at him and said, "Where's your seat belt?"

Flippo looked back at him very nonchalantly and said, "Where's yours?"

The policeman said, "Pull it over," and they had a discussion. Anyway, he didn't give Flip a ticket, but he did tell him if I ever see you on this street again without a seat belt on, I will throw you under the jail.

❧

When asked what was Gary's favorite story, he responded,

Oh, there's so many! He didn't like Elvis Presley. He didn't like Elvis Presley at all, and someone made a hoedown out of Elvis Presley's music, and it was good. We all thought it was great, and we were working in Paris, Texas and getting ready. He and I and Jerry Haag and Ken Bower were all on the stage at the same time. And so, I put this new hoedown on, and he looked at me, and he just threw his mic down on the table, and he said, "I didn't like that GD song in 1955, and I don't like that GD song right now," and he walked off the stage.

And he come back and he looked up at me, and he said, "Do you understand what I mean?"

I said, "I think I got the gist of it!"

"Yeah," I said, "I don't think we'll use that GD song anymore when you're around." But that was Flip!

They (Flippo, Ken Bower, and Jerry Haag) were so much fun to be around. You never knew what was going to happen! It was a good time! We all had some good times!

❧

Flippo, was a favorite of everyone at English Mountain, from the guests in attendance to all the staff that worked there. He always had a kind word to everyone from the owners to the janitors. He would take time to speak to them all and spend time with them, if they felt like talking. He had spent so many years at Kirkwood Lodge in Missouri, so he knew these folks were often overlooked, ignored or in some cases treated with disdain. So, he always took time to make them feel like he was just one of them. He had the knack immediately to make friends with total strangers, whether in the dance hall, on an airplane or at the local coffee shop.

❧

On another occasion, we were having lunch in the dining hall, where we always made it a point to be seated with as many different tables as possible. I happened to be seated at a table of dancers, when Flippo joined several of us, sitting down and removing his ball cap with a big "T" on it. This very prim lady who had joined us asked him, what does the "T" stand for? Without looking up to see who had asked or to acknowledge anyone at the table or any hesitation, he replied "TITS." We all gulped and tried to hold back our laughter and after what seemed like an eternity, this very prim lady burst into laughter as did the whole table.

Only Flippo would do this or get by with it. He was one of a kind who everyone loved. It was actually a Texas Longhorn Cap.

~Jerry Junck, Caller

I'm really glad you're doing this, Larada. Just wanted to tell you that.

Wagon Wheel Dance Hall, Abilene, Texas

Neeca worked for the telephone company, and that's where they found the poles for the rafters and things like that, and they also went around the country looking for wagon wheels because of the name. But also at that time, all guys in that area were pretty much calling to live music. Of course, [there was] not a lot of recorded music yet in 1958. That was just starting, and there was Kalox Record Company in Dallas, Texas that was C. O. Guest, and then Blue Star was in Houston, Texas with Norman and Nadine Merrbach.

Anyway, Flippo had heard Leroy Van Dyke's version of "The Auctioneer." Flip was working; Neeca was working, and he thought that would be a great song to do a square dance, so he bought the record and put it on slow to learn how to do "The Auctioneer" part of it and then started doing it live with bands at square dances.

Jerry Junck. Source: https://www. ceder.net/callerdb/viewsingle.php? RecordId=1620

Somebody who was dancing with him had been to Houston and told Norm Merrbach about it. Norm either wrote Flip a letter or called him. So Flippo wrote it all out and mailed it to him.

And then he was introduced to the Rhythmaires. He said that's the first time he'd ever met the band that became affiliated with Blue Star. And he said, 'We cut that song, and at that time, none of the instruments and the vocals were on separate tracks. Everybody recorded on open microphones—that's what it was like. If you made a mistake, you simply had to start over.' And I asked Flip, 'How many takes did it take? And he said, 'One!' It's truly amazing 'cause he'd never been in a studio before. And he and Norm developed this wonderful relationship. That record made Flippo a star. At that time, if you had a hit record, it literally could turn your career around, and he became a star with that record.

Kirkwood Lodge

Norm and Nadine Merrbach would come up every summer [to Kirkwood], and he would bring some new recordings along, and Flippo would record them there.

Flippo was why people came, and his advertising [was] in the winter time going around, doing these dances. He had the tightest schedule of anybody for 41 years.

⸲⸲

There's nobody like him. Flippo's not a businessman at all. He calls square dances, and Neeca took care of all those bookings. She handled it all. Once Flippo was on a schedule, nobody let him go. Nobody! And he called Margaret Bolts' Outstanding Callers Series on the second Sunday in January for as long as I can remember, and they came over from Des Moines—a bunch of them—and they wanted him to do Des Moines. He said, 'I don't have any days. If Margaret ever lets me go, you can have that Sunday!' And that was late in his career, but they waited nine years to get him. I mean, he had just that tight a schedule.

He's a most interesting guy in the world. If you've known Flippo, you've been had by Flippo, let me tell you! We always see this devil may care guy on the stage; however, if you really know Flip, he is a perfectionist. Very quietly. And I remember a story. He used to do the WASCA festival in Washington, D. C.— seems like 4,000 dancers, and one morning, Beryl Main was there, and I don't remember but every big name you ever heard of was calling this festival. One morning at six o'clock in the morning, somebody went down to the callers' room and Flippo was practicing a singing call. And he's the most famous caller in the world at that time.

And the guy said, "What are you doing, Flippo?"

And he said, "Well, I'm practicing. Do you realize who's out there on that stage?"

He was really a perfectionist. He'll give you a hard time when you're calling with him, but when you first start calling with him, he'll let you go and he'll see how you handle things, and he'll jab you a little while you're calling. He'll be talking to you and stuff, but at no time will he cause you to lose your concentration. He'll give you a hard time, but he's very careful that he doesn't embarrass you.

⸲⸲

~Ken Bower, Caller

The tricks Flippo and his caller friends pulled on each other were outrageous! I heard both sides of "The Stolen Car" story from Ken Bower and Flippo, and they tell two different stories from each—whose truth do you believe?

Here's Ken's version:

Flippo had a sale job on me. "Wouldn't you come down here [WASCA festival in the DC area] and bunk with me?" Flippo asked. And he added, "I've got this big suite." He did have a big suite, and then he said, "Then you take my car back up to the kids you're staying with." [The kids were Whitey and Gladys Puerling in Trenton, New Jersey, a couple who loved to host the traveling callers and was a dear friend of Flippo's.]

And he said, "Then I'll ride home with them, and I can sleep on the way home."

I said, "Okay, I'll do that." So, I rode down with them [Whitey and Gladys].

When we arrived, Flippo said, "Alright, bring your clothes up." I was in the parking garage. And Flippo added, "Don't tell anybody 'cause they'll get on me for having two people in the room, see?" So, he helped me carry my luggage fifteen floors up, carrying my clothes up the back way.

Ken Bower. Source: https://www.ceder.net/callerdb/viewsingle.php?RecordId=907

We went in the suite, and there was a big closet. We hung my shirts up. Flippo went over there and sat, and there were his little tiny shirts. He said, "You can sleep in my room if you want, but don't you wear my shirts." They're about that tiny. [Ken shows with his hands.]

And I stayed for that Saturday night, and I had to leave, so when I left, I took his car, and of course, I had all his clothes in the back. Before I left, I went down to the desk and told them, "Hey, there's a guy up there." I was getting back at him for something. I can't remember what, but I said, "There's a guy up in this room had somebody as a guest, and they didn't pay."

The desk clerk said, "Oh, well, it happens all the time."

I said, "No, wait a minute. I'm the guy that stayed there. He didn't pay for it, see?"

And he said, "Look, I'm not going to go."

I said, "I'll give you ten bucks if you go up there." So, he took the ten bucks. He went up. I took off driving. He just went up there and ripped him up one side and down the other.

Dog gone, I took off, and I got to the first toll booth, and just as I pulled through, here they come—the highway patrol pulled me over. I said, "What'd I do wrong?"

He said, "Well, we're just checking things. We reported a stolen car."

I said, "A stolen car?"

I thought, "Wait a minute. I don't have anything to show them."

He said, "Is this your car?"

I said, "Yeah."

I will never forget this. He looked in the back and said, "That's your shirts in there?"

As Ken told this story, his laughter resounded! "Out of the car!" he ordered. Well, this just scared me to death. Finally, they let me go and I went up to the car where it was. Well, it just scared me to death.

So I left the car at the Puerling's where I was supposed to. It turned out that the guy across the street from them was the captain of the highway patrol, and he was the guy who pulled me over.

~Jon Jones, Caller

Most of us have called him Flippo or Flip. Very few called him Marshall. We first met at a festival in Austin, Texas in the early 1960s. It was just about the time he recorded his first *singing call*,[4] "The Auctioneer" on the Blue Star label. We became instant friends and have been ever since. The Blue Star label was owned by Norman and Nadine Merrbach of Houston, Texas. Their studio, record and equipment sales shop and record storage was attached to their home. Their studio was large enough to dance seven squares, and they had a dance once a month, booking traveling callers. Many *callers* had some good dances there as the dancers were very good and could dance almost everything that was known at the time. Several of the members were local *callers*.

Jon Jones. Source: https://www.ceder.net/callerdb/viewsingle.php?RecordId=1642

In the mid-1970s, I was there calling a dance (all the *callers* stayed with the Merrbach's in their home) and I found out Flip was to be the next *caller* for them. I asked Nadine if she had an old dish cloth or something similar. She said she had an old pillowcase that she did not need. I told them I wanted to write a message to Flip and leave it on the pillow for him. She gave me a Marks-A-Lot [pen] and I wrote a message like, "Jon Jones slept here first." I found out later from Nadine that he got it and took the pillowcase with him when he left stating something like, "I'll get even with him."

Well, for the next ten years, that pillow case showed up on my pillow at many different places. And guess what? It showed up on Flip's pillow at just as many different places as mine. I would find out where he was going to be and either deliver or mail the case to that address with instructions about where to place it. Flip did the same to me. Each time it would have a different message on it from each of us. Once it was on my pillow in the hotel where the CALLERLAB Convention was being held. We had a lot of fun with this, and I do not remember whatever happened to the pillowcase. I think it wound up back at the Merrbach's home, and Nadine kept it for a keep-sake.

❧

On another occasion in the early 1990s, I was a little way north of Beaumont, Texas calling a dance on a Thursday night. I had Friday off and was headed to Louisiana for a Saturday dance. The people I was staying with were good friends and they said I could stay with them until Saturday and they were going to a dance in Beaumont on Friday that Marshall Flippo was calling. I said that would be okay with me. We drove to Beaumont in my car and just as we were pulling into the driveway of the dance venue, Flip pulled in right behind me.

I said, "Watch this." I drove up right in front of the entrance door and stopped. Flip was right behind me and stopped. I got out of my car, opened the trunk, and began unloading my sound equipment.

Flip got out of his car and I said to him, "Hey Flip, what are you doing here?" He said he thought he was calling a dance here tonight. I said that I was calling a dance here tonight.

He said, "Oh gosh (or something like that) I must be in the wrong town." I let him stew for a few seconds and then told him I was kidding, and we were going to his dance. There was a very relaxed look on his face. We had a good time dancing to him that night.

~Curt Braffet, Caller

My Flippo story was while working with him at a weekend at Chula Vista Resort in the Wisconsin Dells, Wisconsin, with Bower, Flippo, Shoemake, and myself.

The callers went out to lunch on Saturday to discuss what we would be doing for the Saturday evening *after party*. After we discussed what skits we would do, we came up with a "list of props" that we need-ed. This particular list included handcuffs, a cap gun, caps, balloons, and then Flip wanted to pick up some 5-hour energy drink for himself. Flip and I set off for WalMart.

Curt Braffet. Source: https://www. ceder.net/callerdb/viewsingle.php? RecordId=2268

As we entered the store, I told Flip that I would buy the cap gun, caps, and balloons because whatever was left over, I could give to my grandkids to play with.

Flip said, "Good, I will get the handcuffs and 5-hour energy drink." We collected our goods. I was walking behind Flip as he's headed towards the checkout line. He was walking (or doing the Flip waddle walk). He made it to the counter, raised his hip and kind of plopped the 5-hour energy drink with the hand-cuffs on top of the box onto the conveyor belt.

The check-out lady looked at the combination that he just put up there, turned and looked at Flip, and before she could say anything, Flip kind of bent down and pointed at her with an excited look on his face, "I just met a girl in the parking lot!"

Dumbfounded she turned to me for help, and Flip pointed his thumb at me and said, "And he's gonna hold the gun on her!" I nodded my head in agreement, and the poor woman said nothing during our whole transaction.

Another weekend I did with the same group (This time in Branson, Missouri). He started telling a joke and Ken Bower bent down behind me and started moaning, "No, no!" That's all I'll say about that one! It's the one about Larry Letson and what he bought for his wife (at the time).

Just another example of his quick wit and shock value comedy he had.

&

~Melton Luttrell – Caller
Letter to Neeca (This was sent before Flippo passed away.)

Where do I start? Was it one of my square dances in 1951 at the country club in Cisco, Texas? I think it was Alvin Cox, a friend Flippo's, that approached me some-time during the evening dance, informing me he was with a friend of his who was wanting to become a square dance *caller* but had never called to a group of dancers, only having practiced with a group of friends at home. He further asked me if I would consider allowing him to call a *tip*[5] and critique his calling ability. I answered that I would be happy to invite him to call, and did so.

Melton Luttrell. Source: https://www.ceder.net/callerdb/viewsingle.php?RecordId=2528

Sure enough, Flip did call, and I remember it well. After the dance was over, Flippo, Al and I met for a brief discussion regarding his calling performance. I was trying to be positive with my remarks but also honest. I remember how difficult that was, because on one hand it wasn't bad, but on the other hand, it was simply awful. The positive thing was that Flip had, and still did, that beautiful, distinct voice. On the negative side, he could not put his foot down to the beat of the music, which made the dancers feel as if they were dancing on a bed of big rocks, constantly stumping their toes. Certainly, I did not put it in those kinds of terms that night, but it was what I was thinking.

I do remember telling Flip that I had attended two different caller schools conducted by Herb Greggerson, along with Dr. Lloyd "Pappy" Shaw, one of the two outstanding square dance giants of their time, and remembered the advice he offered to one of the students at our school. I offered the same advice to Flip: form a square and dance with them as you call. Flippo later told me that Alvin, or one of his friends had a chicken coop that they cleaned out and had just enough room for one square, and that is where Flippo perfected his skill.

That was the beginning of a friendship that endured to this day, some sixty-five years later, and how I cherish those years and memories.

Some of those memories are these, in no particular order:

**In our home on Culver St. in Ft. Worth, sitting at the piano writing square dances, as we attempted to pick out chords, neither of us able to play melodies.

**Later date, same home, same piano, only this time, late at night, long after Sue and Neeca had gone to bed, Jimmie Kate playing every song we ever knew, and Hattie Bell, Flippo and I singing our hearts out. Please note and remember. Someone was always playing, and someone was always singing. Do you think Sue and Neeca bought that? Did I mention that this was two single ladies?

**Remember the time Sue and I visited the Flip and Neeca in Abilene, and they were both at work. We could not get into their locked house but found an unlocked window and crawled through and went to bed. If memory serves me right, Flip was greatly surprised to find unexpected company in his guest bedroom.

**How about the time we called a dance in Austin, our state capital? We were sight-seeing approaching the capital building only a couple of blocks away, when one of the wives saw something that we passed that caught her attention. So. . .what did Flippo do? Just did u-turn in the middle of the street and headed back the other way. . .small wonder we did not end our sight-seeing trip looking through bars.

**The time Flippo visited me and just written a square dance to a *singing call* and wanted to know if I had any connections with someone who might record it. I did not have my record company at the time and wasn't much help. Sure wish I had Square L records up and running at the time. The song was "The Auctioneer." Blue Star recorded it, and the rest is history.

**Back in the late seventies or early eighties, I was calling a dance in New Orleans, Louisiana, and Flippo was calling a dance in Nashville, Tennessee. It was near Christmas time, and we had communicated with each other earlier and agreed to meet at the bus station in Jackson, Mississippi and drive together to our homes in Texas. I had flown to New Orleans, and he was on a driving tour so it seemed like a good plan for me to bus from New Orleans, after my Saturday night dance, and Flip picked me up on his way home. One minor hitch in our plan—the largest snowstorm in the history of the weather records for the south occurred on that day. I remember, as if it were yesterday, the station agent boarding the bus and informing all the passengers that if they were traveling further, they would have to make arrangements or spend the night as all roads in and out of Jackson were closed.

All I could think of was that Flippo and I were both going to miss Christmas at home, and that he was not going to even be able to get where I was in Jackson. I was sitting in the bus station with my suitcase and record case by my side, wondering what it the world was I going to do. And no longer than five minutes later, a snow-covered car with windshield wipers slapping snowflakes as they furiously fell, pulled up in front of the station, and low and behold, there was my dear friend and savior, Marshall Flippo. Flip, you could never know how great it was to see you at that moment. I will always cherish the memory of our trip, crossing the Mississippi river as one of the last cars before they closed the bridge for traffic; the drive home bypassing road blocks for closed roads, driving down the highway seeing no road to drive on, just fence posts on each side barely visible. But with God's help, we made it through to Texas and home in time for Christmas.

**Memories of later years at Kirkwood, with Neeca at home with early labor pains about to deliver her first-born. Flippo was unable to get a commercial flight that would get him there in time and was frustrated as to what to do. It cost him a ton of money, but I urged Flip to hire a charter flight, which you he did. I think we both agree it was worth the money. I suspect, that when Flippo looks at his son John, and knowing how proud Flippo is of him, he knew it was the right decision.

꙼

My Phone Conversation with Melton

Melton described a skit done in Dallas with Flip and Jess Forester:

Well, first of all, you must understand that I've done almost 200 (square dance weekends) of these over the years. We rent a facility or make another engagement with a facility and do what we call a square dance weekend where you have a staff. Flip was on our staff for years. We had, I swear, four weekends a year at that time or five. I forgot which, but Flip always was on one of them. And we had moved it around from place to place, but we ended up in Dallas. I'd just seen what I call a "skit" in Osage Beach when we went down to Lee Mace's Ozark Opry theater as part of our package to Kirkwood. One night we'd always go down to Lee Mace's show which is a country western show, and they had a comedian there that was really good, so we copied this from him.

We took one of our members of our square dancers who was probably six foot three or four—tallest, and my wife had collected all these kind of props, so we had an Indian headdress that we put on him with all the feathers and put some kind of a rope around him and made him look like a real Indian standing out there. And then we took Flip and put him in a squaw dress and put just one feather above his head and all that. His job was—we copied this from the show in Lee Mace's show —was to make this guy laugh because he was like a wooden Indian just standing there.

First of all, Flippo said, "Ah, don't put that on over this," so to do that he had to take off his clothes except for his shorts, and he said that he'd dress over his shorts.

So, Flip did everything known to man to try to get that guy to laugh or to booby slip or make some motion. He stood there; he did his part perfectly. We told him don't laugh at anything. Be a stone-faced Indian, and he stood on that stage for I can't accurately say the time, but it seemed like forever. I'd say maybe four or five minutes, but Flippo [was] doing antics of every sort, taking the microphone and beating on the microphone and scratching on it, and just everything you could think of and he finally could not make this guy laugh. So finally, Flippo turned around, lifted up his squaw dress, pulled down his shorts and mooned the Indian.

Melton laughed, "And the audience couldn't see that, but I could see it, and anybody that was back on the stage could see it, and that just broke ole Jess Forester up. He stood it as long as he could. He just burst out laughing. But that was Flip for you."

❧

I have another one regarding Flippo except he was just a third party in [the] action. We were at Kirkwood, and we'd ski in this part of it. That particular week Frank Lane and I were on the calling staff with Flippo. Flippo was the staff *caller* of course. So Kirkwood had a speedboat to pull skiers with, and so did Flippo. Flippo had his personal boat. I'm not sure which boat we're in, but Flippo was driving the boat. Frank and I were skiing, and we were back and forth—be on one side then on the other side of the boat. I don't know how much you know about skiing, but there's a wake that makes behind the boat that you drive over or ski over. Sort of like an up, down. You gotta hold tight to go over it. So, Frank yelled at me, "Let's change sides."

I said, "Okay." Somebody has to roll up high, and the other has to duck and go under. So, we agreed to try that while we was yelling at each other, so Frank was going to go under me and I was going to go over. So, we started changing sides and about the time that we were supposed, I was supposed to get the rope up real high, I hit the wake and went sorta down to my knees to hold on, and Frank's going under and I caught him right across the neck. My God! You know, that could have decapitated him. But the only thing Flip could think of was how funny it was. He was up there, circling around, coming back to pick us up and laughing about it. Frank was laying there, and I was feeling really bad about it 'cuz I screwed up my part. Frank had a big red spot on his neck where those ropes come across his neck, you know. But to Flippo, it was just funny!

But if you didn't know this about Flippo, he was unreal as a skier. He could ski barefooted even, and I've seen him do it. It was when he was way up in his years. He was really good at it.

❧

The thing that amazes me is how hard he worked at square dance calling, and I've heard a lot of people come up and say, "Boy, that boy is just a natural." Well, hell no, he's not a natural. What he does is he works and learns his trade. For example, when we were going to do a dance together, some place in Louisiana, and I do not recall the place but I do remember us driving together, and he picked me up. But back in the olden days when the *45 records*[6] first started coming out, they had 45 RPM players that you could put in your car and drive along and play them—hook it up through your radio. So we had one of those. I know I had one and he had one, but I would say, at least over an hour of our trip or two hours, he was practicing things for his dance that night.

And, of course, I'll never be Flippo or as good as Flippo, but I don't think I ever practiced a call in my life. I just listened to it, then I can do it or I can't do it. You know, if I know the melody, well then, I could do the dance. When we were at Kirkwood, this is what remind me of it. We'd have a morning session, we'd break for lunch, then we'd have an afternoon session, and if he was calling the afternoon session, he wouldn't come to lunch hardly ever, and a couple times I went down to find out why. He had his records out, practicing what we was going to do for that afternoon—going over and over and over on them, and the guy works at being a square dance caller. Everybody thinks, "Oh, that's natural." After you've done it over and over and over, then you've got it, but all the stuff that you're going to do, he just worked his butt off in practicing and learning all that stuff. So, he was a very hard worker at learning his trade.

~Nasser Shukayr, Caller

When I was a brand-new *caller*, whenever I met accomplished *callers*, I would bombard them with questions. Apparently Flippo doesn't care for non-stop questioning.

My first conversation with Flippo: I was a star-struck young lad. He was trying to be nice.

Me: "Mr. Flippo, what's your favorite song?"

Flippo: "I don't really have a favorite."

Me: "Well, what's one song that you like?"

Flippo: "I like them all the same."

Me: "Is there any song that you liked a lot, back when you first heard it?"

Flippo: "Well, I suppose there's one song that's my favorite."

Nasser Shukayr. Source: https://www.ceder.net/callerdb/viewsingle.php?RecordId=33

Me: "What song is it?"

Flippo: "I like the song a lot, but I never sing it at dances."

Me: "Why don't you sing the song at dances?"

Flippo: "It's probably the title."

Me: "What's the title?"

Flippo: "It's called 'I love you so <expletive> much that I could just <expletive>.'"

❧

Flippo used to smoke cigarettes. At most National Convention centers, the convention centers had a strict No-Smoking rule. But that never stopped Flippo. He'd check in for his calling spot then quietly sneak behind (or even under) the

377

stage to have a cigarette. One time I asked him what would happen if they caught him smoking.

He said, "Nothing would happen to ME. I'd blame it on YOU."

I protested, "But I don't smoke!"

Flippo replied, "Who are they gonna believe? A legend, or you?"

❦

At CALLERLAB conventions, whenever we'd line up for mealtime, Flippo would try to get behind a pretty lady. In the line, he'd reach out and kinda "pinch" the lady, perhaps on the posterior. Then he's shout out the name of (whoever he was in line with at the time), "Jon Jones! You quit pinching that lady right now!!"

❦

A club in the New Orleans area was actually the largest club in the world, with over 800 members. (The Bar-None Saddle-ites of St. Rose, Louisiana). They danced every Friday night. Back in the heyday, they'd dance eighty squares on a floating pecan wood floor. It was awesome. Well, everyone got old, and the club decided to disband. They decided to have their favorite *callers* back in for one last dance. In fact, Marshall Flippo was their VERY favorite *caller*, and he had the honor of calling the VERY last dance ever at that club. I had the honor of calling the NEXT-to-last dance (i.e. the week before Flippo).

I had collected a flyer from the club, advertising their last few dances. I saw Flippo at the CALLERLAB Convention, after I had called and before he had called (i.e. in the week just before their very last dance ever). The flyer had my name and then it added "fun *caller*." Okay, this was years ago. But beside Flippo's name, the flyer had his name ONLY, i.e. it didn't say anything extra about him. (Because his name stands alone. . .apparently my name needed some explanation.

Anyway, I saw it as an opportunity to give Flippo a hard time. So I showed him the flyer, and I showed him where it says I'm a "fun *caller*." I carefully pointed out that HIS name LACKED a designation of Fun *Caller*. I asked him whether he was slipping, i.e. "maybe you used to be fun, back long ago, but nowadays, you ain't no fun no mo." If you don't believe me, just look at the flyer. It identifies the callers who are FUN, and your name is not identified as such. "WHAT DO YOU HAVE TO SAY IN YOUR DEFENSE, Mr. FLIPPO???"

Always the gentleman, Flippo merely said, "Yes, they like you a lot in that area. Way to go."

When you stop and think about all the things he COULD have said (when someone was giving him a hard time), he actually turned that difficult and unusual moment into a quote that I will never forget.

❦

I was calling at a festival with several halls and several *callers*. It's no secret that after the dance, *callers* often go somewhere and party until the wee hours of the

378

morning. Mr. Flippo didn't want to go. I wondered whether he was feeling bad or something, so I asked, in genuine concern, if he was feeling okay. He said he felt fine.

"Well," I asked, "why don't you want to go party with us? You don't like us?"

Flippo replied, in all sincerity, that he's gonna go to his room and study and practice, because if he doesn't do that, then all the young whipper snappers will out-call him.

I responded, "So, while we're out partying, you're gonna practice so that you can show us up tomorrow, right?"

Flippo replied, "No, I'm gonna practice so that y'all don't show ME up tomorrow."

We will never know whether this dialogue was in jest. However, I tend to actually believe it. Flippo was among the Tippity-Top *Callers* for over 50 years. He got that way and stayed that way, by practicing all the time. Even when he coulda, shoulda, woulda gone out and partied. :) You have to truly admire someone who gets to the top, and stays there for decades.

~Shane Greer, Caller

This story may not be funny to anybody else, but every time I think of Flip, I think of this one incident where I was actually calling a festival in Show Low, Arizona. I didn't know he was going to be there. I called Friday night, and then Saturday night I got ready to start the dance, and everybody was squared up, and we were ready to go. When it got to the *singing call*, and I started singing the words, the chorus of the *singing call*, I noticed that somebody was singing with me, and he was actually hidden behind the stage, and they plugged in a microphone. He kind of surprised me. He was there, and so that was pretty funny.

We enjoyed the whole night, the whole evening and the whole dance. We had a good

Shane Greer. Source: Shane Greer

time and then after the dance was over, I was there by myself, and he was there by himself, and he said, "I'm kinda hungry. I'll take you into town, and let's go get a hamburger," so we got into his Cadillac, and we drove into the town of Show Low, and the only thing that was really open was a Sonic. He pulled into this Sonic in that big long Cadillac, and he doesn't want to pull in.

I'm thinking, "Just pull into one of these spots. A ton of them were open."

He didn't want to pull into a spot and order from the car. He wanted to get out and sit down.

And I said, "This is not really the place that we can get . . ."

Flippo said, "Well, right there in the middle, there's a little spot right there in the middle. There's a little picnic table."

And it was warm, and I said, "Okay," so he parks over on the other side, just out of the way, and then we walk up to a little garden area at the Sonic. So we go over there, and we sit down at this picnic table.

"You still have to push the button. We'll have to order. They'll bring it to us." So, he pushes the button; I push the button. The lady or guy comes on and says, "Hey, can I help you?"

"Sure, I will have a cheeseburger and French fries and a Coke."

And Flip said, "I'll have a cheeseburger, and I also want some French fries, and I want a milkshake."

The guy said, "What flavor?"

He said, "Well, I want chocolate. Hey, could you make that really thin?"

And the kid asked, "Do what, Sir?"

He said, "I want a really thin chocolate milkshake."

Nothing on the other end of the line. He kind of looks at me with this funny look on his face, just the way he does. He's dead serious.

And the kid goes, "What do you want, Sir?"

He said, "I wanna milkshake, really thin. I just want a really thin chocolate milkshake. Pour some extra milk in it."

And the kid come back on the speaker and said, "Sir, we don't have any milk."

Serious, he turns around and he looks at me and says, "What do you suppose they're making the milkshakes out of?"

Dead serious. I told my wife that story every time I think of him, and I say, "It's probably one of those that I'm the only one that thinks that's funny." You had to be there to see the expression that he had on his face when he said that but every time I think of him, I think of him saying, "What do you suppose they're making the milkshakes out of?"

~Jim Mayo, Caller

You are aware there are two different kinds of stories: the ones about him and also the ones he tells at *after parties*. I have been hoping for ten years somebody would collect the stories callers told at *after parties*, and Marshall was at the top of the pile for telling those. He probably has them all and so you probably have them all and I'm thrilled to know they are somewhere recorded. I'm thrilled beyond measure to know that those have been captured, because Marshall was among the best at telling those. They're classic among all the traveling callers, and he was foremost among those.

I'm in a fairly unique position because Marshall and I are among the few still living who have been involved from the very beginning which I mark as 1950 for Modern Square Dancing.

Marshall is an absolutely unique person in the entire history. I can't tell you any of the *after party* stories, but I'm sure he told you all of those. All I can do is tell a couple stories that are about my personal interaction with him. Let me start with one: he was often at CALLERLAB conventions, and back many years ago, at

CALLERLAB conventions, we used to throw parties in our room. I started as my first year as Chairman, just thinking there ought to be a party for the board members. That got expanded when JoAnn [Jim's wife] started joining me in 1979. She's a party girl and said we should have one in our room, so we pretty regularly from then on ran what we called the "New England Party" in our room on Monday night, and it grew to be almost an institution. Often, we would end up with fifteen or twenty people, sitting around, talking with each other.

One particular evening, Marshall was sitting on the sofa with Johnny Wedge on one side and JoAnn on the other listening to Bill Peters, Al Stevens and me and a couple of others talking about the technical aspects of calling because we had been developing the teaching means for callers and had come up with the FASR important elements of choreographic control. They stand for Formation, Arrangement, Sequence and Relationship. Those four components are the fundamental elements in managing choreographic patterns in square dancing.

Marshall was sitting on the sofa, and he leaned over to Johnny Wedge, and said, "Do you know what these guys are talking about?" Johnny was a little embarrassed. John was unique in that he had attended what may have very well been the only *caller school*[7] that Marshall ever taught. It was with C. O. Guest in Texas, I think, somewhere near San Antonio in the late 50s. Johnny was stationed at the base down there and had just gotten into square dancing and got interested. C. O. was a teacher of callers; Marshall was not. He never wanted to teach calling. He was happy being a caller.

So, he leaned over to John. John was a little embarrassed, didn't want to appear not to have known everything about calling, and so he started to explain, and Marshall said, "I don't think any of that matters. I just pick up the microphone and call," which was typical of Marshall, always. To his very last dance, I'm sure he called exactly that a way.

Jim Mayo. Source: https://www. ceder.net/callerdb/viewsingle.php? RecordId=429

Pick up his microphone and call! Couldn't care less about the technology of calling. Teaching callers wasn't his business.

That's about the only one that I can share personally. I've had lots of interaction with him, mostly at conventions because he didn't travel into New England very long. He called here when he first started out, and I danced to him fifty years ago and then many, many times, but all the traveling callers came to New England in the early days because it was a hot bed of square dancing, and they could make a lot of money. They could work seven nights a week for three weeks in New England. It was wonderful territory, but Marshall was more western, and after the initial round when a whole lot of other callers started coming to New England, he stayed more west and didn't get up into New England as often. He continued to come occasionally, but he had a regular route that went from sort of central to the western part of the country, so we didn't see him as much after the late 60s as we had before that. It was also a long trip, so he didn't come into this area as regularly as some of the others did. I don't know what his reasoning was, but I knew it was just a fact.

He returned to the *after party* stories, "Well, I'm really thrilled to know that you're collecting his stories and they probably deserve a separate book because it was sort of a classic set of stories that callers told, the traveling callers told at *after parties*, and they were very well rehearsed and practiced because they told the same stories night after night, and they were a wonderful set."

~Dottie Welch, Caller

My first story probably occurred at the San Antonio [CALLERLAB] convention in 2003 or perhaps Reno in 2004. At that time, I was a relatively new, solo attendee and was pleasantly surprised one lunch to have Marshall ask if he could sit in the empty seat beside me. At that moment, one of the "icons" became a friend.

My second story occurred at the Kansas City convention in 2009. A Women Callers dance was scheduled and several of us were waiting our turn. Marshall wandered up the side of the hall saying, "I need a lady. I'm looking for a lady."

No one had responded when he reached me, so I eagerly said, "Yes, I'm not going to pass up an opportunity like this!" We enjoyed a great tip.

There was a dance near Topeka on the Wednesday after that convention to celebrate Dana [Schirmer]'s birthday. I cheerfully drove the 65 miles for the privilege of dancing to Wade Driver and Marshall Flippo and the cueing of Roy Gotta. Those were my only opportunities to dance with and to Marshall Flippo. They are definitely memories to be treasured.

Dottie Welch. Source: https://www.ceder.net/callerdb/viewsingle.php?RecordId=254

~Bill Harrison, Caller

So, I have been dancing to Flip since 1965 at age 8 at our area festival WASCA. He called this festival many years and also traveled through our area annually on a fall tour, and we would not miss him. Then I started calling the Tucson festival for many years in a row, and when Flip moved to Tucson, we always met and visited for many hours during the festival and after. Oh, the stories he would tell about his travels were so funny. This was the highlight of the festival for us to sit and talk. I keep in touch with Flip once a month, and this would not have happened if it were not for our many years while I grew up dancing to him and then the festival bringing us together even closer. I am blessed to be his friend.

Thanks for asking me to put something in your book.

Bill Harrison. Source: https://www.ceder.net/callerdb/viewsingle.php?
RecordId=593

~Bob Nolen, Cuer

First time I ever met Flippo, Dave Taylor had hired us to *cue*[8] an afternoon Square Dance workshop and dance that night in St. Clair Shores in Detroit. I'm cuing the pre-rounds, and all of a sudden, here comes somebody sticking something in front of my face, and it is a telegram.

"This is a telegram for you. You're cordially invited to go F yourself." I wheeled around, and everybody, of course, quits on the floor. They don't know what's going on 'cause I can't say what it says. I cleaned it up. I couldn't believe it.

Bob and Sally Nolen. Source: https://www.ceder.net/callerdb/viewsingle.php?RecordId=2274

🎵

383

Joey Solis. Source: Joey Solis

~Joey Solis, Caller

He was a character, wasn't he? Well, I have three little incidents.

The first one was in 2000. Marshall was doing our state festival, and it was out at the fairgrounds, and I just want to tell you. His reflexes are incredible. We had our Friday night dance going with the state *callers* calling, and Marshall was dancing, and he was in a square that I was in, and we were *promenading*[9] home. And of course, he and his *partner*[10] were the couple behind Bobbie and me. As we were *promenading*, we decided to do our infamous—we're going to wheel around and let out a loud "Boo" and scare the hell out of Marshall and his *partner*. So, we wheeled around and we let out this huge "Boo." Without a blink, I mean, he didn't even hesitate. Marshall took his *partner*, wheeled around and booed the couple behind him. I could not believe it. I mean, that was Marshall. It was wild.

§&

~Sally Nolen, Cuer & Joey Solis, Callers

Now, the second one was in 2007 at the hospital when Marshall got dehydrated [and couldn't call the 50th anniversary festival] and Sally [Nolen] and I went over there to see how he was, and we were going to try to convince him to take his fee because he said he didn't want it, and we just loved Marshall. He did so much for the center. Everybody [on the ASDC (Albuquerque Square Dance Center)] board decided, "We're going to pay him for it," and it turned out to be something else when we got there.

Sally said, "I think I was working at UNM [University of New Mexico] contract work through that period. Anyway, I

Sally and Bob Nolen. Source:
https://www.ceder.net/callerdb/
viewsingle.php?RecordId=2274

decided that I would stop by to see him. So, I went to the hospital, and Joey [Solis was there at the same time.] We walked in, and we were standing, talking, and that's when the nurse came in and said to him, "They want you at X-ray."

And he said, "Okay."

He kinda sat there a minute thinking she would bring a wheelchair or something.

The nurse said, "They want you NOW!"

And he said, "Okay."

And so, he started to get up.

And she said, "Well, you have to put your shoes on."

He said, "Look, I don't have any shoes. All I got is these boots."

She said, "Well, put them on. They want you down there. Do you know where you are going?"

And he went, "Yeah, Okay."

So, the guy was trying to bend. He had a catheter in him and trying to bend over and pull his boots on.

And Sally said, "Wait, Flip, let me help you." So, I [Sally] was bent down and helped him get his boots on, and he kind of waited a minute.

She said, "Well, go on!"

So, he said, "Ah, Okay."

So he stood up. We all kind of looked at each other. So, he stood up with his red long pajamas, the IV pole and the catheter bag was. . . and Joey and I [Sally] were laughing so hard.

Joey remembered Flip in a hospital gown and said, "Now, that is a sight that is etched in my, no, burned into my memory. I will never, never get that out of memory. No matter how hard I try."

That's when he turned around and said, "I don't want to ever hear this story."

And we said, "Yeah, good luck!"

As we were recording this, Larada said, "And then we did it [at his annual dance the next year]!"

Bob [Nolen] added, "And then he saw it again. It was classic!"

My husband, Lin, asked Bob and Sally, "Were you on the stage when they did that?"

Sally answered, "I was standing right next to him."

Bob added, "He knew what was coming when he saw Joey coming around there with that pole."

Joey Solis, Caller Continued

The other one you're very aware of was when he was doing our annual ASDC [Albuquerque Square Dance Center] dance the following year. Somebody—I'm not going to mention their name. You could put the name in, if you want. She dressed up in a sexy nurse's outfit, and of course, I was imitating Marshall in his hospital gown with the IV stand coming. Knowing Marshall, we had to put Jack Daniels or something up there for the IV.

I've never seen Marshall totally lose it. He was calling a tip when this sexy nurse and I come walking through the hall, and he lost it, but he really enjoyed that. I've never seen him enjoy something so much in his whole life. He really appreciated that. Those are my three fondest memories of him.

[I reminded Joey we reenacted this hospital scene again ten years later at Flip's last dance in Albuquerque in 2017, and he had forgotten about that.]

Yeah, he still enjoyed it, but we didn't quite get the same reaction we did the first time.

We both tried to remember his reaction over the mic the first time and agreed Flip said, "What the hell!"

Flip had a strong connection to Albuquerque, and an urban legend around the Albuquerque Square Dance Center is that he financially helped out on the building —which he denied.

Joey stated, "No, he contributed a bunch. In fact, I was going to mention that to you. I thought everybody knew that—with all he gave; he was pretty much a major donor to that center."

I don't think any big time pro caller made you feel as welcomed and part of— almost like his family as Marshall did. You felt comfortable around him. He was just a good ole boy that made you feel good, you know. I think the first time I ever met him, it was like the next year, he knew my name.

ɕ♣

~Tom Crisp, Caller

When I asked Tom to send me his favorite stories about Flippo, he wanted to share his favorite Flippo *Get-Out*s. This is totally technical square dance caller info!

Tom Crisp. Source: Tom Crisp

Zero Box:

Right & Left Thru, Swing Thru, Girls Circulate, Boys Trade, Boys Run, Bend the Line, (Lines with opposites out of sequence)
Pass thru, Wheel & Deal, Centers Touch 1/4, Walk & Dodge, Partner Trade, Touch 1/4
Insides Arch

Outsides Dive Thru
Bow to your partner or Right & Left Grand

Zero Box:

Right & Left Thru, Swing Thru, Boys Run, Tag the Line, face in,
Pass Thru, Wheel & Deal, Centers Zoom, New centers do a U turn back, Left
Allemande

Zero Box:

Swing Thru, Boys Run, Ferris Wheel, Centers Right & Left Thru, 1/2 Sashay,
Zoom twice, Right & Left Grand

Zero Lines out of sequence:

Pass thru, Wheel & Deal, Centers Touch 1/4, Follow Your Neighbor & Spread,
Girls Trade, Boys Run, Boys Trade, All the Boys Pass Thru, Left Allemande

Zero Lines out of sequence:

Pass the Ocean, Swing Thru, Boys Trade
Cast off Three Quarters, Centers Trade, Swing Thru
Cast off Three Quarters, Centers Trade, Swing Thru
Right & Left Grand

Zero Lines out of sequence:

Pass Thru, Partner Trade, Reverse Flutter Wheel, Dixie Style, Trade the Wave,
Explode the Wave, Partner Trade & Roll, Right & Left Grand

Sharon Parker and Ashley. Source: Sharon Parker

~Sharon Parker, Cuer

I am sure you have tons of stories about Flippo. But I would like to share with you a couple of ours. . . I was a teenager. My parents took me out of school to go to a festival south of us. Now this was unusual as my parents would not let me skip school, but for this they wrote a note that I had a "doctor's appointment." When we got to the festival, went into the Friday night dance with Flippo and had a chance to visit with him. He asked how I got out of school to attend. I told him what my parents had done, and he said, "Well, that's okay as my initials are M.D. Flippo." Now I have no idea to this day if his initials are truly M.D.F. - but it gave me my first hint of the character he was. We got to watch him do many of his "skits" over the years, but the rubber ducky was one of my favorites.

Ashley and Flippo. Source: Sharon Parker

When our daughter, [Ashley,] first met Flippo she was a young adult and had been raised with "caller humor." She had on a tee-shirt with a logo on the left chest area. Ashley was with Hunter [Keller] at the time and introduced her to Flippo. He looked at her, directed toward her shirt, and said, "That's a good name for that one, what's the name of the other one?" And gave her a big hug and said it was nice to meet her. Not too long after that, she found one of Flippo's records (33 rpm) in an old record store. She bought the record and took it with her the next time she was to dance with Flip. It now hangs on the wall in her music room.

Hunter Keller, Ashley, and I had run away from home to just dance for a weekend.

⁂

~Jack Pladdys, Caller
Facebook Post - November 5, 2018 (Day after Flippo died)

We all have our greatest memories of an icon. Here's mine. Marshall Flippo was our Michael Jordan. . .our Elvis. . .our Tom Brady. . .our Ali. . . He was the Greatest!!!!

Tony Oxendine, John Saunders (Another icon in the square dance world who passed away), Jerry Story, Marshall Flippo and Jack Pladdys. Source: Jack Pladdys

Here's one on my favorite photos ever!!!! Notice the awesome John Saunders was also in this photo along with Jerry Story and Tony Oxendine. I am so honored to be in this iconic photo.

389

ॐ

~Kandie & Roger Christian, Dancers

[Early in our phone conversations, Flippo told me about Roger and Kandie Christian. Here's their stories.]

Kandie's

I'm sitting here going through pictures trying to find pictures of when Flip was in Alaska 'cause he came up and called our Santa's Swingers Spring Fling in 2012, and then he rescued us, bless his heart, for our state festival in 2013. When I say he rescued us, the *caller* we had canceled on us two weeks before the state festival. Because Flip had been up the year before and had spent a week with us—you know, how he does. You just fall in love with him, and we had this relationship. So, when the *caller* canceled two weeks before the state festival, the next year I called him and asked him if he knew anybody that might be available on such short notice. He was so funny! He was in a car in Michigan riding with someone, but he would be home Sunday evening, and that he would look at the calendar and he would check around and see what he could find. So, in my state of panic, all I could do was say thank you, thank you.

So, Sunday evening I'm sitting by the phone anxiously waiting for it to ring because it was four or five days less than two weeks away. The phone rang and I picked it up, and I was like, "Flip!"

He goes, "Yep! Well, I got your problem solved!"

And I was like, "Oh, thank God!" I had no idea who was coming—he just said I got your problem solved.

Okay, who's coming so we can get a hold of him and we can work it out?

He said, "Darling, you got me."

I was thinking, 'Oh, my gosh!' So, he came back in '13 and did our state festival. We had so much fun with him those two years. It was just beyond wonderful. You just create relationships with that man, and we've just had that relationship ever since, just like so many probably hundreds and thousands of other people. So we've been visiting him in Tucson and calling back-and-forth over the year. And then in the winter, we would get down to Tucson to visit.

ॐ

The first festival was the Santa's Swingers Spring Fling, and it was April 27-29, 2012. I have to tell you the story. That man is just too much.

First of all, our club is really small in Alaska. We're not at the club that has money, and I didn't even know who Flippo was when I was given his name. The caller that we had for our club said, "Hey, why don't you call Flippo?"

Who is that?

And he said, "Marshall Flippo is a great *caller*. He's a national *caller*; he's a world *caller*. Call him up and see if he'll come to Alaska."

Okay, the name just didn't have any impact. It was just another caller. So, I called him up, and I have my usual conversation, "Hey Marshall Flippo. This is Kandie Christian, and I'm with the Santa's Swingers Square Dance Club in Fairbanks, Alaska."

He goes, "Hey, there," and we just started chatting, and I said, "Well, I'm calling to see if you would consider coming to Alaska and calling our Spring Fling next year."

And he goes, "Well, when is that?" So I gave him the date.

He said, "I'll have to look at my calendar."

Okay, but before you even look at your calendar, we have to talk dollars.

He goes, "Yeah."

We're a very small club and, I know you guys outside probably get paid a whole lot. I'm not even really sure what a whole lot is, but I can tell you that we can't afford a whole lot. And this is our Spring Fling. It's a Friday evening, Saturday all day and Sunday until one. We can afford to pay you a fee, buy your plane ticket and then we provide hospitality.

And he says, "Okay, so what are you gonna pay me?"

Well, don't even tell me what you usually get 'cause then I'm going to feel even worse, but we can only afford $500.

He goes, "Really."

Yeah, I really understand if you can't do this. I really do because I know that it's very different outside than it is up here.

"Well, let me think about this," so we chatted a little bit more and then hung up. So, I told the committee, "Well, I made the call."

So, a couple days later, I get a call back.

He goes, "Well, I guess I'm coming to Alaska."

YES! That got us over the first hurdle. I never did find out what he usually got paid, but I figured it was a lot more than that for three days.

And he says, "And you're going to put me up with you?"

Yeah.

"We're going to sleep in the same bed?"

No, Flip. You're going to sleep upstairs in the spare bedroom.

He goes, "Okay."

We talked often over the year, and it got really close. He calls me up one day.

He said, "What's the temperature going to be up there?"

Well, it's probably going to be. . . It's going to be warm. It's going to be in the probably high 50s low 60s.

He goes, "Warm?"

So, we chatted about that for a little bit.

He says, "You know, I'm really afraid that this is going to be cold. I'm really worried I'm gonna freeze my you-know-whats off!"

Flip, it's going to be warm. Oh. I looked up the temperature in Tucson, and I guess you do have a lot higher temperatures than we do.

"Yeah!"

Our club always does something funny for the *caller*. We try to learn about them so we can do something silly and fun, and we had not been able to figure out what to do for Flippo. We really didn't know him yet. I mean, I did go online and

Google, YouTube and listen to him call and shared those YouTube things with the club, but we really didn't know him.

So, I get this call again. He was really worried about the cold temperatures, and now he's trying to figure out if he should get some flannel something to put on because he knows he's going to freeze his you-know-whats off.

I told him, "You'll be fine. We'll put you in one of our long parkas if we have to. You'll be fine."

So, I went back to the club and I said, "You know what? I think I figured out what we're going to do."

And they said, "What?"

Flippo is really concerned about freezing his you-know-whats off.

And one of our naive board members said, "What do you mean his you-know-whats?"

April, he's really, really worried about freezing what's between his legs, Okay!

She goes, "Oh, Kandie," and turns all red.

You guys, we need to make him a fur-lined jock strap, and they looked at me. Poor April's turning purple now.

Everybody else is laughing and said, "Great idea!"

Okay, that's what we'll do for the fun thing for Flippo. So, we did! We went and bought the largest jock strap we could find. Rodney pulled out some fur. I think it was fox, and we cut it, and we lined the outside. That jock strap was this beautiful fur.

And we had to do something for the *cuer*. We went ahead and did a bra for her and lined it in this just regular black fake fur.

So, we get to Saturday night, and at the *after party* is when we give the gifts and do all the fun stuff. So, it was time to give Flippo his gift, so we had the funny one first. I took the bag up and had him and Denise Schmidt up front, and told him a little story about our conversations and him telling me how he was so worried he was going freeze.

Have we kept you warm?

He goes, "Yeah."

You haven't frozen anything yet?

"Yeah."

But we have a little more protection for you, and I handed him the bag. He was looking at me and he's looking in this bag, and he finally pulls the paper off the top of it, and then you could see the fur. So, he's looking at the bag, and he looks up at me, trying to figure out what this is, and then he pulled it out. And, of course, the room just roared! And he looks at this fur-lined jock strap.

And he says, "I need to put this on."

Flippo wearing his fur-lined jock strap gift & Denise Schmidt, Flippo, Kandie Christian & April Boynton, Fairbanks, Alaska, 2012. Source: Kandie Christian

He turns to Denise, and now she's pulled out her fur-lined bra. So, he decides that Denise is going to put this jock strap on him, so Denise takes the jock strap in her hands, and he holds onto her back and steps up and she puts it over one leg and then he steps up with the other one and gets it on, and he pulls it all the way up, and he puffs his chest up and he puts his hands on his hips, and he strutted all the way around the room so everybody could see his fur-lined jock strap.

Denise Schmidt, Flippo, Kandie Christian and April Boynton giving him his serious gift, Denise Schmidt and Flippo and his gift—the Northern Lights gift. Source: Kandie Christian

We had so much fun. He told us when he got home, he hung it on the wall so everybody could see it. He's so good natured, happy, and fun and full of piss and vinegar. He truly is a little boy still—full of piss and vinegar!

Another funny incident involved his confusion about driving around our town. Where we live is in a residential area, and when you come out of our area to get onto a main road, there's a signal. One corner has a JOANN Fabric [store], but you can come to that corner from obviously four different directions. So, the first day, we brought him home from the airport, he saw it on one corner. Then the next day, we left the house, and we came at it from a different direction.

And he says, "You've got JOANN Fabric [stores] on. . ."

And we said, "Yeah, we do." We didn't think much of it—kept going. Well, when we came back from taking him out touring, we came home from one of the other directions. Well, then, we went somewhere else, and we came back from the fourth direction.

He said, "How many JOANN Fabric do you have in this town? I've seen them all over the place."

Flippo, we have one! That one!

"No, you have more than that!" We had lots of laughs about JOANN Fabric stores being on all the different corners in our town which has actually one store. He was just lots of fun.

And of course, after he came up, then we learned from lots of other people who Flippo really is.

[Kandie shed tears as she spoke.] Wonderful, wonderful *caller* and the history that he has in the calling community, so I can tell you we felt so very blessed that this man actually came to Alaska to call our dance for this measly little 500-dollar fee. It was just spectacular. We had a wonderful three-day event. He came in on maybe Tuesday and spent three days with us and took him touring around the northern area, and I think he left on the Monday after, so we had that stretch of time so we could just chat with him and get to know him, and it was just wonderful.

And then it was just interesting. You know how sometimes people say to you, 'We'll keep in touch,' and you never really hear from them. When Flip left, he gave us both this big hug, and he says, 'We'll keep in touch,' and I thought, 'You know what? You're a caller. You're busy! I don't expect it, but thank you so much. We love you, and we're so happy we met you.' Well, we did keep in touch. He called; we called; he called; we called; and then we stopped in Tucson to visit, and then as I said, that following year when the caller we had canceled on us at the last minute, Flippo agreed to come up and again the fee, I'm sure, was way below what he normally gets for a state festival.

He came up and called our state festival that following year in 2013, and again we housed him. He was with us for a week, and for that festival—Thursday, Friday, Saturday and Sunday—and he was the only *caller*. He asked me how many *callers* were calling our state festival. And I said, 'Well, one of course!' I didn't know that festivals out here have two and three and four callers. I didn't know that.

He says, "So what you gonna pay me this time?"

More than five hundred.

He says, "Okay."

Our budget—we pay $1300 for the festival.

And he says, "I'm on my way!"

So, bless his heart! I have no idea what he would have gotten paid out here for a festival, but he came up and called our festival for that small fee. And we had such an incredible state festival, and of course, people knew Flippo. [Other dancers] knew Flippo before I knew Flippo, so they knew when we said Flippo's coming up to call the state festival, [it would be a success]. We had to change immediately our flyers and everything and get the word out that he was coming. We had tremendous attendance in Alaska for that state festival in 2013. It was just amazing, and again we had so much fun with him.

He wasn't afraid to come because the state festival was in July, so he figured he wasn't going to freeze. That's the one where we gave him 'Moose Poop' Christmas decorations, so he was treated to "Moose Poop" as his fun gift.

I'm sure the entire square dance world feels this way—his [death] was such a tremendous loss to the community, and he was so humble. I didn't see an ego in that man, and I think that's unusual for men or even someone who is a nationally ranked *caller* like he is. I just didn't see that ego.

He was loving, and you know, we had been talking before we left Alaska, this summer we had talked a number of times and then he was in the hospital.

Kandie cried, "The last time we talked was about six or seven days before we left Alaska, and our plan had been that we were going to meet in Tucson. We had planned it from the previous year. We'd meet up in Tucson, and he was telling me how his son really wanted him to come back and live with him in Lake of the Ozarks, but he was just feeling like he really wanted to be in Tucson. He was still active and wanted to be where his friends were."

But then that last time we talked, I said, "Are you still in Tucson because you were very sick? What happened?"

He said, "No, I'm living with John in Lake of the Ozarks."

Okay. Well, I think that's probably much better, but I've got to look up where Lake of the Ozarks is 'cuz I don't think that's between Phoenix and Las Cruces.

He goes, "No, but it's not far from Las Cruces."

Okay, but we'll drive up and see you. So that was our plan that we'd get down here (Las Cruces) and we'd figure out what it would take to drive to Lake of the Ozarks, so we could visit him for a couple days while we are down here for the winter, and that was our last conversation.

And he told me, "Wait a minute. My ex-wife and everybody's here and we're all talking and I got to go outside so I can talk to you."

Well, I can call back.

He goes, "No."

So, I said, "OK," so he walked outside and we chatted and that was a week before we left Alaska on October 14 – just a few weeks before he died.

ৡ

I have not seen my husband cry very often, and when we got the message the evening that Flip passed, I got a text message, and I turned to Roger and the tears were just running down my face, and he looked at me, and I told him why, and the tears just instantly welled up in his eyes, and I knew. I knew how much he thought of Flip, but to have him really show that emotion. I thought, "I bet people all over the world are showing that emotion."

Roger's

[Roger, Kandie's husband, shared about the couple of days he had alone with Flip and their shenanigans.]

Roger clarified, "We didn't have shenanigans."

Well, the day after Flip got in, Kandie had to go to Anchorage for a conference for three days, so Flip and I were allowed to run around Fairbanks doing all kinds of loud and crazy things. I showed him some of the spots for breakfast, and he was always interested in breakfast. We went out to the pipeline, cruised around, went up to the museum. He was really an avid museum buff, and we couldn't get him to the auto museum that time, but the next time we did. He was really enthralled with that.

He kept asking me all kinds of questions about Alaska. He'd been up to Juneau probably 20 years prior to his visit to Fairbanks, and of course, Juneau is nothing like Fairbanks. He was interested in the history of Fairbanks, and I did my best to enlighten him as to what was going on, what had happened in the past, and so forth. We basically just kinda hung out and had fun!

With a laugh, Roger confessed, "Oh, yeah. I had to rein him in a couple times."

The one story that I got a kick out of was when he was calling a dance with several other *callers*, and he came out of the men's room, and he had just washed his hands. His hands were still a little wet, and he got up on the stage and shook hands with one of the *callers*. The *caller* knew he had been in the men's room and said to him, "I hope you washed your hands."

Flippo said, "No, never do."

I just remember having all kinds of fun with him. He was a very humble, very down-to-earth person, but he had a heart of gold.

~Darryl Lipscomb, Caller

What can possibly be said about "Flip" that hasn't already been said?

"Flip," as he was passionately known to friends, was larger than life, certainly an icon to the square dance world! Flip was probably the most well known, admired, and respected *caller*, in the history of the activity! He touched the lives of so many dancers, not to mention *callers*.

I am one of those *callers*, who was touched by Flip's magic! I was inspired by Flip at the ripe 'ole age of 12! I first met him in 1959 in the Dallas area, as Flip was calling there. I had heard so many stories about Flip, that I imagined him as a giant Texan!

When I asked my parents where Flip was, they replied, "That's him on the stage."

I asked, "Where?"

My Dad replied, "There, standing on the stage."

I replied, "That little squirt is Flippo?"

I was really disappointed, until he began calling, with that 'manly' voice, in a rhythmic Flippo chant! I, then, forgot about his size. In my eyes, he was, again, that Texas giant!

Darryl Lipscomb. Source:
https://www.ceder.net/
callerdb/viewsingle.php?
RecordId=59

Elmer Sheffield. Source: https://www.ceder.net/callerdb/viewsingle.
php?RecordId=936

~Elmer Sheffield

Well, of course, there are lots and lots of stories with me and Flip. We go back a long way. I met him when I first started trying to become a *caller* over fifty years ago, and we just developed a real relationship. He'd call me, even up 'til just before he passed away, at least once a week, and we would talk just about old friendships and all the things we did together.

Elmer's Birthday Surprise

The thing about the party that the club had for me, they got with my wife, and lot of times when people plan surprise things, it really slips out, but in this case, I was definitely kept in the dark.

We had this dance at the Elks Club. Back in those days we had twenty-five squares at the dance, but I got there a few minutes before, and I just noticed this big refrigerator box kinda sitting back on the stage off to the corner, but since we were using the Elks Club, I just assumed it was something they had there, and it didn't bother me. But just a few minutes before 8:00, I went up on stage, got my microphone and my music and had just put the needle down, and the president walked up on stage.

He said, "Ho, ho, wait a minute. Before we start, we need you to open that box."

And of course, I had no idea what they were planning, but anyway, I just walked over and opened the front of the box, and there was Flip sitting on the chair.

And he said, "Damn, I didn't think you's gonna ever let me out of here."

And of course, he called the dance, and it was great. Another thing about that dance is I found out from the club officers later, when they called Flip and asked him, "You know, you're Elmer's favorite caller. We'd love to have you come and call this special for him. They said how much would you charge?"

And Flip said, "Nothing! If it's for Elmer, I'd do it free."

However, they paid him. They wouldn't let him do it free, but he would have! And it was just a special night. We just really had a good time. There's so many stories. He was just a great friend, a mentor. He taught me a lot of things, and some of 'em I couldn't repeat!

CALLERLAB 2018

And another quick story and this just happened, gollee, so it wasn't too long before he passed away, but we were at CALLERLAB [2018 in Albuquerque]. Before CALLERLAB, Dana [Schirmer] had sent out a thing saying we want to have a special dance there one night with Duets. Any *caller* that you'd like to sing with, send your name and send his name in and we'll program you. Well, I didn't send it in because they're lots of guys I like to sing with, but I just didn't do it.

That afternoon before that night's dance, Dana came to me and said, "Look, I want you to do something for me. I want to surprise Flippo. I sent my name in and asked Flippo if he'd do the Duet with me."

And Flippo said, "You know, I ain't no great singer, but I'll do it."

So, Dana said, "What I want to do when me and him get up there to do our tip, I want to say, 'Wait, there's a young *caller* in the audience that's always wanted to call with you, and if you don't mind, I'll call him up.' I'd like you to come up."

So, sure enough, Flippo and Dana got up on stage.

Dana said, "Wait, Flip, I got this young guy who wants to call with you, and he's here tonight."

And Flippo said, "Well, sure. Bring him up."

And when he called my name, I thought Flippo was going to faint, and it was one of the highlights really because he and myself and Dana got to do a *tip* together, and that was the last time I got to call with him. Of course, he had about retired by then. He was only filling in for people around in his area. He said, 'I've quit the road.' My gosh, he was in his early 90s then, I suppose.

Those are the things that kinda stick out in my mind about Flip. He was just one of the best *callers* that's ever been, but he was just also an entertainer. We always talked about him. There are plenty of *callers* who sing better than Flippo, who had better choreography than Flippo had, but there was something about him that set him above the rest. He could entertain a crowd. He had 'em in his hand all the time.

Kirkwood Lodge

I did like fifteen years at Kirkwood Lodge with him and Ken Bower, and those were some of the best weeks that I ever spent in my calling career, and I've been calling now for, I guess, 51 years. It was just so much fun. I recall one week we were there, and we had three or four couples that came from England. The last night Flippo always thanks everybody, 'we appreciate ya'll coming,' kind of thing.

And he said, "I really want to thank the couples from England. They really added a lot to this week."

And me without even thinking, I said, "Yeah, about $600 a couple!"

And I thought Flip was going to pass out, because you don't get over on him too many times. He's usually the one that's on top of everything, and it was just funny. But those are just a few of things I remember about our relationship. Just a great, great person!

Close Friendship

I can't even recall all the things that we did together because he was a prankster, anyway. We just had a close relationship. Even before he passed away, before he actually went into the hospital last time, he called me at least once a week. He said, "Hello there, friend! This is Flip." (in a raspy voice), and we just talked.

Elmer's Wife & Flippo's Admiration

He knows my wife had a stroke eight years ago. Before that she was--gollee-- she was the life of the party. She kept everybody laughing. She danced with all the older folks and kept them entertained, but once she had the stroke, she's lucky she survived, and of course, has a lot of problems. She can't walk.

He'd say, "Friend, I'm a tellin' you. You are a real genuine person to stay there and take care."

I'd say, "Well, you know, I married her for better, for worse," and this coming March it will be 60 years we've been married.

And I said, "Had it been me, she'd be taking care of me the same way."

But Flippo always bragged on me. He praised me for taking care of her like I do, and like I plan to continue to do so. He compared me to Melton Luttrell. You know, Melton's wife, Sue—I don't remember what her problems were, but she had a lot of problems, but Melton took care of her until she passed away, and Flip would always say, "I really admire you and Melton for staying there with your wives and taking care of 'em."

. . .

Ending

There's so many stories that I can't even recall them all. When somebody mentions something, I say, "Oh, yeah, I remember," but those are the things that I told you that just always stick in my mind because he was such a jewel! I put him at the top of *callers*. If I had an idol, it was Flippo! That's just the way it was. I appreciate you doing this book, and I hope I reserved a copy of it.

Elmer ended with, "Everybody's been had by Flippo."

~John Lewin, Caller

Flippo would set up a *Grand Ocean Wave*[11] which is eight people, side-by-side with a boy on each end, and he would make it sound like it was very technical. [Then] he'd say, "*The two boys at the very end, trade places.*" And you'd just about arrive there, and [then] he'd say, "*Twice*," and everybody would giggle at that.

The other thing was if there was anybody sharing the mic with him, whether it was round dance leader or another caller, if that man had more hair, he would mention it because he was losing all his hair.

The other thing he used to do is he'd call a *Square Thru*[12] and some people would do some kind of a *patty cake routine*[13] that they would wind up [at the right position], and he'd just look and he'd say, "I saw that." But that's the kind of guy he was with the dry humor, you know, but he was quite a character.

~Mike Seastrom, Caller

Marshall Flippo was a "caller's caller." He couldn't tell you about the technical aspects of what he did, but if you observed his calling and danced to him, you knew he had practiced what he called, figured out a way to make it very danceable, and time out perfect. He also used "helper words" at the exact points that were needed to help the dancers succeed. He was calm, collected, and always had a great sense of humor on the microphone.

Flip remembered dancer's names like few *callers* I've ever known. He knew the area where they danced, too. He could also hug and kiss all the ladies in the entire hall and get away with it. Hardly anyone would even notice, except for those of us that knew we could never get away with that kind of behavior. He could also stray into what I would call "grey" or "borderline" areas with jokes or stories, and he could usually get away with that kind of humor without

Mike Seastrom. Source: https://www.ceder.net/ callerdb/viewsingle.php? RecordId=748

offending people. Few of us would ever try to go that far with our jokes or stories, knowing we couldn't get away with it.

Flip was not only a dear friend, but a mentor to me. I admired and learned from his calling in many ways, but it was observing his way of treating other dancers and *callers* that I learned the most.

Marshall Flippo never said anything bad about anyone. He lived by example for me, and although he never explained this behavior in words, it was like he lived the saying, "If you can't say something nice or good about someone, don't say it at all."

Flip respected and treated all dancers and *callers* equally. Whether you were a brand-new *caller* or dancer, or a seasoned veteran in calling and dancing, he treated you with kindness, acceptance and respect and he shared his attention equally.

We talked a lot on the phone, and he always asked about my close family. We shared jokes, stories, and told each other tall tales. He would always say that if my significant others were lonely, he could come over and "take care of them" for me.

Every time we said goodbye from a phone call, he would say, "Goodbye ole' friend, love you." I would tell him the same and it was always as if that would be the last time we would ever speak to each other.

When I learned of Flip's passing, I felt that we had said our "goodbyes" many times. Although I will miss him forever, I am left feeling so blessed that Marshall Flippo was a great ole' friend and mentor, and that he had such a positive impact on my life and the lives of so many others. When I think of Flip, it just makes me smile!

After Parties

Everyone knew Marshall Flippo was good at *after parties*. He was a great organizer and could put together a group of skits, songs, and other entertaining fun things for an *after party* like a pro! He could also put together an *after party* on the fly, or at least he made it look that way. For weekend festivals and big dances, it was usually Flip who put the *after party* program together.

Everyone involved in the *after party* would meet with Flip beforehand, and he would hand out scripts and even costumes so that everyone was involved.

One tall task that we both shared was to do skits at a funeral. It was the funeral of Bob Osgood, the longtime Editor of *Sets In Order* square dance magazine, and the Founding Father of CALLERLAB. It was Bob's wish to have skits at his funeral reception. Since we both had worked with Bob and Becky Osgood over the years, we had many skits we shared at those events, and so it was easy to go back through our notes and pick out the ones we enjoyed most.

One skit that stands out the most in my mind was one that was reportedly written by Becky Osgood called, the Hat Skit. At least two participants sit at a table facing the audience with four different hats to take on and off as a story is read by a narrator.

It was always good to have someone with a minimal amount of hair sitting at the table changing hats. It becomes more about the hats and the story and less about what someone's hair is doing.

Both Flip and I had done that skit many times, but Flip usually did the "changing hats" part, and I usually read the story. That afternoon I had to compete with Flip and do the "changing hats" part, and I knew I had my work cut out for me.

Flip, as I expected, was much better at changing hats, but he also handicapped me by turning and making faces at me every time he changed hats. He had me laughing so hard and my eyes watering so much I could hardly see.

It was a memorable afternoon, a great tribute to a great man and super friend, and a good time was had by all at what could have been a very somber occasion.

Albuquerque, Flippo and my grandson Jack

Anyone who has ever danced or called in Albuquerque, New Mexico, knows what a great square dance center they have there. There are also two hotels adjacent. If you are there for a square dance weekend as a dancer or dance leader you're usually staying at one of those two hotels.

One weekend when I was calling in Albuquerque, I brought my grandson Jack with me, and he was 13 years old at the time. Jack was a great traveler and was my navigator that weekend. When the man at the counter of the rental car agency ask me if I need a GPS unit, I said, "No, I have my grandson Jack with me and he's a great cell phone navigator."

On Saturday morning of the weekend, I got a call from Flip on my phone. It was 8:00 a.m. and he sounded very upbeat. I asked him where he was traveling and he said that he was traveling through Albuquerque on the way to Colorado and was staying at a hotel there. When I asked him what hotel, he said, "The hotel you're staying in."

He said he knew my hotel because he was downstairs having breakfast with the dancers. I woke up my grandson Jack and told him he needed to meet my friend Flippo.

Jack asked, "Who is Flippo?"

I told Jack, "He's someone you'll never forget, and we'll have a couple good laughs for sure."

Jack and I threw on some clothes, and we headed downstairs. After introducing them and after Jack received Flip's, "I've known you for years" greeting, the two sat and talked for a long while. I fetched breakfast for us, and the two of them talked and laughed. Jack always asked about Flip after that.

Flip had a way of talking with people that not only allowed you to feel special warmth, but he had a way of making the conversation about you. He had a way of making whoever he was talking to feel special and respected. It was a quality that I observed many times, and one I always admired. He could always make you laugh too.

"The Auctioneer"

One of the most famous *singing calls* that Marshall Flippo recorded was "The Auctioneer," on Blue Star Records. When I began calling in 1963, that was the singing call to learn. I learned the *figure*[14] that was on the cue sheet and could still call that same *figure* today, but I never analyzed it, I just called it and the dancers did it.

Many years later in the late 1990s, I had a request to bring that singing call with me and use or workshop [teach] the old *figure* at a weekend I was calling. I pulled out the *singing call* prior to the weekend to get a "teaching look" at the *figure* that Flip recorded so many years before. As I analyzed it, I found a place I was not sure about.

I called Flip to ask him about the *figure*, and the phone got quiet. Flip then said, "Damn *figure*! Yep. . .damn *figure*."

I started to respond, but Flippo immediately said again, "Damn *figure*!" Then he said, "Well, I guess we know a lot more about *figures* and dancing these days." We left it at that, and I did the same old *figure* that weekend. The dancers struggled to keep up, but we laughed and had a good time with it, anyway.

Flippo's Last Dance

Lisa and I attended Flip's last dance on New Year's Eve in Green Valley, Arizona, December 31, 2017. It was a magical dance, and we danced every tip.

There were callers and dancers from all over the country in attendance, and he had a short clean story or comment to share about many of them. One that comes to mind is the little story he told about Gary Shoemake. He said he knew Gary in his early years of calling and that Gary lived pretty close to him. He also said that it was great that Gary lived close because he would have him fill in for his local groups when he was on the road. Gary was not only a great caller, but Flip's dancers loved him. He then said that there was one problem. Every time he called home, Gary would answer the phone!

Each *tip* at that dance was themed in obvious and not so obvious ways. Flip was smooth, his timing was excellent, and he was relaxed and having a great time. He was right on the mark with his calling and sense of humor at the age of 90.

When I thanked him after the dance, he was very tired and you could tell he gave it everything he had. I left thinking that I'd feel blessed and proud to call a dance like that any day of the week at any age!

~George & Ann Salwaechter, Dancers

Flip is such a good friend. He has amazing and funny stories with which to entertain us. I'm sure he is telling you many of them. We won't even try to relay them to you, but you might be sure to ask him about hiding money in a toilet paper roll if he hasn't already told you the story.

He truly cares for people and has such a loving heart. He always talks about Mama, so you know he was a good son.

Flip isn't egotistical, even though he has the right to be just that.

Dave Williams from Salida, Colorado, says, "Marshall Flippo is the greatest *caller* ever." That is all he had to say when I told him he could write something about Flip if he wanted. Dave was a great square dance teacher who idolized Flip.

So many of us loved Flip, so it is with a heavy heart that we think of him now. We had just talked to him on Monday and Tuesday before he went to the hospital on Wednesday. He seemed okay then. John emailed on Saturday that he knew Flip didn't want to worry people, but he wanted us to know. At that time, he said he was getting better, but in a day the picture changed.

There was a Going-Away party for Flip at Rincon (Tucson, Arizona) on September 18. He really seemed to enjoy that, but when it was planned, so like Flip, he asked, "Who would come?" There was a crowd of about 60 people. Many of whom contributed money as a gift.

Ann Salwaechter & Flippo.
Source: Harue Okazaki Swift

Later Flip asked if we knew how much money was there. He said he didn't know what to do with it. He thought he would donate it, but between John and us, we convinced him that it was for him and not to give it away. That is just the kind of guy he was.

He will be missed so much.

~Dennis Pabst, Dancer

My parents were Bill and Ethel Pabst. My dad was a *caller*, and every year they went to Marshall Flippo's Lake of the Ozarks Square Dance camp for like 17 years and became friends, and my mom had hazel eyes. So, Marshall always told her that his *singing call*, "Hazel Eyes," was dedicated to her. Her name is Ethel, and he had one thing where he said Ethel every time they twirled like we do now, and that was after my mom.

We went to Germany with them about ten years ago on the tour of the century or whatever. Marshall is famous for all the Frauleins who just loved him, and he loved them. He'd take care of them.

During that time, when you said "Marshall Flippo," it meant "Repair the square." Anytime the other *callers* screwed up or did something bad, "Okay, Marshall Flippo." Everybody would go back home.

My happiest memory is right before my dad died. I moved into Roswell, and Marshall came and did a call in Roswell, and my dad called Flip up, and my dad cried. He knew it was probably the last time he'd see him, and Marshall was just very, very gracious to my dad.

He was friendly to everybody, and he could remember names. The last time I saw him, he remembered Anna's name, [Dennis' wife]. I just couldn't believe it. And I think that was when we went to Laughlin. Marshall called, and it was the last time. We all respected him, and my parents passed it on to us, a second generation. A wonderful, wonderful person. Anytime I saw him, I thought of my mom.

. . .

~Edris Davis, Dancer

We traveled a lot. Some of the *callers* who traveled had their wives with them, but Neeca didn't travel.

John Flippo

At the time when I first met Flippo, they were having the medical problems with John. They were not sure that John was going to live, and they had been married for quite a while before they had him.

Flippo just about worshipped that child. I think they both did.

Albuquerque Square Dance Center

Flippo contributed money to the dance hall. He had the biggest crowds we ever had, and he gave us his entire money back. He helped out a lot. He handed it [paycheck] right back to us.

We were still dancing in the old hall, The Barn, on Washington and Menaul, south of Menaul, and it stayed there for a long time. He came to Albuquerque a couple times a year.

I first met him when I lived in Santa Fe before '65. I don't remember him ever calling over at the Heights. We used to go to the Heights Community Center, and a lot of the traveling *callers* would call over there.

Kirkwood Lodge

Some of my fondest memories with Flippo were at Kirkwood. We played games downstairs with windows overlooking the lake.

One time he knocked on our door at 2:00 am and asked, "Can Edris come out and play?"

~Norma Herron, Dancer

John Flippo

Flippo called a square dance, and of course, they [Flippo and Neeca] had the baby [John] with them. The dance was Saturday night, and several of us met for breakfast on Sunday morning before they left going back home, and they had the baby in a high chair between the two of them. Both of them had a wet washcloth. Every bite that child took, one of them would wipe his mouth. We laughed 'cause all of us there had kids older than his. We have laughed for years about that poor child, having his face wiped so much.

Odessa, Texas

We always teased Flippo about being so short. In 1965, Odessa had their Square Dance Jubilee. The Chuck Wagon Gang and everybody sponsored it, so it was a great big thing, and we'd hired Marshall to come over. This was way back early in his calling,

The decorating committee had just gone all out, decorating the stage. Marshall gets there to put his stuff up on stage, and the decorations are taller than him. So, one member had a construction company, so they ran out in the afternoon and built a thing to put up on stage, so he'd be high enough where everybody could see him. Yeah, and this is back when we had 90-100 squares at the convention.

So, our member got there early, and put it up, and it's a good thing he did because if he'd got there late, nobody would have been able to see Marshall. We have laughed about that every time any of us get together.

On a Personal Level

We had left west Texas and moved to the Dallas area, and then I lost my husband. I'd been out [of square dancing] for a bit and hadn't seen Marshall in like five or six years. It was probably 1970, and I had gotten back into square dancing and walked into one of his dances in Dallas. He remembered me. He remembered that I had lost Joe, my husband, and the whole bit the minute I walked in the auditorium.

That just floored me that the hundreds and hundreds and hundreds of people he deals with for all those years, and then to know who I was just when I walked in. Nobody said anything, but he knew who I was when I walked in, so that kind of memory—that really is something that others need to know something about him, the kind of memory that he had for square dancers that danced very long with him.

~Mike Hogan, Caller

I was 15 years old and attending the Omaha Outstanding *Caller's* Series of which Flip was the *caller* for that dance. It was held at the Livestock Exchange Ballroom in Omaha. It was actually Margaret Bolt who said, "Let's thank Mikey Hogan for letting us use his equipment," so that was my first Marshall Flippo experience.

In forty-two years of calling I never got the opportunity to call with Marshall Flippo until this very last March or April (2017) at the CALLERLAB convention. I record for a guy named Buddy Weaver out of California. Buddy and I are good friends, and one of the songs that he asked me to do was "Green, Green." Now "Green, Green" is a song that was originally recorded by the legendary Marshall Flippo, so

Mike Hogan. Source: https://www.ceder.net/callerdb/viewsingle.php?RecordId=2169

we did it at the CALLERLAB convention, and I invited Flip to come up and to call with us, and he declined. And that was okay because he said, "Go on, Mike.

Go on. I don't call anymore. I'm done, but thank you very much for inviting me. I know you did a great job with this song."

So, I got my buddy, Lanny Weaklend, from Omaha, my buddy, Bear Miller, from Denver, and my buddy, Mike Seastrom, from California, and the four of us started up to do the song, and here comes Flip with his microphone. So, he came up, and he stood right beside me, and we did "Green, Green" together. That's the one-and-only time that I got to call with Flip, and I will cherish that.

Grace and Grant Wheatley. Source: Grant Wheatley

~Grant and Grace Wheatley, Caller & Husband

Many years ago at a Nationals [square dance convention], when the dances had ended on Saturday night, the *after parties* began. The different cities vying for future Nationals tried to entice the dancers to their party by getting the most popular *callers* in the country: Story, Oxendine, Bower, Haag, Driver, Barbour, Flippo, Seastrom, Sikorsky, etc., etc.

It didn't happen often, but one year Grace was invited to one, the most prestigious one. She took three records: a *patter*,[15] a fast *singing call*, and a slow *singing call*. To give the dancers a break, if the caller in front of her went fast, she'd go slow. If he went slow, she'd go fast. If he did a singer, she'd do a *patter*[16] and vice versa. It seemed to me like the ones in front of her were trying more to outdo each other than help the dancers. There was no pause between *callers*. Many of the squares had started to break up. The last *caller* had worn them down with a little help from Denver's altitude. And many of the dancers hadn't heard of

Grace. She wasn't one of the elite full-time *callers*, but three beats into "Crying Time," they were re-formed and dancing.

After she finished, it was just a few seconds before the next *caller* was going. Grace climbed high up into the bleachers to get her coat and record case where she had stashed them. As she reached down to pick up her stuff, a voice that sounded like it was out of breath said, "That was outstanding."

She turned around to thank someone, thinking it was a dancer. It was Marshal Flippo, arguably the best and most popular *caller* with the biggest heart in square dancing. THAT MOMENT was the highlight of the Nationals for us.

ॐ

~Bob Link, Previous Owner of Kirkwood & Dancer

Flippo was a great man. We owned Kirkwood from June 1993 'til October 2000. I loved the eight years I did that. You'll make me tear up thinking about it. How much fun it was!

Anyway, we got the place [Kirkwood], and we weren't square dancers, although I have some hotel and accounting experience. We kinda were like rookies, and that first year we met Flip; he was just a fixture. It was like a group of about thirty seasonal employees. We were only opened six months of the year, and in the winter, his son, John, lived right up on top the hill, and Flip would take off and do his winter tour.

Bob & Sharon Link. Source: John Flippo

He was all over the country, and he'd be back in the spring, and he was the resident *caller*. He was a complete gentleman—what a great guy. He had some bad habits like we all do. He liked to drink a little and smoke a little, but he lived a long life, and it didn't hurt him.

We got along very well, and I adjusted to the system because they had a system, and it was very unique. All a sudden I find myself thrown into this world of rock stars—these guys are gods: Ken Bower, Gary Shoemake, and Lee Kopman.

And all a sudden, Gary said, "Yeah, come out to English Mountain and spend a week with us and I'll show you what we've got."

ॐ

Flip would do his workshops, and we would make sure all that was set for him, and after the first year, we got through our *Basics*[17] and got to *Plus*.[18] We were down there every night for the dances. We became *Advanced*[19] dancers eventually.

He was very supportive of our learning and we learned at a local club, and within the second year, we were down with the *Plus* weeks. We were down dancing, and we would try to learn the *round dance*[20] things and go to workshops. It was like you work all day and then we'd go down, and you're working, but it's not like you're working. It's a dance and an *after party*. You just got to find time to sleep.

In the first three years we had the place, we would travel in the wintertime. While Flip was gone, we'd go down to Sharon's folks, my wife, who lived in Harlingen, Texas. So, we'd go down there and go to the McAllen Festival and visit around to all the parks down there, 'cause we knew all these guys.

When the people arrived at Kirkwood on Sunday, we had to do the introductions. Flippo was always there for that, and you'd introduce all these people from all over the country or the world. We had them from Japan, Germany, England. Groups of ten or fifteen people would come over. Two or three squares would come over to Kirkwood from these foreign countries and spend a week. And it was really wonderful.

I probably ate breakfast with him, I don't know how many hundred times in the eight years that we were there because we ate our meals at the hotel, because we didn't have time to do anything else. Even though the square dancers checked in on Sunday and checked out on Friday, we were opened for regular summer people at the lake there for the weekends, so it was seven days a week, 24/7 job.

From high school seniors in May to summer, families all summer, Flip would be there, and he would do *Basics* for them. He'd get them downstairs and do the "Hokey Pokey" and some of them would do some basic square dancing 'cause a lot of them were rural schools. We still had them coming from four or five states around us, and you'd find out the bus driver had been there twenty years before. Amazing! It was just a unique, unique place, and he was one of the most unique individuals I've ever met.

It was a very exciting time in our lives. We socialized with Marshall Flippo. I think I've even played golf with him once or twice. I would go out with these guys to a local tavern or bar and have a few and visit and do things like that. I became aware quickly how high he stood in square dance. I mean, he was the God Father. Basically, he didn't start it all, but he was the head of the modern square dancing and held that because of his age and the ability he had. He held that position for a long, long time.

We had a group coming from Texas and Minnesota, and of course, they all wanted to have their own *after party*, and the ones from Minnesota'd have the best smoked fish you ever had. And the one from Texas would make all kinds of Texas hors d'oeuvres, and we had several groups that had a rivalry.

My wife, Sharon, went on a square dance weekend with her parents. Her dad was a Rexall pharmacist from northern Missouri, and they were square dancers, and they came down in probably the 50s. After she graduated in '62, Frank Lane and Flip would make a base, and she could climb up and get on their shoulders waterskiing. She remembers doing that and going down that cove.

Flip got along with the people. The kitchen crew at that place was amazing. Some of these girls were driving forty and fifty miles one way to be a housekeeper or something like that, but every employee there loved Flip. That's the truth!

If he had any enemies, I never knew about it. And they didn't come to Kirkwood Lodge! They wouldn't! There was a solid wall of people that were nothing but his friends.

Flip was never a pushy guy. He was never egotistical. He didn't have to be. He was just one of a kind. He'd smile at you and say something, and there never was any hassle.

Flippo was in his 70s most of the time I knew him. I've seen him since we left the hotel when we went out to Tucson a few times where he was wintering, and we would stay out there at Star Pass. We'd call him up and go to have dinner with him. He was always fun. He would always reminisce and talk. What a great guy!

Flip should have had a big ego, but he didn't. I can't tell you the beautiful women that I've seen come up to him, hug him, kiss him. He was just who he was, and he'd just smile.

He had the perfect combination. He could dance you to death and party 'til you fell down.

~Dee Dee Dougherty, Caller

I was three years old when I met Flippo.

Flippo and Dee Dee Dougherty-Lottie. Source: Dee Dee Dougherty-Lottie

~Harue Okazaki Swift

Harue's group from Japan at Kirkwood Lodge in 1992. Source:
Harue Okazaki Swift

This [photo] was 1992 at Kirkwood Lodge. It was my first-time square dancing in the States. I was so excited to meet Flippo and had so much fun. We had twenty square dancers from Japan.

Dancing from left to right: Martha Ogasawara, Tim Marriner, Harue
Okazaki Swift and Marshall Flippo. Source: Harue Okazaki Swift

We came to Kirkwood so we could dance with great *callers* all week and wanted to meet Marshall Flippo. I was very interested in square dance resorts. We don't have any in Japan.

JAPANESE CALLERS & CUERS
~Motohiro ("Moto") Yoshimura, Caller for Square Stars, Tokyo

Marshall Flippo's first visit to Tokyo

Introducing myself, Motohiro Yoshimura, normally called "Moto" for short, a male *caller* who started one of the oldest square dance club in Japan, "Tokyo Square Dance Fukyu-kai." "Fukyu-kai" means "a club to promote our beloved square dancing." This club has over a sixty years history.

So far, we have invited many well-known *callers* from U. S. Among them, Marshall Flippo was the *caller* who gave us a great impact when invited as a featured *caller* to our 26th anniversary, held in Shinjuku area on February 11-12, 1983. He was 57 years old then. This was his first visit to Tokyo with his wife, Neeca.

At this event, we were fortunate enough to have the late Prince Mikasa, the youngest brother of the late Emperor Hirohito, who loved square dance and was eager in promoting the activity. I remember very well that Prince Mikasa and Marshall met for the first time and talked with each other like an old friend.

During the two days, Marshall made his powerful calls, and the enthusiastic dancers in Japan truly enjoyed his call which produced a tremendously super atmosphere. What impressed me was, although he brought approximately 300 phonograph records, they were not in the paper jackets or lyrics cards. He did not mind that all his records were naked. To my surprise, he had no "choreos" nor the lyrics of his singing calls. One of his *singing calls* was the famous "Auctioneer." Dancers came over from distant areas all over Japan in those days when we had only a few round trips a day of the Shin-Kansen bullet trains.

After the dance was over, I, with the late Matt Asanuma, one of the *callers* I worked with those days, went to their [Flippo and Neeca's] hotel for dinner. Then we went down to the hotel bar, and we talked a lot over drinking.

I asked him, "What drinks do you like?"

Without thinking, he answered, "I prefer Sake." That's how I learned he loved the Japanese brew, Sake. No wonder during their stay, we enjoyed Sake every night.

In recent years, I attended the CALLERLAB Convention several times. Every time when I went there, I smuggled Sake for him somehow. By the way, the late Lee Kopman was also one of my best friends, and both of them were there almost every time. I loved the CALLERLAB Convention to meet both of them.

The late Prince Mikasa and Princess Yuriko. Source: Motohiro ("Moto") Yoshimura

Marshall Flippo in Tokyo (1983) with Moto. I love Marshall. I miss him and will do in my coming life. Source: Motohiro ("Moto") Yoshimura

Masaru Wada, Marshall Flippo, Moto Yoshimura, Mike Seastrom, Doc Hiraga at the CALLERLAB Convention in Nashville, Kentucky in 2012. Source: Motohiro ("Moto") Yoshimura

~Kazuhiro Sugitani, Caller for Sumida Circle 8, Tokyo, Japan
Singing Call Experience with Marshall Flippo

It was 1967 in my university days that I started square dance calling. In the *Sets In Order*'s Premium LP record "LUCKY 13th JAMBOREE" of 1964, there was a Marshall's call which made me think to start calling.

His call with lots of rhyming on tempo impressed me so much.

About forty years later, with my wife, Eriko, I attended the National Convention for the first time. It was the 55th held in San Antonio, Texas. The caller of my club at that time was Matt Asanuma, one of the Japanese *callers* whose calls were recorded in the *Sets in Order* Premium LP. I knew he had contacted Marshall beforehand to do a collaboration on his singing call, "She Calls Me Baby."

I was dancing in the convention hall after greeting him [Marshall], then there was a lucky happening. The MC called my name when Marshall was about starting his call. He could not find his partner *caller*, then he wanted me to do a call with him!! Oh, my goodness!! I did a call with that big guy, Marshall Flippo, at my first National!!

This was really the best in my memory.

When [I returned] back home, many people asked me if this was a true story. Yes, it WAS a true story!!

I would like to pay my last respect to the great guy Marshall Flippo from Japan.

Marshall Flippo with myself and my wife Eriko, 2006 in San
Antonio, Texas. Source: Kazuhiro Sugitani

Marshall Flippo loved the "Happi" (Japanese festival coat) with the
headband so much In the Long Beach convention in 2009.
Source: Kazuhiro Sugitani

~Martha Ogasawara

Marshall Flippo is someone who's had an amazing influence on so many
Japanese *callers*, especially any of the earlier *callers*. It's like he was their god. He
was that way for many, many *callers*, but especially in Japan. And I know so many
callers who were so influenced by him, and they slavishly imitated him. Back then
they had limited resources. You wanted to become a *caller*. Where did you go to
find good calling and get good timing? Many people treasured those.

I came into square dancing a little after that, and I remember hearing a recording of Flippo and thinking, "Oh, he's not that good. What's. . . Oh? Really? These people think he's really good?" I kept it to myself, of course. I didn't tell anyone, but it was like, "Oh, okay. Good, but not. . . Huh?"

And then, I took a couple of groups to Kirkwood Lodge, and of course, he was always the main feature, and I forget who it was the first two years, but there were other *callers*. In my mind, it was like I was going for the other callers, and it was like, "Okay, I'll get to hear Marshall Flippo, too, in person."

Once I went there, I said, "Ah!" You have to dance to his calling live to get what he is! And the recorded versions just do not do him justice. I was amazed by the difference between listening to him on tape and listening to him in person and was very interested and enthralled by what the difference was, 'cause a lot of *callers* are kind of the same. They're really good in person, and they're really good recorded, but to me it was like Marshall—you just had to have that aura of

Martha Ogasawara. Source: https://www.ceder.net/callerdb/viewsingle.php?RecordId=463

whatever it is that he projects, and you needed to get beamed with that to realize what a . . . I don't even know what the right word is that I want to use to describe him—inspiring and charismatic—and I'm sure many people have used the same word—man and *caller* he was!

My biggest impressions of him was that big difference and it was like, "Wow!"

---

1. **Caller** — A person who prompts dance figures in such dances as line dance, square dance, and contra dance.
2. **Cuer** — Leader at the front of the ballroom [hall] who tells the dancers, as they dance, what steps to do.
3. **After Parties** — The party after the square dance with skits and a variety of entertainment usually put on by the event staff of callers and cuers. Sometimes dancers participated in skits, too.
4. **Singing Call** — The caller sings parts of the songs. See Glossary for more.
5. **Tip** — A square dance session consisting of two parts, a patter call, and a singing call. See Glossary for more.
6. **45 Records** — The most common form of the vinyl single is the "45" or "7-inch." The names are derived from its play speed, 45 rpm, and the standard diameter, 7 inches.
7. **Caller School** — A training time for new callers staffed with experienced callers.
8. **Cue** —Tell the dancers what steps to do in a round dance.
9. **Promenade** — A walk of some distance around the set by some or all dancers. The active dancers may go as individuals or as couples.
10. **Partner** —From an Infacing Circle Of 8 of alternating men and women, the man's Partner is the next dancer counterclockwise around the circle from him and the corner is clockwise around the circle. For the women, the Partner is clockwise around the circle and the Corner is counterclockwise.
11. **Grand Ocean Wave** — An Ocean Wave is an arrangement of three or more dancers in a line with adjacent hands joined (palm to palm or forearm holds) and dancers facing alternately. Grand notes all eight dancers participate that can.
12. **Square Thru** — Right Pull By (Square Thru 1 has been completed); Face partner and Left Pull By (Square Thru 2 has been completed); Face partner and Right Pull By (Square Thru 3 has been completed); and Face partner and Left Pull By (Square Thru 4 has been completed). Ending formation:
      Back-to-Back Couples.
13. **Patty Cake Routine** — Couples sometimes substitute a whimsical made-up routine for Square Thru Four.

14. **Figure** — 48 beat group of calls that takes dancers from their home position to a Corner for a Swing and a 16 beat Promenade.

15. **Patter** — A single tune, used by a caller as background for a series of calls, with no lyrics accompanying the music. Couples are moved into a variety of formations, but brought back to their home positions before the next set of calls.

16. **Patter** — A single tune, used by a caller as background for a series of calls, with no lyrics accompanying the music. Couples are moved into a variety of formations, but brought back to their home positions before the next set of calls.

17. **Basics** — The beginning CALLERLAB program with fifty-one calls.

18. **Plus** — The CALLERLAB program after Mainstream, adding twenty-nine new calls.

19. **Advanced** — The next CALLERLAB program of square dancing after the Plus Program. In addition to the Mainstream and Plus calls, Advanced dancers and callers are responsible for knowing an additional group of calls divided in A1 and A2 lists.

20. **Round Dance** — Couple dancing in a circle formation, using choreographed routines to a definite arrangement of music.

31

CALLERS FLIPPO WORKED WITH AND SLEPT WITH

F lippo generated a long list of callers he wanted to stories about, and he wanted the stories to be funny. Then he provided a short list of who he slept with! I was shocked he wanted that in his biography. Flip's humor got me once more!

Callers and Cuers Flippo Worked With

Flippo dedicated a large section of our interviews to stories and comments about the callers he worked with, generating a list of sixty-two names and 70,000 words. He thought geographically and listed callers as they came up. So, I could not include all the stories in this book, but you can go to my website and see any cut material in the Private Members Only section.

Several of the callers Flippo talked about influenced his career, and he wanted them recognized at the beginning of this book, identifying them because they were deceased. Frank Lane passed away four days before Flippo did—I'm sure he would have added Frank to this prestigious list.

He mentioned getting help from Gladys Puerling because she "knows how to make thangs funny as hell," but he ran out of time.

Flippo loved his caller, cuer and dance friends and relished all the memories and stories. As he told these stories, he laughed and laughed. He wanted you to join in his contagious laughter!

~About Gary Shoemake

Anytime Flippo had a question about square dancing and his numerous adventures, he'd say, "I'll call Gary. He'll know." Gary was Flippo's main Go-to-Guy!

· · ·

Meeting Gary

I met Gary at a festival I was calling in Lubbock, Texas, and somebody said thar's a caller here from Oklahoma, young guy.

I said, "He's a pretty good-looking ole boy, you know." So, anyway, I didn't thank much more about it, and I'd see him every once and a while dancing. The festival was Friday night and Saturday and Saturday night.

Then on Saturday night, I was invited out to some people's house afterwards. I thank it was the Strong's, but I'm not sure about that. But he was out thar, and I got introduced to him, and we got to talking. He was a cigarette salesman. I forget what company he worked for, but he sold cigarettes. Anyway, he was from Tulsa, Oklahoma, nice-looking guy. So I didn't thank much more about it.

Gary was hired at Fun Valley in Colorado. Mack Henson owned Fun Valley. Mack Henson lived in Abilene, Texas, and I knew Mack real well. I used to deliver bread to him when I run a bread route before I ever started square dancing. And I still run a bread route after I started square dancing and after I started calling. Mack bought this place up in Colorado —Fun Valley, and he hired Gary as his staff caller.

Gary Shoemake. Source: https://www.ceder.net/callerdb/viewsingle.php?RecordId=894

I thought, "Boy, he's doing pretty good, you know." Pretty soon, I heard, "Hey, Ole Gary is moving to Abilene, Texas to be close to ole Mack."

I thought, "Jimminny Christmas!" I'm gone a lot and boy, he's a good-looking guy. He's married, though, but he's sure a good-looking guy. So he tells it a little different than this.

With a laugh, Flip told his version, "I'd be out tour and I'd call home and he'd answer my telephone," but he tells it different.

Gary would say, "Flippo had all kinds of dates. He's turning down more than he could call, and so I asked him if he'd give me some those addresses, and he did. Sometimes I'd call three nights in a row, and I was really up in the world. He'd tell people that I'd get out on tour and when I'd call a dance, the next dance I'd call was four hundred miles away. I would call all of them and that fool would answer my telephone, so he tells it a little different than I do."

Gary became a well-known because of being at Fun Valley just as I did when I went to Kirkwood. That helped both of us get dances.

Governor's Inaugural Ball

The biggest thang him and I called together was the Governor's Ball in Austin,

Texas. We had two hundred squares. Somewhere I've got a letter or two from Governor Preston.

KC Hall in Abilene, Texas

When Gary moved to Abilene, we'd have some dances together thar in Abilene, and out at the KC hall, we had one one night. We had an ole boy that always when he promenaded with the girls, he'd put their arm in thar, you know, and rub their boobies, and he'd squeeze their hands.

But you know people were complaining quite a bit. Neeca and I pulled up to the dance. We was going to go and help Gary put up the sound, and the first thang we heard when we got out of the car, "Get the hell out of here! I don't want to ever see you again, and take those ole bitches with you." He had three bitches with him —three gals that didn't square dance.

So the guy said, "Gary."

He said, "Don't talk to me. Get the hell out. I don't want to even see you again." And so here they come out.

I said, "Neeca, this dance is not starting off too good."

So here come ole _____.

He said, "Oh, Flippo." He thought he was kin to me, and I asked him one night, "How could your name be Smith and you thank down the line thar I'm kin to you?"

Anyway, he said, "Flippo, Gary's run us out. Can you get us back in?"

"No, nay, I can't."

He said, "Flippo, what Gary's. . .?"

"You going to have to leave."

Anyway, I thank that's the last time I seen ole _____. So anyway, he was one of those kind of guys that, and so the gals were pleased that ole Gary run him off.

~About Ken Bower

I was calling WASCA for like seventeen years—WASCA [Washington Area Square Dance Cooperative Association], Washington, D. C.'s spring festival. I was staying at the Park Sheraton Hotel, and we usually had around 5,000 dancers for that weekend, and they had nine callers that called that thang, and I was one of them. Anyway, thar's a couple named Whitey and Gladys Puerling.

When callers—Ken Bower, Arnie Kronenberger, myself were in that area, we'd stay with them and we'd go down and call maybe Atlantic City or down even further south. We'd drive back after each dance back to Whitey and Gladys'. And they were good hosts and hostesses. So, Whitey and Gladys always come to that spring festival. It always started on Thursday.

So, Thursday during the day Ken Bower called me and said, "Hey, I'm over here at Whitey and Gladys'. Do you have an extra bed in your room?"

"Yeah, I got two beds."

He said, "Will you mind me staying thar Thursday and Friday nights? I know thar's a lot of dancers thar. Can I use one of those beds?"

"It's okay with me, if you don't snore."

He said, "You're the one that snores."

But anyway, I said, "Sure, you can," and so he said, "What my plans are—you got to know Ken Bower —is I am going to leave my car here at Whitey and Gladys', and they're getting ready to go, and I'm going to ride up with them. Can I borrow your car to come back here on Saturday?"

"Shit, I need my car."

He said, "No, no, no, you're calling down here after the spring festival. You can ride back with Whitey and Gladys. I'll take your car, drive into New Jersey and go to Whitey and Gladys', pick up my car and go on to Connecticut. I've got some more dates in New England."

"Well, whatever. . .." What else could

Ken Bower. Source: https://www.ceder.net/callerdb/viewsingle.php?RecordId=907

you do? And he came Thursday night, all day Friday, Saturday. Early Saturday morning, we'd been up in Whitey and Gladys' room, and he said, "Give me my car keys. I got to get out of here." And he knew where my car was parked in the parking garage. It still had some clothes in it.

And so he said, "I'll just leave this at Whitey and Gladys', pick mine up and go up into Connecticut."

And I said, "Okay." Anyway, Ken took off, and we were sitting around talked awhile. Ole Whitey drank a lot of beer, so he had a beer or two, and I had a scotch or two. So, about twenty minutes after he left, I said to Whitey and Gladys, "I thank I'm going to bed. See ya'll in the morning."

"Okay."

So, I was going back to my room, and so I was going through the lobby and thar's a bunch of people in the lobby. I'd been thar quite a few times, and I knew that girl on the night desk at the hotel. They had that hotel full.

She said, "Hey, Flippo come here. A guy come by here a while ago. Told me thar was two people in Room C23, your room. Thar's only supposed to be one. He said thar's two in thar."

She said, "Somebody's staying free in that room."

"You're kidding."

She said, "No."

And she said, "You know. Thar's so damn many people here, we don't care what's happening like that."

"What did the guy look like?"

She said, "Well, he's a big tall guy, and he had salt and pepper black hair, you know black hair. It had a few grays in it, you know. It really looked good."

She said, "Flippo, it don't matter at all. Thar's so damn many people here, we're not going to worry about it. Thar's quite a few rooms that have got extra people in them, we're sure."

"Okay. That's enough. I know who that is," so I went back up to Whitey and Gladys' room.

"Guess what that damn Ken did after I lent him my car? That damn Bower went by the front desk and told her thar was two people in my room, and the lady down on the desk said, 'We could care less about that. We don't mind.'"

"But here I was good enough to give him. . . and he went and told thar was two people in thar. I ought to catch him. I ought to catch him."

Oh, Whitey had had quite a few beers.

Ole Whitey said, "He shouldn't have done that. Well, we need to do somethang, and we need to do somethang quick. I'm going to call ole John." John was a retired New Jersey highway patrolman captain who lived across the street from Whitey.

Whitey added, "I'm going to call him and let's report your car as stolen."

"Oh, no, no, no. Let's just forget it. It's alright with me."

"No, no, it was terrible of him," so we called ole John.

"Well, he's not going to like you awaking him up this time of night. It's almost three o'clock in the morning."

Then Whitey assured me, "That's all right. He's going to get in thar in about two hours."

"Well, what about John? You call him this time. . ."

"Ah," he said, "he met ole Ken when he was here. Of course, you've known him awhile. He's a good guy. He won't mind."

Whitey called him up, "We got a Pontiac coming in thar, Texas license. It's Flippo's car, but Ken Bower is in and we want to report the car as stolen. Do you know anybody working tonight?"

He said, "Hell, I know them all."

So Whitey repeated, "We got a guy coming in thar in a Pontiac, clothes in the back of it—big guy, salt and pepper black hair."

"I doubt if they can tell that at night, Whitey."

"Would you mind getting him arrested for the fun of it?"

"That sounds like fun to me."

So John said, "I'll inform all the guys, and they'll know, and the car has Texas license."

So, we get in Sunday. Ole John comes over. He seen us coming, and he comes over thar.

"They got him. He wouldn't even come over and talk to me. He just got into his car and took off." He had to go up into Connecticut.

Whitey said, "You sure?"

John added, "Yeah, they got him. They got him outside the car, put his arms up on the top of the car, and they were patting him down, and he was shaking like a leaf."

Ken said, "No, no, no! I borrowed this car. It's my buddy's car."

The patrolman said, "Yeah, that's what they all say. Well, the car had been reported stolen."

The patrolmen asked, "Are those clothes in the back yours?"

"Yeah, they're mine." The cop reached back thar and took those shirts out that was about. . .?

He said, "Sir, I don' think you can get into this shirt." It was my clothes that was back thar.

Anyway, they got worried about it later on. "What if he tries to run away or somethang like that?" But John said it come out alright.

They finally let him go and said it's all just a joke. Said ole John's in on it. John said later on, "That was probably why he didn't come over."

So anyway, next time I seen him was at Kirkwood—didn't say a word. Didn't say a word about it at all for two years.

So, I called ole Whitey up after I'd seen Ken a couple times, and I said, "Whitey, I don't thank they stopped him. I've worked with him twice. He hasn't said a word about it."

He said, "Well, I'll check with John," so he called me back in about an hour, and he said, "Flippo, they stopped him. I'll guarantee you they stopped him. He's just not telling you."

So, I said, "Well, he hasn't said anythang about it."

That year passed. The next year he was back to Kirkwood, and I'd worked with him two or three times other than that, and he'd never said a word about it. At Kirkwood thar's a ramp that goes up to the kitchen. Below that ramp down on the patio below is where they cook the steaks and the hotdogs and every-thang. Thar's a patio, and thar's place for people to seat down. So, one night I wanted to make a sandwich, so I went through the lobby and went into the kitchen.

Well, I went out the back door which was that ramp. I heard somebody down below—sounded like Ken Bower, "That son of a bitch will never know that they stopped me. I'll never tell him. That dang gum cop stopped me."

So, I heard him say that, so I thought, "Oh, oh, oh! Well, I'm going to listen to this." They couldn't see me, but he had a bunch of his Iowa friends down thar, and he was telling them the whole story.

He said, "They stop me and said the car was stolen." Said, "I told them, 'No, it's my buddy's car.'S"

They said, "That's what they all say. Are these your clothes in the back?"

"And I said—I was so damn nervous, 'Yeah.' So they took out a shirt and it was about two feet high."

The patrolman said, "Sir, I don't think that shirt will fit you. Did you steal these clothes, too?"

He said, "No, I'm telling you. This is my buddy's car. He lent it to me. It's some of his clothes."

"Is he a dwarf?"

He said, "It really did scare me."

"Well, it's been reported stolen."

"Well, it's some kind of joke. Somebody's pulling a joke on me."

And so finally, he said finally they just told me, "Yeah, it's just a story."

"Did you report two people being in a room when they shouldn't be? I think this is a get back on that." So eventually I got the story out of him, but for a long time, boy, he wasn't going to tell me.

❦

~About Gary Shoemake and Jerry and Sherry Haag

Jerry went out in California, and he bought a motorcycle out thar—good, good price on one, but he didn't have no way to get it home, and so I don't know exactly how it went, whether Gary offered to take it or what.

He said, "Boy, I'd buy that motorcycle if I could get it home."

And Gary said, "Well, I got that old van I'm driving."

"I might can get it in the back of it, and I can get it to Carrollton, Texas," which is a suburb of Dallas. "I can get it thar."

Jerry said, "That'll be good 'cause I can get it home from Carrollton."

And so, Gary gets to El Paso, and he calls Jerry and he says, "Jerry, somebody stole that motorcycle out my damn van, and then someone stole all my sound system—just cleared me plum out. Stole everythang I had in the back of that van." And Jerry was disappointed as hell. Anyway, Sherry, Jerry's wife, got in it, and she called Hilton sound system and says, "Has Gary ordered any new equipment here lately?"

"No, we haven't heard from Gary in years. He's got a good sound."

"Well, he told us that it had been stolen."

"Well, he hadn't ordered any new one."

So then she called the El Paso police and said, "Has thar been a report of a motorcycle being stolen or anythang?"

"No ma'am, we don't have any record of that."

So she figured, "Well, how?"

"He's telling us a big ass lie."

So anyway, the way that all ended up was Gary was in El Paso. He thought he's going to go to jail, because the police got into it, and anyway, he told them it was a big story.

~About Jerry Haag

Jerry Haag and I had lots of fun.

Oh, boy! Okay, I'm going to tell you this story, and it's a long one. And I can't remember what hotel it was, but I'm quite sure it was when we were having a weekend in Kansas City. I thank it was the Muehlebach Hotel. It's an old hotel in Kansas City.

The rooms had one door that you opened and they said, "Don't lock your buddy out now. You open that one door, and then thar's two doors—one to the right and one to the left. It's two rooms.

So now if you go to bed and realize you have shut that front door, you got to make sure that it's unlocked so when your buddy comes in, he can get through that door and get into his room."

[To Larada, Flip said,] "Have you got a picture of that?"

Okay. So we's having a big party down almost to the end of the hallway, and Jerry and Ken Bower's room was in one of those big doors. Well, Jerry got up, and he was going to go to bed about 1:30 a.m., and he went on down thar and went to bed and he's laying thar and he thought, "Oh."

They didn't have any keys. They told us they didn't have any keys for those big doors that you go in the front. Anyway, thar's a little alcove thar and then the two rooms, so he thought, "Oh, man, did I shut that door or is it locked?" So he gets up, and he opens his door, and he goes out to see if that door is locked, and he heard, "Click." He looked back, and his door had shut. Here he is in a pair of red bikini underwear.

He goes, "What am I going to do? Well, I'll run down to that room, and get Ken, and he can get in his room and we can call and get me another key or he can go get me another key for my room."

Whatever.

Anyway, so he headed down thar, and he could hear this elevator coming to a stop over to his left side that, so he run and got behind a Coke machine. And thar's three couples come out of the elevator and stood thar.

Jerry said, "I was freezing my butt off. It was cold, and I was naked." And they just kept talking and kept talking and finally they broke up and took off.

"And I run down to the room." It gets funny now.

Jerry Haag. Source: https://www. ceder.net/callerdb/viewsingle.php? RecordId=531

"And I knock on that door."

Well, Beryl Main comes over and looks through the peephole, and he says, "Hey guys, come over here and look at this."

Jerry said, "I was pounding on the door and saying, 'Let me in. Let me in. Let me in.'"

"They're all looking through the peephole and laughing their ass off, and they're not opening the door." So to make a long story short, he finally got in thar, and you know, they finally got him back into his room and everythang, but they had a great big laugh over it. It was funny.

❧

Jerry could have been an actor. Jerry or Ken, either one. They could have both been actors. They were that good.

Oh, they were doing this before I even joined them [Chaparral Record Label], but this is the story I got. They were doing a weekend in Michigan, and Jerry didn't want to do his

"Brenda Flea," so he just didn't bring any of it [his props]. You know where he gets dancing around—"Brenda Flea," they called it. [An *after party* parody and pantomime of Brenda Lee singing "Jambalaya."]

But he didn't bring any of his stuff, so they just kept on and said, "We gonna have it, Jerry. You're just going to have to do it. We don't have much [for the *after party*] and all, and we got to have it."

He said, "I didn't bring it. Forget it!"

They said, "No, we'll fix you up," so they fixed him up.

And Ken was down on the second row, I believe, and Jerry was up on a high stage, and they had fixed him a skirt and everythang, but they didn't realize that when he was up on the stage, that this skirt was kind of split in the front, and you could see everythang—all of his, well, he had a pair of shorts on, I mean regular shorts, underwear.

And so Ken's sitting thar, and he looks up, and that's what he saw first, and these girls were coming from the end of row.

They were yelling at him, "Come down!" And ole Jerry didn't know what the hell was going on. He just kept on dancing around.

Jerry Haag doing "Brenda Flea" pantomime. Source: Neeca Flippo

Another time, at English Mountain, thar's a little stage up that, and we did our *after parties* in one little room thar, one little dance hall, and that's where the restrooms were behind the stage, so that's where Jerry dressed back thar, and he come out and he's doing his dance.

After it's over, he come back thar, "Flippo, come help me." So I run back thar and one of his balloons had a hole in it, and it was shooting water right straight up.

I said, "Jerry, you got to go back out thar 'cause they're giving you a standing ovation. You got to get back out thar and do an encore or somethang. Take a bow."

He said, "I can't. Look at this."

I said, "They'll know better," so he went back, and I thank Gary just played part of a record then. He danced around, that damn water shooting straight up.

Ken Bower and Jerry Haag

Flippo had a motorcycle story he needed to gather details on that we never returned to, but here's another one he told with lots of laughter:

Another motorcycle thang was when Jerry Haag was visiting Ken in Des Moines, and this was before Ken started touring. Ken had a motorcycle, and they got on it on a Sunday afternoon. They were just riding around. They come up on this hill where motorcycles were going up the hill. You know, they'd back off a long way and go right up that hill.

So Ken said, "You want to try it?" They both had a beer in their hands.

"No, no, no, I don't thank both of us on here can make it."

And they had had quite a few beers, anyway, 'cause they decided they'd try this ignorant thang with both of them on the bike. The rest of the bikes were going up one person, you know, just the driver. So they made a big ole circle and thar, and he [Ken] jumped that thang as fast as it'd go, and they started up that hill, but it got almost to the top of that thang, and stalled and fell over backwards with them. Jerry Haag, when it was all over, was still a holding his can of beer. He squeezed it a little, but thar was still beer in thar. Neither one of them was hurt, thank God, but they did make the hill.

I thank it's about all the motorcycle thangs that I have.

~About Beryl Main

Beryl was one of the better callers I ever heard in my life. Really good and good with people, and I have a funny story, but it's all jumbled up.

I called that Gulf Coast Festival in Biloxi, Mississippi for—oh, God, I don't know how many years. And what we'd do is fly into New Orleans, Louisiana and rent a car and go over. Beryl had called and said, "Are you going to rent a car?"

"Yeah, thank I will."

He said, "Well, I have a ride over thar, but I don't have a ride back. Could I ride back with you?"

"Sure." So we get thar—we're leaving out early on Sunday morning, I believe it was. On Friday night, we're up thar, and he's in street clothes, and he usually dresses pretty good with the bolos [ties] and everythang.

Beryl said, "I'm sorry, boys. They lost my bags. I couldn't find it. They said they'd bring it over here if they found it." So he went the whole weekend without no clothes, I mean he just had what he had on. He did go buy a shirt, and I thank a pair of pants from one of the stores that were thar at the festival.

So then on Saturday night, him and I went to a bunch of parties because we had a six o'clock plane out. I thank mine was 6:15 a.m. and his was like 6:30 a.m., somethang like that. Pretty close together. So we never did go to bed that night.

Driving back, I'd drive a while, I'd start nodding off, he'd say, "Flippo, you're going to sleep. Let me drive." Then I'm wide awake. I'd get over in the passage seat. We're driving along. It's not ten minutes until his head is going.

"Beryl, pull over to the side. You're going to sleep." So we kept a changing drivers like that 'til we got back to New Orleans, and we turned the car in and went into the terminal.

He said, "Hey, I got to find that damn bag. I want to try to see what happened,"

Beryl Main. Source: https://www.ceder.net/recorddb/artist_viewsingle.php?RecordId=38

and we saw a big sign that said, "Lost Baggage," and thar was three or four guys sitting at the door of that thang. So, we went up thar and ole Beryl said, "Hey, I lost my bag, and they haven't gotten it to me yet. Would it happen to be in thar?"

And an ole black boy said, "Mr., what's your name?"

"My name is Beryl Main."

He said, "No, I ain't seen nothing like that. And I look at all the names of these thangs when they come in, but I don't remember Beryl Main."

And Beryl said, "Can I look in thar?"

And the guy said, "Sure," so we opened the door, and Beryl walked in and said, "Thar it is right thar."

And the guy said, "Well, that don't have a damn name on it," and the name had been ripped off in moving. He would have never got that bag back unless he found it right then because they wouldn't know what to do with it.

So Beryl said, "That's it."

Then the guy said, "Now, you're going to have to tell me what's in that bag before I'll let you have it."

He said, "Right on the top of my clothes is a pair of cowboy boots."

The guy said, "Let me check that out, sir." He unzipped that damn thang. Thar were the boots.

He said, "Okay. Take the bag." Little ole Beryl was grinning from ear to ear. But that's one of those ole stories.

❦

But Beryl was such a nice person. I called the Permian Basin Festival at Odessa, Texas for, I believe, thirty-three years, and it usually run anywhere from a hundred to a hundred twenty squares. They'd put another caller on thar with me each year. So one time they put Beryl on thar, and we called together, not together, but we were calling every other tip on Friday night and the next morning at the workshop. Well, that's another story goes before this.

At the Saturday morning workshop, Beryl said, "Hey, as soon as this's over, instead of going to eat, will you run over to the car dealer? We don't have a workshop until two o'clock this afternoon. I want to trade my car. I want to get another car."

"Sure, I'll go over thar with you." And so we drove over thar, and let me break into this story a little bit and tell you about Beryl Main. Beryl always had cash on him. I mean lots of money. Anyway, we got over to this dealership, and he said, "Hey, Flippo. This car has 35,000 miles on it."

I said, "Well, Beryl, you've had this a good while, haven't you?"

He said, "The speedometer has turned over twice." Back then, you know, now then you can't do this. It had really 235,000 miles on it.

And he said, "Ah, should I tell them the actual miles?"

"I don't know, Beryl."

He said, "I'm thanking about it. I thank I will. Maybe they won't say anythang about it. Maybe they'll just look at it and thank, 'Oh, boy!'"

This guy looks it over.

Beryl said, "Nobody has ever rode in the back seat. Just a bunch of clothes back thar. We hang them up across thar."

"Boy," he said, "this is a clean car. Why are you wanting to trade it off at 35,000 miles? It's just kind of broke in."

He said, "Oh, I'm starting to have pay for little thangs on it. The heater went out the other day, and I had to get a new heater, and I don't like that. I'm going to get another car."

He said, "We've got the car for you." So, the guy gave him one hell of a price.

I thought, "God. I believe I'll try this."

At that time, cars weren't as high as they are now, way back thar. The guy says, "It's going to be $11,000 difference."

And ole Beryl said, "How do you want me to pay for this? Cash?"

The guy said, "What?"

"Cash?"

He said, "No, I won't sell it to you with a check."

He said, "No, no, not a check. It's real money—cash!"

The guy said, "Well, that's $11,000."

And Beryl said, "Well, what a minute." He went out thar and opened the trunk of this old car. His bags in thar, and he pulled out a little sack, reached down thar and brought a wand of money out thar and counted $11,000 out!

And the guy said, "Good Lord! What if somebody robbed you?"

"Nobody's going to rob me," Beryl said, "I'll fight 'em."

And then, about two months later, I saw Beryl on the road. Our paths crossed on tour, and I said, "Beryl, that's not the car you bought thar in Odessa."

He said, "No, damn thang. Flippo, don't ever try to cheat anybody!"

"Why not?"

He said, "That damn car was the biggest lemon I have ever seen. Hell, thangs were falling off of the damn thang. Everythang was wrong with that car. I had to trade it off, and I got this—it's a pretty good one."

"Where did you trade off at?"

He said, "I believe it was at Columbus, Ohio. I just couldn't stand it anymore, so I traded it off."

Beryl said, "Don't ever try to cheat anybody! Look here. Had a damn lemon that was just worse than the car I given them, and I just got tired of it. I traded it off."

He said, "One thang about this one is it is okay except I bought a tank of gas in Michigan, drove around, got on the damn freeway, and I was on the ramp, and my damn car stopped."

"This new car?"

He said, "Yeah, this new car. I had the next day off, thank the Lord because, I thought, 'Hell, I'm going to have to call AAA and they can call me.'"

They said, "We'll try to find out why your car stopped."

Beryl said, "Okay, I'll be staying at this motel over here."

He said, "After a while, they called me up about an hour later and said, 'We found your problem.'"

He said, "Oh, thank the Lord. Is it going to be a long time?"

He said, "It will be awhile."

He said, "What's wrong with it?"

He said, "Your gas tank was full of water." So he went back to the station thar, and they gave him, I forget what they give him. Price of gas back anyway, but they put a new tank on thar.

~About Frank Lane[1]

Anyway, thar's a couple other good stories about Frank. Barbara, his wife, and I both got him on one. He could not see that Barbara would ever beat him in anythang or me either. I never beat him in anythang hardly. But we got him one time. It's a long story.

I used to call out at Frank's ranch. He built that building out thar in Estes Park, Colorado. I used to call around the fourth of July every year out thar. That's when they were having their caller's college, and I would go in and visit with some of those callers that were in thar, and then that night I would call a dance, and the next day I would leave and go back to Kirkwood.

It was nice and cool. He had those wooden windows that would raise up. Beau-

Frank & Barbara Lane. Source: https://www.ceder.net/callerdb/viewsingle.php?RecordId=832

tiful. Great, great floor. Boy, he protected it. Nobody took any drinks across the floor, on the floor, anythang. It was a beautiful floor.

Anyway, I can't thank of his name. He's a caller, and he had somethang to do with the government of Canada at the capitol. I can always remember her name and cannot remember his. Her name was Catherine. I thank she started it with a C, too.

Catherine and Barbara were back in the kitchen, I guess, cleaning up after we had a little *after party* snacks. So, anyway, the guy from Canada, Catherine's husband, got us all down on our knees. Thar was about ten or twelve of us.

He said, "I've got a game here that's played with five dice. It's a very simple game once you know, you never tell."

So he said, "It's called Petals Around the Rose."

So he threw those dice out thar, and he said, "Thar's four petals around the rose." Well, accidentally I seen what he might have been talking about 'cause thar was two 3s out thar, so I thought, "Well now, thar was four dots around the middle dot." So, I thought, "Maybe, I might have this." I just lucked into it.

So he throws them out thar again. "Six petals around the rose." Well, I said, "Three 3s." The rest of them were even. See three 3s. Six petals around a rose, and so he said, "Does anybody got it? Very easy game. Once you know, you never tell. Petals Around the Rose."

Then he'd sling them out thar, you know. The third time, I forget what thar was—a couple of 5s. I thank thar was a couple of 5s. The rest of them were all even. So fives. So, one, two, three, four around that one. One, two, three four around the other.

I said, "Eight petals around the rose."

He said, "That's right."

And ole Frank jumped up—not really. He raised his head, "You've seen this before."

"No, I haven't. I just lucked into it, I thank. Maybe."

And he threw again and sure enough, I had it. Well, Frank's going berserk. So we played, hell, I guess, we played a good forty some-odd minutes, and Barbara and Catherine came over. And then they were just standing thar looking over us.

He said, "Oh, how ya'll doing? This is a just a game I'm playing here called Petals Around the Rose, played with five dice. Once you know the secret, you do not tell nobody."

He said, "It's called Petals Around the Rose." Boy, he threw them out thar, and Barbara didn't say anythang, but the next time he threw them out thar, she said, "Thar's six petals around the rose."

He said, "Barbara, that's right!"

Oh, she just kept going. Ole Frank went up on his knee, "Oh, no, no, no, she just guessed that!" So, he only threw them two more times, and then Frank could see she had it. So, anyway, it was really funny. I was staying with Bob and Paula Nickalaus from Denver, so we were going to have leave. They had to get up early the next morning, so we took off, and as I was leaving, I was looking for Barbara.

I said, "Barbara, did you tell him? I'll never, never speak to you again. Now just write that down."

She said, "Flippo, let me tell you somethang. I would not tell him, if it was on his deathbed."

This was in July. September he came over to Kirkwood to do his week over thar. I was behind the snack bar, back in the corner, right thar next to the dance floor, really, and the counter.

I guess thar was five or six of us behind that counter. This was Sunday afternoon, and people were coming in for the week. So some of them would stay upstairs, you know, and go off to their rooms. But some would come down, and we'd have a little bull session down thar behind the snack bar. Here come Frank and Barbara. Frank's shaking his hand like he's got dice in them.

He said, "They've got a very simple game here, boys, played with five dice. It's called Petals Around the Rose. Once you know, you never tell, and the stupid people get it first."

He would not give up, so I said, "Dang you, Barbara. I wouldn't speak to you if you told him, and I'm not speaking to you."

He said, "No, no, no. She didn't tell me. Flippo, I went to bed that night, thanking, 'What the hell?'"

Oh, before I left he already had some paper out and a pencil, and he was writing down each turn, you know.

But anyway, he said, "We went to bed that night."

"Not to sleep?"

"I finally dozed off a little while, but I was going out early to play golf."

So he said, "I was trying to thank what the heck could that be? Pretty simple game."

He said, "On the seventh hole, I was fixing to tee off, and it hit me. Oh, it's that middle dot on the dice. That's what the rose is. I'll bet you money. I'll bet you money."

He said, "I had five dice in my pocket on the golf course."

He said, "I started throwing them, and I started guessing, and I quit right thar. Quit playing golf." For him to quit playing golf, it's very serious.

Anyway, he went back over and said, "Barbara, see if I've got it here."

She said, "Now, I'll tell you if you got it, and if you haven't got it, I'm not telling you nothing."

"Two out thar. And six round it."

She said, "You got that one right." So then he found out he got them all right, but it was a funny thang because that Barbara and I got it so fast. That's the second time that I got him.

※

The third time and probably the first time. The first time I ever got him, this was before the other two I just told you about. We were playing golf in Hayward, California. Both couples of us were staying thar with Bob and Nita Page. Bob was a caller thar, called for Gingham Squares. Frank called [as a guest caller] for Gingham, but I didn't. I called over at the south San Francisco High School.

So we're out on the golf course, and I never even come close to. . . .. On the 18th hole, I had a putt from here to Albuquerque, way down at the bottom of the green, and he's up thar almost to the top, and he had the pin.

He said, "I'll tend the pin. If they just get close to—ha, ha, ha."

I said, "You know, if this goes in, you owe me fifty cents."

He said, "Yeah! Ha, ha, ha! If it goes in."

So, I hit the ball and hit it right in the sweet spot. I thought, "Well, it's going to get thar." And I kept a looking at it. He kept a looking, too. He pulled that flag out; that ball fell right in that hole. Frank reached down and got that ball and threw it over into a pond.

And I said, "Damn Frank."

He said, "I owe you fifty cents and just shut up."

"Wait a minute, wait a minute. I'm not going to shut up. You threw my dollar and a quarter ball into the pond. Now you owe me fifty cents. Like hell you do. You owe me two and a quarter."

He said, "You'll never get that. I'll give you the fifty cents, but I ain't paying for that ball." And he never did.

But that's the three thangs. We worked together four weeks a year and two weekends a year for thirty-six some odd years—two at Kirkwood, one at Asilomar and one we had of our own. I got to know him pretty well.

We started down at French Lake, Indiana at the French Lake Sheraton. It was an old spa. It had a good dance floor and everythang. We danced thar quite a while. We never did put out any brochures or flyers—nothing. We'd sell forty-eight squares out every week, every time we had the thang. A lot of Michigan people come down.

Anyway, we worked thar I don't know how many years. I wouldn't even guess. But then we got to seeing dog turds on the stairwells and all that stuff, so Frank said, "We're getting out of here." But the floor was excellent. Excellent floor. So we moved over to the university of Indiana thar at Bloomington. We moved thar into their Student Center. Anyway, we stayed thar until they kept going up on their price, so we moved out of thar.

And we went to Purdue. And they had a nice dance floor thar, and square dancing had started to put out flyers. And this has been over the years, you know, and finally we started an effort to put out flyers to get more people in. I'd say we were at Purdue for about six years. And they had a really good cafeteria. It was the best place of the two universities to eat.

At Purdue, the crowd got so small, we moved out to a Ramada Inn in Effingham, Illinois. We were pulling in anywhere from fifteen, twenty, twenty-five squares, but it had fallen off so much that we were lucky to get anybody.

I worked with Frank two weeks at Kirkwood, one week at Asilomar and two weekends a year—one weekend in French Lake and . . .. [Flip never remembered the second weekend he did with Frank.]

~Lee Kopman

Lee was late coming down for a workshop one time, and I was up on the stage gettin' the amplifier all ready and the lights on and everythang. So, everybody's squared up, and they said, "Call us a *Challenge*, Flip?"

I said, "I can't. Oh, wait a minute. Wait a minute. I got some cards up here that Lee's left up here. I'll read 'em."

I said, "Whoa, whoa. I can't read Jewish."

But Lee's got the worst handwriting in the world.

Lee Kopman. Source: http://www.sdfne.org/

~About Ed Gilmore[2]

Ed Gilmore—well, when you say "Ed Gilmore" to a square dance caller, it's almost like talking about God.

Ed Gilmore sat thar 'til the sun started coming up with you all night long, drink coffee and smoke cigarettes. We'd just shoot the bull and a lot of places that he'd called said, "Well, we'll be up all night 'cause he's going to want to sit around and talk and smoke cigarettes and drink coffee."

He loved to talk square dancing, and he had so many brilliant ideas about square dancing that callers now use, and they don't even know where it come from, but I can't thank of any.

I didn't work with Ed.

Ed Gilmore on cover. Source: *Sets in Order*, November 1961

But Ed was probably the granddaddy of smooth dancing. Ed and Bob Osgood were close, close friends. Ed was buried as a pauper. I remember we took up money. I know I 'member donating for a headstone for him, so they finally got a headstone out in the graveyard where he's buried but oh—sad, sad note thar. I believe he was buried in Yucaipa, California.

It's sad, yeah, because he meant so much to square dancing at that time. He's part of CALLERLAB starting and everythang. Really sad.

But Ed was one real good human.

~About Ed Gilmore and Joe Lewis

I have a funny story about me and Ed Gilmore and Joe Lewis. Joe Lewis was kind of my idol. Joe Lewis was Melton Luttrell's big idol, and of course, Melton was mine; therefore, I met Joe Lewis and went to quite a few of his dances. Had him in Abilene a couple times. He played the accordion and called at the same time now. I don't know how he did it. He got to thank about what he's calling and where his fingers supposed to go, but he did that.

Anyway, I was calling in Dallas, and Joe and Claire, his wife, came out to the dance and said, "Hey, pretty soon you're calling over in Sherman-Denison."

"Yes, sir."

He said, "Come and stay with us in Dallas. It's seventy miles over thar. We'll go to the dance with ya."

And I thought, "Stay all night with Joe Lewis! Man alive."

So I said, "Okay," and I got into Joe's house at one o'clock in the afternoon, and we're talking and everythang and having some coffee, and Claire was fixing supper, and Joe said, "Come on, Flippo. Let's go to the airport. I got to pick up a guy."

So we're about halfway to the airport and I said, "Who you picking up?"

He said, "Ed Gilmore." Well, now, I was already tightening up because of Joe Lewis was going to go to one of my dances. He'd been to some of 'em, but him and Claire would have gotten to go to my dance over at Sherman, so I thought, "Well, maybe Gilmore won't want to go to the dance."

So, we went on, had supper and everythang, took off over thar, and Gilmore went with us.

And the reason I was concerned was that Sherman-Denison club was go-getters. I mean, they were wilder than hell but always had a good time. They had one ole boy over thar named Johnny. We called him Crazy Leg's John. He could kick to the ceiling.

Joe Lewis, Ed Gilmore and all the callers I knew—Frank Lane, a bunch of them—they didn't like that kicking going on, and that swinging-style *dosado* and all that. Well, ole Johnny was one of those. He could kick to the ceiling and let out a Ute band—everybody would holler and going on, you know.

Larada, fixing to call the first square up on the stage, got 'em squared up, and I looked and over to the left was Joe and Claire Lewis in a square with Crazy Leg's John.

I thought, "Oh, my God!" Ed Gilmore was sitting over to the side.

The first right and left grand ole Crazy Leg's Johnny kicked up way in the air and let out a war hoop. People all a hollering, and Ed Gilmore—I'll never forget his face. His mouth was opened. He was lookin' like, "What did that guy just do?" And of course, when he met his wife and *dosado*, well, he took her and threw her up in the air and swung her around.

And Ed was still. . .. He looked like he'd been hit with oblivion. And so, what's up? He cut ole Johnny out of that square as slick as I've ever seen.

And ole Johnny was wondering, "Who in the hell is this guy?" So he's kind of standing over thar, kinda lookin,' and so, he tried to cut 'em out, but he wasn't too good at cutting anybody out. Ed wouldn't cut out, and so he lucked out, and he cut out Joe Lewis. So bang, bang, bang. Boy, everythang's going, they're kicking and everythang, and Joe cut out Ed Gilmore.

Ed Gilmore, he didn't take five steps 'til he cut out Crazy Leg's John again, you know, and ole John, "Look at that guy."

So Joe didn't like the kicking at all, especially when Claire was in the square and all that swinging high and swinging-style *dosado* stuff and so anyway, after the dance, I thank they took ole Johnny to the side. They weren't going to change Johnny.

But later on, Joe Lewis and Johnny became real good friends which was really odd, but now Ed Gilmore said on the way back to Dallas, "I've never seen a dance like that in my life."

But Ed didn't get out that much. He hung around California a lot. He was from Yucaipa—really a well-thought of guy. A lot of good recordings. I had one at one time, and I thank I've lost it. I don't know where it might be. Might be in the shed in Tucson.

~More About Arnie Kronenberger

Arnie, he was bashful.

Every year we'd meet out in Palm Springs— Frank Lane, Arnie Kronenberger, and Bill Hagadorn who owned Kirkwood at the time. That's why we'd go to Palm Springs 'cause they went thar and spent four months every year. And so, we'd always go to Palm Springs after my California tour and meet up with 'em and usually have dinner with Bill and Arnie and Frank and I, and the girls would fly in. I know Neeca flew in one or two times, and Barbara was with Frank.

And Arnie Kronenberger was a great caller from LA, and in fact, aside from Betty [Casey], he called to a square in New York from LA one time when TV first started. He was a very, very good caller.

Arnie Kronenberger. Source: http://www.sdfne.org/arnie-kronenberger/

And what we did, we all four [men] played every one of those Bob Hope golf courses out thar. We were out thar about a week, and we'd play golf every day. And we'd play at Bermuda Dunes, Indian Wells. We played two more, I know. [Indian Wells and Thunderbird CC] The ones they use at the Bob Hope classics.

Anyway, the first dinner, we'd always go out when everybody got thar. So, anyway, I'm sitting thar with the Kronenberger's. Neeca is on one side and Arnie's on the other. We're talking, and after a while, I noticed Arnie laughing—kind of giggle.

An aside: Flippo said, "By the way, knock out all the giggles except this one."

I'd turn around and look at him and he'd shut up, you know, and look at me. So we'd go on and we'd be eating and I could hear, "Ha, ha, ha, ha!" And I'd look at him right sharply and his face would sober up.

So about the third time he did this, I said, "What in the hell are you laughing about?"

"Well," he said, "I guess I'll tell the whole thang. Jan's going to kick me out of here if I tell it, but I'm going to tell, anyway. Of course, we live in LA, and we got here a night early. We were downstairs, but we wanted the upstairs in a two-story motel." And I believe that's where we all stayed in the same motel except Bill and Betty—they had a condo thar.

"Oh," he said, "We wanted the top story, but we were told we don't have one [room on the top floor]. Well, we stayed down below, but today they moved us up to a top floor. So we moved up thar, and here we are, and we'll waiting on you all. We have nothing to do except to get in the "Thralls of Ecstasy."

"We were in the "Thralls of Ecstasy" about two o'clock in the afternoon, and all of a sudden we heard this key turning the dang gum door, and the door opened. I did a double back flip out of the bed, and the guy just closed it, and said, "Oh, I'm sorry."

"And so, it wasn't five minutes we got a phone call. I answered the phone. The guy said, 'George?'"

I said, "Hell, no. This ain't George. Who do you want?"

He said, "Well, George was in that room last night, and he give me a key to the room in case I need to freshen up or anythang."

"But George is not here anymore and don't you dare open that door again. You just interrupted a session that will never happen again. You just ruined our party."

He could hear people laughing in the background, so this guy—whoever it was —had already went back, told his friends about what had happened.

We were laughing like hell when he said, "That damn door opened and somebody said, 'George' and I done a double back flip out of the bed."

We had a lot of fun out thar.

❧

One time out thar, they were pretty good golfers, but we teed off. I believe we were at Bermuda Dunes, and Arnie hit a golf ball about, I'd say, thirty yards farther than any of us. He was not that big a hitter.

But we said, "Jimmeney, boy."

Arnie said, "I've been playing golf quite a bet now. I'm getting a little better."

We said, "Good Lord, a mercy."

He said, "I've even took some lessons. Man, I'm hitting the ball pretty good."

And we said, "Well, that's farther than the pro's been hitting them. My God, it's a way out thar."

He said, "Yeah, yeah, yeah, I've been taking lessons."

And so we get out thar. Of course, we all hit up toward the green, and it's a long hole and kind of like a mesa. In other words, we were down below and it was kind of hilly. And ole Arnie picks up his ball, and he hits it long again.

We said, "Arnie, you're so good."

So we get up thar on the top of this mesa, and hell, thar's a damn pond of water up thar across the sand dunes. Arnie was in the cart that I was in, and we're driving along and he said, "Oh, man, no!"

I said, "What's wrong?"

He said, "You know, I hit that ball pretty good. I hope it didn't go in that water."

"I bet. Well, hell, I've got extra balls. I'm sure you do, too."

He said, "Yeah, yeah, yeah."

When we get up thar, we cannot find that ball.

And I said, "Arnie, you just hit it too damn far. I can't believe how you're hitting that ball."

And we're looking and looking. I said, "Arnie, if the ball is gone, take out another ball. Let's play this. Go, go, go!"

And he said, "Ah, man, help me look a little more."

"No! We've looked long enough. We've looked here for five or ten minutes, and we're going to have people coming up our backs after a while if we don't get going."

So he said, "Oh, damn. Okay." So he took out a ball and hit it.

"Hell, you didn't hit that thang far."

He said, "No, no, I kind of dug it, but I did get across the water."

"Yeah, you did, but not very much further."

So we're driving around thar, he's laughing, "Hee, hee, hee." I looked at him like I looked at him in the restaurant—and driving on, and he continues to laugh.

"Arnold, what the hell you laughing about? You've been laughing this whole trip."

He said, "Flippo, I paid ten dollars for that ball, and it's a souped-up ball, and I's really gonna take ya'll."

"No! It wasn't how you was hitting that damn ball so far."

He said, "It went in the water my first time to hit it. I paid ten dollars for it."

Dumb shit. We had a lot of fun out thar—a lot thangs happened. One time we were playing in a sandstorm out thar, and I remember hitting my ball and watching it. It goes out a piece, and it starts going back and we're all looking at it. Oh man, it landed right at my feet. That wind was blowing so hard, and of course, it wasn't a very happy day. All those days were good out thar except that one day we had a hell of a sandstorm.

❧

We's at Remuda Dunes. First time we played it I know we's up on number one tee early in the morning, and it was gorgeous.

And Arnie said, "Wonder what the poor folks are doing today?"

"Course, after we paid the fees thar, we's pretty poor."

~About Dave Taylor[3]

Ohhhhhh weeeee! Ah, Dave Taylor. Dave Taylor is dead now. You know he died just here a while back, bless his heart. We did a lot of stuff together. He worked, I don't know how many years at Kirkwood. Of course, I worked with him out thar, and then we did a Sunday afternoon in Detroit, him and I. It was our last one 'cause I remember us talking about it 23 years. We talked about going on, trying to get 25, but none of us could get our days we wanted to have it, but we always had a good crowd. He was very popular in Detroit. Also, he moved to Chicago. He got very popular in Chicago. Good caller. He's good with people. He knew his material really.

Flippo asked me if I had danced to Dave Taylor and I hadn't.

Well, you'll have to go to the Pearly Gates to dance to him now, I thank.

Dave Taylor on cover. Source: *American Squares*, November 1964

Probably Dave was the most funny at CALLERLAB. He MC'd it one time, and I thank it was the funniest damn show I have ever seen. I mean, he had a comeback for everybody. He was very quick-witted. Really a neat guy. He dressed up neat and everythang. He was just one of those good people.

~About Dick Jones

Put Dick Jones' name on thar, too. He's gone. He was from the east coast.

Dick Jones worked at Kirkwood a few years, and we'd play golf. Great caller. Of course, I's amazed at his calling.

We'd go out to play golf, and I enjoyed playing golf with him. He's a very, very good golfer, but he would address the ball, and I'd thank, 'Dick, when are you going to hit this son-a-bitch?' And he'd waggle, wiggle, waggle, wiggle, waggle, and he'd go back, and I'd thank, 'I don't know when he's going to swing this time.' Oh, no, here'd come his wiggle again.

Dick Jones. Source: Neeca Flippo

I mean, he'd have like twenty-five to thirty wiggles, waggles—whatever you call 'em. Waggles, I guess is the word, and you'd thank, "Oh, please hit the ball." And when he hit it, he hit a long, long way and straight most every time. He's a big guy and a very nice fellow.

Dick and I went out and played golf early every morning, and a couple other guys with us.

☙

Absolutely a wonderful caller, him, and what was her name? Dick and Artie. But she's a very out-spoken person, and he was more on the quiet side. But she was kinda boisterous and a nice lady.

It took a couple weeks, but in our last two interviews, Flippo wrestled with Dick's wife's name and finally in the second to the last interview, he said, "Ardie."

~About Hotsy & Joan Bacon

When I was calling in the Cincinnati area, I called thar once a year, and I would always stay with Hotsy and Joan. Now her name is spelled J-o-A-N. You'd thank it'd be Joan, but it's [pronounced] Joann.

Hotsy was a square dancer. He's somewhat of a caller. I believe it might be Harold, but all I've ever heard is "Hotsy," and I'm sure that come from his last name being Bacon. So I imagine somebody nicknamed him "Hotsy" right off.

Now they lived up in Hamilton, Ohio which is right thar, just right out of Cincinnati, and we'd go down thar to cross the river into Kentucky and call.

I'd always sleep in the feather bed they had upstairs. Just in passing, John went with me one year before he went to college.

I thought, "I'm going to have to get a motel 'cause I know they don't have another room." They had just one upstairs bedroom, and that was it. Before I got thar, they wrote me a letter, and they said, "We understand that John's with you. Come on and stay with us. You can sleep in the same bed."

And I knew John had never slept in a feather bed, but we had a lot of fun sleeping in that southern bed. We woke up and thar was sunk place where our bodies were, you know. John was flabbergasted about that feather bed, but he liked the food!

Joan was probably the best cook I met on tour or anywhere. She was just a farm girl that knew how to cook.

Joan called me along about Christmas time this year [2017] and so good hearing from them. If I could just come by thar one more time and get one of Joan's meals.

☙

We were coming home from a dance in Covington. It was about twenty miles difference between their house and crossing the river. They took one of those ole stores, like Penney's or Sear's or somethang like that, thar in Covington that was vacant and made a square dance hall out of it, and all the square dance clubs around thar used it. They had a good wood floor in it. They had a little trouble with the sound, but they fixed it, and Jerry Helt. I told you that name would come to me. Jerry Helt, an ole caller friend of mine, called down thar of a morning.

Jerry Helt on cover. Source: *Square Dancing*, October 1979.

~About Jerry Helt

Jerry Helt lived down in southern Ohio, and he used the dance hall in Covington. He used it like of a morning. He'd go out on the street and get 'em to come in. "Come on in. We'll do a little square dancing." He was very good at it. A lot of clubs used it. I can't even thank of the club that had me in thar, but that's terrible. But I went in thar quite a few years.

Anyway, ole Jerry done a lot of calling out in California. He'd go out thar every year, and I saw him at—I believe it was Osgood's funeral or Becky's funeral. I guess it was Osgood's funeral that he called a square dance with all the people that were thar, with us all sitting down, and he's a very accomplished guy. Very, very intelligent. Ole Jerry Helt lived down thar close to Portsmouth, down in that area, down in Ohio.

Well, thar's a funny thang about her [Jerry's wife]. She came to a dance I's calling in Midtown which is about halfway between Cincinnati and Dayton. I's calling that festival, and I got the sound up, and here she come.

"Hey, Jerry sent you this record. Put it on. And he said it'd really make a good square dance."

"Jerry sent it to me?"

"Yes, put it on thar. Let's listen to it. You got your sound all up."

"Jerry Helt sent me a record, and you want me to put it on right now?"

"Yeah, put it on. Let's listen to it. I haven't even heard it."

"You'd have to have a shotgun right up to my head for me to put a record on that Jerry Helt had sent me."

She says, "Well, damn it!" I can see her just as plain as hell. I can't call her name.

She said, "Damn it. You can turn the music way down low and listen to a little bit of it." So I turned it way down low and it was, "Let's All Get Drunk and Go Screw."

I said, "Do you see why I wouldn't play it out loud?"

But little ole thangs like that that come back in your memory, and they're great memories that you never thank of, not until you talk to somebody like you, and then little ole thangs like that but were fun, you know.

Then he shouted, "Kathy! Kathy! Kathy with a K."

~About Al and Bob Brundage

Al and Bob Brundage. Source: http://www.sdfne.org/

When I asked Flippo, "Do you have any funny stories on Al?"

You know, I don't thank I've got a thang on him. I worked with him all that time. He was kind of like Bob [his brother]—in other words, it would be hard to get somethang on Bob.

❦

Let's see. Bob Brundage. I thank I knew one of his wives, but I don't know whether he had two wives or not, but it seemed like way back thar, I met a wife of his. Now whether it's just the only wife or second wife or third wife, I don't know.

He's been in Albuquerque a long time.

I met Al before I met Bob, and I met him [Bob] back East. When I heard he lived in Albuquerque, [it] was a big surprise to me, so why he went thar I don't know.

Well, he took me through the Archives [The *Sets in Order* Square Dance Society's Hall of Fame's portraits]. That's the only time I was through the Archives thar, and I thank some callers went through thar the Archives this time [CALLERLAB 2018 in Albuquerque].

But Bob was sure good to me in Albuquerque. As long as he could, he drove me, went to the dances, drove me out after the dances. Then he got to where he couldn't drive at night, so bless his heart. [Bob Brundage died the Monday afternoon of CALLERLAB, 2018 when it was in Albuquerque. He was to be on the Legends panel and died that afternoon].

~About Earl Johnston

Now Earl Johnston. The first time I worked with him thar was eighty-eight squares thar in Connecticut. And those books that come out that you sign [The Century Club collect signatures from any new caller danced to. The object was to collect one hundred.]

Well, of course, he'd signed 'em all 'cause he lived thar, but between each tip, I'd go to the hallway and sign books while they played two rounds and he called his tip, and I'd sign books all that time. Thar was eighty-eight squares. Everybody had a book, so I'd sign books all through that break, and every break except the very last one. I didn't even go back to the hallway, but I thank I signed all of them, probably. But it was a hell of a chore.

Earl Johnston. Source: http://www.
sdfne.org/

I worked with Earl quite a bit.

~About Al "Tex" Brownlee

The first festival, The Permian Basin Oil Show, I ever called in my life, was at Odessa, Texas, with Al Brownlee. One year they'd have the dance in Odessa; the next year it would be in Tulsa, Oklahoma.

He went on to be known as "Tex" Brownlee—good, good caller. Good person, good with people.

Al "Tex" Brownlee handcuffed Flippo at festival in Fontana, North Carolina. Source: Neeca Flippo

It's Fontana, North Carolina. That was the first time I'd ever been to Fontana, so Tex'd been the staff caller in Fontana for a long time—about as long as I was in Kirkwood. So the first time I was thar to call, they handcuffed me to this pole and left me thar for a round. I thought they'd let me loose, and they made me stand thar for another square dance tip, then he finally let me loose. And he was also a deputy sheriff.

ॐ

I 'member that dang gum festival I called with him. We went out to the Strong's house in the afternoon for supper, and Neeca and I were already dressed for the dance, and we got out thar about 3 o'clock, I guess. Tex comes out, and he had nothing on but just casual clothes, and so after supper, he come walking out of thar, and he was a dressed like Cal Golden.

Cal Golden wasn't even close to Tex. Tex was a tailor, and so he made a lot suits. He started selling those suits, and boy, they were all sparklers, you know, and so, after supper, we was all talking in the living room. He came in. He had a black thang on, and it was fringe down the sleeves, fringe all the way down to the bottom of his pants. The front of it was poppies outlined in white, and it was just some kind of suit.

He said, "Thank anybody will notice me tonight?"

He told me, "Now Flippo, the way I dress will hold me 'til I put the needle on that first record, and then. . ." But, ah, good Lord, he was so good. He's gone now, so is Jean. She had Alzheimer's—they were just wonderful people.

446

I always enjoyed being around him. I've got another story about him and how quick-witted and everythang he was. Have you got time for it?

&.

This don't have anythang to do with the festival I called with him, but it's a funny story. I know all the people that were. They all went out to somebody's big home thar in Odessa for an *after party* after a dance. I was not thar. This was a dance that I was told about.

Anyway, it was some kind of festival—big crowd. Anyway, they went out thar, and thar was about twenty to twenty-five people out thar, this big ole home, and they were eating. Tex was getting drunker and drunker.

And Bobby King said, "I'm going home, Tommy."

She looked at Tommy White and said, "Tommy, will you make sure that Al gets home OK?"

Al "Tex" Brownlee. Source: http://www.sdfne.org/

So, you know, Al is Tex. I knew him as Al, then they started calling him Tex.

So Jean, Tex's wife, says—it's about one-thirty or two o'clock—"Tommy, will you make sure he gets home wherever he is?" Thar's people in all rooms, you know, and she never did get back.

Tommy said, "I sure will get him."

And she said, "Well, Beverly [Tommy's wife] and I are going home, so you bring ole what's his name home with you. Take him home. Make sure he gets home!"

Tommy said, "I'll make sure he gets home." Now Tommy's about six foot seven, and he's not that big a bone, but he's a slender guy. Tex weighed 116 pounds—that was his top weight. And I was taller than him. Little guy, little guy.

So, Tommy said, "Well, along about four o'clock, I hadn't seen him in about an hour or so. Where the hell is he?" So he started checking all the rooms. Well, way in the back bedroom, thar's ole Tex. He's laying across the bed, sound asleep.

He said, "I just gathered him up in my arms and carried him out, and people who were still thar were hitting at him and he never woke up. Oh, man. He was sound asleep, sound asleep."

Tommy said, "Went out, propped him up against the car. I got my car unlocked. I opened that door, and I got him in the passenger seat, and he just kind of just collapsed over. I drove him home, so I got to his house, and I went around and opened the door, and I reached in and picked him up, and I carried him to the front porch."

And I thought, "Oh, God, I hope she left that door open 'cause I don't have a key. I bet she's sound asleep."

Anyway, he said, "I set him down thar on the porch, and he just laid back against the wall. That ole head was limp as hell, and I tried the door and it was open, so I gathered him up in my arms and took him in thar and laid him down on the couch. Jean had left the door open."

So, he's fixing to leave. He put him on the couch, so he was just sound asleep, anyway. Jean didn't wake up.

"I was going to tiptoe out. Light was on. Lamp was on above Tex's head. I was tiptoeing and then I got to thanking, 'Nay, oh boy! I better loosen his shirt.' His tie was on, but his bolo was always up, the top button buttoned, you know."

He said, "I just loosen that tie and open his shirt, so it won't be so tight around him."

Tommy said, "That son of a bitch."

I said, "What's wrong?"

He said, "Well, I went over thar and unbuttoned his shirt, pulled his bolo down. I started to take his coat off. I pulled it back, and he stood straight up and said, 'OK, Tommy, I'll take it from here.'"

He'd been waiting that whole time and said, "Thank you, Tommy, I'll take it from here." He's just a really fun guy. He's summin'.

&a.

We's doing a festival. He'd bring up a little damn *hash call*—not too often but every once in a while—and he'd ride in on a stick horse, on a broom, and he had a whole entourage with him. He had a whole bunch of his friends with him.

So, he'd just come in that back door, and he'd ride that damn stick horse—an old broom. Put an old mop mane on it, and here come that whole bunch right up to the stage, you know, and he got up on the stage, and everythang got kind of quiet, and he got off of that thang and just kicked the hell out of it.

And he said, "You lousy old horse. Son of a gun, I'm so tired, I can't move another minute."

He said, "Damn it." He kicked that ole broom. I thought I'd die when he kicked that horse. He was a good, good caller, recorded some on Blue Star.

~About Harue Okazaki Swift

Flippo and I met on Wednesday afternoon after CALLERLAB 2018 in Albuquerque, and Harue Swift, a Japanese-American caller from Arizona, stopped by with a picture of her dancing in 1992 with Tim Marriner and Flip.

Flip's response, "Yeah, I was kind of bald then too, wasn't I? And that's you? You know, we could have been man and wife."

In his goodbyes to Harue he said, "Good luck with your calling. *Flutter*."[1] Flip encouraged her with pronouncing this call.

He continued, "You know, she understands that square dancing so well, and she is working so hard on her diction and everythang. Bless her heart. And she's really gung ho."

Flippo & Harue—The last dances Marshall called at Rincon West.
September 13, 2015. Source: Harue Okazaki Swift

~About Melton Luttrell

When asked if he had any stories about Melton Luttrell, Flippo replied:

A looooooooooong story but funny as hell! Ole Melton. Now I might have this a little wrong. I'll check with him, but he changed the story, didn't change it, but I just heard it wrong and told it wrong probably. He gets through calling in Joplin and is headed home down the Will Rogers Turnpike in Oklahoma. He has a flat.

His right rear tire was flat, so he gets out and he's got a one-handle lug wrench, and the ole car was old. But anyway, he bent that handle on that damn one-handle lug wrench to where he had no leverage at all.

Melton Luttrell. Source: https://
www.ceder.net/callerdb/viewsingle.
php?RecordId=2528

So, he said, "How in the hell am I going to get that tire off?" And he had it jacked up and everythang.

So, he looked across the turnpike, and thar was a kid riding around on a little ole motor scooter—looked like maybe he's on his Daddy's farm. It's on the other side of the fence. He looked across four lanes and the median, and then thar was a steep hill that went down and then he could walk up to that fence where that kid was riding around.

He thought, "Oh, boy!" He said he couldn't get nobody to stop, so he thought, "Well, maybe this kid. . .." So, he went over two lanes of traffic, down through the median, over another two lanes and then down this steep hill where this kid was. "If he comes around again, I'll see him."

So yeah, here he comes. Here he comes, so he stopped him, and he said, "Your

Dad wouldn't have a lug wrench up at the house, would he?"

"He's got a four handle one up thar."

Melton said, "Boy, I would sure love to borrow it."

The boy said, "I'll be right back." Boy, and he took off.

After a while, the kid came back with a four handle, so they both walked across thar. He got all the lug nuts off, took off, put the old spare on thar, and so he was offering this kid money, and the kid wouldn't take it.

He followed him all the way back across, down the steep hill, down to the fence where the kid had parked his motor scooter.

And he said, "Now please, take this money," and he argued all the way across, but the kid wouldn't take it.

So Melton said, "I just reached in my damn pocket, pulled out a five dollar bill and threw it to him."

He said, "Now you take that. Don't leave it laying thar."

Melton went back up the hill, and he saw him pick it up and take off, so he got back over thar and he said, "Where are my keys?" He had put the ole flat tire in the trunk and slammed the trunk lid.

He can't even start the car. "Where are my keys?"

So, he's looking and looking and looking. He couldn't find them, so he thought, "Well, hell! They're here!" Took the back seat partly out and he couldn't get back. Thar was a wall between him and the trunk from the back seat.

He couldn't get through that way, so he said, "I know they're back thar." So he gets out, and he's trying to stop cars. He's just had it. He said, "At first, I just kind of leaned up against the fender, and the car would go by and I'd hold up my hand and he would just keep going."

Finally he said, "Boy, I was out thar both hands like I's trying to stop them."

Finally, a guy stopped.

Melton said, "Can you help me? It's about four miles down thar to the place where you get food, gasoline and that kind of stuff. See if they got somebody down thar that can help me. I've locked my keys in my car."

And the guy said, "Well, I'll tell somebody." Sure enough, after a while thar come a service truck back, and he just drove across the median and up thar right behind Melton's car, and he said, "What's wrong here?"

Melton said, "I thank I locked my keys in the car. I cannot find them, and I had a flat. I put my flat tire in the back, slammed the trunk."

The guy said, "Oh, man! I don't know. I can't get it open, but I do know a locksmith who can get it open."

He said, "Well, let me go get that locksmith."

Melton said, "Would you?"

He said, "Yeah, I'll get him, and I'll bring him back. He's got all kinds of tools." So, he went. After a while, here he comes back in forty minutes, I guess it was, and he had that locksmith with him.

The locksmith started trying to get it open with different tools and different keys.

He said, "Damn it! It's on the other ring. I've got another ring and that key that fits that old car thar is on that other ole ring."

He said, "I'll go get it."

So ole Melton said, "I'll appreciate it." And so, they took off in the service truck again. So, Melton had to relieve himself.

"Where can I go? Thar's no trees or nothing to get behind. Oh, the big ditch over thar. Nobody can see me down in thar. I'll go over thar."

So he went across the two lanes, then he went across the median, went across the other two lanes, went down the hill. He was relieving himself, and thanking, "Oh, man," and he happened to look down, and he was pissing on his keys.

He said he must have pulled them out when he pulled that five dollars out of his pocket and threw at the kid. So he goes back, and he gets up to where he can see his car, and thar's a highway patrolman looking, and the guy had left his locksmith tools on Melton's trunk. You know, you got to have a permit to have locksmith tools. So, anyway, a great big ole red faced, red-headed patrolman had his back to him, and he was looking at these tools.

Melton got across the two lanes and said, "How you doing?" But it scared the hell out of him.

The patrolman turned around and went, "Whoa! Whoa! Is this your car?"

Melton said, "Yes, sir."

He said, "These your locksmith tools?"

"No, it's a long story."

The ole boy said, "I've got all day."

He said, "Well, now, I have to tell you this story, and it's kind of a long story, but the locksmith's gone. He's coming back. I tell you it's his tool."

The patrolman said, "Yeah, that's what they all say. But I'll be waiting here. Have you got a story to tell? I don't care how long it is. I'm not leaving." So Melton told him the story and said that guy started laughing, turning red in the face and just laughing up a storm. But, see, it was a funny story.

So here comes the locksmith back with the other set of tools. He gets out of the truck, and Melton said, "Here's twenty dollars. Take your tools. I'm leaving."

The guy said, "Whoa, whoa! Wait a minute. I'm going to get it open."

He said, "No. That's all."

The patrolman said, "Ask him."

And Melton said I just took on off, and I'm looking in the rear-view mirror and this patrolman bent over his hood laughing like hell and telling them the story.

I probably don't have it exactly right. I'll talk with Melton and see if it's okay to put it in thar. I'm sure it will be.

⌘

Melton was really a stickler about making dates. If he was booked somewhere, he made it. He hadn't never missed one except one time he was sitting thar at home, watching TV, the phone rang.

It was somebody from Memphis said, "Melton, where are you?"

"I'm watching TV. How you been? I'll see you next month."

"No, Melton, you supposed to be here today. We're all here ready to dance and you're not here." They were already in the hall.

He said, "Oh, my goodness. Let me look."

"Oh," he said, "I looked and you're right. I was supposed to be thar. I'm so sorry. I'll come over and call you a free dance any time you want me, let me know."

ॐ

Melton Luttrell was a dear friend with Joe Lewis. Melton lived in Fort Worth, and Joe lived over in Dallas, so they visited quite often. We had Joe down in Abilene two or three times. He spent the night with us, Neeca and I. We had a piano, so we'd stay up in the wee hours of the morning, playing the piano and singing, you know.

Melton was usually thar, too. We just sing into wee hours of the night, but Melton always wanted Joe to play some ping pong. Melton was a ping pong ace.

I'll tell you, he can play ping pong. Joe never would, so every time Joe'd come and visit [at Melton's lake house], 'Come on, let's go down in the basement. We'll play some ping pong.'"

"Nay, I don't thank I want to, Melton."

So, one time, he said, "Oh, boy! You ask me every time let's go down. Okay, I'll go down thar and play." Joe beat him two points.

But the final now—Melton said, "Come on, come on. Play another game."

"No, that's it."

Flippo sang, "Never did play him another game!"

ॐ

Melton Luttrell singing with a square dance band. Source: Neeca Flippo

Flippo talked a lot about this picture of Melton with the band:

Now you could dance to Melton before I ever started calling. Now you've got that down thar, haven't you?

I'll go from the left: Coon Dawson on the fiddle. C like a coon. Double O-N.

Coon. Dawson. D-A-W-S-O-N. Then on the rhythm guitar in the white shirt is Al Parks. Thar's Melton standing up at the microphone—the tall guy. Behind him is Travis Palmer on the bass fiddle, the upright bass. P-A-L-M-E-R. On the piano was Gerald Parks, that's Al's brother. Gerald Parks. Beautiful—great, great musicians. Now, he's hidden back in thar somewhere.

Probably the best square dance band I ever, in my life, called with. These kids lived around Eastland and Cisco, 'round that area over thar. Mean to tell you, they were such a good band. We used bands all the way through the 50s pretty well.

Flippo didn't know the name of the band. "But Melton will know." [I emailed Melton, and we talked about this picture, and the band really had no name.]

They used to play over in Breckenridge regularly on Saturday nights if they didn't have a square dance thang, and they'd pick up a guy that was really good on the saxophone, named Bob Myers. M-Y-E-R-S, and you couldn't get into the dad gum dance hall hardly over thar. None of them were singers, only just music and boy they could make some music.

Thar's three couples with us, that seemed like every time that they were going to play over thar. They did a lot of square dance numbers on Saturday nights, I mean, gigs, but when the square dance ended, they'd go over to the American Legion in Eastland, but when they had these guys, you couldn't get in the hall hardly.

~About Bill & Phyllis Speidel

He was a good, great caller thar in the Lincoln area. He's very, very well known. He called a long time with a guy named Kenny, and I can't thank of Kenny's last name. They did a lot of festivals together, but they weren't on the staff at Kirkwood. Ah, anyway, they sang together until Kenny got married, and the wife didn't like square dancing, so pretty soon, they fell out of it, just Bill.

His wife is still alive. Phyllis's a helluva cook, I know that, one wonderful cook.

Bill & Phyllis Speidel. Source: http://www.squaredancene.org/fame/speidel.php

Bill Speidel was the funny guy. Bob Fisk wore a hat to the *after party* one night, and he sang "Kansas City Star." He pantomimed it. Later on, Bill used that same hat to make a cake in which was a nice-looking hat. He was doing magician tricks, and he was really good, too. He'd dress up in a damn tuxedo and everythang, and he's a magician. So he had a wand up thar. He had an assistant.

Well, everythang that he did was wrong. He had a bottle of whiskey thar; course it was iced tea. Every time he'd look and see if he done summin' wrong, well, he'd take a swig of that, so, then he's gonna make a cake in that hat, and he'd shake it around and shake it down and say some funny words. He had some good words that sounded like a magician. And he looked back at the hat, then swirl it around and nothing was happening, so he'd reach over and take a big swig of that whiskey.

So then he worked some more and put some water in thar. He'd say some words, and he'd look in thar and it wasn't making a cake or anythang, so he'd grab the ole bottle again and take another drink. This went on two and three times when he'd take a drink.

The last time that he said, "Abracadabra," or whatever the words were, he looked at the hat, nothing had happened in thar, so he just put the hat on, and of course that flour and stuff just started running down his face.

We had a little snack bar at Kirkwood over on the side and kinda to the right of the podium. And to the left, thar's a door that you go outside, and thar's two sinks thar and a little snack bar, 'cause when we had high school seniors thar, we'd make malts and stuff thar for 'em.

So the hat ended up over thar on the side of the sink—it looked like hell. Anyway, we were talking towards the door. I was talking with Bob, with Bill and his assistant, Ken, and Phyllis was thar—nobody else in the hall. We were talking about three to five minutes.

Well, Bob Fisk had some really good friends, and they'd do anythang in the world for Bob, and this guy come in and started warshing that hat, and Bill kept a lookin' at him over thar and lookin' at him, and everybody kind of lookin' at him.

Finally, the guy saw Bill lookin'.

He said, "You almost ruined ole Bob Fisk's hat. I'm fixing it up for him."

And Bill said, "That's not Bob Fisk's hat. That's my hat. That hat was borrowed from me for Bob Fisk's act."

"Oh." The guy just dropped the hat and took off.

And Bill said, "Damn it. I should not have told him that for a long while—'til he got the hat cleaned." But he just dropped it.

Bill Speidel was probably the funniest guy on two legs that I had ever met. He couldn't say anythang wasn't funny.

Flippo referenced his favorite picture from Kirkwood Lodge, "The picture you see of me and Fisk laughing our ass off. The guy standing thar. You just see the profile of him. That's Bill Speidel."

~About Ray & Harper Smith

Ray and Harper Smith probably taught more Texas square dancers than anybody, and they're the ones that originated the *after party* skits and stuff, and we could shoot 'em.

But I worked with Harper. Harper was on the staff at Kirkwood for one week, and so was Ray. They're both gone now. They had different personalities. Both of them were good.

Harper and Ray Smith on cover: Source for Ray Smith: *Sets in Order*, August 1961

~About Wade Driver

Wade Driver—Waaaade Driver.

Well, I was headed to the studio with Norman Merrbach, the producer and owner of Blue Star Records in Houston, and he said to me, "I have a young caller coming in, going to record a number. He just moved here from Georgia. His name is Wade Driver, and he's a pretty good caller, I understand, but he's coming in to do a number."

And I said, "Oh good. Will I get to meet him?"

"Oh, yeah, we'll hang around 'til he gets here. I'm going to produce his record." And so, I just got through recording mine, and this kid come in thar and introduced him all around, so he got in thar, and boy, he was blowing the heck off of that record. You could tell he really had practiced. He was going to get it through the first time, come hell or high water.

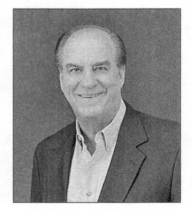

Wade Driver. Source: https://www.ceder.net/callerdb/viewsingle.php?RecordId=848

Well, he had his eyes closed. Thar was a big glass wall between us and him. We were sitting out where the engineer was doing all the little knobs and everythang

455

that they got. At that time, we would call our number and we'd call it at the same time the band played it. He'd be the one in the glass cage.

So, they went along a long time 'til they started getting a little better, a little better and pretty soon, we'd start doing the tapes, but he was calling, that sucker, and he was doing a good job. His eyes was closed. He's singing, and I went up and just mashed my face against the window thar, and he was about halfway through, and he kind of opened his eyes and lost it and then he had to do it all over again.

He said, "I don't know who you are—just met you, but I thank we're going to be friends."

I forget what Norman put it on, but he put it on one of his labels and it went pretty good, and Wade did it really well. Of course, Wade's going to do a good job.

But he became a really, good, good friend, and he really has success with that Rhythm Records, and he knows music so well.

A lot of times, guys that could sing, we had 'em sing [at *after parties*]. When we worked with Wade, he always sang a song. He wasn't in too many skits.

~About Cal Golden

Cal Golden. Source: http://www.sdfne.org/

I 'member the first time that I met Cal Golden was before he was overseas so long. You know he was over in Germany. But he was some kind of guy that ordered all the food and stuff like that.

Before he went over, I met him. First time I met him, I believe it was Biloxi,

Mississippi.

And he said, "Flippo, if I don't make it calling, I'll become the governor of Arkansas." [By the way, he never became the governor.]

And I 'member that, and after that, I didn't see him for years until one time he came into a weekend Al Brundage and I were having.

~About Jerry Story

Before Jerry was a really big hit, he was really good anyway, and if he came by—I was told this by one of the Chaparral boys and I don't know which one. Maybe it was Gary. I don't know. That was before I was a Chaparral guy.

"Oh," he said, "Every time Jerry comes by, we let him call, and he brings the house down, so we decided to quit letting him call when he comes by."

Jerry Story. Source: https://www.ceder.net/callerdb/viewsingle.php?RecordId=1233

Jerry Story & Tony Oxendine. Source for Jerry—see above. Tony - https://www.ceder.net/callerdb/viewsingle.php?RecordId=754

~About Jerry Story & Tony Oxendine

Oh, Oxendine. Oxendine. I cannot tell you a couple of stories because we were all drunk. But they were funny.

And we were so drunk that my son had to drive us home. My son was a bartender down at the Lake of the Ozarks. We were so dad gum drunk—all three of us. This is a hell of a story.

My son said, "Dad, you're not driving home."

Jerry said, "I'll driiiiive home."

Back to Kirkwood is what we were talking about. I lived thar, and they were thar for a week.

And John, Flippo's son, said to Jerry, "No, you're not driving home either. Neither one of you three. I'm gonna to tell my bar maid to take care of the bar. I'm gonna drive you home, back to Kirkwood." So he did.

So I don't know whether—no, you shouldn't put this in the book.

We's headed toward the kitchen, because we's going to raid the kitchen—make us a sandwich and all that stuff at Kirkwood. Story saw a golf cart.

"I wonder if the keys in that thang?"

Sure enough, they were, and I said, "Guys, that's the . . ."

Story was the driver, and if you have ever ridden with Jerry Story, it's an experience. It was one of the maid's golf cart, and it had a little like a pickup bed in the back. It's little. Somebody had built a little wooden one around it. That's where they carried their sheets and stuff.

They put me back thar, and anyway, we went for one hell of a ride. It's really a wonder that we hadn't killed ourselves.

Randy Dougherty. Source: https://randydougherty.com/

~About Randy Dougherty and Jerry Story

Anyway, when we were on tour later on with ole Randy [Dougherty] and the bus, he had fixed that ole bus up and thar's six or seven of us went on tour. I believe it was six. And ole Randy let Jerry drive that damn bus one night. And I knew we'd never see light again because Jerry is. . .. He's not a reckless driver, but he just drives like a maniac.

~About Jerry Junck

This story is about golfing with Jerry Junck, John Flippo, and myself and Leonard Peterso, from Rockford, who was a good golfer.

Anyway, Leonard had been down at a retirement village. He and Marilyn moved down thar a long time ago, but he's really from Rockford, Illinois. We all went golfing, the four of us.

My son, John, teed off first, and thar's a little ole brook that run right in front of us. It wasn't a creek, just a little ole babbling brook. It was running water. And so he teed off first, and he hit the ball up thar. Just barely did clear the little babbling brook, and it was not a very good drive.

Mr. Junck says, "Oh, that gives me a lot of confidence, John. Thank you for doing that. I feel like I can really hit it now." And

Jerry Junck. Source: https://www.ceder.net/callerdb/viewsingle.php?RecordId=1620

he hit a golf ball that went across the brook and hit a big ole rock and came right back at us.

And I 'member Leonard said, "Everybody down, everybody down."

The ball went over our head and back behind us under a tree. And anyway, we played that day and had lots of fun, but not a very good job except Leonard. Leonard always played well. Anyway, we had a good time that day, but that started it off.

🐍

Jerry Junck is a great friend, and he drove all night and everythang to get down to my whatever [Farewell to the Road dance] that we had in Abilene. And then he, let's see, then when I had my retirement on New Year's Eve, he drove a long way on that too.

🐍

He's got a toupee. [Anytime Flippo talked about Jerry, he made a joke about his beautiful hair being a toupee.] He's got a beautiful head of hair. He's not losing any of it either. Jerry is a very, very fine friend. He's just one of those guys that you really become close to. That's one thang I hate about retirement 'cause I miss seeing a lot of the guys, you know that I got to see at least once or twice a year.

🐍

459

Jerry and I still talk together on the phone, probably—it'll average four times a month. And he calls me, or I call him. Same way with Shoemake. Probably I talk with Jerry more than I talk with anybody, any caller that was close to me or I was close to them, whatever.

I talk with Chuck and Gary Shoemake the most. I talk with Jerry about as much. In fact, I just talked to Jerry day before yesterday, I believe it was. Great friends, and they'll always be friends, but I just won't see 'em like I used to see them.

Now one thang about Jerry. I'll get to see him when I'm here [with his son, John] 'cause he does a week at Kirkwood with Bobby Baier in August, so I'll get to see him then.

~About Mike Seastrom

I went to Asilomar with Osgood for years, and one time Bob told me, "Flippo, I've got a guy working for me—young guy—going to be a great caller."

"What's his name?"

He said, "Mike Seastrom," but I immediately forgot it and then later on when this guy was getting really, really good, I remembered that's the one that ole Osgood told me about, and it was, and he turned into a super caller and a dentist.

I asked him if he could work on my teeth, and he said, "Sure, I can."

I said, "Well, I'll send 'em to you."

I just like to be around him. He's one of those guys that you like to really be around, and he's got that Lisa with him now, and he's just dead set on life. That's it for him. He says so. I guess that's it.

Mike Seastrom. Source: https://www.ceder.net/callerdb/viewsingle.php?RecordId=748

Mike was on the staff with us in Laughlin. It was Ken Bower and Gary Shoemake and Mike Seastrom and me. Mike and this other guy done the baseball [skit for an *after party*. It was "Casey At the Bat."]. It's the story about baseball. The way they had it set up, Mike was the baseball player. I don't know whether thar's pictures of him or not, but it was hilarious, the skit was.

It was Mike and Lin, [my husband] and then the guy that had the skit up. He did it a couple times. The guy that came up with the skit and brought all the props and stuff like that. [Chuck Babcock from Garden Grove, California.]

Mike Seastrom in "Casey at the Bat" skit at Laughlin, Nevada January 7, 2014. Source: Larada Horner-Miller

I had seen it other places, but not as good as Mike. Mike was extraordinary. And of course, the guy behind him had to be on the ball, too.

460

Any skit you put Mike in, he went all out, and he should have been an actor. And then he pulled teeth with Hollywood stars.

§∎

In one of our last interviews, Flippo mentioned that he wanted to go to Mike and Lisa's wedding in May 2019 saying, "I'll try to do that, but I can't keep track of it."

~About Singing Sam Mitchell

Singing Sam—the best voice I have ever heard in my life. I'm talking about pop stars, western stars, everythang, Sam Mitchell.

I just begged him, "Get somebody and get your ass off to county western!"

He said, "Ah, nah. I like square dancing."

Good caller. He loved to play golf. Betty was his wife. He had a little heart problem. Betty didn't like him to go out so much, but she usually showed up in the middle of the week and by that time, we'd played two or three days of golf.

"Don't tell Betty I went out three days in a row."

Started out at Tucson, Arizona, when I first met him. I hadn't heard him call. I'd heard of him. And then he moved to

Sam Mitchell. Source: http://www. sdfne.org/

Michigan. While he was in Michigan, I stayed all night with them a couple times. One time, we went to the Michigan State football game. I 'member that.

§∎

And then one time Bob Fisk was visiting them, and I believe this was on a Saturday.

Sam said, "Well, I got to go down into Ohio." And at this time, Bob Fisk had an airplane, and he'd flew into Lansing, Michigan, where Michigan State is.

He said, "Sam, let me just fly you down thar. We can spend a little more time at home, and then we'd come back at night and save you that ole long trip in the car."

So Sam said, "That's a good idee." So Bob flew him down thar, and they took off back to Lansing after the dance at night time, and they get into the air and Sam asks Bob, "How many night hours have you had in flying?"

And Bob looked at his watch and he said, "About 15 minutes." They made it home safely.

§∎

461

Sam Mitchell was coming to Kirkwood one time, threw a cigarette out his car, and it went into the back seat, and he didn't know it and the damn car caught on fire. I mean, the back seat just burned all to hell. And he had, I believe, all of his kids with him.

And anyway, I know he lived in Florida. At this time, he was headed to Kirkwood. He went by the route of South Carolina where he had read somethang about a dental guy, and he got all his teeth pulled and new teeth put in. And of course, he suffered all week long.

He'd come and do his workshop or do a number at night, and he'd go right back to bed. But he really sung to death the damn thang.

A great guy—a tall guy and at one time, he was a singing waiter, I believe, in Kansas City. Also, I thank he was a policeman at one time, I believe that was in Kansas City, too. But then, I didn't know him at that time.

And he wrote a song that was just a terrific song, but he's afraid that it was too heavy. It wasn't heavy patriotic. He was afraid the government would get after him if he released it, so he never did do anythang with it. I can't remember all of it. He had a whole bunch of verses to it, and it was a neat song.

I said, "See somebody to record that for you."

"No, no, no, I'm afraid of the government." So anyway, he never did get it recorded.

He'd sing at our *after parties*. We'd get him to sing some songs, and I guarantee you if it didn't raise the hair up on the nape of your neck, you wasn't alive. He just had a voice that was just out of this world. I could sit here and listen to him from now until I die. But he really did have a good voice.

But I guess he probably wasted it all on square dancing or not. I don't thank he wasted it, but if he would go and get an agent and do some Country Western 'cause he could. Better voice than Jim Reeves! I guarantee you it was a better voice, and I just loved Jim Reeves and his voice. But Sam Mitchell had him beat.

~About Max Forsyth

Max Forsyth was a great caller from Indianapolis. I stayed with them. He was a very exciting caller. In fact, this park right here [Rincon West RV Resort, Tucson, Arizona] that I'm in he was here, he opened it, and I thank he was here eighteen years, and he wanted to retire. So they got Shane Greer to come and take his place.

Anyway, Max was a really, really good caller.

Max Forsyth. Source: http://www.sdfne.org/max-forsyth/

Grace & Grant Wheatley. Source: Grant Wheatley

~About Grant & Grace Wheatley and Festus

While we were looking through one of Neeca's photo albums/scrapbooks, I noticed a letter from Grant Wheatley.

"Did you know Grant?"

With a laugh, I answered, "Oh my God, Yes! What a fun guy!"

Well, they used to come, oh, and was at. . .. Let me see, where was Roswell? No, where the hell did I meet them? It was either Roswell or Silver City.

You know, I never did take an umbrage at the letter and Festus. I never did. And anyway, he was quite a character.

See Grant's Festus article and his letter to Neeca in Appendix H.

~About Charlie & Bettye Procter

Charlie was such a good, good friend, and he worked Asilomar for a good while thar after Manning and Nita didn't come back, and we always had such fun with him.

Fun, fun *round dance* teacher[s] that really knew their stuff. They called him "Ole Rubber Legs" 'cause of the way he danced.

I equated them with Manning and Nita Smith. The Smiths and the Hamiltons were the top two in the USA for a long while. Frank Hamilton and Manning and Nita Smith. Now Manning and Nita were excellent *round dancers*, but they put a lot fun in it.

Frank and Carolyn Hamilton were like the Chaffees. In other words, I equate the Chaffees in my era with Frank and Carolyn Hamilton because they were so precise and everythang. Darlene Chaffee's gone now. He's still alive.

Charlie was precise to a certain point. He wanted you to do every step correctly, but he wouldn't want your toes to be out thar the same distance and all that kind of stuff. Charlie and Bettye Procter were really, really fun. They had a great, great following, and they were originally from the Dallas area.

She was quick-witted as she could be. They're both gone now, but Judy's still alive—that's their daughter. She lives in Paris, Texas. And looks just like her Momma did at a young age. Beautiful woman. I thank they got a boy or two that's still alive.

When you lose a child, it really bothers you for the rest of your life. They were walking home one night and this little kid hit one of Charlie's kids over the head with a trombone. Yeah, it's what killed him. And that was sad, but anyway, they were fun, fun people.

They worked Asilomar; they worked Kirkwood; and they were the ones that suggested. . .Chaparral Weekend. Labor Day weekend had been in Kansas City, and then we found a better deal in Oklahoma City, so we went thar, and then Charlie had moved. He kind of retired. I believe Bettye had died.

I know I was a pallbearer, but I thank she had died before Charlie moved out thar. Anyway, he got in touch with Gary [Shoemake] and Ken [Bower] and said, "Well, thar's a great facility out here [Paris, Texas] if you all want a use it, I thank I can get it," and so he did. I believe he did the rounds first two or three years. Oh, I can't remember when Bettye died, but he got it for us and we went out thar and that whole town was so good to us.

Charlie & Bettye Procter. Source: Neeca Flippo

§ê.

Well, now, when Bettye died, we went out to the graveyard, out to the cemetery, and I was a pallbearer. Frank Lane was a pallbearer. Well, thar was six of us, and when we [were] transferring her over to that thang they put 'em down into the grave with, we almost dropped it, and Charlie's sitting on the front row.

Charlie says, "Next time, I'll run git some younger pallbearers."

§ê.

Now Bettye was a wit. She's a quick wit.

Charlie bought ole Bettye a red convertible. I believe it was a convertible, but it was red, and Bettye was a pretty woman. A trucker tracked her going north, said, "Break for that pretty lady thar in that red car going south. Won't you whip that thang around and come on up north with me?"

And she said, "Well, buddy, I'm sorry to tell ya. I didn't get this car going north when I should be going south."

❦

Ah, I got to talkin' about Bettye, and, course, I worked a lot with Bettye and Charlie. I know lots of funny thangs.

After Asilomar one year, Charlie and I went up thar somewhere in the Bay area, and he was doing the rounds and I was doing the squares for this club, and it had a stage that had a rug on it, but it dropped down about two or three feet. The middle part was pretty big. Well, each side had a lower side to it. About, I say two to three feet. Well, Charlie fell off of that thang 'cause the rug looked the same.

So, later on in the dance, I thought, "Well, that's kind of embarrassed ole Charlie. I'll play like I fell, too." So I made a big noise, and I played like I fell, too, and Charlie come running up thar and said, "You clumsy son of a bitch. Can't you see that."

Charlie was very quick-witted. Charlie knew all the *rounds*. He never looked at a cheat [cue] sheet at all, and he'd *cue* all those damn rounds. I don't know how he did it. Never a cheat sheet, but he had that kind of memory, I suppose.

Every once in a while, he'd peek at the new round, and he'd go back and look at somethang, but as far as him cuing, you never seen him look at a cheat sheet or nothing, boy! He just stood up thar and cued it from memory.

He was very good, very good, very good. You don't see that—anyone doing that anymore.

❦

But Charlie and Bettye lived in Red Oaks in the Dallas area a long time, and they had an exhibition group that was well known at most Nationals. I forget what they called the group.

[Flippo always wrote down any information he needed to get and a couple interviews later—in fact in the second to the last interview we did, he had found the name of the Procter's exhibition group: Let's Dance.]

They're both deceased now.

~About Ted Frye

Ted Frye and Jessie. I stayed with them most of the time when I was in Knoxville. Ted Frye and I became real close friends. He was a realtor and done pretty well at that job. He was a big guy.

I 'member the first—I don't know whether it was the first Cracker Barrel that

465

I had ever seen. It was thar in Knoxville. We'd go thar for breakfast, and he'd order that Uncle Herschel. Two biscuits would come with it and gravy. So, he ate ten biscuits one morning.

"God," I said, "How can you eat all of that?" But he'd say to the waitress, "Can I get a couple more biscuits?"

She'd say, "Yeah." She'd bring him just one. He'd eat it. Then, he'd say, "Ma'am, can I get a couple of biscuits?"

So, I thank he ate ten. But he was big, you know. He had, I guess what you'd call, the place to put it in his stomach and everythang.

❧

He had a record company of his own. I'm trying to thank of name of it. [Pioneer Records and Square Tunes] Ohhhhhh boy. But he did pretty good with his recordings, too. He recorded either in Nashville or Knoxville, and he had some really good recordings.

Ted was really, really a good caller, but he'd just as soon not call, and so every year I'd go in thar, I'd return from calling, and I'd say, "Well, now you gotta get back in it 'cause you like it."

He said, "I do, but I'm busy as a realtor and all—selling homes and stuff like that." And so, he'd promise me every year, "I'm going to start up a beginner class, and I'm going to start back—I promise you this!"

Next year, I'd go in and I'd say, "How's your class?"

"Oh, Flippo! I never did start it!"

And so, he became quite ill after so many years, and I guess the last time I remember him was in his home in Knoxville, and he still looked pretty good, talked good and eveythang, but he was on his last legs, I understood. I don't know what all he had, but he died.

Now Jessie's gone, so they're both gone. The kids are still around—I got to know the kids pretty well. After we'd have a square dance, well the kids would go with us to some honky-tonk. The kids, you know, they were good.

Ted Frye was really, really a great friend. I miss him, I just miss him very much, especially—well, I don't get around thar anymore, but especially when I went up to English Mountain or somethang like that, and I had to go up to Knoxville. I called Jessie and talked with her, but I really miss ole Ted Frye. He was a good one.

Good caller, Larada, good caller, I mean it. He's the smoothest guy I have ever seen. His voice just made it smooth for some reason, but he was really a good smooth caller.

I don't know who bought that label if anybody did, whether it went defunct or not. What the heck? I can't thank of the name of the label and I used those records so much. Oh, God! Well, I'll put it on a little note down here. Ted Frye—F-R-Y-E, I thank. Yeah. Ted Frye records, record label. I'll find out what it is.

~About Dee Dee Dougherty-Lottie

Ah, I knew her when she was a baby. I knew her and her brother both, Randy, when they were just kids. Their mother and daddy danced in Minneapolis, and that's where I first met her. She became real good, well, so did Randy. They both became real good callers.

Well, you know, I was gonna to say I used to put her on hais quite a bit.

She's different in her calling. I remember I called the song "Alabama Jubilee" a zillion times. She and I were doing the "Alabama Jubilee" in Birmingham, and so we decided the last number of Saturday night we'd do the "Alabama Jubilee."

I thought, "Hell, thar's no problem here. I've called it all my life—all my calling life." And what I did wrong was let her start it, because she is so different. I could not find the frigging tune.

Flippo & Dee Dee Dougherty-Lottie. Source: Dee Dee Dougherty-Lottie

I swear I was sweating blood when that thang was over, and she said, "Man, it's going."

I said, "Man, it's going. Hell, I can't keep my damn tempo."

But she's different. I went to one of her dances one time, and I was really, really impressed with what that gal can do, and she gets that whole damn floor up. Of course, everybody likes her, and I just love her.

~About Bob Yerington

Bob Yerington—Shirley's still alive. Bob died quite a few years ago. Bob'd always do a week at Kirkwood, and he just had people come back year after year after year. You know they were coming back because of Yerington.

He worked with Bobby Newman I thank a couple of years at Kirkwood. Bob Yerington had really good fans in from Houston, and they'd come every year, boy, to hear ole Bob Yerington.

He was from Muscatine, Iowa.

He used to wear those ole blue boots. I 'member that. Oh, golly. I remember sitting over thar and a room full of people at Kirkwood—big room—and it was just full of people, and we'd tell stories and stuff like that.

Bob & Shirley Yerington. Source: Tom Manning

Bob was pretty good at *after party* skits, too. Well, he was probably good at everythang he ever did, but I can't thank of anythang funny right now.

I talked to Shirley just every once in a while, just around Christmas time is when I call her. I sent her a Christmas card each year. I get one back, so I guess it's

467

her. I talked with her here not too long ago, and she's doing fine. They still live on Main Street.

~About Bobby Newman

I know after an *after party* broke up one night at the big room [at Kirkwood], some of us had to walk through the Terrace Room, where we danced, to go home. I didn't have to, but a lot of 'em did, and so, we'd been telling pretty raunchy jokes with all those people in that big room, and everybody's having a good time, maybe a few drinks.

But Bobby Newman had turned that amplifier on and started calling, so we just squared up. I thank thar was two squares or maybe just one. I believe thar was just one 'cause thar wasn't that many up thar, and he knew them all and we'd been telling real raunchy jokes and everythang, and he says, "Square 'em up, and I'll be your f**king corner. And your f**king partner," and he's saying the word.

And he said, "We're going to f**king dance right now."

And he said that a hundred times. Thar was an ole boy, and he [Bobby] didn't know it that came in, and he's just down thar by the tape recorders. Thar's a tape recorder shelf down thar. We get through it, and we's starting leave the building down thar from the Terrace Room.

We's just going to our rooms, and this guy said, "Oh, Bobby, you know that was good, man. I got that on tape."

Bobby said, "You don't have it."

"Yeah, I . . ."

He said, "Give me."

He said, "Whoa, whoa, whoa, whoa!"

Boy, he made the ole boy give him that tape. Thar was no way—no way!

I don't believe Yerington was in the hall at that time. I don't believe Shirley was either. I don't thank Bob and them would have ever done that around those two.

Bobby Newman was from Paducah, and he worked down in the valley of Texas. He had an RV park down thar—Sunshine somethang. Then he retired from that, and he went to work for a fence company and still doing it—still with that fence company, and he ought to be about ready to retire now, but he was an excellent caller and good people. He and Nancy were just loved by anybody that ever got around 'em. They're just that kind of couple. She's a little girl, little tiny thang.

~About Chuck Goodman

Chuck Goodman was from New Orleans. He built a hall down in New Orleans that'd hold about sixty squares, and he'd have a beginner class. Thar was another little hall with a tree right in the middle of it. Now you danced around the tree.

I stayed with 'em a billion times. He had a real nice home. Opal was a really, really good cook, and she *cued rounds*.

So, what he would do is we'd meet with the local *callers* thar. He would have beginner classes the same night as the big dance that they have. Maybe it was once a week, and it'd always be fifty or sixty squares thar. But he'd have local *callers* and him. I know when I was in thar a few times, he would be designated to teach.

One time when I was thar, he wasn't at the dance, but what happened is they would start about an hour later than the regular dance, and as soon as the regular dance was over, he would really try to get everybody over to the little hall. Sometimes it was too crowded, but a lot of the old dancers went over and danced with the new dancers, so, they had the night all ready, and as soon as they finished, he just took them into the club. I thank he had 560 people probably, but anyway, it added up to sixty squares or fifty squares. [seventy squares] And he had them as members.

He told me one time, "Flippo, people want me to hire this guy. Thar's two or three people that asked me to hire him, and I said, 'I didn't know him.'"

But he said, "I hired him, and it was the worst dance I'd ever seen in my life, and the guy was embarrassed about it, but he wasn't capable calling to what we were used to dancing, and it was just a bad, bad dance. And he was staying with us."

And Chuck said, "Along about three o'clock in the morning, my alarm went off in the house, and I went to the back door, and I heard noise thar, and I went to the back door, and it was him, trying to get out. He had his suitcase and everythang, and when he tried to get out, he was just going to sneak out, you know, and get out of thar. When he tried to open that door, the alarm went off."

He said, "Flippo, he's just running around in a circle, looking and saying, 'What in the hell am I supposed to do here?'"

But Chuck said, "I guess he's so embarrassed over that."

જ

One of the nicest guys that you'd ever want. It was him and Opal. Both were just good people, but he was kinda firm on how that hall was run, and actually people would help him. He was such a good guy. Well, when he was able to come to the dance, thar was people that—I mean—a lot of people, maybe ten to twenty people that stayed after the dance and cleaned up that hall and it was just as good as it was when they walked into it.

But he didn't designate 'em, they just volunteered, and so I said, "How do you get your club to pick up?"

"I started cleaning one night, and three or four other people come along and pretty soon, thar was a bunch of people. Pretty soon, I backed out of that—just let 'em have it."

And she cooked one of the best—I don't know how she did it—but it was the best fish dinners I ever ate, and some kind of a white gravy that was just excellent.

~About John Davis

John Davis & Charlotte—I just wonder if Charlotte's still alive. Johnny Davis had sugar diabetes. I thank finally lost one of his legs, yeah, down around the ankle. Really a bright guy. He called *Advanced* about as good as I ever heard anybody call it, and he recorded on. . .. Larada, I can't remember what the damn labels were? I'm having troubles with square dance labels today. [Grenn, Inc. from the Internet]

But he had a real big hit way back thar called "Big Daddy," and everybody and their dogs were calling it. And I've still got that ole record somewhere, I'm sure, but he had a really big hit thar.

He lived in Ohio. I want to say around Cincinnati, and I've been to their home, but can't remember whether it was in Cincinnati or not, but down south Ohio.

Thar's a funny story here on him. Well, I don't know whether it was somethang funny or not. I know he got in trouble. Thar was a girl dancing right in that front square, right in front of him at Kirkwood.

Johnny Davis. Source: *Sets in Order*, December 1966.

Well, the podium wasn't very tall off of the floor and one of the squares were right in front of you, and so this gal had a wig on, and she come around thar, and Johnny and I were calling one together, and all of a sudden, she came around thar, and ole Johnny just reached down, took her damn wig right off. Well, the gal just laughed like hell, but Charlotte was livid.

Boy, she got ole Johnny after the tip. She took him outside, and I imagine read the riot act to him 'cause he came back in, and he was kind of a meek little guy.

He got that off of thar so easy, and she just laughed—it was a nice wig. But I hadn't paid much attention to it. She came around one time, and he just reached up and took her damn wig off.

Funny thangs happened!

Charlotte was a perfect—I said perfect—caller's wife. People loved her, and she kept him in line. What great person she was.

After he died, Charlotte come out to a couple dances I called thar—I called in Dayton. Were they around Dayton? I believe they were around Dayton, but anyway, she came out thar a couple times after John had died. Then I guess it was a few years, and she didn't show up, so the last time, that's been a long time ago. But I got her number from somebody thar, and I called her, and she was doing fine. She had a job, and she liked it. And they had two kids, and they grew up, and neither one of 'em had sugar diabetes, so that one ended.

And now I don't know where those kids are, but they're middle age now. I don't know whether Charlotte's still alive or not. I better check up on that and see.

~About Johnnie Wykoff

Oh, Johnnie Wykoff was great. I first met him in Indianapolis when I called thar for Max Forsyth. Max would have me in thar once a year, and he introduced me to Johnnie. Johnnie was—how can I say it—an excellent caller, but he knew music so well.

Johnnie Wykoff started recording on Blue Star, but when he moved to Houston then, he did so well in Houston. He was so well-liked and became probably Houston's most popular caller. After Norman [Merrbach] died, he bought Blue Star from Nadine and done a great job with the recording and producing.

When John died, they had a memorial for him. They could hardly hold all the people, he was so well liked. His memorial was really great, and then they had another one later on for him, and it was great, too. He was so well liked in that area.

He was married to Star.

He asked me to call a couple weekends with him, and I guess we did maybe four or five weekends together, and he was very good at getting thangs put together and everythang—putting the weekends together, making programs, and all that stuff. He was very articulate at that!

Let me see—funny thangs about John. Star wouldn't let John drink any thang intoxic. . .'til I came to town. So he was always glad to see me come to town, so he could have a scotch or two, you know.

Johnnie Wykoff. Source: https://www.ceder.net/recorddb/artist_viewsingle.php?RecordId=24

He had heart problems, and I thank he died on the lot of like a K-Mart or somethang. He died in his car.

But he was in Houston quite a few years. When I first met him or talked to Max Forsyth about it later on, Max said, "Johnnie said after he heard me call, he said, 'Now he should stick with country western music.'"

So, I stuck to a lot to country western music, just on his say so. Then when he took over Blue Star, I's still recording for them, so I done some work for John. I stayed with him and Star when I was in Houston after Merrbach died.

We always had a lot of fun when we're together.

~About C. O. Guest

C. O.'s been dead a good while. His wife, Chris, is still alive and a wonderful woman.

Anyway, C. O. couldn't hardly see. He had real thick glasses and not making fun of his sight or anythang, just some funny thangs happened.

Big Daddy Bussey—B-U-S-S-E-Y. Big Daddy Bussey was a caller in Oklahoma City. He hired ole C. O. to come call for him. C. O. drove from Dallas to Oklahoma City.

They were headed to the dance that night and it was getting dark, and Big Daddy said, "C. O. put on the breaks."

And he said, "What are you doing?"

C. O. said, "Thar's some people walking across the road up thar."

"No," he said, "C. O. That's a shadow of a telephone pole."

And so Big Daddy said, "During the dance, C. O. was a kind, lovely person."

And he was calling the dance for Big Daddy, had a big ole crowd and way back in the back the roof sloped down, and thar was a pole holding part of the roof up back thar, and C. O. kept a saying this one tip, "We need a couple in the back, need a couple in the back," and they're all looking. They're all waiting.

Finally, Big Daddy run up thar and told him, "C. O., they don't need a couple back thar. It's a guy leaning up against a pole with his arms thar."

But C. O. was a really, really a nice person, a typical Texan. Lovely to talk with, just a nice personality. Chris is still alive, and the last time I saw her, she was at that dance we did—well, they still do—in Paris, Texas.

~About C. O. Guest & Billy Lewis

C. O. Guest and Billy Lewis started with—I believe it was Blue Star or one of Merrbach's labels. He had two or three labels, and they started down thar with Merrbach down in Houston, and then they formed their own company called Kalox—K-A-L-O-X and were very, very successful with that label, and a lot of good hits. Of course, both of 'em could call real well, C. O. and Billy Lewis.

~About Billy Lewis

Billy's still alive. I believe Billy's wife—I'm not sure of this—so, but I kinda thank it was Mary. I could be wrong [sung out], Larada, like I been quite a few times.

The last time I saw him was I was surprised to see him, really. It was in Waco, Texas quite a few years ago, but a long time after C. O. had died and the label had become defunct.

He came out, and he said he's started calling again and had a little club over in some town thar close to Waco, but that's the last time I saw Billy. I thank he's still alive. He was one of those younger guys.

~About Pancho and Marie Baird

Pancho and Marie Baird. I believe they were from Santa Fe. I wasn't around 'em too much. I called with 'em a couple times when they had the band. We had the bands all the way through the 50s, and they kinda died out, and then we went into record music.

Pancho called, and they had a band. I forget what Marie played, but they had a good band that was well-thought of—square dance band.

The first time I met 'em, I guess was in El Paso. They were playing, and you didn't have to tell 'em too much about a song. They could pick up, you know, if they didn't know it, just hum a little bit, they had it.

I wasn't that well acquainted with 'em, but I had seen 'em at different dances. We always talked a little bit, and then I thank I called with 'em twice—once in El Paso and once in Odessa.

I knew they were excellent. He was a good caller, too—very good.

Pancho and Marie Baird & the Git-fiddlers Band. Source: Neeca Flippo

~About Jim Brower

Jim Brower could have been a pro golfer back in those days. When he was young, he said, "Yeah, I could have made it, but it didn't pay anythang. I couldn't survive on it even if you won a tournament, you didn't win very much."

So, it was a way back thar. He was a very good golfer. I played a lot of golf with him. Jim is the first one that I know of that would say, "Keep smilin', ya'll. Keep smilin', ya'll." He'd always put the "ya'll" on the end of it, so Jim was really, really well-thought of in the New England area. They booked him up thar, and course, they just thought he hung the moon. With his accent up thar and everythang, and "Keep smilin', ya'll."

Jim Brower. Source: http://www.sdfne.org/

And he's the first one also when a square broke down thar in Kirkwood, and he'd probably used this before, but he stopped and said, "I need to help that square back thar. I called it wrong for ya'll. Would you square up, and I'll try to call it right." He didn't blame them a bit. He laughed. But a good friend. He worked here at Kirkwood many a year.

Let me see—who took his place when he retired? I believe Bob Yerington took his place, but I'm not sure of that. Jim Brower had a good week. Jim was an avid golfer, avid square dance caller—excellent square dance caller, typical Texan.

He was not boastful or anythang like that. I'm not saying he was that way—being from Texas. Sometimes they thank you're stuck up or better than everybody else, and that wasn't the case with Jim Brower. He never changed his talk or anythang—Texan throughout! He was from Texarkana, Texas. Texarkana—three states thar in one word: Texas, Arkansas, and Louisiana. They're all right thar in that little niche.

~Bronc Wise

The only funny story I really know for sure is, happened here at Kirkwood. This one I know for sure 'cause the waitress waited on him would not lie if she had a gun put to her head.

On Thursday night, it was fried chicken night, and they had on each plate two monstrous pieces of chicken, and of course, at Kirkwood at that time, if you wanted another piece, you could ask for another piece. They bring another piece. So, so I was eating, I was eating supper back in the kitchen about where I usually eat thar back on a table back thar for the employees. Well, I's eating supper back thar, and June came through the door from the dining room, said, "Mona, give me two more [pieces of] chicken. That one guy back thar has already eat his. . .."

Bronc Wise. Source: https://www.ceder.net/callerdb/viewsingle.php?RecordId=581

"Well, June, you just took 'em out thar."

"I know. He grabbed one up and started eating it as soon as I put it down thar. Rest of the people haven't even started, and he's already eaten two pieces. He wanted two more pieces."

So Mona said, "Well, good." She sent two more pieces out thar. Anyway, June came back and said, "That guy can eat. He's a big guy."

I said, "Who is it?"

She said, "That caller for this week." So I look around the corner, and opened the door and stuck my head out. It was Bronc Wise out thar sitting at that table. So, we had eight at a table—eight people or six at a table or four at a table or two at a table. We had those different kinds of seating.

But he's sitting at a six. After a while June come back in and she says, "I cannot believe it."

I said, "What's wrong?"

"Well." Said, "I gave him those two pieces of chicken. He ate 'em, and the lady next to him said, 'Oh, I can't eat that second piece,' and said he just reached over grabbed it and said, "I'll take it."

So, I said, "Well, he's a big guy. He's probably trying to get a little energy up or summin'."

So then, it wasn't too long. I's about through with my food. I'm a very slow eater, but I'm about through with my food, and I's getting me a piece of pie and here come June through the door, "Mona, Mona, two more pieces of chicken, please for this guy out here."

And Mona said, "I can't believe that. How many does that make?"

"Eight!"

Eight big pieces of chicken—no, it was nine. I believe it was six or seven. Anyway, anyway, it was a lot more than I could ever eat.

Nice fellow—I like him.

Bronc's Response:

I was like 25 at the time! Kirkwood's restaurant was heaven for me! After that happened, he and I played poker with a couple other guys. After that broke up around 2, Flip told me that if I wanted something, just look in the fridge in the kitchen. I did. . .found cold fried chicken!

The next morning Flip was saying, "Listen! Listen!" The cook staff was complaining that the police who patrol the place at night ate all the cold chicken!!!

"Them damn po-lice!"

Ted Clements. Source: https://www.ceder.net/callerdb/viewsingle.
php?RecordId=2480

~About Ted Clements

Well, you know, he never did get up to the level, you say, like a Shoemake or a Bower or anythang like that, but let me tell you—the ole boy can call a square dance, and I was really—yeah. Really, really impressed with his calling, and he's got a good thang going over thar in Las Cruces.

~About Darryl McMillan

[This happened at Chula Vista Resort, Wisconsin Dells, Wisconsin.]

Well, thar's one funny thang. I don't thank it's funny, but Darryl McMillan thanks it's hilarious. He's a caller, very good caller from Alabama. He was on the staff, but we were going to parties one night, and it was still when they had the ole wooden buildings, and it was spread out all over everywhere.

We were going a long, and Darryl said, "Now, make sure this next party has somethang to eat. If they don't have anythang to eat, we'll just skip it."

So anyway, we were going along and we had a drink in one hand, a sandwich in the other. We was going to another party, and it had snowed some, but it had kind of melted away, but under the trees was still snow and ice.

Well, we're walking along, and my heel hit that dad gum ice, and I actually saw my feet out in front of me, and I went "plow down," right straight down on my back.

And Darryl looked down and said, "Flippo, if you're not hurt, that's funny as hell."

So Flippo said, "Well, you just now become my ex-friend."

But he's a good one, and we went the way around and was getting pretty high. I guess if I hadn't had a few, I'd probably killed myself, but I slipped. You know, I don't really remember being sore over it. I must have fell just right. A lot of funny thangs happened, but they leave your mind, you know.

A very, very, very good caller, and he and Ann were just super folk. They live up in Alabama. He's still calling—calls a lot. Hangs around a little with Elmer Sheffield.

Darryl added, "The sandwich Flippo was eating was an egg sandwich. When he fell, he reached to break his fall, and he landed right on top of the sandwich. When we got to the next party, I told everyone that Flippo was eating a "pressed" egg sandwich.

Darryl McMillan. Source: https://www.ceder.net/callerdb/viewsingle.php?RecordId=2210

Elmer Sheffield. Source: https://www.ceder.net/callerdb/viewsingle.php?RecordId=936

~About Elmer Sheffield

Oh, boy. One of those humans that I could not be like that, I don't thank, but Margie had her stroke, and he just takes care of her every day. He takes her to

Nationals and to CALLERLAB and everythang, and you know—got to get her all dressed and everythang.

❧

He and Paul Markham were contacted to do the first gay national [square dance] convention in Seattle.

Elmer couldn't remember who was the lady and who was the man, so he had a lot of trouble on that. Had to call a lot of memory stuff. But the next night, I thank thar was two squares of the ladies dressed in orange shirts or some other kind of shirt—men's shirts, whatever, and the men were normal like in Levi's and whatever. And said he got by okay then.

He said they treated Marge like she's a queen. They really did take care of her.

I know they called a second one, which was in Denver, I believe, and then I don't know if they called any more or not.

❧

He came to Kirkwood many a time.

Lee Kopman, Flippo, and Dave Hodson. Source: Neeca Flippo

~Dave Hodson

Dave Hodson—now I don't know whether to really say anythang about this or not, but Dave Hodson come to me at a Challenge week here at Kirkwood with Lee Kopman, and so, I don't know. About the middle of the week or summin', he said, "Flippo, how do you call a Plus dance?"

I said, "What?" (sang what) I said, "What?"

He said—I guess you could say a well-known Challenge caller came and asked me, or summin' like that.

And he said, "You know, when I got out of class, I went right into Advanced and then into Challenge. I went right by all the Plus and all that stuff, and they asked me to call a Plus dance, it scared me to death. I won't even take one."

I said, "Oh, Dave, you wouldn't have a bit of trouble if you'd just study the list a little bit."

He said, "I don't even know how to do some of the damn figers."

~About Larry Letson

OK, now, ahhhh, Larry Letson. Larry Letson.

Kick his ass. I haven't seen him in a long, long time. We talk to each other on the phone at least once a month, and so I haven't seen him in a while.

I picked him up one time, and I wasn't even going to let him in the car. He looked like a neon sign coming at me. I had a rental car. He was getting off of some flight in Indianapolis, Indiana. I decided to wait for him, and I could not believe what he had on. But anyway, he's a good one. He's really a good guy.

ᕦ

Some of the stuff I tell that's funny on him, I can't tell.

ᕦ

Larry was very innovative with his calling, and he had some really good square dance movements that he come up with and not any different *Basics*, but the *Basics* we have, he used, and he come up with some really good stuff. He was good with people. He was very well liked in the valley of Texas down thar at the RV park that he called [a retirement dance community in south Texas] for before him and Vickie busted up.

Of course, he called a lot with Story and Oxendine, and he was on their label.

Larry Letson. Source: https://www.ceder.net/callerdb/viewsingle.php?RecordId=1311

ᕦ

We took a tour together, and I thank we had ten dances all lined up from Indiana all the way down to New Orleans, and just one town after another, and we had a lot of fun, but it was a just two friends.

≈

He came to pick me up. I flew into Indianapolis, and Larry's supposed to pick me up thar. Larry wore different clothes, and he had on—what do you call those tight pants? I don't know. He had a bright orange shirt with, I believe blue through it and those tight pants.

Of course, just fit in with his red hair. He picked me up, and when he got out of the car—well, I's waiting on the curb, and he came, and he got out of the car to help me with my luggage, and he lit up the whole street. I mean, he was really bright.

I said, "I don't thank I'm going to get in the car with you—people are lookin'!"

≈

One time, we had rented a car in Chicago at CALLERLAB at Drake's. Well, he's down the hall from me, one room. So, the day we's supposed fly out of thar, it's getting pretty, pretty dangerous.

Not having a choice, I said, "Well, we're going to run late. Now we got to git to that airport."

He said, "Oh, yeah, be right thar."

"Well," he grumbled.

I said, "I'll be downstairs," and so he's coming down, and he got the car and drove around, picked me up, and we were running late, I mean to tell you, we were running late. We had a rental car we had to turn in, so we git pulled up thar where they'll check your baggage on the curb, and got our bags out and our tags.

I said, "Are you gonna run. . .?"

He said, "Ah, they'll find it." He left that car right thar.

And later on, I asked him if he ever found out anythang about the car.

He said, "Oh, yeah, they sent me a bill looking for it," and I said, "I ought to pay half of it."

He said, "Oh, no, you don't want to pay half of this!" So I don't know what kind bill he got, but, anyway, "Oh, they'll find it."

We went on and caught our airplane but just barely.

≈

Ole Larry—he's a really good friend. I miss him a lot, you know, seeing him around the square dance circle, but if that's what he wants—Lowe's—that's what he's gonna get. He just won't come back to calling. Story and everybody begged him. Oxendine begged him. I've begged him—he ain't comin' back. You beg him, and he said, "No, no. Never again."

I knew his mother and dad real well. And his dad just had a heart attack, but he's okay. He's back home. His momma died, and they were a neat couple, too—Bill and Betty Letson—just really friendly.

We went on a cruise with 'em one time, and they were on the same plane, and Larry was in the back. It was me and my second wife, and then across the aisle from us was Bill and Betty.

So somethang's happening in the back, and we kinda looked back thar. Larry was saying somethang to one of the stewardesses—I thank they call 'em Flight Attendants now. But they were all laughing, and she looked back thar and said, "Flippo, that's not my son!"

I said, "Well, what you do? Get 'em mixed up at birth? What are you saying?"

Good family. Betty's died now, and Bill is still alive, living in Lafayette, Indiana, where Purdue University is. That's where Larry's working now at Lowe's at Lafayette.

❧

When Flippo was talking about Bob Sumrall, he said, "I don't know anythang really funny about Bob Sumrall. Excellent caller. Compared to Letson, he was laid back. Letson was a bang, bang, banger."

❧

A clean story about Larry Letson does not exist. Just talked to him the other day, and he did show up in Green Valley that time [New Year's Eve Dance in 2017—Flip's last contract].

Grand Square Square Dance Club Callers, San Antonio, Texas
~About Joe & Cricket Young

Joe and Cricket Young—just like the bug. They were good people. Their daughter and only child is still alive. She married John Thompson, a caller. Joe retired from the Army—he also retired from the post office and the VA. They're both gone now.

Joe and Cricket Young—very fine caller, a very good organizer, very good with people. Had to perform the ole Heimlich on him one time at a restaurant.

When I ran off the highway between Houston and San Antone, Joe got thar fast. He was a good friend.

I always stayed with Joe and Cricket when I went to San Antone. I called for their Grand Squares club. I called their anniversary dance, I don't know how many years. I'll try to find that out, too.

He was a very good teacher, square dancing-wise, good dresser. He's always neat as a pin, neat as a pin, a good golfer, and just really genial.

Seemed like somethang happened at Cricket's funeral, and I can't bring it up to save my neck. My computers down! Yeah, ah God! I went to the funeral. It was a monstrous funeral. She was well-liked, well, her and her husband, too. Joe was caller for two or three clubs in San Antone.

But Joe never recovered [after Cricket's death], you know. Joe and Cricket were as close as a couple I've ever seen—they were. He met her when he was in the Army, and they married, and they were married umpteen years.

Both of them just really good people, and, I thank. He was four years older than she was. He's eighteen, and she's fourteen. And I guess she got her parent's permission to marry. I don't know how that all happened, but I know she was very young when married. They didn't thank it'd last, but it did.

Yeah, [Silence] Joe Young, Joe Young—seemed like all these years that I stayed with 'em—year after year after year after year, and I can't bring anythang really funny. It'll probably come to me, come to me after we hang up.

~About Chris Crisler

When Joe died, Chris took over the Grand Squares.

Chris bought a brand-new van that had those thangs on the top, you know, those railings on top of the van. You see them for decoration or whatever. Fasten 'em down to whatever. So, he said to Joe and Cricket, "Let's go up to Dallas to the National, ah, no to CALLERLAB, and we'll go up in my brand-new van."

So, they git to this parking garage, and he says, "Damn, I don't know what the height of this thang is, so we'll ease by and figure." It had a bar hanging down thar. You know, you can't go any higher than this.

So he said, "I don't know. Hey, Joe, get out. Let's see if it fits."

So Joe got out, and he said, "You can make it! You can make it." So Joe got back in, and they went on in. Chris said, "Oh, thank you, Joe."

Anyway, later on, he said, "I'll pick ya'll up at the lobby. We'll go somewhere to eat. I'll go git the van." Well, he gits the van. Well, he knew it was low enough to go under, but [now] it wasn't. When everybody got out, he drug those bars right on the top of his van. Everybody got out, and it wasn't as full as it was when they went in.

Chris has passed away now. His widow's still alive. I know the last time that I called for them, Chris was still alive. His wife's name is Allene. Chris and Allene Crisler. It's Crisler—C-R-I-S-L-E-R.

When Cris died, Wayne Weston took it over. He's the caller now for Grand Squares.

❦

~About Bill Wright

Probably one of the best callers I ever heard. I really liked Bill. He lived in San Antone, too. Excellent caller. I can't thank of any funny thang right off. I thank he might be at an assisted living thang now.

He had a great Army life—it was Air Force. I forget what he ended up at, but he had a couple of sons. Now I'm not too sure of this. I'll ask Don [Winkler] that too. Don knows everythang.

❦

Bob Fisk. Source: Neeca Flippo

Callers I've Slept With

When Flippo and I made the list of callers he wanted to tell stories on, he added another list, "Callers I've Slept With," and named one person—Bob Fisk! So here's that story! He chuckled throughout this whole story!

This one couple, Guy and Vi Kinder, lived east of the river thar in St. Louis—one of those towns. They lived in Granite City, Illinois. They moved to Phoenix, and they were having the Phoenix Festival, and Bob Fisk and I were to call it. Well, right before the festival, their children came to visit them, and they either called us or wrote us a letter, saying, "You'll have to sleep in the same bed because our kids come in, if you don't mind."

So, I called Bob, and he said, "Well, keep your hands off of me."

Bob Fisk was a very good-looking guy. The girls kinda slobbered over him. It was like if you hear Jerry Story's name; you know immediately who they are talking about. Well, back thar, when Bob was traveling all over and everythang, if you said some girl asked you about Bob, all they had to do was say, "Can you do a song about Bob Fisk?"

So after the festival was over, a month or so, I was dang gone in West Virginia, and this little ole gal come up—pretty little girl—and said, "Have you seen Bob lately?"

"I had to stay in the same bed with him out thar in Phoenix."

"You did!"

"Yes, he kinda disappointed me."

She said, "What?"

"Well, before he went to bed, he took his toupee off."

She protested, "He don't have a toupee!"

"Yeah, you're the only one that don't know that, but he's got a toupee. That hair is not his."

And she said, "Noooo."

"Yeah. What really got me is right before he got into bed, he took his teeth out, put them in a glass thar by the bed."

"He don't have false teeth."

Bob had a really good smile, you know.

"Everybody knows he's got false teeth."

She said, "He don't!"

"Yes." And I had to laugh.

She said, "You son a bitch!" Anyway, I thought that was a good story, so I'm telling it around, and I get to Trenton, New Jersey. And I said, "Gladys, I want to tell you a story about Bob Fisk," so I told her the story, and she said, "Oh, my God! Just a minute." And she went and got a *Sets in Order* magazine where Osgood had put him [on the cover] as Caller of the Month and found a picture of him.

And she said, "Flippo, I'm going to blow that up. Before you leave here, I'll give you some flyers."

So, so she took that picture, blew it up, made him bald-headed and made him with no teeth and a big smile, no teeth and so I was carrying this around and it said, "Bob Fisk" underneath it. I was carrying this around and showing it to people. I had a whole bunch of 'em. So I was putting them on bulletin boards and everythang.

So I went down to Evansville, Indiana. They had a Sunday afternoon dance, and I was to call it. Bob Fisk was to come in the next month. Well, they took the picture.

"Oh, give me that picture. Give me that picture." They couldn't wait to get that damn picture, so when he come in thar the next month, they had a big pot up on the stage, and they had blew that picture up even bigger, and his picture was in front of that pot, and underneath the picture was a sign said, "Donation for Fisk some new teeth and a new toupee."

So, he got in thar, and I heard the tape of when he got in thar.

Before he ever started calling, he said, "Well, from this picture here, I know who's been here. Yes, I had to sleep in the same bed with him in Phoenix. He's found out that I had a toupee and I had false teeth, but I found out somethang about that little bastard." That's what he said on the microphone about that little bastard.

He said, "He's queer!"

So, I had to quit telling the damn story. Great times!

Whew! Flippo, the master storyteller, square dance caller and friend, relished each story he told and crafted it as best he could. He loved these people mentioned and wanted to pay a special tribute to his lifelong friendships! Right now, I can feel Flip hiding behind each of these stories, chuckling and whispering, "Thar are so many more I could have told!"

---

1. **Flutter[wheel]** — The right-side dancers leave their current partner and Right Arm Turn with each other a full turn, each ending where they started. Halfway through this motion, they take a couple handhold with the other dancer (i.e., the one they were originally facing directly), and the second half of the Arm Turn is completed with each new couple working as a unit.

DO YOU WANT MORE?

When I finished transcribing the thirty-seven interviews with Flippo, I had over 258,000 words, so I realized I had a dilemma: this book was going to be gigantic! Flip shared over 70,000 words in stories about other callers and dancers. After talking with John Flippo, we decided to cut a large chunk of those stories. I cut what didn't pertain specifically to Flip, like the chapter on the Kirkwood employees.

So because you bought this book, you have access to **ALL** cut material—it's housed on my website in a Members-Only section. To access that material, email me at MOFlippo@earthlink.net with proof of purchase, and I will give you entry into the restricted area. Then you can browse and enjoy the "extended stories" of Marshall Flippo.

Here is a sampling of the stories, articles and memorabilia that will be in the private Members-Only section of my website at: http://www.laradas.books.com

- Letters & Notes from fans
- Articles
- An original copy of the call sheet for "The Auctioneer"
- The Old Mule Skit

Flippo's Stories about

- Kirkwood EmployeesTwo Good Cooks
- Tex Brownlee & the Skunk
- Explosion & Jerry Haag
- Walt Faulkner

APPENDIX A – CHRONOLOGY OF MARSHALL FLIPPO'S LIFE

DATE —EVENT

September 2, 1927—Born in Tuscola, Texas
September 2, 1944—Volunteered and joined the Navy
1946—Bill Hagadorn bought Kirkwood Lodge.
September 2, 1948—Released from the Navy
February 25, 1949—Married Neeca
1951—Flippo & Neeca started square dancing
1952—Started calling in a chicken coop
1953—Started teaching square dancing at Abilene Recreation Depart
1954—Rented the Hayloft to teach square dancing
1956-March, 1961—Taught beginner classes at the YMCA, Abilene
1957—Went to Kirkwood Lodge on vacation for first time - Les Gotcher, caller
1958—Flippo & Neeca joined with three other couples in Abilene, Texas, and built the Wagon Wheel Square Dance Hall.
1958—Skipped Kirkwood Lodge & went to Arkansas and worked with Les Gotcher
1958—Recorded "The Auctioneer" in Houston with Blue Star records owned by Norman & Nadine Merrbach and began recording with Blue Star Records
1960—Bill Hagadorn asked Flippo to become the resident caller at Kirkwood Lodge
1961—Signed on as resident caller at Kirkwood Lodge in Osage Beach, Missouri
1960 - 2002—For 42 years Marshall spent 6 months at Kirkwood Lodge and 6 months on the road touring. He is known as the "Ambassador" of square dancing.
June 8, 1963—John Flippo, Flippo's son, born
1964 - 2000—Started calling annually at two events at Asilomar with Bob & Becky Osgood for thirty-six years

September 11, 1967—Norman Merrbach gave Flip Gold Record for recording one million records.

1970—Inducted into the *Sets in Order* American Square Dance Society Hall of Fame & picture on May cover of *Sets in Order*

1971—Was one of the "Founding member" of CALLERLAB

1971 - 1981—Served on the Board of Governor's for CALLERLAB

January 19, 1971—Called at the Inaugural Ball for Preston Smith in Austin, Texas with Gary Shoemake

1972—Flippo & Pat Munn bought Kirkwood Lodge

1972—Received Gold Record for selling one million records

April 8 - 10, 1974—Attended 1st CALLERLAB Convention

1977 — Quarter Century Award

1981—Received the Milestone Award from CALLERLAB

March 27, 1984—Sent a crippled boy from Minnesota some records and information about himself

1984—Received Award of Excellence from CALLERLAB

1985—Started recording with Chaparral

1991—Divorced Neeca after 42 years of marriage

2004—Half-Century Award

September 1, 2007—Inducted into the Texas State Callers' Hall of Fame honoring Texas Callers who have called for more than 25 Years in Texas and contributed to the overall success of Square Dancing in Texas

April 19, 2011—Received the Gold Card Award from CALLERLAB.

2016—Received the "Caller's Lifetime Achievement Award" from CALLERLAB

September 2 - 4, 2016—Called at last Chaparral Labor Day Weekend in Paris, Texas

September 5, 2016—Retired after 64 years of calling at "Farewell to the Road" Dance, Abilene, Texas

May 12 - 14, 2017—Honored last Contract in New Mexico - New Mexico State Square and Round Dance Festival, Albuquerque, NM

December 31, 2017—Honored last Contract - New Year's Eve - Green Valley, Arizona

September 18, 2018—Attended Farewell Party in Tucson, Arizona - 60 in attendance - Flippo moving to Missouri to live with John

November 4, 2018—Marshall Flippo died

APPENDIX B – ITINERARY OF USS LANDER

USS LANDER

(AUXILIARY PERSONNEL ATTACK 178)

KEEL LAID:	OCTOBER 9, 1944
CONSTRUCTED BY:	THE OREGON SHIPBUILDING CORPORATION
LAUNCHED:	NOVEMBER 19, 1944
COMMISSIONED:	DECEMBER 9, 1944
NAMED FOR:	LANDER COUNTY, NEVADA
HOME PORT:	MARE ISLAND, SAN FRANCISCO, CALIFORNIA

CRUISE OF THE USS LANDER (APA 178)
(DECEMBER 1944—DECEMBER 1945)

ARRIVAL DATE	LOCATION	DEPARTURE DATE	DISTANCE (MILES)
DECEMBER 7, 1944	ASTORIA, ORE	DECEMBER 20, 1944	350
DECEMBER 21, 1944	SEATTLE, WASH.	DECEMBER 24, 1944	1100
DECEMBER 27, 1944	SAN FRANCISCO	DECEMBER 29, 1944	500
DECEMBER 29, 1944	SAN PEDRO	JANUARY 12, 1945	200
JANUARY 13, 1945	SAN DIEGO	JANUARY 22, 1945	60
JANUARY 23, 1945	OCEANSIDE	JANUARY 28, 1945	120
JANUARY 28, 1945	SAN PEDRO	FEBRUARY 9, 1945	2218
FEBRUARY 15, 1945	PEARL HARBOR	FEBRUARY 20, 1945	2357
FEBRUARY 28, 1945	ENIWETOK	MARCH 3, 1945	1500
MARCH 14, 1945	IWO JIMA	MARCH 20, 1945	700
MARCH 22, 1945	GUAM	MARCH 23, 1945	1100
MARCH 27, 1945	ENIWETOK	MARCH 28, 1945	2350
APRIL 4, 1945	PEARL HARBOR	APRIL 4, 1945	125
APRIL 5, 1945	MAUI	APRIL 6, 1945	125
APRIL 6, 1945	PEARL HARBOR	APRIL 12, 1945	90

(CON'T. NEXT PAGE)

Page 1 itinerary of the USS Lander. Source: *USS LANDER 1945*

CRUISE OF THE USS LANDER (APA 178)

(DECEMBER 1944—DECEMBER 1945)

ARRIVAL DATE		LOCATION	DEPARTURE DATE		DISTANCE (MILES)
APRIL	12, 1945	MAALAEA BAY (MAUI)	APRIL	28, 1945	96
APRIL	28, 1945	PEARL HARBOR	MAY	13, 1945	20
MAY	13, 1945	HONOLULU	MAY	20, 1945	2350
MAY	28, 1945	ENIWETOK	MAY	29, 1945	1370
JUNE	2, 1945	ULITHI	JUNE	3, 1945	1259
JUNE	7, 1945	OKINAWA	JUNE	10, 1945	1228
JUNE	17, 1945	ULITHI	JUNE	18, 1945	869
JUNE	20, 1945	MARCUS	JUNE	23, 1945	1358
JUNE	27, 1945	ENIWETOK	JUNE	30, 1945	325
JULY	1, 1945	ROI	JULY	2, 1945	60
JULY	2, 1945	KWAJALEIN	JULY	3, 1945	2225
JULY	9, 1945	PEARL HARBOR	JULY	10, 1945	2068
JULY	17, 1945	SAN FRANCISCO	AUGUST	4, 1945	4143
AUGUST	16, 1945	ENIWETOK	AUGUST	25, 1945	1356
ANGUST	28, 1945	ULITHI	SEPTEMBER	2, 1945	845
SEPTEMBER	5, 1945	LEYTE	SEPTEMBER	5, 1945	663
SEPTEMBER	7, 1945	MANILA	SEPTEMBER	9, 1945	52
SEPTEMBER	9, 1945	SUBIC BAY	SEPTEMBER	9, 1945	130
SEPTEMBER	10, 1945	LINGAYEN GULF	SEPTEMBER	20, 1945	1474
SEPTEMBER	25, 1945	WAKAYAMA, JAPAN	SEPTEMBER	26, 1945	1588
OCTOBER	1, 1945	SUBIC BAY	OCTOBER	1, 1945	584
OCTOBER	3, 1945	LEYTE	OCTOBER	6, 1945	449
OCTOBER	8, 1945	TALOMA (DAVAO GULF)	OCTOBER	9, 1945	14
OCTOBER	9, 1945	PAKIPUTAN STRAIT	OCTOBER	14, 1945	1811
OCTOBER	21, 1945	MATSUYAMA, JAPAN	OCTOBER	26, 1945	1480
OCTOBER	31, 1945	SAIPAN	NOVEMBER	1, 1945	5235
NOVEMBER	14, 1945	SAN FRANCISCO	NOVEMBER	29, 1945	5200
DECEMBER	15, 1945	GUAM	DECEMBER	16, 1945	5450
DECEMBER	28, 1945	SAN PEDRO			

TOTAL 56,597

Page 2 itinerary of the USS Lander. Source: *USS LANDER 1945*

USS Lander — Copyright. Source: https://www.navsource.org/archives/10/03/03178.htm

APPENDIX C – MORE BURMA-SHAVE JINGLES

Here's your opportunity to enjoy more classic Burma-Shave jingles!

General *Patter*[1] Jingles

I went to town
in my little red wagon
hind wheel off
and the axle dragging.

ॐ

Up the river
and around the bend.
When you meet your honey,
You're gone again.

ॐ

Rope that yearling,
brand that calf,
meet your honey
with a once and a half.

For this last one, he added the rest of the call, "*It's a once in a half and a half all around, whirligig, whirligig, whirligig around.*"

ॐ

You can't go home
if you're going by the mill
'cause the bridge washed out
at the bottom of the hill.

&

The big creek's up
and the little creek's level.
Plow my corn
with a double shovel.

&

Possum on a fence post.
Chicken on a rail.
They'll take a drink
from the water well.

&

Plus Patter Jingles

"Here's a couple of *Relay the Deucey*[2] or *Spin Chain the Gears*[3] patter. These are usually in the same *hash call*.[4] If you do one, you do the other."

She had one big breast
in the middle of her chest,
and an eye in the middle of her nose.

So says I
if you look her in the eye
You're better off looking
up her nose.

&

Flippo added more explanation, "If you do *Relay the Deucey* twice, you use this one coming up, which is almost like the first one."

It ain't no woman
and it ain't no man,
and it don't wear
very many clothes.

&

So says I
if you look her in the eye
You're better off looking
up her nose.

---

1. **Patter** — A single tune, used by a caller as background for a series of calls, with no lyrics accompanying the music. Couples are moved into a variety of formations, but brought back to their home positions before the next set of calls.
2. **Relay the Deucey** — Plus Call — From Parallel Waves or Eight Chain Thru (in which case dancers first step to Parallel Waves). It can be done left-handed and is called Arky
   Arm Turn 1/2;
   Center 4 Arm Turn 3/4 as Others 1/2 Circulate;
   Wave Of 6 Arm Turn 1/2;
   Center Wave Of 4 Arm Turn 1/2 as Others (do a Big) Diamond Circulate;
   Wave Of 6 Arm Turn 1/2;
   Center Wave Of 4 Arm Turn 3/4 as Others move up.
3. **Spin Chain the Gears** — Plus Call — Each end and the adjacent center dancer turn one-half (1800). The new centers of each ocean wave turn three-quarters (2700) to form a new ocean wave across the set, as the other four dancers do a U Turn Back (turning in toward the center). The centers of the wave Trade and then release hands with each other. Four dancers on each side of the square now form a four-hand star and turn the star three-quarters, forming a new wave across the set. Centers of this wave Trade momentarily reforming the wave across the set. The two outside pairs of dancers of the center wave now turn three-quarters (2700) as the other four dancers turn back (turning away from the center).s
4. **Hash Call** — Same as Patter — A single tune, used by a caller as background for a series of calls, with no lyrics accompanying the music. Couples are moved into a variety of formations, but brought back to their home positions before the next set of calls.

APPENDIX D – INTERNATIONAL TOURS

Flippo called in the following countries

- Japan—several times
- Germany—with Tom and Gina Crisp three times: 2002, 2007 & 2008
- Spain, Morocco, and Majorca—April 15–30, 1973 with Bob and Nita Page
- England—with Dave Taylor and [Flippo's second wife]
- Canada

Cruises

- February 21–March 3, 1974—Cruise to Mazatlan, Puerto Vallarta, Manzanillo and Acapulco with Bob and Nita Page[1]
- February 21–28, 1981—Eight Day Caribbean Square Dance Cruise with Bill Speidel[2]
- February 7–14, 1987—Caribbean Cruise with Chris and Rita Vear, Bill and Phyllis Speidel, and Art and Fran Moore[3]
- March 21–28, 1992—Seven Day Caribbean Promenade Cruise with Ken Bower, Wade Driver, Jerry Haag, Larry Letson, Tony Oxendine, Gary Shoemake, Scott Smith, and Jerry Story[4]
- March 20–27, 1994—Top of the Line Cruise with Ken Bower, Wade Driver, Jerry Haag, Tim Marriner, Randy Dougherty, Larry Letson, Tony Oxendine, Gary Shoemake, Scott Smith, and Jerry Story[5]
- May 23–30, 1996—Seven Days on The Western Caribbean. Top of the Line Cruise with Ken Bower, Tim Marriner, Randy Dougherty, Jerry Haag, Tony Oxendine, Wade Driver, Larry Letson, Scott Smith, Jerry Story, and Gary Shoemake[6]

- March 22–29, 1998—Seven Days in the Southern Caribbean. Top of the Line Cruise with Randy Dougherty, Larry Letson, Tim Marriner, Tony Oxendine, and Jerry Story.[7]
- March 26–April 2, 2000—Seven Days on The Western Caribbean. Top of the Line Cruise with Randy Dougherty, Larry Letson, Tim Marriner, Tony Oxendine, and Jerry Story.[8]
- April 14–21, 2002—Seven Days on The Southern Caribbean. Top of the Line Cruise with Tony Oxendine, Jerry Story, Randy Dougherty, Larry Letson, and Tim Marriner.[9]

---

1. *Sets in Order* (December 1973): 75.
2. *Sets in Order* (December 1980): 67.
3. *American Square Dance* (July 1986): 38.
4. *American Square Dance* (May 1991): 28.
5. *American Square Dance* (June 1993): 90.
6. *American Square Dance* (October 1995): 14.
7. *American Square Dance* (April 1997)" 22.
8. *American Square Dance* (December 1998): 7.
9. *American Square Dance* (September 2001): 47.

APPENDIX E – CHEK-A-KALLER LEGEND

See picture collage for this in Chapter 19.

CHEK-A-KALLER KONTEST

CORRECT LIST OF CALLERS

1. Frank Bedell
2. Dick Enderle
3. Ted Frye
4. John Hendron
5. Marv Lindner
6. Vaughn Parrish
7. Ray Smith
8. Bob Wright
9. Billy Lewis
10. Bob Dubree
11. Dan Robinson
12. Johnny LeClair
13. Lee Kopman
14. Birdie Mesick
15. Bob Frye
16. Mick Howard
17. Mel Roberts
18. Ernie Kinney
19. Frank Lane
20. Jerry Haag
21. Ken Bower
22. Roger Chapman
23. Charlie Baldwin
24. Al Brundage
25. John Walter
26. Max Forsyth
27. Manny Amor
28. Harry Lackey
29. Bob Wickers
30. Don Belvin
31. Beryl Main
32. Les Gotcher
33. Marshall Flippo
34. George Jabbusch
35. Bill Gracey
36. Marlin Spies
37. Bob Osgood
38. Dave Taylor
39. Tex Brownlee
40. Dick Steele
41. Jack Johnson
42. Ken Anderson
43. C. O. Guest
44. Sam Mitchell
45. Harper Smith
46. Bob Yerington
47. Jay King
48. Les Chewning
49. Chel Chave
50. Buzz Brown
51. Chuck Dillenbeck
52. Bruce Johnson
53. Don Williamson
54. Decko Deck
55. Bob Augustin
56. Louis Calhoun
57. Bev Tallman
58. Lee Helsel
59. J. Fred Muggs
60. Rich Anderson
61. Walt Wentworth
62. Lee Schmidt
63. Bud Redmond
64. Bob Fisk
65. Ralph Silvius
66. Earl Johnston
67. Fred Christopher
68. Darrell Figg
69. Cal Golden
70. Bob Page
71. Jerry Helt
72. Kip Garvey
73. Allen Tipton
74. Buck Fish
75. Dick Jones
76. Jack May
77. Jack Lasry
78. Osa Mathews
79. Marv Labahn
80. Harry Tucciarone
81. Doc Gray
82. Dick Leger
83. Phil Adams
84. Archie Howell
85. Jim Copeland
86. Jim Brower
87. Don Ashworth
88. Ken McNabb
89. Jim Mork
90. Ron Schneider
91. Joe Abbott
92. Jim Pearson
93. Johnny Davis
94. Cal Brazier
95. Francis Zeller
96. Sal Fanara
97. Frannie Heintz
98. Dave Hass
99. Deuce Williams
100. Mal Minshall
101. Don Atkins
102. Bill Peters

Source: Stan Burdick, *Square Dance,* (August 1971): 56.

497

APPENDIX F – FLIPPO'S RECORDINGS & REVIEWS

The core list below was compiled at Vic Ceder's website https://www.ceder.net, and I explored in *Sets in Order* and *Square Dance* magazines to find some of the missing records and references to specific records. Thirty-two songs did not have a review or reference in either *Sets in Order* or *American Square Dance* magazine.

Marshall Flippo recorded over 224 records for fourteen recording labels. He received two gold records for sales over a half a million and one million while he was at Blue Star.

"A historic moment in the square dance music industry occurs in 2005, when Blue Star Records becomes the only label to release its 1,000th record. Appropriately, MARSHALL FLIPPO records the vocal for 'BLUE BLUE DAY' on Blue Star 2501."[1]

As I researched, I saw the power of promotion the two magazines had in the square dance world. I also saw how popular Flippo's songs were, so I wanted to share them with you.

The list below shows the title, the album (if identified), which square dance magazine listed and reviewed it, and the date(s) listed and/or reviewed.

KEY
*** – Song without reviews or comments in either magazine.
SA – Review found in Flippo's scrapbook/album but not dated

Blue Star Record Label[2]

1. A Donut and A Dream. *Sets in Order*, July – September 1973; *American Square Dance*, June and July 1973
2. A Hundred To One. *Sets in Order*, June – August 1977; *American Square Dance,* May – August 1977

3. Alabama Bound. (*Fun Level Square Dances Album*) (*50 Basics Album*).
4. Alabama Jubilee. ***
5. All by Myself. *Sets in Order,* April and May 1965; *American Squares,* March 1965, May 1965

6. All I Ever Need Is You. (*Marshall Flippo Calls in Stereo Album*). *Sets in Order,* March and April 1972; *American Square Dance,* February – May 1972
7. All I Ever Need Is You. *Sets in Order,* June and July 1979, August – October 1979; *American Square Dance,* July 1979, August 1979, September 1979
8. Anytime. *Sets in Order,* June, August, September, and November 1982, April and May 1983; *American Square Dance,* July, August, September, and October 1982
9. Arizona Double Star (*Flippo Flips Album*). *Sets in Order,* June 1961
10. At Two To Two Today. *Sets in Order,* March – June 1982, April and May 1983; *American Square Dance,* March – June 1982
11. Back on My Mind Again. *Sets in Order,* April and May 1979; *American Square Dance,* April 1979
12. Be Nobody's Darling But Mine. *Sets in Order,* July and August 1980, October 1980,
13. Beautiful Lady. *Sets in Order,* December 1982, February – May 1983; *American Square Dance,* November and December 1982, January 1983
14. Because I Love You. *Sets in Order*, May and June 1971; *The New Square Dance*, April – June 1971
15. Blue Blue Day (1000th Recording for Blue Star). *American Square Dance,* March 2005
16. Blue Eyes Don't Make an Angel. *Sets in Order,* April – June 1984; *American Square Dance,* March – June 1984
17. Blue Is the Color. *Sets in Order,* September – December 1978; *American Square Dance*, September – November 1978
18. Blue Moon of Kentucky. *Sets in Order,* March and May 1964; *American Squares,* March – May 1964; *American Square Dance,* September 1973
19. Blue Side of Lonesome. *Sets in Order,* September and October 1967
20. Blue Sioux City Five. *Sets in Order,* July 1963; *American Squares,* June 1963
21. Break My Mind. *Sets in Order*, June and July 1979, August – October 1979; *American Square Dance,* July – September 1979
22. Bright and Shiny. *Sets in Order,* August and September 1963; *American Squares,* July and August 1963
23. Bundle of Love (*Flippo Flips Album*). *Sets in Order,* January and February 1969; *The New Square Dance*, November 1968
24. Bundle of Southern Sunshine. *Sets in Order,* June and June 1961; *American Squares,* June and July 1959
25. Call Me Baby. *Sets in Order,* May and 1962; *American Squares,* May and June 1962

26. Call Me Up When You've Got Nothing to Do. *Sets in Order,* February 1961; *American Squares,* February 1961
27. Cielito Lindo. *Sets in Order,* March 1959, June – October 1969; *American Squares,* April 1959
28. Coward of The County. *Sets in Order,* April – June 1980; *American Square Dance*, April – June 1980
29. Crying My Heart Out Over You. *Sets in Order,* January and March 1974, October and November 1982, April and May 1983; *American Square Dance*, October and November 1982
30. Crying on My Shoulder. *American Square Dance,* January – March 1974
31. Dancing in The Street. *Sets in Order,* November and December 1965, September and October 1975; *American Squares,* October 1965; *Square Dance,* January 1966; *American Square Dance*, August – October 1975
32. Dime A Dozen. *Sets in Order,* September 1963; *American Squares,* August 1963
33. Diminishing Star (*Flippo Flips Album*). *Sets in Order*, June 1961
34. Dixie Bell. *Sets in Order,* May and June 1971; *The New Square Dance,* May and June 1971
35. Don't Be a Baby-Baby (*Marshall Flippo Calling New Dances and Old Favorites Album*). *Sets in Order,* March 1962; *American Squares,* February 1962
36. Don't Let the Good Life Pass You By (*Marshall Flippo Calls in Stereo Album*). ***
37. Dream Train. *Sets in Order,* June and August 1964; *American Squares,* June 1964
38. Every Street's A Boulevard (*Marshall Flippo Calls in Stereo Album*). *Sets in Order,* February 1972; *The New Square Dance,* December 1971; *American Square Dance,* January 1972
39. Fairweather Sweetheart. *Sets in Order,* July 1966; *Square Dance*, June 1966
40. Fence in the Moon (*Fun Level Square Dances Album*). ***
41. First Thing Every Morning (*Souvenir Record Album*). ***
42. Flippo's Honey Mixer/ Flip side, Cecelia. *Sets in Order*, November and December 1970, January 1971, December 1982, February 1983; *The New Square Dance,* November and December 1970; *American Square Dance,* December 1982
43. Foolin'. *Sets in Order,* December 1959, January 1960; *American Squares,* December 1959, January and February 1960
44. Fortuosity (*Marshall Flippo Calls in Stereo Albums*). ***
45. Gentle on My Mind (*50 Basics Album*). ***
46. Get It Right. *Sets in Order,* August – October 1981, April and May 1983; *American Square Dance*, August, September, and November 1981
47. Give Me Back My Heart. *Sets in Order,* January – March 1971; *The New Square Dance,* January – April 1972
48. Going Down That Lost Lonesome Highway (*Fifty Basic Album*). ***
49. Gonna Swing That Gal Tonight. *Sets in Order,* February – June 1969

50. Good Morning. *Sets in Order,* July – November 1970; *The New Square Dance,* May – September 1970
51. Hangin' Around. *Sets in Order,* March – June 1983; *American Square Dance,* March – May 1983
52. Happy *(Flippo Flips Album). American Squares,* June 1961
53. Happy Heart *(Marshall Flippo Calls in Stereo Album).* ***
54. Happy Pair. *Sets in Order,* June 1961
55. Heart Full of Love. *Sets in Order,* March 1959; *American Squares,* March 1959
56. Heart Full of Love. *Sets in Order,* January and February 1979
57. Heart of My Heart. *Sets in Order,* September – December 1981, April and May 1983; *American Square Dance,* October and November 1981
58. Hello Dolly. *Sets in Order,* May – July 1964; *American Squares,* June 1964
59. Hometown Sweetheart. *Sets in Order,* June and October 1970; *The New Square Dance,* June and September 1970
60. Hooked on Cowboy Clothes and Country Music. *Sets in Order,* January – May 1983; *American Square Dance,* February 1983
61. How I'd Like to See You Again. *Sets in Order,* June – August 1978, October 1978; *American Square Dance,* June – August 1978
62. I Can't Quit *(Marshall Flippo Calling New Dances and Old Favorites Album). Sets in Order,* March – May 1962; *American Squares,* March 1962
63. I Get the Blues When It Rains. *Sets in Order,* December 1966, January 1967; *Square Dance,* November 1966, January 1967
64. I Love You Most of All. *Sets in Order,* April – June 1980; *American Square Dance,* April – June 1980
65. I Saw Your Face in The Moon. *Sets in Order,* April and May 1976; *American Square Dance,* April – June 1976
66. I Still Love You. *Sets in Order,* July – September 1984; *American Square Dance,* July and August 1984
67. I Was Just Walking Out the Door. *Sets in Order,* May 1967
68. I Wonder Whose Baby You Are Now. *Sets in Order,* April – July 1976; *American Square Dance,* May and June 1976
69. I Wonder Why *(Marshall Flippo Calling New Dances and Old Favorites Album). Sets in Order,* April – June 1960; American Squares, April and May 1960
70. I'll Have Somebody Else. *Sets in Order,* April 1978; *American Square Dance,* April and June 1978
71. I'm A Swinger. *Sets in Order,* April – August 1968
72. I'm Sorry If My Love Got In Your Way. *Sets in Order,* May – August 1975; *American Square Dance,* April – July 1975
73. I've Got a Song To Sing. *Sets in Order,* July and August 1972; *American Square Dance* – June and July 1972
74. If the World Keeps on Turning *(Marshall Flippo Calling New Dances and Old Favorites Album). Sets in Order,* September and December 1959; *American Squares,* October 1959
75. In Fort Worth, Dallas or Houston. *Sets in Order,* September, October,

and December 1971; *The New Square Dance,* September, October 1971,
and November 1971

76. In Your Heart. *Sets in Order,* June – August 1968, January 1969

77. It Do Feel Good. *Sets in Order,* October – December 1975; *American
Square Dance,* October – December 1975

78. It's A Sin To Tell a Lie. *Sets in Order,* December 1974; *American Square
Dance,* September – December 1974, January 1975

79. James. *Sets in Order,* May and June 1963; *American Squares,* April and
May 1963

80. Johnny Jingo. *Sets in Order,* June and July 1962; *American Squares,* June and
July 1962

81. Kingston Town (*Fun Level Square Dances Album*) (*50 Basics Album*). ***

82. Linger Awhile (*Fun Level Square Dances Album*). ***

83. Long Rocky Road. *Sets in Order*, January, March, and April 1970; *The
New Square Dance,* April 1970

84. Louisiana Swing. *Sets in Order,* May – October 1970; *The New Square
Dance,* May 1970

85. Love Bug Itch. *Sets in Order,* May – August 1974; *American Square Dance,*
May and July 1974

86. Love Put a Song In My Heart. *American Square Dance,* April – June 1976

87. Marshall Flippo Calls the First Nighter. *American Square Dance*, August
and September 1974

88. Marshall Flippo Sings Em and Swings Em In Stereo. *Square Dancing,*
January 1970

89. Melancholy Baby. *Sets in Order,* May 1978; *American Square Dance,*
April 1978

90. Million Dollar Smile (*Flippo Flips Album*). *Sets in Order,* May and June
1961; *American Squares,* May and June 1961

91. Monte Carlo Or Bust (*Marshall Flippo Calls in Stereo Album*). *Sets in Order,*
April – June 1972; *American Square Dances,* March – June 1972

92. Morning of My Mind (*Marshall Flippo Calls in Stereo Album*). ***

93. Mountain Star (*Fun Level Square Dances Album*). ***

94. My Ideal. *Sets in Order,* February and April 1963; *American Squares,*
February and March 1963

95. Nobody's Darling but Mine. *Sets in Order,* July and September 1980;
American Square Dances, July – September 1980

96. No One Will Ever Know. *Sets in Order,* September, October, and
December 1984; *American Square Dances,* September – November 1984

97. Norman (*Marshall Flippo Calling New Dances and Old Favorites Album*). *Sets
in Order,* March 1962; *American Squares,* February and March 1962

98. Nothing to Do With You. SA

99. Old Phonograph Records. *Sets in Order,* June – September 1967; *Square
Dance,* July 1967

100. Old Side of Town. *Sets in Order,* July and August 1980; *American Square
Dances,* July and August 1980

101. Once a Day (*Marshall Flippo Calls in Stereo Album*). ***

102. One Beside You (*Marshall Flippo Calling New Dances and Old Favorites Album*). ***
103. Out Behind the Barn. *Sets in Order,* December 1981, January and February 1982, April and May 1983; *American Square Dance,* December 1981, January and February 1982
104. Paradise Called Tennessee. *Sets in Order,* April and June 1984; *American Square Dance,* April and May 1984
105. Partner That Nobody Chose. *Sets in Order,* March – June 1982, April and May 1983; *American Square Dance,* April – June 1982
106. Pass Thru and Around One (*Fun Level Square Dances Album*). ***
107. Philadelphia, U. S. A. *Sets in Order,* July 1959; *American Squares,* August and September 1959
108. Pretty Blue Eyes. *Sets in Order,* July – September 1980; *American Square Dance,* July – September 1980
109. Put on Your Dancing Shoes. *Sets in Order,* December 1981, January and February 1982, April and May 1983; *American Square Dance,* December 1981, January and February 1982
110. Quicksilver (*Flippo Flips Album*). *Sets in Order,* May 1961; *American Squares,* May and June 1961
111. Rainbow Girl. *Sets in Order,* May – October 1970; *The New Square Dance,* May 1970
112. Rainbows Are Back in Style. *Sets in Order*, June and July 1968, January and February 1969
113. Rich Livin' Woman (*Marshall Flippo Calls in Stereo Album*). *Sets in Order,* August 1965; *American Squares,* July and August 1965
114. Ring and a Star (*Fun Level Square Dances Album*). ***
115. Rose of San Antonio. *Sets in Order,* January 1969, August and September 1977; *American Square Dance,* June – September 1977
116. Rotten Little Song. *Sets in Order,* July – September 1975; *American Square Dance,* July – September 1975
117. Round and Round. *Sets in Order,* May – July 1962; *American Squares*, May and June 1962
118. Sally G. *Sets in Order*, October – December 1975; *American Square Dance,* October 1975
119. Say Something Sweet. *Sets in Order,* April and May 1965; *American Squares,* April and May 1965
120. Sheboygan. *American Squares,* February 1962
121. Smile, Darn You Smile. *Sets in Order,* June 1962; *American Squares,* June and July 1962
122. So This Is Love. *Sets in Order,* June – September 1971; *The New Square Dance,* June – August 1971
123. Somebody Else's Date (*Square Dance Calls with Marshall Flippo*). *Sets in Order,* September, October, and December 1960; *American Squares,* May, September, and November 1960, April – June 1975; *American Square Dance,* February – June 1975
124. Somebody Stole My Gal. *The New Square Dance*, October 1971

125. Somebody's Knocking. *Sets in Order*, May – July 1981; *American Square Dance,* May – July 1981
126. Something Nice About You. *Sets in Order,* June 1977; *American Square Dance*, May 1977
127. South Pacific Shore (*Flippo Flips Album*). *Sets in Order*, May and June 1961; *American Squares*, May and June 1961
128. Southern Rain. *Sets in Order*, March – June 1981; *American Square Dance*, April – June 1981
129. Square Thru Dixie (*Flippo Flips Album*). *Sets in Order*, June 1961
130. Star Right, Star Bright (*Marshall Flippo Calling New Dances and Old Favorites Album*)***
131. Summer Vacation. *Sets in Order,* January – March 1984; *American Square Dance*, January – April 1984
132. Swing Her Easy, She Belongs to Me. *Sets in Order,* January 1961; *American Squares,* January 1961
133. Swing That Girl Tonight. *Sets in Order*, March 1969
134. Swing That Maid. *Sets in Order,* June 1963; *American Squares,* May and June 1963
135. Swing Your Baby Now. *Sets in Order,* January and February 1961; *American Squares,* January and February 1961
136. Swinging with You (*Square Dance Calls with Marshall Flippo*). *Sets in Order,* September and October 1960; *American Squares,* May and September 1960
137. Summer Sounds (*50 Basics Album*). ***
138. Take Me Along. *Sets in Order,* April – June 1960
139. Tearing Up the Country. *Sets in Order,* July and September 1973; *American Square Dance,* September 1973
140. Tell Maude I Slipped. *Sets in Order,* August and October 1968, February 1969; *The New Square Dance,* October 1968
141. Texarkana Baby. *Sets in Order*, January and February 1967; *Square Dance,* March 1967
142. That's Where My Baby Used to Be. *Sets in Order*, December 1967, January – March 1968, April and May 1968
143. The Auctioneer (Original). *Sets in Order*, November 1958; *American Squares,* November 1958
144. The Auctioneer. *Sets in Order*, February – May 1968, July and August 1968; *American Squares,* May 2002
145. The Caper. *Sets in Order,* July – September 1962; *American Squares,* July and August 1962
146. The Name of The Game. *Sets in Order,* June and July 1969, September – November 1969; *The New Square Dance,* July 1969; *American Square Dance*, September 1973, September 1976
147. There's Not a Star In Texas. *Sets in Order,* December 1977, January – March 1978; *American Square Dance,* November and December 1977, January – March 1978
148. Things. *Sets in Order,* November 1969, February 1970, September –

December 1984; *Square Dancing*, December 1969, January 1970; *The New Square Dance,* December 1969; *American Square Dance,* September – November 1984

149. To Think You've Chosen Me. *Sets in Order,* December 1969, January and March 1970; *The New Square Dance,* January 1970

150. Today's Tear Drops. *Sets in Order,* September, October, and December 1967, January and February 1968

151. Tootle Dee Doodle Dee Doo. *Sets in Order,* July – December 1969; *The New Square Dance,* September 1969

152. Trail of the Lonesome Pine (*Fun Level Square Dances Album*). ***

153. Traveling Minstrel Man (*Marshall Flippo Calls in Stereo Album*). *Sets in Order,* June, July, and September 1971; *The New Square Dance,* June - August 1971; *American Square Dance,* January 1973

154. Truly Fair. *Sets in Order,* January – March 1966; *Square Dance,* January – March 1966

155. Under The "X" In Texas. *Sets in Order,* January – May 1977; *American Square Dance,* November and December 1976, January – April 1977

156. Vacation. *Sets in Order,* December 1963, January 1964; *American Squares,* December 1963, January 1964

157. Wake Me Up Early in The Morning. *Sets in Order,* December 1972, January – March 1973; *American Square Dance,* December 1972, January 1973

158. Walk Right Back (*Flippo Flips Album*). *Sets in Order,* May 1961; *American Squares,* May 1961; *The New Square Dance,* March 1971

159. Walkin' and Talkin'. *Sets in Order,* July 1960, December 1974, January – March 1975; *American Square Dance,* December 1974, July and August 1960, January – March 1975

160. Walk Don't Run (Flippo Flips). *Sets in Order,* June 1961; *American Squares,* June 1961

161. We Should Be Together (Flippo's 100th Release). *Sets in Order,* July – October 1976; *American Square Dance,* July – October 1976

162. West Virginia Memories. *Sets in Order,* March – June 1983; *American Square Dance,* March – May 1983

163. When My Blue Moon Turns to Gold. *Sets in Order,* March – May 1967

164. When the Whippoorwill Sings. *Sets in Order,* April – June 1965; *American Squares,* April and May 1965

165. Who Can? (*Marshall Flippo Calling New Dances and Old Favorites Album*). ***

166. Wonderful Feeling (*Fun Level Square Dances Album*). ***

167. You Call Everybody Darling. *Sets in Order,* March – May 1966, September and October 1977; *Square Dance,* April – July 1966; *American Square Dance,* August – November 1977

168. You Can't Take It with You. *Sets in Order,* October, 1965; *American Squares,* September and October 1965

169. Your Love Put a Song in My Heart. *Sets in Order,* April and May 1976

170. Marshall Flippo Lets His Hair Down on Blue Star. *Sets in Order,* June and November 1966, January and February 1967, December 1967
171. Smooth and Easy Danceable Squares by Marshall Flippo. *Sets in Order,* October and November 1967

Dance Ranch Record Label (The Old Merrbach Masters Updated)

1. Auctioneer Grande. *American Square Dance,* June 2006

2. Beautiful Lady. *American Square Dance*, December 1993, January 1994
3. Blue Eyes Don't Make an Angel / Cindy Lou. *American Square Dance,* April 2006
4. I Never Knew / Cutie's Due at Two To Two Today. ***
5. Spending My Summer Vacation / Classic Pretty Lady. *American Square Dance*, October 2007
6. Dance Ranch Round-Up 81 with Flippo/Belt/Fisk. *American Square Dance,* October 2002

Bob Cat Record Label

1. Mention My Name. ***

Chaparral Record Label

1. A Love That Just Won't Die. *American Square Dance,* December 1992, June – September 1993
2. Another Square Dance Caller. *American Square Dance,* February – September 1990
3. Believe Me. *American Square Dance,* July 2001
4. Fond Affection. *American Square Dance*, November – December 1989, January 1990

5. Friend in California. *American Square Dance,* June – August 1995
6. Green Green. *American Square Dance,* May – September 1992, December 1992, January 1993, March – May 1993, November and December 2001
7. I Can't Give You Anything but Love. *American Square Dance,* February – April 1992
8. If You're Gonna Play In Texas. *Sets in Order*, November and December 1984, January – December 1985; *American Square Dance,* October – December 1984, January – December 1985

9. Loose Talk. *American Square Dance,* June – August 1995
10. Major Breakdown. *American Square Dance,* January – June 1988
11. Mrs. Right. *American Square Dance,* November and December 1993, January – October 1994, December 1994, January – May 1995
12. Oklahoma Hills. *American Square Dance,* August and September 1993, November and December 1993, January – April 1994
13. One Thin Dime. *American Square Dance,* July – December 1987
14. Oo-Wee Baby. *American Square Dance,* June – November 1990, February and March 1991, June – December 1991, May 1992
15. Please Don't Talk About Me When I'm Gone. *American Square Dance,* January – September 1986, March and April 2003
16. Roadrunner Romp. *American Square Dance,* November 2001
17. Sea Sick Susie (*Marshall Flippo Calling New Dances and Old Favorites Album*). ***
18. Shine. *American Square Dance,* November and December 1988, January – October 1989
19. Somebody Special. *American Square Dance,* January and February 1992
20. Sunday Morning. *American Square Dance,* March and April 2003
21. Time. *American Square Dance,* January – October 1988
22. We've Got The Memories (with Gary Shoemake and Scott Smith). *American Square Dance,* September – December 1990, January – March 1991, June – December 1991
23. Welcome To (Lake Of The Ozarks). *Sets in Order*, November and December 1984, January 1985; *American Square Dance*, October – December 1984
24. Why Are You Pickin' On Me. *American Square Dance*, October – December 1986, January – June 1987

Desert Gold Record Label

1. Right or Wrong. *American Square Dance*, December 2003, July 2006

E-Z School Record Label

1. Texas Star. ***

ESP Record Label

1. Let A Smile Be Your Umbrella.
   American Square Dance, May –
   December 2001
2. MTA. ***
3. Old Fashioned Love. *American Square
   Dance*, October 2003
4. Traveling Minstrel Man. *American
   Square Dance*, February 2008

Source: https://www.ceder.net/
callerdb/viewsingle.php?
RecordId=927

Four Squares Record Label

1. Buffalo Gal. *American Square Dance*,
   December 1987, February 1988, April
   1988, June 1988, August 1988,
   October 1988

Rhythm Records Record Label[3]

1. As She's Walking Away. ***
2. Muddy Water. *American Square Dance,*
   July and August 2009, November
   2009
3. One In A Million. *Sets in Order,* May
   1983; *American Square Dance*,
   June 1983
4. Turn Me Loose and Let Me Sing. ***
5. When It's Christmas Time in Texas.
   ***
6. Wrong Road Again. *American Square Dance,* August 2004

Source: https://www.ceder.net/
callerdb/viewsingle.php?
RecordId=927

Source: https://www.ceder.net/
callerdb/viewsingle.php?
RecordId=927

Riverboat Record Label

1. Howling' At the Moon. *American
   Square Dance*, March 2008

Source: https://www.ceder.net/
callerdb/viewsingle.php?
RecordId=927

Source: https://www.ceder.net/callerdb/viewsingle.php?RecordId=927

Royal Record Label

1. Blue Virginia Blues. ***
2. Dance Time In Texas. *American Square Dance,* December 2000
3. 2010 "Square Dance Music" (with Patty Greene, Tony Oxendine, Justin Russell, Johnny Preston, Hunter Keller, Randy Dougherty, Jerry Story. Special Guests • Dick Rueter • Marshall Flippo). *American Square Dance*, December 2009, January 2010

Square Dancetime Record Label

Source: https://www.ceder.net/ callerdb/viewsingle.php? RecordId=927

1. Diamond Oo Wee Baby (The DIAMOND PROGRAM is designed for use in school classes and in EASY SQUARE DANCE PROGRAMS. Music Courtesy of Chaparral Records). *American Square Dance,* March – December 1992, February and March 1993, May – July 1993, November and December 1993, January 1994

Square Tunes Record Label

Source: https://www.ceder.net/ callerdb/viewsingle.php? RecordId=927

1. Someday Soon. *American Square Dance*, March 2009
2. Someday Soon. ***

Sets in Order **Record Label Albums**

1. **Luck 13 Jamboree Souvenir LP Album** — Thanks to all of these callers, Marshall Flippo, Ed Gilmore, Lee Helsel, Jack Jackson, Earl Johnston, Arnie Kronenberger, Frank Lane, Johnny LeClair, Joe Lewis, Bob Page, Bob Ruff, and Bob Van Antwerp, who contributed their time and calling ability, and Bob and Becky Osgood, MC. And thanks to the Balance, Blue Star, Grenn, J Bar L, MacGregor and *Sets in Order*

recording companies, this unusual collection has become an actuality. NOT FOR SALE. FREE WITH NEW SUBSCRIPTION. *Sets in Order,* August and September 1964

2. **The Official Magazine of Square Dancing Presents 1967** — Al Brundage, Marshall Flippo, Ed Gilmore, Bruce Johnson, Earl Johnston, Arnie Kronenberger, Frank Lane, Johnny LeClair, Joe Lewis, Bob Page, Dave Taylor, Bob Van Antwerp, and Bob Osgood, MC.

3. **The Official Magazine of Square Dancing Presents 1969** — Marshall Flippo, Lee Helsel, Bruce Johnson, Earl Johnston, Arnie Kronenberger, Frank Lane, Bob Page, Bob Van Antwerp, and Bob Osgood, MC.

4. **American Square Dance Society 1970 "Red"** — Al Brundage, Bill Ball, Marshall Flippo, Earl Johnston, Johnny LeClair, Bob Page, Wally Schultz, and Dave Taylor.

5. **American Square Dance Society presents 1971** — Marshall Flippo, Ed Gilmore, Lee Helsel, Earl Johnston, Arnie Kronenberger, Jack Livingston, Beryl Main, and Dave Taylor.

6. **American Square Dance Society presents 1972** — "Avocado" Basic Program of American Square Dancing (Basics 1-50). Don Armstrong, Bob Dawson, Marshall Flippo, Melton Luttrell, Jim Mayo, Earle Park, Wally Schultz, Bob Van Antwerp

7. **American Square Dance Society presents 1974 Sound "Documentaries"** — "Orange" Extended Basics Program of American Square Dancing (Basics 1-75). Johnny Davis, Marshall Flippo, Earl Johnston, Lee Kopman, Beryl Main, Gaylon Shull, Dave Taylor, Don Williamson

8. **American Square Dance Society presents 1975** — Johnny Davis, Marshall Flippo (Skillet Lickin'), Earl Johnston, Lee Kopman, Beryl Main, Gaylon Shull, Dave Taylor, Don Williamson, and Bob Osgood, MC.

9. **American Square Dance Society presents 1978** — Don Beck, Frank Bedell, Wade Driver, Bob Fisk, Marshall Flippo (Darkness), Cal Golden, Lee Kopman, Jim Lee

10. **American Square Dance Society presents 1983** — Marshall Flippo (Cindy), Jerry Helt, Dave Taylor, Frank Lane, Jim Mayo, Mac Letson, Stan Burdick, Dick Leger, and Bob Osgood, MC

11. **American Square Dance Society 3 Sound "Documentaries"** — "Purple" 11 Experimental Movements of American Square Dancing. Marshall Flippo, Ed Gilmore, Lee Helsel, Earl Johnston, Arnie Kronenberger, Jack Livingston, Beryl Main, Dave Taylor

12. **American Square Dance Society presents 1984 Premium Records** (4 Albums) — Bob Van Antwerp (The Basic Program), Mike Seastrom (The Plus Program), Marshall Flippo (The Mainstream Program), Bronc Wise (The A-One Program)

Blue Star Long Play Albums

1. **Flippo Flips** — (Walk Right Back, Diminishing Star, Bundle of Southern Sunshine, Hash, South Pacific Shore, Square Thru Dixie, Million Dollar Smile, Sides Cut in Varied, Quicksilver, Arizona Double Star). *Sets in Order*, June 1962, September and October 1965, September – December 1968; *American Squares*, June 1961, January 1964
2. **New and Old Favorites**. *Sets in Order*, June 1962
3. **Marshall Flippo**. *Sets in Order*, September and October 1965
4. **Fun Level Square Dances** — (Ring and a Star, Trail of the Lonesome Pine, Pass Thru and Around Two, Linger Awhile, Pass Thru and Around One, Fence in the Moon, Mountain Star, Alabama Jubilee, Wonderful Feeling, Kingston Town). *Sets in Order*, June 1962, September and October 1965, September 1968, November and December 1968; *American Squares,* May – August 1962, January 1964, August 1964
5. **Great Flippo Calls**. *Sets in Order,* September and October 1965
6. **Everybody Dances When Flippo Calls**. *Sets in Order,* September and October 1965, September – December 1968; *American Squares,* August 1963, January 1964
7. **Beginner Dances**. *Sets in Order,* September and October 1965, September – December 1968; *American Squares,* July 1964
8. **Marshall Flippo Calling New Dances and Old Favorites** — (I Can't Quit, Who Can?, Don't Be A Baby, Baby, Dixie Styles, I Wonder Why, One Beside You, Norman, Star Right, Star Bright, If the World Keeps on Turning, Sea Sick Susie). *Sets in Order*, September – December 1968; *American Squares*, March and April 1962
9. **The Best Collection of New Squares Yet**. *Sets in Order,* August 1964, September and October 1965, September 1968, November and December 1968
10. **More Dances for Fun Level Dancing** — (First Thing Every Morning, The Auctioneer). *Sets in Order,* August 1964
11. **Marshall Flippo Calls Square Dances to Double Your Dancing Pleasure**. *Sets in Order,* September and October 1968
12. **Smooth Dancing**. *Sets in Order,* September – December 1968
13. **Smooth and Easy Squares**. *Sets in Order,* September – December 1968
14. **Marshall Flippo Calls in Stereo** — (Rich Livin' Woman, Every Street's A Boulevard, All I Ever Need Is You, Monte Carlo or Bust, Morning of my Mind, Traveling Minstrel Man, Don't Let the Good Life Pass You By, Happy Heart, Once A Day, Fortuosity). *The New Square Dance,* December 1971; *American Square Dance*, January 1972, April – December 1972, January 1973, March – December 1973, January – August 1974
15. **Flippo Calls A Terrific Dance**. *American Squares*, January 1964
16. **Marshall Flippo Sings Em and Swings Em**. *Sets in Order,* August 1969, September – November 1969

17. **12 Dances Called by Marshall Flippo**. *Sets in Order,* October –
    December 1971, January and February 1972
18. **Marshall Flippo Calling the Kirkwood**. *Sets in Order*, April –
    December 1972, January – December 1973, January – September 1974;
    American Square Dance, April – December 1972, January – April 1973
19. **Marshall Flippo Calls**. *Sets in Order*, April – December 1972, January
    1973; *American Square Dance,* April 1972
20. **Marshall Flippo Calling the 75 Basics Plus 7 Extra Basics** (Two
    different records) — *Sets in Order*. September, October, and November
    1974, February – November 1978, April – September 1979 (Most Popular
    LP Albums), October 1979 – June 1980 (Most Popular Albums), July –
    September 1980 (Most Popular Blue Star Albums), October – December
    1980 (Blue Star Albums and/or Cassettes), January – November 1981 (LP
    Albums), January – September 1982 (LP Albums), January – September
    1983 (LP Albums); *American Square Dance,* October and November 1974,
    March – November 1978, July – December 1979 (Most Popular LP
    Albums), January – September 1980 (Most Popular LP Albums),
    February – April 1981 (Most Popular LP Albums), May – November 1981
    (Most Popular Blue Star Albums), January – September 1982 (LP
    Albums), February 1983 (LP Albums), March 1983 (LP Albums), April
    1983 (LP Albums), May 1983 (LP Albums), June 1983 (LP Albums), July
    1983 (LP Albums), August 1983 (LP Albums), September 1983 (LP
    Albums), January 1984 (LP Albums & Cassettes), February 1984 (LP
    Albums & Cassettes)
21. **Marshall Flippo Calling the Mainstream Plus Basics**. *Sets in
    Order,* August 1976 – December 1976, January – May 1977, February –
    December 1978, April – December 1979 (Most Popular Albums), January
    – June 1980 (Most Popular Albums), July – September 1980 (Most
    Popular Blue Star Albums), October – December 1980 (Blue Star
    Albums and/or Cassettes), January – November 1981 (LP Albums),
    January – August 1982 (LP Albums), January – June 1983 (LP Albums);
    American Square Dance. October – December 1976, January – August
    1977, March – November 1978, July – December 1979 (Most Popular LP
    Albums), January – October 1980 (Most Popular LP Albums). **TWO
    DIFFERENT ALBUMS:** October – December 1980 (Most Popular
    LP Albums), January 1981 (Most Popular LP Albums). **ONE ALBUM:**
    February – April 1981 (Most Popular LP Albums), May – November 1981
    (Most Popular Blue Star Albums), January – September 1982 (LP
    Albums), February – September 1983 (LP Albums)
22. **Marshall Flippo Calling 10 Singing Calls**, accompanied by The
    Merelene Singers (includes Marshall's 100th release on Blue Star). *Sets in
    Order*, August – December 1976, January – May 1977, February –
    December 1978, April and May 1979 (Most Popular LP Albums), July
    and August 1979 (Most Popular LP Albums), September – December
    1979 (Most Popular Albums), January – June 1980 (Most Popular
    Albums), July – September 1980 (Most Popular Blue Star Albums),

October – December 1980 (Blue Star Albums and/or Cassettes), January – April 1981 (LP Albums); *American Square Dance*. October – December 1976, January – August 1977, March – September 1978, November 1978, July – December 1979 (Most Popular LP Albums), January – December 1980 (Most Popular LP Albums), January 1981 – April 1981 (Most Popular LP Albums)

23. **Flippo Calls the 50 Basics** — (Patter, Going Down That Lost Lonesome Highway, Patter, Gentle on My Mind, Patter, Kingston Town, Patter, Summer Sounds, Patter, Alabama Bound). *Sets in Order,* February – December 1978, April – December 1979 (Most Popular Albums), January – June 1980 (Most Popular Albums), July – September 1980 (Most Popular Blue Star Albums), October – December 1980 (Blue Star Albums and/or Cassettes), January – November 1981 (LP Albums), January – September 1982 (LP Albums), February – September 1983 (LP Albums); *The New Square Dance*, October and November 1971; *American Square Dance,* January – December 1973, January – July 1974, October and November 1974, March – November 1978, July – December 1979 (Most Popular LP Albums), January – December 1980 (Most Popular LP Albums), January – April 1981 (Most Popular LP Albums), May – November 1981 (Most Popular Blue Star Albums), January – September 1982 (LP Albums), February – September 1983 (LP Albums), January and February 1984 (LP Albums & Cassettes)

24. **The Great Flippo Calls a Bunch of Dances** — *American Squares,* August 1963

25. **The Best Collection of New Squares** — *American Squares*, August 1964

Marshall Flippo's Hilton Record Player. Source: John Flippo

1. Buddy Weaver, "Blue Star Redefining Square Dance Music," December 13, 2019, http://www.buddyweavermusic.com/bluestar.php
2. Blue Star Record Label's Web Site: http://www.buddyweavermusic.com/bluestar.php
3. Rhythm Records Record Label Web Site: http://www.rhythmrecords.biz/

APPENDIX G – LIST OF CALLERS WHO ATTENDED FLIPPO'S LAST NIGHT, DECEMBER 31, 2017

National Callers:

- Ken and Dee Bower, Palm Desert, California
- Bob Lottie & Dee Dee Dougherty-Lottie, Mesa/Casa Grande, Sun City, and Florence, Arizona
- Wade and Healy Driver, Spring, Texas
- Patty Greene, Monroe, North Carolina
- Jerry Junck, Mesa, Arizona
- Vic and Shauna Kaaria, Redlands, California
- Larry Letson, Lafayette, Indiana
- Tony and Kim Oxendine, Sumter, South Carolina
- Mike and Lisa Seastrom, Thousand Oaks, California
- Mike Sikorsky, Apache Junction, Arizona
- Gary Shoemake, Sevierville, Tennessee

Local Callers:

- Glenn Condit, Tucson
- Tom and Gina Crisp, Sonoran Stables, Tucson
- Rick Gittelman and Patty, Tucson
- Don Haney and Sandy, Voyager RV Resort, Tucson
- Wendy Krueger, British Columbia, Canada
- Juanita Portz, Sierra Vista
- Janet Shannon, Tempe
- Mike Smithers, Sierra Vista
- Harue and Bryan Swift, Sierra Vista
- Bill Reinders, Green Valley

APPENDIX H - FESTUS ARTICLE & LETTER

Nice try, Albuquerque: Tried to sneak Flippo through and keep him to yourself. It was pure accident I spotted the little sign on the east bulletin board announcing Marshall Flippo was coming. Now there was a name I had heard of. *News Notes* mentioned him last year, describing a dance he called and saying how terrific he was. I had also heard many callers and dancers brag about the greatness of one Marshall Flippo. I figured if guys who were not famous (legends in the Albuquerque area like Buddy Jones, Louie Martinez, Jimmie Carter) could be so doggone good, this fellow must be a ring-tailed ding dong doozey and vowed to make the dance. Monday or not, secret or not.

Six of us closed our stores three hours early, jumped into our cars and drove for the Duke City [from the Gallup, New Mexico area]. We arrived in time to grab a quick bite at the 76 Truck Stop and change into dancing clothes. (I am not sure some of those truck drivers had ever seen a real live square dancer before). Sometimes it is hard to tell if people are genuinely showing their appreciation or making sport. Anyhow, we received a standing ovation and signed quite a few autographs.

I can't believe how poorly folks kept the secret. The ASDC [Albuquerque Square Dance Center] had more people than a New York subway at rush hour. I asked where the great man was and someone pointed to two gentlemen talking to each other. In my mind I had pictured the marshal as being like that other famous marshal, Matt Dillion, of "Gunsmoke." Sure enough, there he towered in all his majesty: big, tall, good-looking. He was talking to an older, rather short fellow, who in comparison looked rather seedy. I decided the little man must be the marshal's sidekick, like Festus. This Festus looked like an ex-jockey turned racetrack tout, old enough to have ridden Man O' War or Seabiscuit. I went over to the big fellow and asked if he were the marshal. He must have thought me a rube because he gave the name of an ex-president of the U. S. (Jimmy Carter). Festus chuckled, joining the levity at my expense. I decided to leave and return when they were not in such a jocular mood.

I smiled with knowing confidence when Marshall Dillion walked up to the stage and picked up the microphone. They hadn't fooled me. But then he handed the microphone to Festus, and Marshall (Festus) Flippo called one of the best dances I ever heard. I would count myself among his legion of fans if he hadn't closed with this statement, "Keep her between the ditches and don't let anybody pass you." He didn't know my wife, the driver, takes everything a caller says literally, and does it with conviction. He probably didn't know there would be a convoy of dynamite trucks heading west that night whose frustrated drivers were not allowed to pass the little old lady wearing funny clothes in the Buick. It was the worst ride of my life!

By the Red Rock Rambler, Grant Wheatley

Grant's Letter to Neeca

POB 1336
Gallup, NM 87301-1336

24 June 1982

Dear Mrs. Flippo,

I would like to apologize to both you and Marshal for the "Festus" article. It was intended originally only for the eyes of those who live in Gallup and read the "Grand Mouth," our local newsletter. Then through an unfortunate series of events, it got the bit in its mouth and went for a stroll.

First it got sent to the "News Notes" because it was a slow month, and I thought it might brighten up our "Club News." But instead of leaving it in that section where only the most diehard readers would have discovered it, the editor featured it and even sent a copy to you. Then I heard from a couple colleagues of my wife Grace that they were taking it to Caller Lab to show Marshal. And finally, just when I was starting to feel the monster had run its course, some clown in Kentucky got ahold of it and sent it to Stan Burdick.

I have been beside myself with embarassment and shame. Here I am a fat little nobody from the smallest community in New Mexico (Cousins, NM --I have to drive 30 miles to Gallup for my mail) making sport of the most famous square dance caller in the world in a national magazine.

I would have apologized sooner, but did not know your address. The other night Jack Glynn mentioned he would be seeing Mr. Flippo at a Caller's College in Estes Park. I am going to ask him to deliver this note to you.

Thank you for the gracious note you sent the "News Notes" I am enclosing a copy of the "Grand Mouth" which mentions the article and also the latest for your amusement.

God Bless,

Grant

Grant's Letter to Neeca. Source: Neeca Flippo

APPENDIX I – GLOSSARY OF SQUARE DANCE & ROUND DANCE TERMS

Round Dance Terms

Cue — Tell the dancers what steps to do in a round dance.

Round Dance Cuer or Cuing Staff — Leader at the front of the ballroom [hall] who tells the dancers, as they dance, what steps to do.[1]

Rounds — A round dance song.

Round dancing — Couple dancing in a circle formation, using choreographed routines to a definite arrangement of music.[2]

❧

Record Size Terms

33 1/3 Records — A vinyl record format characterized by a speed of 33 1/3 rpm, a 12- or 10-inch (30- or 25-cm) diameter, and use of the "microgroove" groove specification. Introduced by Columbia in 1948, it was soon adopted as a new standard by the entire record industry.[3]

45 Records — The most common form of the vinyl single is the "45" or "7-inch." The names are derived from its play speed, 45 rpm, and the standard diameter, 7 inches.[4]

78 Records — An early type of shellac-based phonograph record that played at 78 revolutions per minute.[5]

Square Dance Terms

Advanced — The next CALLERLAB program of square dancing after the Plus Program. In addition to the Mainstream and Plus calls, Advanced dancers and callers are responsible for knowing an additional group of calls divided in A1 and A2 lists.

After Party — The party after the square dance with skits and a variety of entertainment usually put on by the event staff of callers and cuers. Sometimes dancers participated in skits, too.

Allemande Left — an Arm Turn by the left (plus a Step Thru as the dancers head toward their next dancer interaction).[6]

Basic — The beginning CALLERLAB program with fifty-one calls.

Barge Thru — Square through four and then pass through in the middle. Variations: *1/2 Barge Thru, 3/4 Barge Thru, Barge Thru.*

Beau — the left-side dancer (the Boy's normal position).[7]

Belle — the right-side dancer (the Girl's normal position).[8]

Bow to your partner, corners all — It is traditional at the beginning of a dance to honor your partner and corner by (men) bowing to your lady, and (ladies) curtsying to your man.[9]

Break — The middle break in a singing call is called a break. See singing call Definitions.

California Twirl — Dancers raise joined hands to form an arch and exchange places with each other by having the woman walk forward and under the arch along a tight left-turning semicircle. The man walks a slightly wider right-turning semicircle. Dancers have exchanged places, passing right shoulders, and are both facing in the opposite direction from which they started.[10]

Caller — A person who prompts dance figures in such dances as line dance, square dance, and contra dance.[11]

Caller School — A training time for new callers staffed with experienced callers.

Calls a Tip — see Tip.

Challenge — The CALLERLAB program after Advanced which has five levels, the most difficult level of square dancing ranging from C1 (easiest) to C2, C3A, C3B (also called just C3 or full C3) and C4 (most difficult).

Circle to the left, go around the hall — Dancers join hands with adjacent dancers to form a circle and move the circle in the indicated direction, or to the left if no direction was given.[12]

Corner — From a Squared Set of Normal Couples, each dancer's Partner is the adjacent dancer, and each dancer's Corner is the next dancer "around the nearest corner of the square" from them.[13]

Courtesy Turn — Left hands joined in front, the left-side dancer (the Beau) places his/her right hand behind the other dancer's back. The right-side dancer (the Belle) places her/his right hand in the small of his/her back to join the other dancer's right hand. As a couple turn to the left 1/2 way (Beau "pushing" the Belle) to face in.[14]

Crossfire — Plus — As the centers begin to Trade, the ends Cross Fold. Upon completing their Trade, the centers release hands and step straight forward forming an ocean wave or mini-wave with the dancers they are facing.[15]

Dip and Dive — Alternating arching (High) and ducking or diving (Low) down a line of alternately facing couples. Traditionally, an active couple leads to the right to circle half and then does a "Dip and Dive Six." They dive through the first couple, arch over the next, then do a California Twirl on the outside to dive and arch across to the starting point. Each couple, when they reach the outside, do a California Twirl to dip and dive back through to starting point.[16]

Dive Thru — One couple makes an arch by raising their joined hands, while the other couple ducks under the arch. Both move forward. The couple making the arch does a California Twirl.[17]

Do Paso — Left Arm Turn with partner until facing corner and release armhold. Right Arm Turn with corner until facing partner and release armhold. If there is no further instruction, Courtesy Turn partner to end facing the center of the set.[18]

Dosado — Walking a smooth circular path, dancers walk forward, passing right shoulders, slide sideways to the right, walk backward, passing left shoulders, and slide slightly to the left to return to their starting position.[19]

Dosido — What has come to be called Do Paso except that in the Texas Dosido the arm turns continued for an indeterminate period until the caller gave the next call. "Partner left and corner right and keep on going if it takes all night." [20]

Elbow Swing — like a right and left grand but you went all the way around each person.

Figure (Flippo's version: figer) — almost always causes each woman to progress to a new man. Once this has happened, she temporarily takes on the Head/Side identity and home position of that man.[21]

Flutterwheel — The right-side dancers leave their current partner and Right Arm Turn with each other a full turn, each ending where they started. Halfway through this motion, they take a couple handhold with the other dancer (i.e., the one they were originally facing directly), and the second half of the Arm Turn is completed with each new couple working as a unit. [22]

Flyer — (same as Square Dance Brochure) — Advertisement for Kirkwood's schedule and calling and cuing staff.

Grand March — An opening ceremony at a ball that consists of a march participated in by all the guests.[23]

Grand Ocean Wave — An Ocean Wave is an arrangement of three or more dancers in a line with adjacent hands joined (palm to palm or forearm holds) and dancers facing alternately. Grand notes all eight dancers participate that can.[24]

Grand Right and Left — Same as right and left grand.

Hash (numbers) — Same as Patter — A single tune, used by a caller as background for a series of calls, with no lyrics accompanying the music. Couples are moved into a variety of formations, but brought back to their home positions before the next set of calls.[25]

Heads — From a Squared Set, at the start of the tip, the Heads are the two opposing couples who are facing toward or away from the caller.[26]

Hot Hash — A special tip with no pauses between formations. The tempo of the music is increased, adding to the difficulty.[27]

Join Hands, Circle to the Left — Dancers join hands with adjacent dancers to form a circle and move the circle in the indicated direction, or to the left if no direction was given.[28]

Levels of Square Dancing — Basic, Mainstream, Plus, Advanced, and Challenge.

Mainstream — The CALLERLAB program after Basic, adding seventeen new calls.

Middle Break — The middle break in a singing call is called a break. See singing call Definitions.

One Night Stands (One-nighters) — A one evening square dance that has a party atmosphere and a few *Basics* are taught. The objective is to get people up dancing and having a good time.

Partner — From an Infacing Circle Of 8 of alternating men and women, the man's Partner is the next dancer counterclockwise around the circle from him and the corner is clockwise around the circle. For the women, the Partner is clockwise around the circle and the Corner is counterclockwise.[29]

Pass Thru — Dancers move forward, passing right shoulders with each other and end back-to-back.[30]

Patter — A single tune, used by a caller as background for a series of calls, with no lyrics accompanying the music. Couples are moved into a variety of formations, but brought back to their home positions before the next set of calls.[31]

Patty Cake Routine — Creatively couples sometimes substitute a whimsical made-up routine for Square Thru Four.

Plus — The CALLERLAB program after Mainstream, adding twenty-nine new calls.

Promenade — A promenade is a walk of some distance around the set by some or all dancers. The active dancers may go as individuals or as couples.[32]

Relay the Deucey — Plus Call — From Parallel Waves or Eight Chain Thru (in which case dancers first step to Parallel Waves). It can be done left-handed.

1. Arm Turn 1/2;
2. Center 4 Arm Turn 3/4 as Others 1/2 Circulate;
3. Wave Of 6 Arm Turn 1/2;
4. Center Wave Of 4 Arm Turn 1/2 as Others (do a Big) Diamond Circulate;
5. Wave Of 6 Arm Turn 1/2;
6. Center Wave Of 4 Arm Turn 3/4 as Others move up.[33]

Right and Left Grand — If necessary, men turn up to 90 degrees to face promenade direction and women turn up to 90 degrees to face reverse promenade direction. Dancers blend into a circular formation as they Right Pull By, Left Pull By, Right Pull By, Left Pull By.[34]

Right and Left Thru — Right Pull By; Courtesy Turn.[35]

Right hand lady — From a man's perspective when squared up at home, the woman diagonally to his right.[36]

Seesaw — Men face partner (usually returning to home position from doing an

All Around the Left Hand Lady) and pass by left shoulders as ladies move into the center. Men loop to the left around partner and walk forward to starting position as ladies move back out to place.[37]

Sides — From a Squared Set, at the start of the tip, the Sides are the two opposing couples who are standing perpendicular to the caller.[38]

Singing Calls — A singing call is most often done to a recognizable song with known lyrics. The caller mixes in the dance calls between sections of song lyrics. Generally a singing call uses a pattern where each person dances a portion of the song with each of the other dancers in the square before returning to their original partner at the end. The purpose of singing calls is to relax, dance as a group, and enjoy the song and the caller's performance.[39]

Snaparoo — What Frank Lane called a *Star Thru* — See *Star Thru* Definition Below

Spin Chain the Gears — Plus — Each end and the adjacent center dancer turn one-half (180o). The new centers of each ocean wave turn three-quarters (270o) to form a new ocean wave across the set, as the other four dancers do a U Turn Back (turning in toward the center). The centers of the wave Trade and then release hands with each other. Four dancers on each side of the square now form a four-hand star and turn the star three-quarters, forming a new wave across the set. Centers of this wave Trade momentarily reforming the wave across the set. The two outside pairs of dancers of the center wave now turn three-quarters (270o) as the other four dancers turn back (turning away from the center).[40]

Square Thru — Right Pull By (Square Thru 1 has been completed); Face partner and Left Pull By (Square Thru 2 has been completed); Face partner and Right Pull By (Square Thru 3 has been completed); and Face partner and Left Pull By (Square Thru 4 has been completed). Ending formation: Back-to-Back Couples. [41]

Star Figures — The designated dancers form a star by stepping forward if necessary and placing the appropriate hand in the center of the formation. Forming the star may require a dancer to individually turn in place up to 3/8 of a turn. Dancers turn the star by walking forward in a circle around the center of the star. The distance traveled may be specified in fractions of a star full around, or until some condition is met (e.g., Men Center Left Hand Star, Pick Up Your Partner with an Arm Around, Star Promenade). [42]

Star Thru — Man places his right hand against woman's left hand, palm to palm with fingers up, to make an arch. As the dancers move forward, the woman does a one quarter (90 degrees) left face turn under the arch, while the man does a one quarter (90 degrees) turn to the right moving past the woman. [43]

Spin Chain the Gears — Plus — From Parallel Waves or an Eight Chain Thru formation.

1. Arm Turn 1/2;
2. Centers Arm Turn 3/4 as Ends U-Turn Back;
3. Very Centers Trade as Outsides slide inward to form two Stars;
4. Star 3/4;
5. Very Centers Trade;
6. Center Wave Cast Off 3/4 as Others U-Turn Back by flipping away from the center of the set.

Ends in Parallel Waves. [44]

Square — Consists of four couples. Each square consists of "two head couples" and two "side couples." The person directly to a couple's left in the formation is referred to as their "corner." [45]

Square Dance Brochure — Advertisement for Kirkwood's schedule and calling and cuing staff.

Swing — Dancers step forward and slightly to their left, use a ballroom hold, and rotate clockwise as a unit for four or more beats of music. As dancers end the swing, the woman continues turning to her right (unrolling along the man's right arm) until she is facing the same direction as the man. [46]

Swing Thru — Those who can turn 1/2 (180 degrees) by the right; then those who can turn 1/2 (180 degrees) by the left. [47]

Tip — A square dance session consisting of two parts, a patter call, and a singing call. The patter call consists of a rapid-fire sequence of spoken calls, which lead the dancers through intricate and unpredictable patterns. There is usually background music to provide a basic beat, but the emphasis is on dance as an intellectual exercise. In the singing call, the moves are much more predictable. The caller usually sings a popular song with the calls interspersed between the phrases and the emphasis is on dancing to the music. [48]

Trade By — The couples facing each other pass thru, the couples facing out do a partner trade to face in. [49]

Visiting Couples — One couple would go to another couple in the square and would do the calls directed. Popular calls during the '50s.

Walk Around Your Corner — Dancers face their corners. Walking forward and around each other while keeping right shoulders adjacent, dancers return to their original position, with their backs toward their corner. [50]

Wash your clothes and wring them out. Hang them on the line, sunny side out — Wash your clothes and wring them out. - Older unstandardized call with no definition. Hang them on the line, sunny side out – Circle facing out.

Weave the Ring — Dancers do a no-hands Right and Left Grand.[51]

---

1. Wikipedia, "Round dance," April 29, 2019, https://en.wikipedia.org/wiki/Round_dance
2. Corvallis Gazette-Times, "Square Dance Glossary," January 21, 2010, https://www.gazettetimes.com/square-dance-glossary/article_a0b68d40-070c-11df-a303-001cc4c002e0.html
3. Wikipedia, "LP Records," March 6, 2020, https://en.wikipedia.org/wiki/LP_record
4. Wikipedia, "Single (music)," March 15, 2020, https://en.wikipedia.org/wiki/Single_(music)
5. Dictionary.com, 2020, https://www.dictionary.com/browse/78
6. *CALLERLAB Basic and Mainstream Definitions* (March 10, 2017): 18.
7. Vic and Debbie Ceder, "ceder.net," March 17, 2020, https://www.ceder.net/def/courtesyturn.php
8. Vic and Debbie Ceder, "ceder.net," March 17, 2020, https://www.ceder.net/def/courtesyturn.php
9. https://acme-corp.com/teamGuest/R/2_426/sd101/Bow%20to%20Your%20Partner.htm
10. *CALLERLAB Basic and Mainstream Definitions* (March 10, 2017): 37.
11. Wikipedia, "Caller (dancing), December 8, 2019, https://en.wikipedia.org/wiki/Caller_(dancing)
12. *CALLERLAB Plus Definitions* (December 22, 2014): 10.
13. *CALLERLAB Basic and Mainstream Definitions* (March 10, 2017): 5.
14. Vic and Debbie Ceder, "ceder.net," March 17, 2020, https://www.ceder.net/def/courtesyturn.php
15. Vic and Debbie Ceder, "ceder.net," March 17, 2020, https://www.ceder.net/oldcalls/viewsingle.php?RecordId=3772
16. Vic and Debbie Ceder, "ceder.net," March 17, 2020, https://www.ceder.net/oldcalls/viewsingle.php?RecordId=228
17. Vic and Debbie Ceder, "ceder.net," March 17, 2020, https://www.ceder.net/oldcalls/viewsingle.php?RecordId=3838
18. *CALLERLAB Basic and Mainstream Definitions* (March 10, 2017): 30.
19. *CALLERLAB Basic and Mainstream Definitions* (March 10, 2017): 12.
20. Vic and Debbie Ceder, "ceder.net," March 17, 2020, https://www.ceder.net/oldcalls/viewsingle.php?RecordId=236
21. *CALLERLAB Basic and Mainstream Definitions* (March 10, 2017): 6
22. *CALLERLAB Basic and Mainstream Definitions* (March 10, 2017): 51.
23. Merriam-Webster, https://www.merriam-webster.com/dictionary/grand%20march
24. Vic and Debbie Ceder, "ceder.net," March 17, 2020, https://www.ceder.net/oldcalls/viewsingle.php?RecordId=440
25. Corvallis Gazette-Times, "Square Dance Glossary," 2020, https://www.gazettetimes.com/square-dance-glossary/article_a0b68d40-070c-11df-a303-001cc4c002e0.html
26. *CALLERLAB Basic and Mainstream Definitions* (March 10, 2017): 6.
27. Corvallis Gazette-Times, "Square Dance Glossary," 2020, https://www.gazettetimes.com/square-dance-glossary/article_a0b68d40-070c-11df-a303-001cc4c002e0.html
28. *CALLERLAB Basic and Mainstream Definitions* (March 10, 2017): 10.
29. *CALLERLAB Basic and Mainstream Definitions* (March 10, 2017): 5.
30. *CALLERLAB Basic and Mainstream Definitions* (March 10, 2017): 6.
31. Corvallis Gazette-Times, "Square Dance Glossary," 2020, https://www.gazettetimes.com/square-dance-glossary/article_a0b68d40-070c-11df-a303-001cc4c002e0.html
32. *CALLERLAB Basic and Mainstream Definitions* (March 10, 2017): 15.
33. Vic and Debbie Ceder, "ceder.net," March 17, 2020, https://www.ceder.net/def/relaythedeucey.php
34. *CALLERLAB Basic and Mainstream Definitions* (March 10, 2017): 20.
35. *CALLERLAB Basic and Mainstream Definitions* (March 10, 2017): 35.
36. *CALLERLAB Basic and Mainstream Definitions* (March 10, 2017): 64.
37. Vic and Debbie Ceder, "ceder.net," March 17, 2020, https://www.ceder.net/oldcalls/viewsingle.php?RecordId=378
38. *CALLERLAB Basic and Mainstream Definitions* (March 10, 2017): 6.
39. https://www.majorkeys.org/square-dance-terminology.html
40. *CALLERLAB Plus Definitions* (January 31, 2018): 7.
41. *CALLERLAB Basic and Mainstream Definitions* (March 10, 2017): 38.
42. *CALLERLAB Basic and Mainstream Definitions* (March 10, 2017): 21.
43. *CALLERLAB Basic and Mainstream Definitions* (March 10, 2017): 37.
44. Vic and Debbie Ceder, "ceder.net," March 17, 2020, https://www.ceder.net/def/spinchainthegears.php
45. Corvallis Gazette-Times, "Square Dance Glossary," 2020, https://www.gazettetimes.com/square-dance-glossary/article_a0b68d40-070c-11df-a303-001cc4c002e0.html

46. *CALLERLAB Basic and Mainstream Definitions* (March 10, 2017): 21.
47. *CALLERLAB Basic and Mainstream Definitions* (March 10, 2017): 47.
48. Corvallis Gazette-Times, "Square Dance Glossary," 2020, https://www.gazettetimes.com/square-dance-glossary/article_a0b68d40-070c-11df-a303-001cc4c002e0.html
49. *CALLERLAB Basic and Mainstream Definitions* (March 10, 2017): 52.
50. CALLERLAB *Basic and Mainstream Defintions* (March 10, 2017): 38.
51. *CALLERLAB Basic and Mainstream Definitions* (March 10, 2017): 52.

APPENDIX J – ADDITIONAL REFERENCES

Books

Betty Casey, *Dance Across Texas,* University of Texas Press (1985).
Betty Casey, *The Complete Book of Square Dancing [and Round Dancing],* University of North Texas Press (2000).
Bob Osgood, *As I Saw It,* Humbug Enterprises (2017).
Bob Sumrall, *Do-Si-Do,* (1949).
Jim Mayo, *Step by Step Through Modern Square Dance History,* (2003).
John W. Jones, *Square Dance Fundamentals,* Jones Street USA, LLC, (1970).
Lloyd and Dorothy Shaw, *Lloyd Shaw and the Cheyenne Mountain Dancers.*
Lloyd Shaw, *Cowboy Dances,* The Caxton Printers, Ltd. (1949).
Richard Severance, *A Step in Time: The American Square Dance,* (2018).

URLs

Andeles, Andy. "RIVCO Indio a Few Minutes with Marshall Flippo 2011." November 12, 2011. https://www.youtube.com/watch?v=wvH3B8t4awQ

Andeles, Andy. "RIVCO Marshall Flippo Ticket Story November 2014." November 7, 2014. https://www.youtube.com/watch?v=F3OUt-yuLM8

Arizona Public Media. "Marshall Flippo." June 21, 2016. https://www.youtsbe.-com/watch?v=i6jITivozQQ&t=12s

Bricker, Darin. "Marshall 'Flip' Flippo Funeral." January 19, 2019. https://www.youtube.com/watch?v=wmQNwcPpPqc

Bricker, Darin. "Marshall Flippo – It Makes Me Laugh." February 9, 2019. https://www.youtube.com/watch?v=yuEmRBGr70w&fbclid=IwAR1D-U7gToOwdctfpjtiVR00xaz1UupRTHEvUIeh_gEJK2bH0BiQpvNxXBA

Bricker, Darin. "Marshall Flippo — Wagon Wheel Reception." January 19, 2019. https://www.youtube.com/watch?time_continue=7&v=QSU0hsE00P8&fbclid=IwAR3VjGZwlmZbNw2s3H6LtsR7n4FMh0aNsCmDf9K-9LyghQH1rYToyI7Xjq4

Brundage, Bob. "Flippo, Marshall: SIO Hall of Fame, CALLERLAB Milestone." October 20, 2007. http://www.sdfne.org/marshall-flippo/

CALLERLAB. "2016 CALLERLAB Convention Life Time Achievment Award." April, 27, 2016. https://www.youtube.com/watch?v=eNAxdsZq16A

Farrar, Dennis. "Marshall Flippo receives CALLERLAB'S Gold Card Membership." May 7, 2011. https://www.youtube.com/watch?v=ms4fb3PnQkg

Hardy, Chuck. "Marshall Flippo's Schedule, 2000-2001." 2000. http://www.chuckandgerry.com/clubhouse/mflippos.html

Horner-Miller, Larada. "Celebration of Marshall Flippo in Albuquerque, New Mexico." March 20, 2016. https://www.youtube.com/watch?v=m92CcYxnmBA

Horner-Miller, Larada. "Flippo Signaling to Stop 'The Auctioneer.' in Albuquerque, New Mexico." March 24, 2020. https://youtu.be/CGpQKk9MLSc

Horner-Miller, Larada. "Flippo & 'I Just Don't Look Good Naked Anymore.'" March 24, 2020. https://youtu.be/HTD_XHHFr5g

Leroy Van Dyke singing "The Auctioneer." https://www.youtube.com/watch?v=WaVTxiPBJgM

Lipscomb, Darryl & Sheffield, Elmer. "Marshall Flippo is the King." September 7, 2017. https://www.youtube.com/watch?v=c232iIORnl4

SquareDanceHistory2, "10th National Square Dance Convention, Detroit." 1961. https://www.youtube.com/watch?feature=player_detailpage&v=0Q3y8Er8pzg#t=680

Square Dance History Project. "Visit With the Legends, 2010." 2010. http://squaredancehistory.org/items/show/1138

Square Dance History Project. "Visit With the Legends, 2011." 2011. https://squaredancehistory.org/items/show/1139

Square Dance History Project. "Visit With the Legends, 2012." 2012. https://squaredancehistory.org/items/show/1140

Marshall Flippo Song Bytes

From the Square Dance History Project
1958 — "The Auctioneer" — https://squaredancehistory.org/items/show/160
"The Auctioneer" Remake — https://squaredancehistory.org/items/show/161
1961 — Patter — http://squaredancehistory.org/items/show/1098
1970 — "Mary Ann" — https://squaredancehistory.org/items/show/1428
1970 — "New World in the Morning — http://squaredancehistory.org/items/show/1099
1970 — Patter — https://squaredancehistory.org/items/show/1427

From Other Sources
Pass Through and Around One Patter — https://squaredancehistory.org/items/show/467
"Down Yonder" — https://archive.org/details/78_down-yonder_norman-merrbach-margaret-patrick_gbia0024978/02+-+Down+Yonder+-+Marshall+Flippo+-+Margaret+Patrick.flac
"When It's Christmas Time in Texas" — https://www.socialzon.me/videos/watch/AihkOFB8OIk

News

Barchfield, Vanessa. Arizona Public Media. "A Promenade Down Memory Lane With Square Dance Caller Marshall Flippo Recorded Interview." September 2, 2016. https://radio.azpm.org/s/41490-the-life-of-square-dance-calling-legend-marshall-flippo/

Fulton, Loretta. Abilene Reporter News. "Flippo bids road farewell at Abilene's Wagon Wheel Hall." August 31, 2016. http://archive.reporternews.com/lifestyle/flippo-bids-farewell-to-the-road-at-abilene-part-at-wagon-wheel-hall-3b37d818-b4e9-4e85-e053-0100007-391932211.html/

Singleton, Adam. Big Country Homepage. "One Last Dance for Veteran Square DanceCaller." September 2, 2016. https://www.bigcountryhomepage.com/entertainment/ktab-4u/one-last-dance-for-veteran-square-dance-caller/543158758

Websites:

Blue Star Record Label, Buddy Weaver Owner — http://www.buddyweavermusic.com/bluestar.php

Country Dance & Song Society — https://www.cdss.org

Sets in Order Website — All 444 issues available to see! — http://newsquaremusic.com/sioindex.html

Square Dance Foundation of New England, Inc. — http://www.sdfne.org/

Square Dance History Project — https://squaredancehistory.org

Yellow Square Dance Council — http://www.squaredancemontana.com

ABOUT LARADA

Larada Horner-Miller is a poet, essayist, and accomplished multi-genre author who holds a bachelor's degree in English, with a minor in Spanish and a master of education degree in Integrating Technology into the Classroom. She is the accomplished author of four award-winning historical fiction, memoir, and poetry works plus three self-published cookbooks.

Larada Horner-Miller

Her most recent book, *A Time to Grow Up—A Daughter's Grief Memoir* has won many awards including being a 2018 Book Excellence Awards, Finalist in the Memoir category at the New Mexico-Arizona Book Awards and a 2018 Independent Press Distinguished Favorites Award in the Memoir category.

Horner-Miller has also been a past National presenter at the Women Writing the West Conference and is currently the creator of Memoir Workshops for others who want to share their family's legacies through words.

Larada and her husband, Lin, enjoy being nestled in the mountains above Albuquerque, New Mexico, near the village of Tijeras. When not writing books, this passionate, energetic, and enthusiastic woman loves to spend time kicking up her heels at square and round dancing gatherings, traveling, knitting, and reading. As co-manager of her family's southeastern Colorado ranch, she enjoys spending time exploring her family's historic ranch and reminiscing with her brother and his children about their mom, dad, and granddad.

To learn more, visit https://laradasbooks.com/

Contact:
    Larada Horner-Miller
    Larada@icloud.com
    www.laradas.books.com

Books Published:

This Tumbleweed Landed, 2014
When Will Papa Get Home?, 2016
Let Me Tell You a Story, 2015
A Time to Grow Up: A Daughter's Grief Memoir, 2017

Cookbooks Published:

From Grannie's Kitchen, Volume 1 — Pies, Cakes & Christmas Candy, 2014
From Grannie's Kitchen, Volume 2 — Beverages, Bread, Cookies, Meats, Vegetables, Mis. & Records of a Rancher's Wife, 2015
From Grannie's Kitchen, Volume 3 — Casseroles, Mexican Dishes, Relish, Sandwiches, Salads & Desserts, 2016

REVIEWS PLEASE

Book Reviews are so important to how online stores market books! After reading Flippo's biography in any of the formats, please go to Amazon.com and rate the book and write a review—I would appreciate it so much!

Index

British Columbia, Canada, *515. See also Krueger, Wendy*

Brochure, *110, 148, 158, 183, 251, 434, 524, 527*

Brower, Jim, *118, 309, 473. See also Kirkwood*

Brownlee, Al "Tex", *273, 309, 445–447, 485. See also Fontana, NC; Handcuffed; Permian Basin festival*

Brownwood, TX, *75–76. See also Abilene A's; Harrison, John Ray*

Brundage, Al, *173, 192, 220, 222, 227, 311, 444–445, 457, 511. See also Atlantic City, New Jersey; Thanksgiving*

Brundage, Al & Bea, *311*

Brundage, Al & Bob, *444–445*

Brundage, Bob, *192, 318, 332, 444–445, 532. See also Albuquerque, NM; CALLERLAB*

Buchheits, *300. See also Kirkwood*

Buffalo Gap, TX, *28, 30, 46. See also Stockton, Anna (A'nt Anner); Stockton, Bill (Uncle); Stockton, Charlie (Uncle)*

Buick Day, *175–176, 518. See also Puerling, Whitey*

Burdick, Cathie, *158, 271. See also American Square Dance magazine; Burdick, Stan; Square Dance Magazine*

Burdick, Stan, *158, 222, 265, 271–272, 274, 279–280, 284, 511. See also American Square Dance magazine; American Squares magazine; Burdick, Cathie; Square Dance Magazine*

Burgess, Mrs., *33. See also Wylie*

Burma-Shave Jingles, *9, 89–91, 284, 491–493. See also Wilson, Joel (J. C.)*

Bussey, Big Daddy, *471. See also Guest, C. O.*

Butterfield, TX, *35*

C

Caldwell, NJ, *174*

Califone, *84, 178*

CALLERLAB, *16, 100, 122, 217, 219–224, 226–233, 246, 253, 281, 284, 305, 309–314, 331–332, 337, 350, 356, 371, 378, 380–382, 398, 401, 406, 412, 414, 417, 436, 441, 444–445, 448, 477, 479, 481, 488, 522, 524–525, 528–529, 532. See also Osgood, Bob*

Camdenton, MO, *126, 147, 364. See also Kirkwood*

Camp Pendleton, CA, *67. See also Navy*

D

Record Label
Duet(s), *398. See also
CALLERLAB*
Dun, Eddy, *76–77. See also
Abilene A's*
Durant, OK, *187*

E

E-Z School Record Label,
509. See also Recordings
Easter Parade, *248–249. See
also Puerling, Whitey;
Spain*
Easterday, Irv & Betty, *173.
See also Atlantic City, New
Jersey; Brundage, Al;
Thanksgiving*
Eastland, TX, *453*
Effingham, IL, *434*
El Cajon Boulevard, *42. See
also Curry, Thurman; San
Diego, CA*
El Centro, CA, *43*
El Paso, TX, *43, 425, 472*
Eldon, MO, *114. See also
Hagadorn, Bill; Kirkwood*
Elks Club, *397–398. See also
Sheffield, Elmer*
Elliott-Hamil Funeral Home,
*353, 356. See also
Elmwood Memorial Park;
Memorial Service*
Elmwood Memorial Park,
*356. See also Elliott-Hamil
Funeral Home; Memorial
Service*

Emperor Hirohito, *246, 412.
See also Japan
(Japanese); Prince Mikasa*
England, *235, 249, 399, 409,
495. See also Taylor, Dave*
English Mountain Resort,
*156, 367, 408, 427, 466.
See also Shoemake, Gary*
Eniwetok, *52, 54. See also
Navy; USS Lander*
Equator, *56–57, 60. See also
Navy; Pollywog(s);
Shellbacks*
Equivalency Test, *34. See
also Navy*
ESP Record Label, *509. See
also Recordings*
Estes Park, CO, *431. See also
Lane, Barbara; Lane,
Frank*
Eulogy, *353–354. See also
Luttrell, Melton; Memorial
Service; Shoemake, Gary*
Eureka Springs, AR, *111, 364.
See also Gotcher, Les*
Evans, Hazel, *81–82. See
also Evans, R. H. 'Hub'*
Evans, R. H. 'Hub' , *39–40,
53, 81–82. See also Evans,
Hazel*
Evansville, IN, *483*
Exeter, *249–250. See also
England; Taylor, Dave*
Eyes, Derek, *76. See also
Abilene A's*

F

H

I

Lander
It ain't no woman, *492. See also Burma-Shave Jingles*
Iwo Jima, *39, 50, 52–54, 60, 81. See also USS Lander*

J

Jackson, Bob & Patti Ann, *339–340. See also Tucson, AZ*
Jackson, Jack, *112, 124, 510. See also Kirkwood*
Jackson, MS, *165, 374*
Jackson, OH, *178*
Jambalaya, *133, 427. See also Brenda Flea Skit; Haag Jerry*
Japan (Japanese), *50, 54–55, 57–59, 62–64, 235–242, 244–246, 258, 265, 267, 345, 352, 356, 409, 411–412, 414–415, 448, 495*
Jeffus, Stan, *319, 355, 365. See also Memorial Service; Paris, TX*
Jimmie Kate, *374. See also Luttrell, Melton; Martin, Hattie Bell*
JOANN Fabric Store, *394. See also Christian, Kandie & Roger; Fairbanks, AK*
Johnson, Bruce, *111, 206, 220, 222, 511. See also CALLERLAB; Kirkwood*
Johnson, Dee, *131. See also*

Kirkwood Employees
Johnson, J. J., *321, 334, 336–337. See also Sheehan Johnson, Mary*
Johnson, J. J. (Source of Pictures), *333, 335. See also Sheehan Johnson, Mary*
Johnston, Earl, *172, 220, 222, 445, 510–511. See also Johnston, Marian*
Johnston, Marian, *172. See also Johnston, Earl*
Jones, Ardie, *442. See also Jones, Dick*
Jones, Buddy, *517. See also Albuquerque, NM*
Jones, Chuck, *11–12. See also Osgood, Bob*
Jones, Dick, *153, 199, 441–442. See also Jones, Ardie; WASCA*
Jones, Fenton "Jonesy", *83*
Jones, John W., *531*
Jones, Jon, *229, 311, 353, 355, 371, 378. See also Carroll-Jones, Deborah; Jones, Shirley*
Jones, Kayla, *353. See also Jones, Vernon*
Jones, Shirley, *311. See also Jones, Jon*
Jones, Vernon, *314, 353. See also Jones, Kayla*
Joplin, MO, *449*
Jordan, Wally, *76. See also Abilene A's*
Juaire, Ed & Pat, *271. See also American Square Dance magazine*

M

Wright, Bill, *203, 481*. *See also Grand Squares Square Dance Club*

Wykoff, Johnnie & Star, *470–471*. *See also Blue Star Record Label*

Wylie, *9, 28, 32–35, 39, 75, 83, 355*. *See also Abilene, TX*

Y

Yamaguchi, Sekiko, *245*. *See also Japan (Japanese)*

Yerington, Bob, *118, 136, 467–468, 473*. *See also Kirkwood ; Yerington, Shirley*

Yerington, Shirley, *467–468*. *See also Yerington, Bob*

YMCA, *8, 82, 86, 280, 487*

Yokohama, *63*. *See also Baseball; Japan (Japanese)*

Yokosuka Harbor, *58, 62, 235, 239*. *See also Japan (Japanese); Navy*

Yoshimura, Motohiro (Moto), *412–414*. *See also Tokyo*

You can't go home if you're going by the mill, *492*. *See also Burma-Shave Jingles*

Young, Joe & Cricket Young, *202–203, 480–481*. *See also Grand Squares Square Dance Club; San Antonio (Antone), Texas; Thompson, John*

Youngblood, Lillian, *131*. *See also Kirkwood ; Kirkwood Employees*

Yuba City, CA, *193–194*. *See also Marysville, CA*

Yucaipa, CA, *196, 436–437*. *See also Gilmore, Ed; Smith, Pete*

Yuma, AZ, *43*. *See also Curry, Thurman; Hitchhike (Hitchhiking)*

YWCA, *272*

CPSIA information can be obtained
at www.ICGtesting.com
Printed in the USA
BVHW071913200720
584132BV00002B/2/J